THE MIXTECS OF OAXACA

The Mixtecs of Oaxaca
Ancient Times to the Present

Ronald Spores and Andrew K. Balkansky

University of Oklahoma Press : Norman

Library of Congress Cataloging-in-Publication Data

Spores, Ronald.
The Mixtecs of Oaxaca : ancient times to the present /
Ronald Spores and Andrew K. Balkansky
pages cm. — (The civilization of the American Indian series ; volume 267)
Includes bibliographical references and index.
ISBN 978-0-8061-4381-1 (hard cover)
ISBN 978-0-8061-6743-5 (paper)
1. Mixtec Indians—History. 2. Indians of Mexico—Oaxaca—History.
I. Balkansky, Andrew K., 1967–
II. Title
F1221.M7S76 2013
972'.7401—dc23
2013000925

The Mixtecs of Oaxaca: Ancient Times to the Present is Volume 267
in The Civilization of the American Indian Series.

The paper in this book meets the guidelines for permanence and durability
of the Committee on Production Guidelines for Book Longevity of the
Council on Library Resources, Inc. ∞

For Mary Elizabeth "Betsy" Smith

It was a common belief among the native Mixtecs that the origin and beginnings of their false gods and rulers was in Apoala, a town in the Mixteca, which in their language they call *yuta tnoho*, which is "River where the rulers came from," because they are said to have split off from some trees that grew from that river and that have special names. They also call that town *yuta tnuhu*, which is "River of the lineages," and this is the more appropriate name and the one that fits it best.

Fray Antonio de los Reyes
Arte en lengua mixteca (1976 [1593]: Prologue, I)

CONTENTS

Contents

ILLUSTRATIONS

TABLE

PREFACE

This book conveys the essence of what is known of the Mixteca and its people (Ñudzahui, or currently, Ñusabi or Ñusauvi★) from the time of its earliest human occupants until the present moment, but it is by no means all that is known. The Mixtecs and their neighbors, the Valley Zapotecs, together constitute one of the "nuclear areas" for the growth of primary civilizations in antiquity. Before now, however, it has been hard to relate the Mixtecs—and their numerous linguistic variants—to the broader comparative schemes of world civilizations. The Mixtec have unusual traits, and the region has been underserved in terms of sustained anthropological inquiry. Yet the Mixteca's oldest cities were contemporary with Monte Albán I, and its

---

★For present purposes, and to standardize the text, the authors—with modest orthographic modifications for the purpose of better understanding—have adopted the sixteenth-century Teposcolula dialect vocabulary of Mixteco as presented in the *Vocabulario* of Francisco de Alvarado and the *Arte* of Antonio de los Reyes. Not only are there multiple dialects of the Mixtec language now and in the past, but it is virtually impossible to adequately represent the numerous linguistic variants (see Josserand et al. 1984). Like Latin in the case of the medieval and Renaissance romance languages, the majority of sixteenth-century native texts written in Mixteco were rendered in the Teposcolula variant (see Terraciano 2001). It is also to be kept in mind that the Mixteco of Alvarado and Reyes was far closer to the pre-Hispanic and early Colonial culture of the region than are modern forms rendered some four centuries later. Such terms as *yuhuitayu, ñuu, ñuhu, yya, yya canu, toho, tay ñuu, tay situ ndayu, aniñe, siqui,* and *tay toho* that appear frequently here follow closely the form and meaning that they had in the sixteenth century, when they first appeared in European script. The "proper" form of rendering native terms and meanings is the subject of constant debate among Mixtec scholars. We have neither the time or space or the scholarly expertise to engage these arguments. We present the concepts as we have come to understand them in their sixteenth-century contexts, and for the present at least, we leave the scholarly debates to the scholars.

native writing system among the most celebrated in all of Mexico. Much has changed, too, in the past fifty years, including a revolution in our archaeological knowledge of the Mixteca, as well as intensive and ongoing work with documentary materials and ethnographic activity that makes it possible to generate a book covering the full scope and character of the Mixteca and its peoples.

This is not our first effort of this kind. The senior author published a synthetic volume on the Mixtec in 1967—which was, not incidentally, the year the junior author was born. We mention these facts to emphasize the multigenerational nature of our work and the extent to which knowledge of the region and its peoples has grown in recent years. The present volume, then, is meant to be a compilation of existing research and a stepping-stone for future generations of students whom we sincerely hope will improve upon our efforts. We cannot cover all that is known about the Mixtecs in this single volume, but look instead at certain key turning points in the development of Mixtec civilization and at those questions that animate our ongoing research. We have attempted to apply a convergent methodology, whereby we employ archaeological, biological, linguistic, ethnohistoric, and ethnographic data in order to form a more complete picture of Mixtec culture over three millennia. Our bias is toward archaeology and ethnohistory, in that—within the larger domain of anthropology—those are our own specializations. We find, however, that our specializations would be inadequate were we to ignore the vital knowledge derived from the other subfields of anthropology. While we hope that the reader will consult our prior publications, it is absolutely essential that we all make active use of the works of numerous authors in the bibliography and several others that we have not cited specifically.

Our concern in the present volume is with tracing the emergence and evolution of Mixtec culture from the origins of the earliest settled farming communities, around 1500 B.C.E., through to the rise of the towns and cities that made up the Mixtec state, with its distinctive social system, technology, religion, writing, and great art and architecture, and then following the remnants of this still-living culture and the Mixtec people as they spread far and wide through Mexico and the rest of North America. We are, then, concerned with three thousand years of adaptation by the Mixtec people, first to the Mixteca, then to the contiguous regions and cultures of Oaxaca, Puebla, and Guerrero, then to greater Mexico, and eventually to the far-flung lands and peoples of the United States and Canada. How did prototypical Mixtec culture emerge from the preexisting congeries of egalitarian farming communities scattered about the three zones of the Mixteca—the Alta, Baja, and Costa of western Oaxaca, southern Puebla, and easternmost Guerrero? How did the pre-Hispanic Mixtecs adapt to the transformations of the Spanish Conquest and three centuries of Colonial control? What accounts for the persistent features of Mixtec culture, and how have many thousands of Mixtec migrants adapted to the world beyond the Mixteca? We consider the origin of the Mixtec kingdom, variously called *yuhuitayu*, *señoríos*, or *cacicazgos*, and of the Mixtec themselves through pre-Hispanic, Colonial, and modern times.

In order to achieve our objectives, we must go back into remote antiquity before bringing the archaeological record forward and making contact with the very different source material of written history. The point of convergence is the Mesoamerican Postclassic period, roughly the last six hundred years before Spanish contact that saw the greatest florescence of Mixtec culture, and where events and personalities recorded in codices remain the stuff of legend and history. In many ways, however, the great expansion of the Mixtec is an ongoing process, as the residents of the many migrant communities scattered across North America can attest. The past is always present for hundreds of thousands of native speakers of the multiple dialects of Mixteco, as well as such related languages as Trique, Chochona, Amuzgo, or Chatino, Zapoteco, Cuicateco, Nahuatl, or Tlapaneco, who shared in a common cultural tradition, many still living in the Mixteca, others having migrated far beyond its boundaries.

A great many scholars have contributed to our understanding of these questions, some long past, others still hard at work. We nonetheless owe special debts to France V. Scholes, Alfonso Caso, Wigberto Jiménez Moreno, Ignacio Bernal, and John Paddock (RS), and to Gary Feinman, Joyce Marcus, and Charles Spencer (AKB). They are the scholars, the models of excellence, who pointed us in the right direction at critical junctures in our professional lives, and showed by way of example how to think as anthropologists, archaeologists, and historians. We should also mention in this context our prior collaborations with Stephen Kowalewski and John Monaghan, both of whom have influenced our work (we like to believe this has been mutually beneficial), and who are able and no doubt willing to identify any number of inadequacies in what follows. We also gratefully acknowledge the collaboration of our preeminent Mixtec *codicistas*, Maarten Jansen, Aurora Pérez Jiménez, and Manuel Herman Lejarazu, who have considered the great literary, historical, and artistic works of the Mixtecs in exquisite detail and have vastly enriched our knowledge and appreciation of the codices. Dawn Stricklin, it should be noted before closing, made essential editorial contributions to the present volume. We would not have gotten the manuscript off to press without her. We must also acknowledge the important contributions of two highly insightful and helpful reviewers of the original manuscript, who contributed very significantly to the final product. Lastly, we dedicate this book to Mary Elizabeth Smith. Her good humor is legendary, and her studies of codices and other historical materials achieved so much with so little fanfare—all the best traits for any Mixtec specialist to follow.

PART ONE

THE MIXTECA
IN ANCIENT TIMES

1

THE MIXTECA
AND THE MIXTECOS

Oaxaca is a region of unusual geographic and ethnic diversity, small communities, small farms, and minor industries. Against this varied contemporary setting, the rich and diversified cultural traditions of Oaxaca have developed over the past several thousand years. At least sixteen major ethnolinguistic groups occupied Oaxaca at the time of the Spanish Conquest.[1] Some groups, like the Mixes, Chontals, and Mazatecs, remained isolated in remote mountainous areas from which they have emerged only in recent decades. Others, most notably Mixtec- and Zapotec-speaking peoples, operated in the mainstream of Mesoamerican society, with far-reaching exchange networks, urban states, and highly developed religion.[2] They were among the originators of Meso-american civilization. Modern Mixtecs may be found almost anywhere on the North American continent, while their homeland remains a region of great beauty with a spectacular history, with vast but underdeveloped resources and great potential for development, but with limited opportunities at present for material advancement.

Our approach in this book consists of following the course of development among the Mixtec from their earliest beginnings to the present, focusing on transformational events: urban origins and development; the emergence of the state and a complex social system; technological innovation; the emergence of writing, great art, and science; religious transformations; catastrophic epidemic; collapse and cultural reformulation; and conquest and colonization that pertain to ancient and Colonial times. Wars of independence

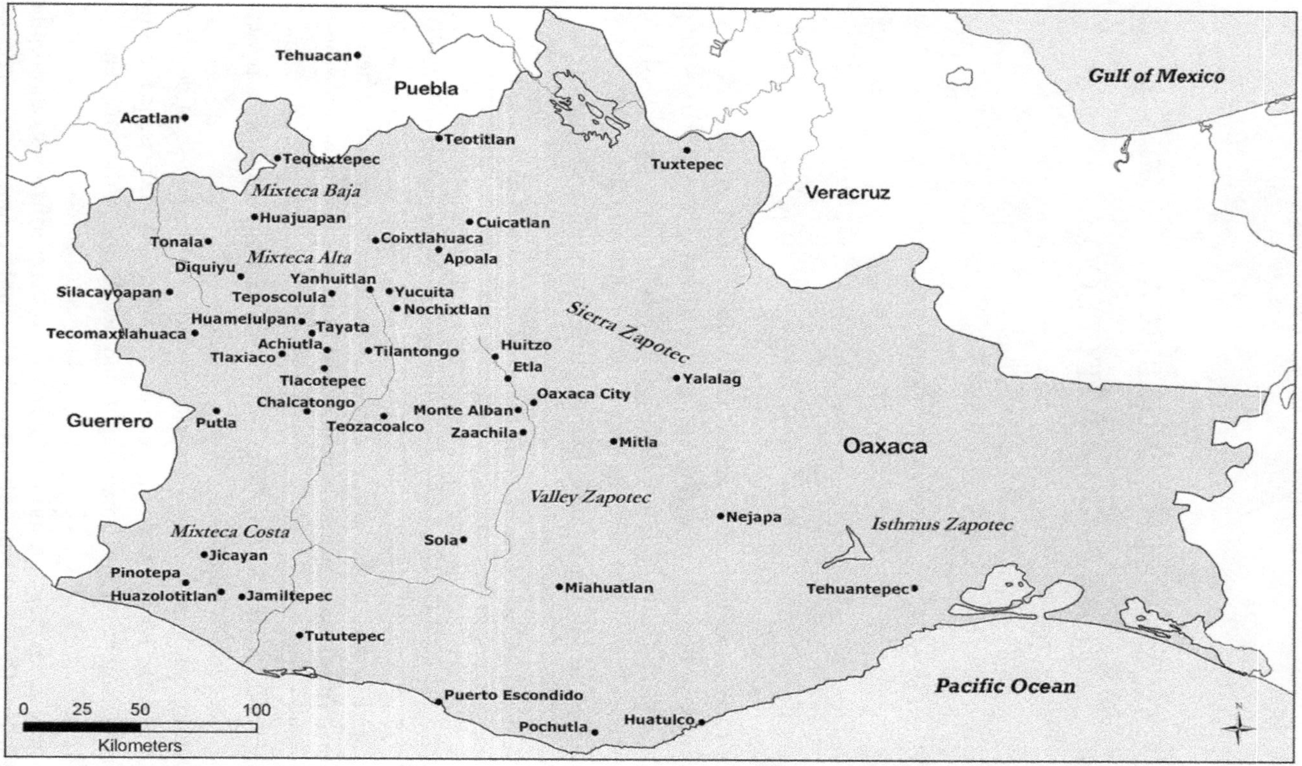

Figure 1.1. Map of the state of Oaxaca, showing important places of the Mixteca Alta, Baja, and Costa.

and revolution followed, and the modern era of economic globalization and mass migration characterizes the present. We consider anthropological studies of the Mixtec to have reached a critical density, which upon synthesis and further study should yield data and theoretical observations of considerable interest to scholars worldwide. We begin with the relevant background to the Mixteca and the Mixtecos, their archaeological, historical, linguistic, and environmental parameters before considering the prehistory in greater detail than in any of our prior efforts. The second half of the book covers the Spanish Conquest and colonization and continues into the contemporary era of the Mexican nation-state. We must delay all of that, however, and before getting to the "good stuff" make a few remarks about our methods and explain why we frame the presentation as we do.

CONVERGENT METHOD

We have always viewed our work as situated within the entire Mixteca, both as it exists today and in the past, and sought ways to conjoin the several subfields of anthropology into a broad, and we hope convincing, approach to the Mixteca and the Mixtecos. This is not a new idea. As with many things in the study of Oaxacan peoples and places, we trace the roots of a conjunctive-historical or "convergent" method to Alfonso Caso.[3] Caso, his closest collaborators Ignacio Bernal and Jorge Acosta, and Wigberto Jiménez Moreno began a tradition of integrative studies that is still followed—bringing the results of archaeological excavations together with the study of ethnohistory, and situating analyses of writing and the calendar alongside regional settlement surveys. Caso's studies of ancient Mixtec settlement, writing and the calendar, Colonial maps, land transactions, and eye-witness accounts form important elements of the research from this era (1930s to the 1960s) and still contribute to our view of Mixtec cultural development as a continuous and unfolding process.

What the convergence of aims and methods means in practice varies among researchers, but for us it involves, minimally, the use of complementary data for looking back in time as well as for the present and into the future.[4] Julian Steward described this approach as "the elementary logic of working from the known to the unknown" and then remarked that for areas like Mesoamerica, "where many of the more conspicuous sites were only recently abandoned and where a connection between historic and prehistoric cultures was obvious, it was almost an inevitable approach."[5] We take it as axiomatic that explanations tempered by several sources of information almost always prove to be the more enduring. We likewise view the documented behaviors, attitudes, practices, knowledge domains, and beliefs of native Mesoamericans as the right and proper starting point for our research.[6] Ethnographic and historical documentation thus becomes a yardstick against which we measure modern, historic, and pre-historic sequences of development.

Our emphasis on documented behavior is far more revealing and more reliable than the empirically empty theoretical approaches that are often employed in Mesoamerica. There are good reasons why we continue to use results generated in the 1930s, 1940s, and 1950s, and it has to do with their empirical utility.[7] What strengthens this approach is the use of parallel lines of evidence, including materials recovered through systematic excavation and survey as well as observations drawn from systematic study of the documentary record. Yet we remain mindful that the Postclassic period in Oaxaca wherein all convergent approaches must demonstrably come together is barely subdivided chronologically. This means that the last six hundred years or more of Oaxaca prehistory is only a rough sketch archaeologically, thereby masking all of the oscillations the historical sources tell us characterized each small polity. The considerable dynamism and flux of the Postclassic is difficult to approach in this circumstance, and earlier periods require still greater interpretive conservatism.

THE SCIENCE OF ARCHAEOLOGY AS APPLIED TO THE MIXTECA

Archaeology, as a branch of anthropology, is a set of techniques and methods applied to the study of material remains of past cultures. Although the discipline is ancient, archaeological methodology and objectives have evolved steadily over the last century. We can readily trace this development in Oaxaca, both in aims and methods, from the late nineteenth-century era of Marshall Saville and Leopoldo Batres to the mid-twentieth-century work of Alfonso Caso and Ignacio Bernal, and more recently to John Paddock, Kent Flannery, Steve Kowalewski, Charles Spencer, Bruce Byland, Marcus Winter, and many others.

Systematic archaeological research began in the Mixteca in the early 1930s, with limited surface survey in the central region and excavations in two major sites, Yucuñudahui and Monte Negro. In the late 1940s, reasonably extensive excavation was conducted at Coixtlahuaca, and in the 1950s limited exploration was carried out at Yatachío of Tamazulapan. Generally speaking (as outlined in chapters 2 and 3), these were rather individualized investigations aimed at gaining knowledge of developments at particular loci and/or relationships between the Mixteca Alta and Monte Albán.

Beginning in the mid-1960s, however, the objectives of archaeological research shifted to a more regional and processual orientation that combined extensive-intensive regional survey and associated selective excavations. This demanded the honing of specific methods, including the formation of a systematic pottery typology-chronology for the region, ecological and geomorphological studies, and an emphasis on cross ties between sites both within the Mixteca and beyond (see results from the Vanderbilt University Nochixtlan Valley Project, the University of Michigan Prehistory and Human Ecology of the Valley of Oaxaca Project, and the somewhat later Valley of Oaxaca Settlement Pattern Project).[8] More recent and current archaeological studies (1990s to the present) are the direct descendants of the mid-1960s to 1970s projects and are discussed in detail in subsequent chapters. Among the more important recent developments in the archaeology of the Mixteca have been the expansion of the regional survey program and the excavation of the urban capital at Yucundaa-Teposcolula.

These collective efforts required planning and coordination among numerous individuals and several academic and research institutions. The information presented in this book is derived directly from this highly productive and creative archaeological base. Without it, and the collaborations on which it is based, most of the material and related interpretations and conclusions presented here would not be possible.

The Ethnohistorical-Ethnological Foundation

The most productive approach to the study of Mixtec culture and history is a convergent methodology that incorporates the methods and results of historiography, archaeology, linguistics, geography-geology, and ethnology. Each category provides a specific set of techniques for exploiting and processing cultural information. Taken together, however, the sum of the parts of this method of study eclipses the substance and value of any one of the individual approaches. At times we have referred to the larger focus as ethnohistory, or "documentary ethnology."[9] In the present context, however, it is more useful to reserve the term "ethnohistory" for our explicit use of conventionally written or pictorial manuscripts and their conversion to raw ethnographic and historical data, with at least some diachronic penetration being provided by oral history. The framework of analysis, however, is anthropological, therefore not relying exclusively on one sort of study or information, to the exclusion of other data and approaches.

Figure 1.2. Archaeological survey of Inguiteria, the Postclassic capital of Coixtla-huaca; the surfaces not yet cut by erosion have artifacts and house remains in place, showing that most of the erosion is post abandonment.

The ethnohistorian is in a position to search for solutions to anthropological problems and may engage in empirical research or test hypotheses as effectively as any other social scientist. There are many possible lines of inquiry into the nature of socioeconomic organization of a community or region and its relationship to demographic fluctuation or technological innovation. For example, as with the Mixteca, it is possible to investigate connections between a political capital, or *cabecera*, and its subordinate communities and between the community and the province or state and the factors that may contribute to changes in those relationships over time. Also over time can be examined the nature of a system of beliefs as well as conceptual and institutional changes and their broader cultural relationships.

Several features of the ethnohistoric approach should be mentioned. First, documentary ethnology allows for consideration of long developmental sequences, some covering decades, others—as with the Mixteca or the valleys

Figure 1.3. Excavation of Building E-4 at Yucundaa–Pueblo Viejo de Teposcolula, near the royal palace. Laura Diego Luna (standing) is one of the excavators.

of Oaxaca or Mexico—extending from before the eleventh century to modern times. Conventional ethnographic studies are largely restricted to the present, but the ethnohistorian can focus on the past and the present and observe cultural developments through long periods of time. Second, the documentary approach allows for detailed synchronic-functional analysis at any point in time for which documentation is available, as, for example, the case of the ancient political system, the *yuhuitayu*, *señoríos*, *cacicazgos* or kingdoms of the Mixtec. Third, documentary ethnology can employ one of the most scientific methodologies in anthropology, for its basic data are highly susceptible to verification and authentication. As long as the documentation upon which a study is based is extant, anyone can examine that exact same documentation, retrace the investigator's steps, and reach their own conclusions regarding the reliability of cultural inferences. Obviously, documentation can provide a breadth of exposure to cultural details that are generally not possible for the archaeologist, yet it retains the diachronic dimension that is not accessible to the conventional ethnologist. We reiterate, however, that the best approach is one that combines *all* of these methods and orientations by an individual or, as is more often the case, through collaboration of several investigators.

The first major category of resources for the Mixteca are the native picture manuscripts of the pre-Hispanic era and their Colonial derivatives and native European illustrative, artistic, and cartographic sources created from the time of the Spanish conquest to the early twentieth century. The media of presentation are stone, primarily deer skin, bone, and native paper. The vast majority of these illustrated sources by now have been published separately in collections, or as relevant components in many articles and books. Pictographic documents have been most plentiful from the Valley of Mexico, from Oaxaca—especially the Mixteca—and from the Maya area.

An extensive body of unpublished manuscript sources has been used in the preparation of this book, and the senior author is first and foremost an ethnohistorian. Most of these materials are preserved in three major repositories: the Archivo General de la Nación, Mexico City; the Archivo General de Indias, Seville; and the Archivo Histórico del Poder Judicial del Estado de Oaxaca, in the city of Oaxaca. Also of great importance have been materials housed in the more specialized archives of the world, such as the Bancroft Collection at the University of California, the Latin American Library at the University of Texas, the Bodleian Library of Oxford University, and the *bibliotecas nacionales* of Mexico and Spain. There are, of course, abundant published sources, many of which have been used in the preparation of this book and which are listed in the bibliography. Several of the more important archives and libraries are worthy special mention.

Archivo General de la Nación, Mexico City (AGN)

This is the richest repository of manuscript materials in America relating to the Mixteca during the Colonial period. Its holdings are divided into several dozen *ramos*, or sections. Although there are indexes, guides, and extensive bibliographies relating to the holdings of the AGN, there is absolutely no alternative to consultation of the originals or their exact copies.

The preparation of this book relies on materials from six sections of the AGN:

Ramo de Civil: records of civil litigation involving both natives and Spaniards.
Ramo de Indiferente General: a collection of short reports and grants or denials of individual privileges, orders for investigation, or resolution

Figure 1.4. Cathedral, left, and Archivo General de Indias, Seville, Spain.

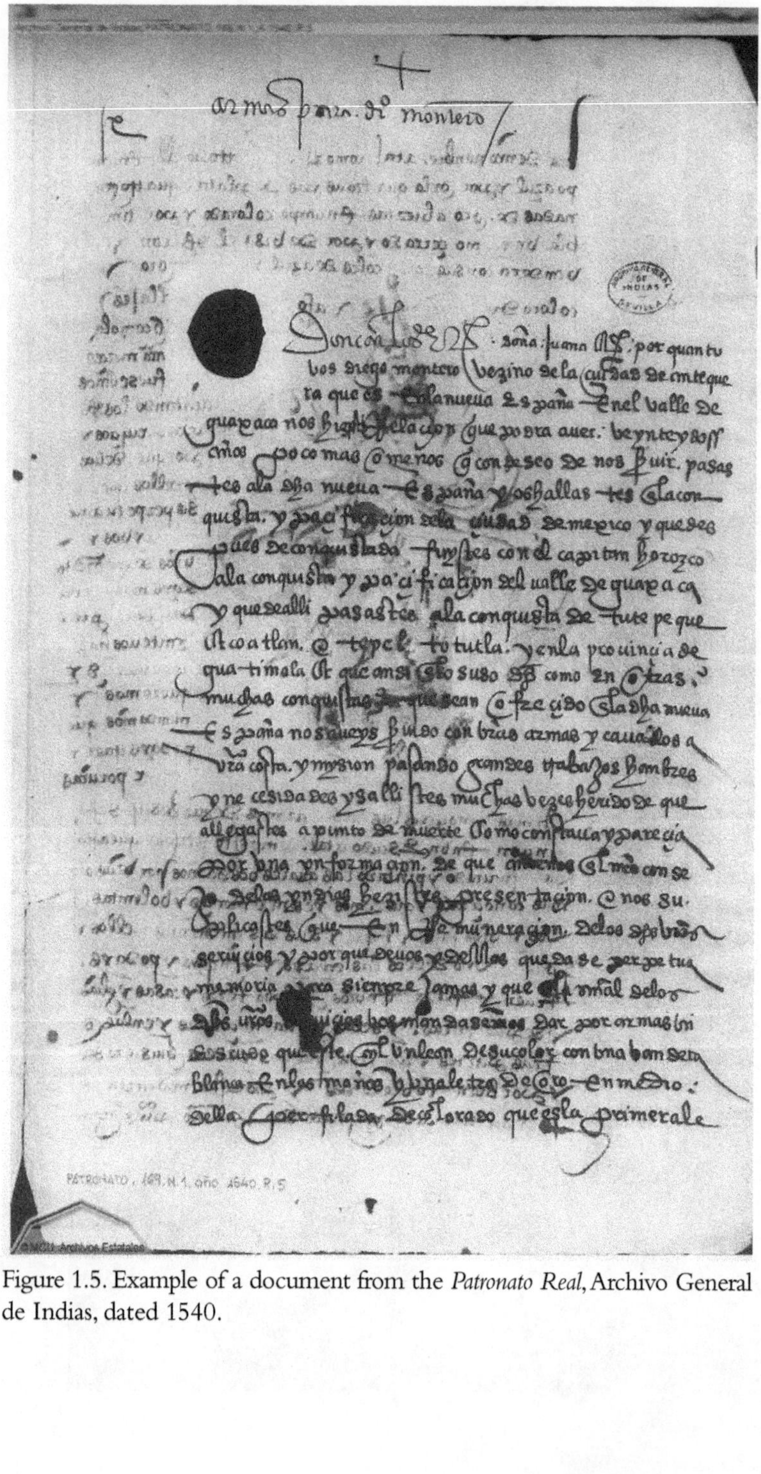

Figure 1.5. Example of a document from the *Patronato Real*, Archivo General de Indias, dated 1540.

of all manner of conflicts involving natives, Spaniards, and religious and civil institutions.

Ramo de Indios: litigation, grants and prohibitions, reports and orders for investigation of all matters relating to natives.

Ramo de Inquisición: records of investigations and processes relating to matters of heresy, idolatry, treason, and other violations of the "divine order" as defined by the Crown and the office of the Spanish Royal Inquisition throughout the Colonial period, and involving natives from the time of their conversion to Christianity until the mid-1570s, when they were exempted from inquisitorial jurisdiction and process.

Ramo de Mercedes: royal grants of privilege or entitlements to both natives and Spaniards.

Ramo de Tierras: a voluminous collection of lawsuits regarding public and private lands and resources involving natives, Spaniards, communities, and religious, secular, and corporate institutions and agencies.

Archivo General de Indias, Seville (AGI)

The AGI consists of 43,000 bundles, or at least 80 million pages, of original documents housed in the sixteenth-century Casa Lonja de Mercaderes in Seville, Spain. It is the largest and most valuable repository of original documentation relating to the history of the Spanish Empire in the Americas and the Philippines. Although there are earlier and later documents, the vast majority relate to the period from 1492 to the 1820s. Investigators have access to original documents, to microfilm, to photocopies, and, increasingly, to digitalized impressions.

The AGI is arranged in *ramos*, the most important for the study of Colonial life in Oaxaca being the following:

Audiencia de México: a vast collection of thousands of bundles of documents relating to the governance of New Spain from 1519 until the end of Colonial times. Whatever the subject—social, political, economic, or religious—any research project on Colonial New Spain–Mexico would be incomplete without reference to the documentation found in this *ramo*.

Contaduría: an enormous collection of primarily economic documents relating to Spain and its empire from medieval times to the nineteenth century. It contains incredibly detailed accounts, reports, audits, wills, censuses, and inventories all aimed at controlling the wealth and expenditures resulting from Spain's vast economic enterprise.

Escribanía de Cámara: a large *ramo* containing millions of pages relating to the economic and political matters of Spain and its vast empire from medieval times to the end of the empire, as well as wills and litigation over estates and dispensation of inherited wealth.

Indiferente General: as the title suggests, this branch of the archives is a great collection of documentation of all types relating to Spain since medieval times. It is an extremely varied resource, requiring painstaking consultation in order to find and utilize relevant materials.

Justicia: one of the greatest documentary collections ever assembled concerning all matter of justice and legal matters relative to Spain and its vast empire from Islamic-medieval through Colonial times and on into the twentieth century. The documentation is incredibly detailed and partially cataloged for general purposes of reference and research. It would, however, be erroneous to assume that such lists and indices cover anywhere near all the subject matter or potential of this grand *ramo*. They do not.

Patronato Real: a vitally important collection of documentation involving the right of the Spanish Crown to control both civil-military and religious organization and dispensation in the empire and related matters in the New World. As is readily apparent, this authority extended to every conceivable type of activity, and this is reflected in the highly diversified contents of Patronato documentation.

Biblioteca Nacional de México, Mexico City (BNM)

These holdings contain abundant documentation, books, picture manuscripts, maps, censuses, reports, works of art, and architectural renderings, with strong emphasis on resources from the Colonial period and the nineteenth century.

Biblioteca Nacional de España, Madrid (BNE)

Similar in its holdings to the National Library of Mexico, the BNE eclipses that facility in terms of the extent of its collections and the antiquity of its resources, which extend back to Roman and medieval times.

Archivo General del Poder Ejecutivo del Estado de Oaxaca (AGEO)

Although of minimal utility for studies relating to sixteenth-century Oaxaca, the AGEO is of inestimable value for a complete study of multilevel government, vital statistics, and general history of the region from the seventeenth century until the present. Although incompletely organized and cataloged, with sufficient dedication investigators can glean abundant valuable information from this underutilized collection.

Archivo Histórico del Poder Judicial del Estado de Oaxaca (APJO)

This is an indescribably important archive for localized research in the specific areas of Oaxaca from about 1535 through the twentieth century. It is organized regionally from documentation gathered in this fine facility in Oaxaca from the *juzgados de primera instancia* (courts of the first instance) throughout Oaxaca, and it is most notably valuable for research on the Mixteca (from the Teposcolula archives) and the Sierra Norte de Oaxaca (from the Yalalag archives) for the Colonial period and to a lesser extent for studies involving documentation from the Huajuapan, Etla, Juchitan, Tehuantepec, Ejutla, and Yautepec archives. Like the AGEO, the APJO is inexplicably underutilized.

There are guides of varying utility to all of the noted sections (*ramos*) of the AGN and AGI and lesser archives, and the great *bibliotecas* of Mexico, Spain, the United States, and other European countries, but thorough, reliable exploitation requires painstaking, page-by-page review of the original documents or consultation of reliable photocopies or transcriptions. Even good guides or indexes are always lacking in the descriptive detail necessary to cover all areas of possible inquiry, so. any study that relies solely on these guides would be woefully inadequate. As may be obvious, a working knowledge, if not mastery, of Spanish paleography is absolutely essential to adequate utilization of these documentary resources.

There are no shortcuts in ethnohistorical research, and no manner of digitalization, or other recent technical contrivance, can substitute for finding, reading, and interpreting the sources. For this task, the ethnohistorian must hone a set of specific techniques and methods that are every bit as precise and demanding, if not more so, as for any archaeologist, ethnologist, historian, geologist, biologist, or linguist. Moreover, it is essential that the ethnohistorian working in Mexico understand governmental and religious organization and institutions in Spanish Colonial and Republican times. Studies often fail to consider these institutions and their possible effect on all aspects of life. An understanding of governmental structure, function, and hierarchy is essential in order to evaluate the context within which particular sets of documents were produced, or to understand why they were produced in the first place. Context, as well as content, is an essential consideration in ethnohistorical research.

The employment of documentary sources contained in archives through-out the world, together with the prudent use of abundant primary and secondary sources in printed form, can be applied to a nearly endless stream of anthropological problems. The ethnohistorical approach has already produced abundant positive returns in Mexican anthropology, but future contributions utilizing a more conscious and systematic methodology will result in ever better ethnological studies. Additionally, these studies provide models for application not only to Mexico but to Spanish America in general and to all areas of the world where any substantial corpus of ethnohistorical documentation exists.

There, it is done. We may now return to the Mixtec, to their environment, language, and culture as it has developed over the past three millennia and more since the advent of village life. The Mixteca of today is considered by some to be one of Mexico's poorer regions. Such evaluations, however, may betray a lack of knowledge on the part of the commentator about the area and its history and potential. "Undeveloped" or "underdeveloped" are generally preferable and more accurate designations for the region than "poor," "impoverished," or "backward." In times past, the Mixteca was among the most productive and densely populated regions of pre-Hispanic Mexico. Natural resources are abundant, and means both technological and social were found to sustain agricultural production at least until the time of the Conquest. We begin with the natural environment and cultural geography. The environments of the three major subregions of the Mixteca are varied, even internally, and this variation is one of the keys to understanding the Mixtecos.

Environment and Geography

As a cultural and geographic area, the Mixteca constitutes the western third of the modern state of Oaxaca, plus adjacent portions of southern Puebla and easternmost Guerrero. It is an extensive and diversified region extending approximately 260 kilometers from southern Puebla to the Pacific Ocean and 175 kilometers from eastern Guerrero to the western edge of the Valley of Oaxaca and the Cañada de Cuicatlan. Altitudes run from sea level to over 3,000 meters. Topography ranges from rolling to irregular to severely fragmented, and physical barriers join time and distance to channel human movement and interaction. Climate, depending on altitude and topography, ranges considerably in temperature and precipitation; the only certainty is the annual change from dry season to wet, and of course the likelihood of being surprised by the weather.[10]

Figure 1.6. Valley of Putla, with the Postclassic archaeological site La Azteca atop mountain in right background; below, the Colonial-era sugar *hacienda*, Trapiche la Concepción, established around 1550.

There are no broad, open plains or basins in the Mixteca. Even relatively open valleys are broken and uneven. Short, seasonally fluctuating streams constitute the principal hydrographic features of the area. Surface or near-surface water is generally in short supply, and the sufficiency of rainfall varies from year to year and region to region. The Mixteca is normally divided into three regions, the Mixteca Baja in the north and northwest; the Mixteca Alta in the central and eastern zone; and the Mixteca de la Costa (Costa Chica or Mixteca Costa) in the southwest and south. Diverse topography and climate result in multiple microenvironments, and the historical and cultural developments in the Alta, Baja, and Costa have been notably affected by this geographical diversity.

The "nuclear area" for the development of Mixtec civilization, and the central focus of the present book, is the Mixteca Alta;[11] but we seek to understand the Alta within the context of the whole Mixteca and, secondarily, with the rest of Oaxaca and Mesoamerica.[12] The Mixteca Alta is a cool, relatively moist, starkly folded and microenvironmentally diversified area of mountains, high hills, canyons, and valleys. Zones of human occupation range from 1,650 to 2,500 meters. The Mixteca Baja is a topographically diverse, hot, and semiarid zone in which occupation extends from 750 to 1,650 meters. The Mixteca Costa rises from sea level at the Pacific Ocean to 750 meters in the north and consists primarily of a narrow coastal plain backed by irregular "foothills," with a hot and relatively humid climate and dense plant growth. Although the known earlier development of the Mixtec tradition is found most prominently in the Alta, by the Classic period, and even more prominently the Postclassic period, Mixtec-speaking peoples and their institutions extended across the three Mixtecas, into the Valley of Oaxaca, and as far east as the Isthmus of Tehuantepec.

Although often called one of Mexico's poorest regions, the Mixteca, in reality, is rich in natural resources, usable land, forests, minerals, and has a climate favorable to growth of a variety of crops. Although the region is lacking in expansive valleys, agriculture is entirely feasible throughout the region, where for thousands of years Mixtec farmers have adapted to the narrow valleys as well as the mountains, ridges, and slopes, including areas where terraced fields could be created. Water derived from seasonal rainfall, and to a limited degree from natural springs, creeks, and rivers, is normally adequate to support wild plant growth and to sustain seasonal agriculture in the drier areas and year-round farming elsewhere.

In the uplands of the region, Mixtec farmers grew and subsisted upon a basic dietary complex of corn, beans, and squash, with heavy supplementation from such domesticates as *maguey* (agave), cactus, chili peppers, avocados, *chia* (amaranth), and *zapotes* (a wide variety of fleshy and colorful fruits). Although the daily diet was derived from cultigens, the Mixtecs also collected a great variety of wild plants, nuts, tubers, cacti, and fruits that were utilized as food, for medicine, and for numerous practical and ceremonial functions.[13] In areas favorably disposed for such crops, primarily the lower and coastal areas extending from around Putla south to the Pacific, *cacao* (the cocoa bean or seed pod from the tree *Theobroma cacao*, used to make chocolate), cotton, peanuts, and tobacco were grown.

The only domesticated animals of importance were the turkey, the dog, and quite possibly ducks. They figured in the diet and ritual activities of the Mixtec, but none was developed for work. Numerous wild animals were hunted for food, for clothing, and for ritual-ceremonial purposes.[14] Access to some forms, such as deer or turkeys, was limited to the noble classes. Other wild forms, such as rabbits and many rodents, snakes and other reptiles, jaguars and other wild cats, coyotes, and *javali* (wild pig) were important to the Mixtecs. Birds, large and small, were hunted for food or for their valuable plumage or captured for ritual sacrifice. Fish and shellfish, and where available sea mammals, were also important, especially in the Costa, but these forms were also traded to the Mixteca Alta and Baja.[15]

Substantial pine and oak forests, as well as a heavy concentration of gigantic *sabinos* or *ahuehuetes* (cypress trees) along stream banks, are found in the higher reaches of the Mixteca Alta and Baja, and the Costa produces a variety of usable hardwoods, palms, and climbers. Wild plant life is most abundant and most varied in the Costa, but dozens of usable wild roots, bulbs, beans and nuts, berries, vines, leaves, bark, resins, mushrooms and other fungi, and other edibles grow throughout the Mixtecas.

Plentiful mineral resources were utilized by the ancient Mixtecs.[16] Salt was found in abundance in the region of the Costa stretching from Pinotepa to Tututepec, and from veins of salt production in such scattered areas as San Felipe Ixtapa, Teposcolula, Santa María Salinas, San Bartolo Salinas, and San Ildefonso Salinas in the region of Santiago Tamazola in northwestern Oaxaca, and Zapotitlan Salinas in southern Puebla. At least three of these areas continue to produce high-quality salt (Zapotitlan, San Bartolo, and Santa María Salinas) and have structural remains and abundant pottery dating from at least the Classic period. Similar evidence of early "industrial sites" can be found in numerous localities along the Pacific coast from the Guerrero border to Puerto Angel.

Other mineral resources were the abundant limestone used in construction and for production of lime, *endeque* (Mixteco: *ndique*, a soft, incompletely formed limestone used extensively for construction in the Mixteca Alta and Baja), and basalt or volcanic tuff employed in the production of grinding implements such as *manos*, *metates*, and *molcajetes* from Archaic times until the present. Large deposits of high-quality chert utilized in stone-tool production are found extensively in the Mixteca Alta, most notably at the vast quarry at Classic-period Yucuñudahui[17] and at a source located approximately half-way between San Felipe Ixtapa and Yolomecatl in the Mixteca Alta. A third known chert source is at Chilapa de Díaz.[18]

Excellent clays for pottery production are found in numerous specific localities in all three Mixtecas. Some of the better-known sources are in communities that continue to produce pottery, many of which are nearly indistinguishable from pre-Hispanic wares: Acatlan, Puebla; Silacayoapilla and Ayuquilla, Huajuapan; Santiago Tamazola, Silacayoapan; San Andrés Montaña and San Juan Mixtepec, Juxtlahuaca; Cuquila, San Antonio Nduaxico, and Magdalena Peñasco, Tlaxiaco; Santo Domingo Tonaltepec, Teposcolula; San Miguel Adequez and San Pedro Cántaros Coxcaltepec, Nochixtlan; and Jicayan, Tlacamama and Mechoacan, Jamiltepec. Given the undoubted importance of these quasi-industrial centers with respect to the modern economy and the direct connections with ancient pottery production in the Mixteca,[19] it is curious that so few have been studied. The notable exceptions are Acatlan, Puebla, studied by Louana Lackey, and Jicayan, Oaxaca, studied by Fran Ahern.[20] Investigation of pottery production and related cultural factors in these communities should have the very highest priority in future ethnographic and archaeological research in the Mixteca; it is, based on current trend lines, a dying art.

Another important mineral resource was mica, found in widely scattered areas but utilized heavily as an inclusion in pre-Hispanic pottery, particularly in the Mixteca Baja, for use in ritual and ceremonial attire as inferred at Tayata, and as "cut-sheet" offerings in burials, most prominently observed in excavations in such sites as Yucunama, Cerro de las Minas, Huamelulpan, and Yucuita, and in surface survey of dozens of sites in the Alta and Baja. Other important mineral resources were gold, silver, alabaster, jadeite, and a vast array of pigments used in artistic painting, pottery decoration, and textile dying or as cosmetics.[21] Except for mineral pigments, which are found virtually universally, the sources, manner of extraction, and distribution of these substances, particularly jade, is incompletely known. The best study of these more rare resources and their use would be Alfonso Caso's study of Tomb 7 at Monte Albán.[22]

THE LINGUISTIC EVIDENCE AND MIXTECA PREHISTORY

The major language of the Mixteca in prehistoric and modern times is Mixteco. There are numerous dialects of this complex three-tone language, and it is, in turn, fairly closely related to Cuicateco and Trique; a little more distantly related to Mazatec, Chocho, Ixcateco, Popoloca, Amuzgo, and Tlapaneco; still

Figure 1.7. Fernando Reyes, a weaver from Santa Cruz Tayata, master of a dying art.

more distantly related to Zapoteco, Chatino, and Chinanteco; and quite distantly related to such languages as Otomi of central Mexico, Chiapaneco of the Isthmus, and Mangue of Central America.[23]

According to the linguistic studies of Otomanguean culture history by Kathryn Josserand, Marcus Winter, and Nicholas Hopkins, sometime around 4500 B.C.E., Proto-Otomanguean split into two major branches.[24] The western Mesoamerican branch eventually divided into a northern subbranch that included Otopamian and Chinantecan languages and a central subbranch consisting of Tlapanec and Chiapanec-Mangue languages. Starting from the Puebla area, the latter cluster eventually pushed far to the south into Chiapas and Central America.

The eastern Mesoamerican branch of Proto-Otomanguean split into a subbranch consisting of Amuzgo and Mixtecan languages, and a second subbranch was comprised of Popolocan and Zapotecan. With respect to the Amuzgo-Mixtecan subbranch, Amuzgo split off during the centuries between 3500 and 2500 B.C.E. About 2000 B.C.E., around the beginning of the Formative period and early village life, Trique split off from Mixtecan, and around 500 B.C.E. Cuicatec became a separate language. Josserand and others believe that sometime during the seventh century Mixtec was diversifying into its five major dialectical groups, and that this diversification continued until

Figure 1.8. Palm-leaf baskets, or *tenates*, in Zaachio, Nochixtlan; this tradition goes back to pre-Hispanic times.

after the Spanish Conquest.[25] It is interesting that this linguistic diversification occurred in tandem with the cultural disruptions of the Epiclassic period 600–900 C.E. that we discuss in subsequent chapters.

The major dialectical areas are:

1. The Central and Eastern Mixteca Alta: that includes the Yanhuitlan-Nochixtlan Valley, Teposcolula, Tamazulapan, Coixtlahuaca, Apoala, Tilantongo-Mitlatongo-Peñoles, and the Valley of Oaxaca. A non-contiguous outlier of Mixtec speakers in Coatzospan in the Mazateca speak a dialect that may pertain to the Central and Eastern dialectical area.

2. The Western Mixteca Alta: the area lying south and west of the Yanhuitlan-Nochixtlan Valley, centering around Tlaxiaco and Achiutla and terminating to the south in the Chalcatongo–San Miguel el Grande area.

3. The Northern Mixteca Baja: the upper Río Balsas drainage, including Chigmecatitlan and Acatlan, Puebla, Huajuapan de León, Tonala,

Figure 1.9. Modern *endeque* mine in Coixtlahuaca; blocks of this kind were used in pre-Hispanic construction.

and Silacayoapan. Northern Mixteca Baja dialects relate more closely to the Central and Eastern Mixteca Alta regions than to the Western Mixteca Alta area, but due to somewhat inadequate dialectical study, firm conclusions on internal complexity, external relations, and linguistic history are not yet feasible.

4. The Southern Mixteca Baja: the area around San Juan Mixtepec and Santiago Juxtlahuaca–Tecomaxtlahuaca and Putla, and extending to the Metlatonoc area of eastern Guerrero. Southern Mixteca Baja dialects relate rather closely to dialects in the western Mixteca Alta area.

5. The Mixteca Costa: includes Ixtayutla, Jicayan, Pinotepa, and Tututepec on Oaxaca's Pacific coast. According to the authors, "this dialect group is both recent and relatively homogeneous, formed by two major population movements which probably originated in the region of San Juan Mixtepec, reaching the coast by the tenth century."[26] These observations as well have strong archaeological parallels that we discuss later on.

It would be difficult to argue with the authors' conclusions that "the combination of linguistic with archeological data as well as ethnohistorical

Figure 1.10. Emelia Ramírez Santiago and her pottery, Santo Domingo Tonaltepec, Teposcolula; another tradition descended from pre-Hispanic antecedents.

information can and should form the basis for greater understanding of the social and cultural development of the Mixtec."[27] Unfortunately, progress toward these noble objectives has been painstakingly slow. Intensive archaeological surveys (and in rare instances excavations) have been completed, are under way, or are planned for the immediate future in the valleys of Nochixtlan, Tamazulapan, Tilantongo, Teposcolula, Huamelulpan, Tlaxiaco, Achiutla and the Costa, along with Coixtlahuaca-Tequixtepec, but vast areas of the Mixteca Baja; the borderlands between Oaxaca, Guerrero, and Puebla, the Chalcatongo-Yosondua area; and the broad expanse between Putla, Ixtayutla, and the Costa remain virtually untouched by systematic archaeological surveys and excavation.[28]

Although the linguistic work of Josserand and Hopkins has been monumentally important, they are the first to admit that much dialectical and historical linguistic research remains to be done. Just now the Mixteca Baja

Figure 1.11. Mixtec dialect areas. Redrawn from VUPA 31, map 1.

would appear to be most urgently in need of linguistic attention. The opportunities are there, but a lack of motivated personnel and appropriate planning and funding, the great distances, and difficult accessibility have conspired to inhibit attainment of the convergent goals set out by both linguists and archaeologists. Also, virtually no progress has been made by archaeologists to define linguistic groupings on the basis of purely archaeological data.[29]

The Ñuiñe problem in the Mixteca Baja, the nature of the relationship of Ñuiñe art and iconography to the Mixtec language, culture, and history demands coordinated archaeolinguistic research.[30] The recent expansion of the regional survey program in the Mixteca Alta likewise has gone forth without attention to the linguistic implications of the inferred relationships among sites and subregions of the Mixteca. One encouraging note is the linguists' findings that the coastal dialects of Mixtec relate to the highlands to the north and that the Mixtec penetration of the area began during the tenth century. This fits exceedingly well with conclusions drawn from the historical record that Mixtecs, many of them associated with the imperial machinations of Lord Eight Deer, moved into the area that quite likely was previously occupied by other groups, probably Chatinos.[31]

THE PROTOHISTORIC MIXTEC COMMUNITY

When Spaniards arrived in Oaxaca in the 1520s they found a native political system controlled by hereditary elite and articulated by martial and voluntary alliances and military conquest. The Mixtec system consisted of a constellation of small states, the pre-Hispanic *yuhuitayu* or Colonial-era *cacicazgos*, extending from southern Puebla to the Pacific coast and from the Valley of Oaxaca west to Guerrero.[32] Bilateral kinship reckoning, rules of inheritance, and requirements of status-group endogamy had channeled power and property among royal-class nobles throughout the Mixteca since the tenth century, if not before. Although much of the area came under the political-tributary control of the Culhua-Mexica (or Aztec) Empire in the early sixteenth century, there was virtually no outside interference in native political, social, and economic institutions, and there was a high level of independence in the Mixtec system of government.[33]

As the Spanish established control over Oaxaca, they not only tolerated the preexisting political system but reinforced the authority of the traditional rulers and incorporated them into their plan of acculturation, economic exploitation, religious conversion, and systems of social welfare and conflict resolution.[34] Native lords, called *caciques* by the Spaniards, remained in authority in their communities, and the rights and privileges of the rulers and their families were reinforced and protected both in theory and practice. Although males occupied official positions of authority as governors of native communities, women were recognized as legitimate *cacicas*; held great wealth in land, houses, livestock, and movable property; were entitled to specific services from the communities making up their *cacicazgos*; and functioned as regional entrepreneurs.

During the pre-Hispanic era, the population of the Mixteca was concentrated in communities of varying size and function. The larger communities were urban centers, internally diversified and serving to integrate surrounding rural communities and also to link them to comparable clusters of cities and towns. This constellation of city-town-village provided the matrix of Mixtec culture during the centuries preceding the Spanish Conquest. And it was within this geopolitical context that Colonial acculturation and the transformation of Mixtec society took place, after a few critical changes imposed by the Spanish.

What follows is a brief overview of the structure of the Mixtec community. We describe the urban dimensions of Mixtec settlement and link these field observations to relevant documentation. What emerges is a revised model for the Mixtec "community kingdom," noting that these are in fact separate, although interactive, categories (the place of residence versus the institution of the *cacicazgo*).[35] The purpose of the ethnohistorical model in this instance is to give a sense of what we are looking at archaeologically in the sites and regions of the Mixteca, and for what is salient in an anthropological sense. It is a model to be tested through archaeology. For the present, it helps us to link our household excavations with the larger region's settlement pattern. What, after all, do all those dots, blobs, signs, and squiggles mean on our survey maps? "Sites" are not analytical constructs so much as bits of data to be combined, sorted, and squeezed of useful information. It is the community and its constituent elements that we are trying to reconstruct.

Pre-Hispanic Background to the *Cacicazgo*

Pre-Hispanic Mixtec government was based on direct rule by a minimal hierarchy composed of rulers and principal men. Although only a small ruling caste and a relatively few *principales* were involved in government, traditional bonds of loyalty between rulers and subject populations served to integrate and perpetuate numerous little kingdoms, or *cacicazgos*, throughout the region.[36] The *cacicazgos* were linked by aristocratic marital alliances and through trade and a regional ceremonial complex. Economic activity extended beyond *cacicazgo* boundaries, but subsistence needs were met within the local sphere. The ancient Mixtec world was, for the most part, defined by the sky above, the land below, and the visible horizon.

Social activities were organized around the community and the administrative-ceremonial center. Even under Culhua-Mexica domination, government remained uncomplicated by bureaucracy or massive labor or military mobilization. There was little concern for, or involvement with, the world beyond the Mixteca. Economic ties extended to other regions of Mesoamerica, but political action was localized, at least until late Postclassic times, when alliances were formed with Zapotecs of the Valley of Oaxaca and probably with other groups. Although marital-political alliances often articulated polities that were quite separated within the Mixtec sphere, linking mechanisms were simplified and direct and without an overriding superstructure. This situation changed with the Spanish Conquest. The Spanish nonetheless quickly discovered the virtues of the native system of government and simply built an administrative superstructure atop the native one.[37]

The Ethnohistorical Mixtec Community

Despite the evident variation of late pre-Hispanic Mixtec communities in spatial extent, in demographic parameters, and in their prior settlement histories, monumentality, and prominence based on historical documentation, there is a shared structure recognizable in most if not all Postclassic and protohistoric communities in the Mixteca. The model community exhibits a combination of four components: a civic and commercial center, or *cabecera*, inclusive of numerous *barrios* or residential wards; several outlying settlement clusters (the variously termed *sujetos*, *estancias*, *ranchos*, or hamlets); one or more unique ceremonial precincts often at a remove from the urban core of the community; and farming and collecting lands in the fully rural areas, although agricultural features were also found even in the most urbanized settings. These characteristic traits constituted the Mixtec community from roughly 1500 to the time of effective Spanish occupation around 1528 and, we believe, for many centuries before European contact.

The first component of the Mixtec community was of course the concentrated civic and commercial center, or *cabecera*, of the urban capitals. These were zones composed of dwellings, governmental facilities (which may coincide with elite households), ceremonial sites, a market plaza, possibly defensive alignments and/or guard stations, and other structures. Centers were usually located on level or gently sloping ground. Frequently, as at Coixtlahuaca,

Yucuita, and Chachoapan, these centers lay at the margins between steep mountain slopes and relatively level valley farmlands. In other instances, as at the *pueblos viejos* of Teposcolula, Tamazulapan, Nochixtlan, and Tilantongo, or at Huazolotitlan, centers were located on relatively high hills or promontories overlooking valley lands. It is not clear whether the variation in environmental setting was chronologically significant or suggestive of other factors.

The center was divided into wards, or *barrios*, of variable size and number. Some of the wards were occupied by families devoted to the service of the community ruler; others were taken over by free commoners who were farmers, merchants, or artisans; also residing in the center were the hereditary ruler and his family and members of the local nobility. There is no convincing evidence that the Mixtec *barrios* constituted discrete kinship or corporate property-holding units of the type reported for other areas of Mexico. The documents make frequent mention of *barrios* as residential and political units while making no reference to kinship as an organizing factor, but additional research is needed to clarify this matter. The community of Tejupan consisted of a center without dependencies. This was highly unusual for an important place and merits further investigation, although like other large sites it was divided into *barrios*, each governed by a noble appointed by the ruler-*cacique*. Yanhuitlan had more than twenty residential precincts, each supervised by members of the nobility, as well as numerous dependent settlements. Other important Postclassic communities fell somewhere between these extremes.

The second component of Mixtec settlement was the set of outlying dependencies or hamlets. These carry the designations *sujeto*, *estancia*, *aldea*, or *rancho* and were integral components of the Mixtec community. Dependence was indicated by place names or "hill signs" on the pre-Hispanic picture manuscripts and by glyphs and Spanish glosses after the Conquest. Each hamlet consisted of a number of dwellings clustered in an open and rather informal pattern. The hamlets of a community were separated from each other and from the center by fields and irregular terrain at distances ranging from several hundred meters to several kilometers. Often the semi-self-sufficient hamlets were isolated from their center by ranges of mountains as well as considerable distance.

The third component of the Mixtec community was the "disembedded" ceremonial place or places, which were usually located adjacent to (not necessarily within) the concentrated urban center. This zone was most often situated on a mountain or hilltop, in a cave, at a spring, or in association with some unusual natural configuration. Oftentimes the monumental areas of more ancient sites were reutilized for this kind of less public and smaller-scale ceremonialism. Achiutla exemplifies this pattern, but it is also found at Tilantongo, Yucundaa-Teposcolula, Tututepec, and other late pre-Hispanic communities.[38] This ceremonial precinct would be in addition to, but separate from, the more public ceremonial areas present within *cabeceras* and *barrios* and would be places for ruling elites to commune with ancestral spirits and for offerings and sacrifices. The several caves of the "Great Causeway," the monumental raised avenue that surrounds Yucundaa-Teposcolula, are clearly dedicated to important ritual-ceremonial activities. The hilltop, meanwhile, is covered with some of the most impressive public spaces in any of Oaxaca's Postclassic kingdoms.

The fourth component of the Mixtec community consisted of the lands surrounding the center, the hamlets, and the disembedded ceremonial spaces. These lands were devoted to agriculture or were utilized for the hunting of wild game and for the collecting of vegetal materials, minerals, and wood for construction and fuel. Much of this terrain is uninhabited to the present day and remains a commons for living Mixteco communities. Prehistorically, it is important to realize, not all of these lands were "rural" but were functionally integrated with the various residential and urbanized settings. The Mixteca is characterized by an interlacing network of steep-sided mountains, ridges, buttes, and narrow dissected valleys, excepting only a small stretch of coastline. The Mixtecs adapted to this situation of limited arable land by developing the remarkable system of *lama-bordo* or *coo-yuu* (cross-channel or gully) terrace farming on the slopes, canyons, and arroyos of the region.[39] This innovation made it possible for the Mixtecs to vastly expand production not only to sustain a large population but to meet the needs of an increasingly demanding ruling aristocracy and, eventually, to satisfy the tributary requirements of the Culhua-Mexica Empire.

Such was the Mixtec community as derived from historical documentation. The question that inevitably arises is, where did it all begin? That, as we will see in the first half of this book, is becoming more apparent from recent archaeological research, although gaps remain. Apart from the senior author's excavations at protohistoric Yucundaa-Teposcolula (ca. 1250–1550), we must retreat a thousand years before reaching the early urban capitals at Monte Negro, Yucuita, and Huamelulpan, for which we have a comparable convergence of regional survey and excavated information. We fall back another thousand years before finding a suitable exemplar of the pre-urban situation in the junior author's study of the Tayatas (ca. 1300–300 B.C.E.). As it happens, the first gap just mentioned coincides with the series of collapses during the Classic to Postclassic transition. The second or earlier gap relates to the flux,

Figure 1.12. Artist's reconstruction of Yucundaa–Pueblo Viejo de Teposcolula, early sixteenth century, based on recent archaeological discoveries. Artist: Enrique Martorell.

if not chaos, evident in settlement shifts during the Middle to Late Formative and the initial growth of cities. These are issues with broad resonance within Mesoamerica but also globally, fitting schemes of the rise and fall of ancient civilizations around the world.

MIXTEC URBANISM

At the Spanish Conquest, Mixtec communities ranged in size from the low hundreds to tens of thousands of inhabitants. Six communities—Coixtlahuaca, Teposcolula, Yanhuitlan, Achiutla, Tilantongo, and possibly "greater Tlaxiaco" in the Mixteca Alta—and Tututepec in the Mixteca Costa—had pre-Conquest populations exceeding ten thousand. Putla, situated on the edge of the Mixteca Baja as it descends toward the coast, likewise approached this size class. In each case, however, the population was widely distributed over a community territory of forty to sixty square kilometers, and in the case of Tlaxiaco, Yanhuitlan, and Achiutla, the bulk of the population was resident not in the *cabeceras* but rather in the outlying *barrios*, *sujetos,* and other subject communities. Among the Mixtec, the urban configuration was situated in the cluster of settlements surrounding the capital, inclusive of the several components enumerated above.[40] It is therefore not the size of the capital or *cabecera* that matters, but the functional integration of the whole—including the undifferentiated settlements, the external relationships, and the exploitation of resources, marketing, craftwork, and agricultural production.

It is clear that at the Spanish Conquest the basic patterns of the Mixtec community described here were found to exist among groups of people speaking the Mixtec language, carrying what has been described as Mixtec culture, and residing in the region called the Mixteca. We believe that the configuration of Mixtec culture as it was known at the time of the Spanish Conquest was formed and functioning at a time no later than the onset of the Postclassic in the tenth century, and for certain cultural patterns long before then. Certainly, the dispersed "clustering pattern" seen during the Postclassic precedes urbanism in the Mixteca and was present since at least the Middle Formative. This conclusion is drawn from statements in the available sixteenth-century documentation, from the analyses of native picture manuscripts, and from the growing foundation of the archaeological record.

The linguistic evidence gathered above indicates that speakers of the Mixtec language were present for the past four thousand years and that the Mixtec cultural pattern, with some exceptions, had already begun to form by

1000 B.C.E. Urban states were in place by 300 B.C.E., if not somewhat before. The *cacicazgo*, an institution arising from the Mixtec community configuration as a "superorganic" means of integration, was present no later than the onset of the Classic period. Oral traditions recorded by Torquemada, Herrera, and Burgoa would tend to suggest a more recent arrival or emergence of the Mixtec people and their historically documented institutions, but this seeming discontinuity has more to do with contemporary dynastic politics than the more realistic time depths arising from linguistic and archaeological research. Our excavations at Tayata and Yucundaa-Teposcolula, the excavations of Monte Negro, Huamelulpan, Cerro de las Minas, and other sites, and more than four decades of archaeological survey in the Mixteca provide ample support for such an inference.

The Functional Configuration of Mixtec Cities

We have discussed the form of Mixtec cities, and we will consider the reasons for their origins in the next chapter, but what were their urban functions? During late pre-Hispanic times, the idealized Mixtec community was composed of a socially and economically diversified capital settlement; one to several outlying towns, villages, and hamlets; one or more ritual-ceremonial activity areas that were integrated into the capital center and its nearby environs, but also in many instances at points removed from populated centers; and farming and collecting lands, oftentimes at some remove from occupied areas but also found integrated within urbanized settings. The *cooyuu* terrace system would be an example of intensive agricultural features being integrated into the urban plan. This loosely nucleated entity that we call "the community" was the basis for the elaboration of Mixtec culture and remained largely intact even after the Spanish Conquest. It was, in short, the dominant structuring feature of Mixtec life. We do not, however, see this as mere happenstance but rather view it as serving fundamentally adaptive functions.

Archaeological settlement patterns illustrate the basic community pattern, replicated again and again in our surveys and reconstructed boundaries of the *yuhuitayu*. We have already alluded to the fact that Teposcolula, Achiutla, and Yanhuitlan, among many other late pre-Hispanic communities, deployed their populations to maximize food production. This pattern is at least as old as urbanism, such that Huamelulpan's core settlements extended along parallel ridgelines within easy reach of the nearest available bottomlands. Terrace farming enhanced this situation, best seen in the truly monumental

coo-yuu system that descends from the summit of Cerro Volado/Huamelul-
pan down to the valley floor.[41] The settlement clusters of earlier times,
surrounding sites like Tayata and pre-urban Yucuita, were directly adjacent
to the best lands and the confluence of river channels. But what did this
settlement system actually do in terms of integrating the region socially, politically, and economically? Why was urbanism so persistent over many
centuries, despite the presumptive strain on the land, to say nothing of the
dynastic tumult recorded in historical documentation?

We can put this discussion in a comparative context with brief reference
to the concept of "agrarian urbanism." Kowalewski and others have proposed
that Mixtec cities functioned as "key brokers in an agrarian economy."[42]
This is one way to understand the pre-Hispanic Mixteca and more generally
the nature of Mesoamerican cities.[43] There were not, after all, good examples
of specialized industries leading to urbanism and states in Mesoamerica,
least of all in the Mixteca, where full-time specialization outside of farming
and a limited number of priestly and political functions was absent. Also
absent were economic drivers typical of other kinds of early states, including
metallurgy—present in Mesoamerica in later times but nonetheless limited—
or for that matter animal husbandry, or long-distance trade in bulk commodities, or maritime traffic—all of no consequence except possibly late in
the sequence.

Agricultural production in pre-Hispanic Mesoamerica was nonetheless
extraordinarily intensive, dependent on human hand-labor without the inter-
cession of draft animals, wheeled vehicles, or plows.[44] In the Mixteca Alta and
Baja, settlement patterns and agricultural terracing were integrated within
a specific pattern of organization comprised of multiple settlements—designated as *cabeceras* and *barrios* during historical times—that had existed since at
least the fourth century B.C.[45] The agrarian form of urbanism meant that cities
coordinated the many locations and forms of agricultural production—for surplus, for exchange, and for the diverse members of society residing throughout the outlying settlements in each small kingdom. The role of rulers and
urban institutions were especially needed to moderate relations among the many
kingdoms, in which microgeographic variation led to differing constellations
of goods and levels of production in a given year.

We encourage the reader to keep these considerations in mind in the
next several chapters as a way of understanding the early appearance of the
settlement cluster and the continuance of the idealized community form
well into Colonial times. The extent to which the Mixteca's productive

resources can be returned to a sustainable basis in the present depends as much on the social dimensions of the Mixtec community as it does on land and water.

GOING FORWARD

In studies of the Spanish Conquest and Colonial period, one frequently expressed view is that native Mesoamericans were defeated by the Spaniards and existed thereafter as a dominated, subjugated, and seamless underclass with little or no power over their own lives or their relationships with the Colonials. Insofar as the Mixtecs are concerned, the image of the down-trodden native masses simply does not conform to social reality. Mixtecs and other indigenous peoples played an active role in the Colonial culture that was forming around them. They were not passive nonactors in a "Great Game" controlled by the Spaniards. On the other hand, never was there significant organized resistance, or a concerted effort by natives to overthrow Spanish control.[46] That occurred only during the Independence era of the early nineteenth century and as a result of the agitation and leadership provided by disgruntled *criollos* and *mestizos* rather than the primarily native communities.

The natives played their own game of adaptation and accommodation, and except for their understandable failure to adjust to an unintended biological extermination from European diseases, the strategy worked quite well. They survived in their towns and villages, and they managed to retain much of their traditional way of life, or they devised an acceptable mix of European and native customs. This does not mean that all Mixtecs were placed below *mestizos*, *criollos*, and *peninsulares* (European-born colonists) in the class system. Some Mixtecs ranked above other Mixtecs, some Spaniards above other Spaniards, and Mixtecs ranked both below and above Spaniards depending on the circumstances. Most natives ranked at the lower end of the social hierarchy, but clearly not all. We delve into these matters more fully in the second half of this book.

It is clear that the Mixteca is a prominent regional variant of the Mesoamerican cultural tradition from the Early Formative period until the arrival of the Spanish in the sixteenth century. A fair amount of archaeological, ethnohistoric, linguistic, and ethnological study has been conducted in the area since the mid-1930s, and within the past decade the pace of research has quickened. More and more attention is being directed to the region and its development, and a new generation of students is finding it to be an attractive area of research—at once uncrowded, underworked, and open to newcomers, yet challenging in terms of the big questions confronting anthropologists, archaeologists, historians, and linguists. This culture area, encompassing some 45,000 square kilometers, is not the Valley of Oaxaca, the Valley of Mexico, or the Maya area. It is something related but different, and one day, very soon, the Mixteca will assume its rightful place among the well-known civilizations of Mesoamerica and the ancient world.

2

THE RISE OF
MIXTEC CIVILIZATION

Prominent among the great civilizations of Mesoamerica were those that developed in and around the central valleys of Oaxaca and in the area of western Oaxaca known as the Mixteca. The Valley of Oaxaca has been under continuous archaeological and ethnohistorical observation since Alfonso Caso's initial studies of Zapotec writing in the 1920s and excavations of Monte Albán that began in 1931. Quite possibly the development of civilization in the Zapotec area is better understood and more adequately documented and described than for any comparable region of Mexico. Although under scientific scrutiny since the mid-1930s, and intermittently until recent times, the archaeology of the Mixteca could only be described as "understudied." That situation, however, is rapidly changing. A new era of archaeological research has put almost everything we thought we knew about the Mixteca to the test. The objectives of this research have been to discover the cultural origins and evolution of Mixtec society from the earliest pre-pottery cultures, to early farming villages, and on to the level of cities and states as they evolved up to the Spanish Conquest.

Our account of the rise of the Mixtec civilization during the Formative or Preclassic period (ca. 2000 B.C.E. to 200 C.E.) relies on the pioneering explorations of Caso, Jorge Acosta, Ignacio Bernal, and Eulalia Guzmán and later projects that began in the mid-1960s.[1] We draw heavily on this earlier research and upon complementary results from the modern regional surveys of the Mixteca and, of course, the excavations at Cerro de las Minas,

Table 2.1

MIXTECA CHRONOLOGICAL SEQUENCE AND SELECT LOCATIONS

Years	Period	Select Sites	Cultural Characteristics
1521–1820	Spanish Colonial *Cacicazgos*	Nueva Antequera, Teposcolula, Yanhuitlan	Conquest and aftermath Colonial documents
900–1521	Postclassic	Achiutla, Coixtlahuaca, Guiengola, Putla, Tilantongo, Tututepec, Yanhuitlan, Yucundaa	Zapotec-Mixtec alliances Eight Deer, Mixtec codices Tututepec's coastal empire Polychrome, metallurgy
600–900	Epiclassic	Jaltepetongo, Ñuiñe sites, "Survivals" in Nochixtlan Valley	Monte Albán's collapse Ñuiñe, coastal art styles
200–600	Classic	Cerro de las Minas, Cerro Jazmín, Yucuñudahui	Origin of *yuhuitayu* "Second wave" urbanization Excavation of Yucuñudahui
300 B.C.E.–200	Late/Terminal 1 Formative	Cerro Jazmín, Huamelulpan, Loma Sandage, Monte Negro, Yucuita	Mixtec urban tradition Monte Negro excavated
2000–300 B.C.E.	Early/Middle Formative	Etlatongo, Tayata, Yucuita, Yucunama	Monte Albán founded Writing begins in Oaxaca Early villages, ranking "Cruz" defined at Yucuita
>2000 B.C.E.	Archaic	Yuzanú	Foraging, incipient cultivation
>8000 B.C.E.	Paleo-Indian	Coxcatlan Cave (Tehuacan)	Hunting and gathering

Huamelulpan, Monte Negro, and Yucuita.[2] These early urban centers have been known for several decades, but with some optimism we now point to the excavation of pre-urban villages in Etlatongo, Tayata, and Yucunama that provide the first real glimpse into the archaeological precursors of the Mixtec cities and states.[3] We focus mainly on the Mixteca Alta at this point, because documented settlement extends much further back in time in the Alta than for either the Baja or Costa. The Mixteca Baja moreover is best known for its Classic period "Ñuiñe sites," which we discuss in the next chapter; the Mixteca Costa meanwhile was occupied by Chatino-speaking populations and was not inhabited by Mixtecs, so far as we know, until Postclassic times.

Mixtec society underwent fundamental evolutionary change over three thousand years ago with the emergence of village life and social division into "ranks" and political systems called "chiefdoms" and again over two thousand years ago with urbanization and the formation of the state. These changes parallel developments elsewhere in Oaxaca and in Mesoamerica. The Valley Zapotec prehistoric record is especially noteworthy, and we mention it frequently.[4] Where else would you find two primary civilizations, interacting and mutually influential over thousands of years, evolving in parallel and occupying nearly the same physical space, but at the same time divergent in many aspects of their cultural development? Mixtec-Zapotec interaction underlies much of what we deem important about the Formative period that culminates in the rise of urban states. But based on a virtual revolution in archaeological research in the Mixteca that has accelerated since the mid-1990s, we find that prior assumptions about the Mixtec as being derived or secondary to the Zapotec or primarily a Postclassic phenomenon are no longer tenable.

We are able to discuss with some clarity the ways that the Mixtec differentiated themselves from other ancient Mesoamerican peoples during the Formative and the reasons why we reject older notions of the Mixtec originating from sources external to the region. Simply put, we see no lag in development compared to the Valley Zapotec, Olmec, Maya, or other Mesoamerican peoples. External influences, while present, are only that, influences; they are not of themselves prime movers but rather interactive variables that worked in tandem with the Mixteca's own internal dynamic.[5] We politely suggest that our colleagues who do their research in other regions attend to these facts and bring the Mixtec into their own comparative treatments of Mesoamerican civilization.

Archaic Pre-Pottery Cultures

The evidence of human occupation in the Mixteca in the years prior to the development of agriculture and pottery and village life is quite sparse (the Archaic period runs from approximately 8000 to 2000 b.c.e.). There is no late Pleistocene record in the Mixteca to speak of, apart from chance finds of extinct fauna, and no clear indications of the coexistence of humans with these animal forms in the entire region (the Valley of Mexico, the Valley of Tehuacan, Puebla, and the Valley of Oaxaca are comparatively well represented in these areas). A Coxcatlan-type projectile point has been recovered on the slopes of Yucuñudahui-Yucunoo of Chachoapan-Coyotepec, indicating that during the early Archaic period, sometime around 7000 B.C.E., hunter-gatherers were roving over the Nochixtlan Valley.[6] Despite instances with suggestive but inconclusive results, we simply do not have a record of continuous human development spanning the Pleistocene/Holocene boundary comparable to Coxcatlan Cave and the Tehuacan sequence or the Valley of Oaxaca.[7]

In 1968 archaeologists from the Instituto Nacional de Antropología e Historia (INAH) excavated a site containing a mammoth mandible in an arroyo on the northwest boundary of Nochixtlan, and many other terminal Pleistocene fossils, mainly mammoth vertebrae, teeth, and long bones, have been recovered in the valleys of Nochixtlan, Tamazulapan, Coixtlahuaca, Tilantongo, Teposcolula, Huamelulpan-Tayata, and elsewhere. We are frequently shown such items by local people while on survey but have never found them in context (the reports of discovery are sometimes decades old). Except for the Nochixtlan recovery, and two other more recent recoveries, in Tequix-tepec and on the slopes of Cerro Jazmín, none of the discoveries were made in controlled excavations, and no related cultural materials have been found.

Several caves and rock shelters have been surveyed in the Mixteca Alta, but none has yielded evidence of human activity during the pre-pottery or Archaic period.[8] In the early 1960s Richard MacNeish found some pro-mising cave sites located along the old Panamerican Highway running from Tamazulapan in the Mixteca Alta through Huajuapan and Chazumba in the Mixteca Baja, but none has been systematically investigated. Survey of the central Mixteca Alta, or the approximate triangle between Tlaxiaco, Tepos-colula, and Tilantongo, recovered a number of Archaic-style projectile points, "early looking" lithic scatters, and undated rock-art sites.[9] There are some dozen such sites from this zone where future studies of the Mixtec Archaic might begin. These open-air and rock shelter sites are similar to ones found on the Peñoles survey,[10] suggesting considerable potential for a widespread but as yet undefined Archaic presence in the Mixteca.

Stephen Kowalewski and associates made a special effort during their survey to investigate suspicious lithic scatters, caves, and other potential Archaic sites, afterward concluding: ". . . the rather thin archaeological remains would say that the people of the Mixteca Alta prior to the second millennium B.C.E. were nomadic gatherers and hunters and that there were not many of them. Such a conclusion may be premature, because some Archaic sites may be invisible to us because of erosion or deposition and because there has never been a full-scale project in the Mixteca Alta specifically aimed at finding Archaic deposits."[11] It is probably significant that chance finds of Archaic projectile points more commonly occur in the Valley of Oaxaca than in the Mixteca Alta, to say nothing of the extensive cave deposits at sites near Mitla excavated by Kent Flannery.[12] But we remain hopeful that future investigators, perhaps following MacNeish's lead in the Mixteca Baja, will generate something more substantial than we have managed to do.

The open-air site of Yuzanú, near Yanhuitlan, was excavated in 1955 by José Luis Lorenzo.[13] At first believed to be a pre-pottery site, with artifacts consisting of various scraping tools, chipping debris, fire-cracked rock, and a hearth (most likely a *maguey*-roasting pit), the location yielded a radiocarbon date of about 2000 B.C.E., close to the time of farming settlements in the Nochixtlan Valley. Rather than being pre-pottery, the site was probably contemporaneous with pottery-using sites, but specialized or temporary and thus lacking in pottery.[14] Archaic or not, Yuzanú will remain an enigma until comparable material from the Mixteca becomes available.

With ongoing and planned surveys of the region, it is probable that evidence of human activity during the Archaic period will eventually be found in the Mixteca. Although at present there is little indication of significant occupation in the region on a level comparable to Tehuacan or the Valley of Oaxaca, only intensive survey and excavation focused on the period will yield answers as to what occurred in the Mixteca prior to the onset of village life.

EARLY VILLAGES, RANK SOCIETIES, AND CHIEFDOMS

The long pre-urban period that Mesoamerican archaeologists call the Early and Middle Formative was a time of substantial change, growing social complexity, and increasing differentiation among regions (approximately 2000 to 300 B.C.E.).[15] It was also a time when substantial sites in many regions were in contact, each of them sharing a set of trade relationships sometimes subsumed under the name Olmec. This may be a misnomer: the mix of local styles and pan-Mesoamerican motifs that appeared on pottery trade wares in many cases originated or had their foremost expressions in highland regions rather than the Olmec heartland on the Gulf Coast of Mexico. Analysis of this style has nonetheless prompted considerable theorizing about the role of Gulf Coastal peoples in the emergence of Mesoamerican civilization.[16]

By the onset of settled village life in the Mixteca (around 1500 B.C.E.), we can accurately describe the inhabitants as being speakers of Mixtec.[17] Half a millennium later, societies of considerable internal complexity appeared on the scene. These "rank societies" had permanent forms of social inequality, expressed in regional site-size hierarchies and differential access to goods among households including valued trade items and various kinds of ritual paraphernalia; when such societies continued to grow and subdivide, and when some villages or settlement clusters expanded into adjoining regions, we can reasonably speak of the presence of chiefdoms.[18] We see these changes manifest in growing site sizes among a subset of the larger villages, in regional site hierarchies, and in status gradients, craft activity, trade relationships, and burial treatment. We would also expect to find evidence of permanent, institutionalized leadership. Chiefdoms are significant for their intrinsic interest, often being called "flamboyant" owing to their elaborate material culture, but also because they are the archaeological precursors to states.[19]

The Early and Middle Formative saw major sites appear throughout Mesoamerica, including Chalcatzingo in Morelos, San Lorenzo Tenochtitlan in Veracruz, Paso de la Amada in Chiapas, La Blanca in Guatemala, and San José Mogote (Etla on the map) in the Valley of Oaxaca.[20] We may now begin adding sites from the Mixteca Alta to this list, most known only from survey but others, notably Tayata, from excavated results.[21] The Mixteca Costa site of Charco Redondo was an important center by the Middle Formative, although it is doubtful that Mixtecs were living there at this time.[22] We cannot say much about the Mixteca Baja at this point, only that there is an archaeological background in the region at least as far back as the Middle Formative.[23] This new understanding of pre-urban times in the Mixteca is relevant to the Valley Zapotec and ultimately to the origins of Monte Albán and other Oaxacan cities. There is a much larger area than before from which one must consider the nature of the influences and the direction of evolutionary change.

Archaeological investigations conducted between 1966 and 1976 by Vanderbilt University and INAH reveal that as early as 1350 B.C.E.[24] Mixtec farmers had established themselves in four or five villages in the Nochixtlan Valley.[25] Most important among these early sites were Yucuita and Etlatongo. These were small communities covering no more than a few hectares but located adjacent to the best, most fertile farmlands along the Yucuita River and at the juncture of the Yucuita and Yanhuitlan rivers at Etlatongo. We also have evidence for occupation of the "interior" of the Mixteca Alta, west of the Sierra de Nochixtlan, at Tayata, where surveys and excavations located several small occupations from the phase of incipient village life and an uncalibrated radiocarbon date of 1250 B.C.E. Teposcolula likewise has early sedentary sites and some glimmerings of regional hierarchy. Pottery cross-ties from these Early Cruz sites in the Mixteca Alta align with the Valley of Oaxaca and to a lesser extent the Tehuacan Valley.[26]

Regional surface surveys elsewhere in the Mixteca suggest that much of the area was very sparsely populated during the initial sedentary phase.[27] It is nonetheless clear that the earliest sedentary villages were located in somewhat larger valleys and in sites adjacent to the best soils and water sources. This is not surprising but becomes significant later on, when settlement patterns shift away from these optimal conditions. The Mixteca Alta, specifically, was likely attractive to the first farmers—it has higher average rainfall than either the Valley of Oaxaca or Tehuacan, and highly fertile soils when pristine and not eroded. While little is known of the Mixteca's initial Early Formative settlements and their inhabitants, it is probable that their lives closely paralleled those of residents of the Valley of Oaxaca to the southeast.[28]

Growth in Settlement Hierarchies

There was substantial site expansion by the late Early Formative.[29] This was also the time of significant social change at San José Mogote and other emerging chiefly centers. Etlatongo, Xacañi, and Yucuita had become important centers in the Nochixtlan Valley.[30] This observation seems generally true for the Mixteca Alta, based on the regional surveys as well as excavations at Tayata. William Duncan and others, for instance, describe a unique set of human cremations from Tayata, from contexts that appear to have been transitional between Early and Middle Formative.[31] One of the cremated individuals was found in a seated position, suggestive of authority in Mesoamerican societies; the other was prone, or lying face down.[32] This same excavated context from Tayata also contained numerous fired-clay figurines, many of which displayed attributes and attire consistent with an elevated social rank.[33] These results, in conjunction with settlement patterns from the Tayata Valley and adjacent regions, are compelling evidence for the emergence of a permanent elite class and social hierarchies at local sites as well as regional levels. This process evidently began in the late Early Formative and was in place throughout the Mixteca Alta, Baja, and Costa by Middle Formative times. This sequence of development runs more or less in parallel with the Valley Zapotec.[34]

The Teposcolula Valley had at least seven sites totaling 36 hectares in combined size.[35] Loma Mina was the largest of these villages, measuring 12 hectares. Tayata was at least 24 hectares.[36] Nochixtlan held four emergent polities each with clusters of surrounding sites, the largest of these being Yucuita at 65 hectares.[37] Other settlement clusters besides those located in Tayata,

Figure 2.1. Burial of an adult female, cremated in place at Tayata as the Early Formative period ended. The pit was dug for the interment and cremation, and the deceased placed face down over the fuel.

Teposcolula, and Nochixtlan were centered on Tejupan and Tlacotepec. Each of these "head towns" and their satellites persisted albeit with changes across pre-Hispanic times and in fact into the present—a remarkable example of continuous cultural development. These clusters or "valley pockets" of settlement were buffered by mountains and horizontal distances of 6 to 10 kilometers from edge to edge. Kowalewski and others estimate that the eight settlement clusters mentioned above represent a combined total of five thousand persons at this time.[38] The Mixteca Alta's range of site sizes, major and minor centers, site clustering, small polities, and the buffer zones between them are all comparable to survey results from the Valley of Oaxaca and elsewhere in highland Mesoamerica.[39] This widely shared settlement pattern is suggestive of high degrees of interaction among many comparable, although ethnically distinct, societies.

Middle Formative settlement expanded still further, with the original core settlement clusters growing into hierarchically integrated "superclusters."[40]

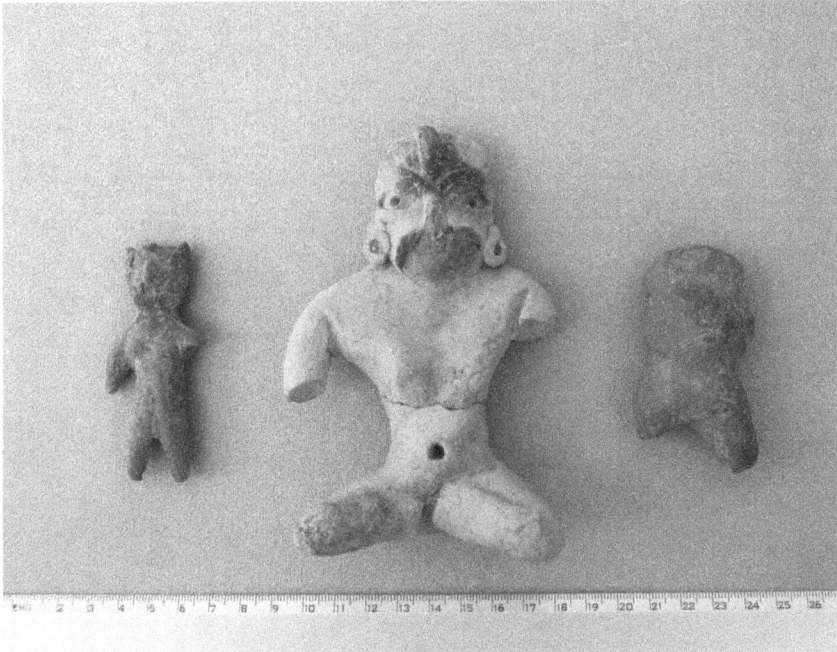

Figure 2.2. Seated figurine with various elite accessories from Tayata, from the same household context as the human cremations. This figurine was one of several from the site that was defaced and burned intentionally.

Kowalewski and others argue "that the settlement clusters were political units and that they formed larger polities, the superclusters," where "the basal political unit is the settlement cluster, not the single settlement or village."[41] Tayata was one of the superclusters, the "hub" of four valley pockets, with subsidiary site clusters extending outward into smaller valleys, stopping only at the borders of neighboring superclusters that originated in Tlacotepec and Teposcolula. Tayata was itself 77 hectares in size, and probably more, given the extensive erosion wearing its edges away. Tayata was the largest of the superclusters, with 356 hectares of combined occupation and a mid-range population estimate of 6,225. These size estimates are comfortably within the range of what demographers and archaeologists consider urban, but we defer this discussion of proto-urbanism until later. What is especially compelling is simply that settlement structure of the Middle Formative Mixteca was virtually identical to what was observable at the time of the Spanish Conquest, although the demographic scale was not what it would become.

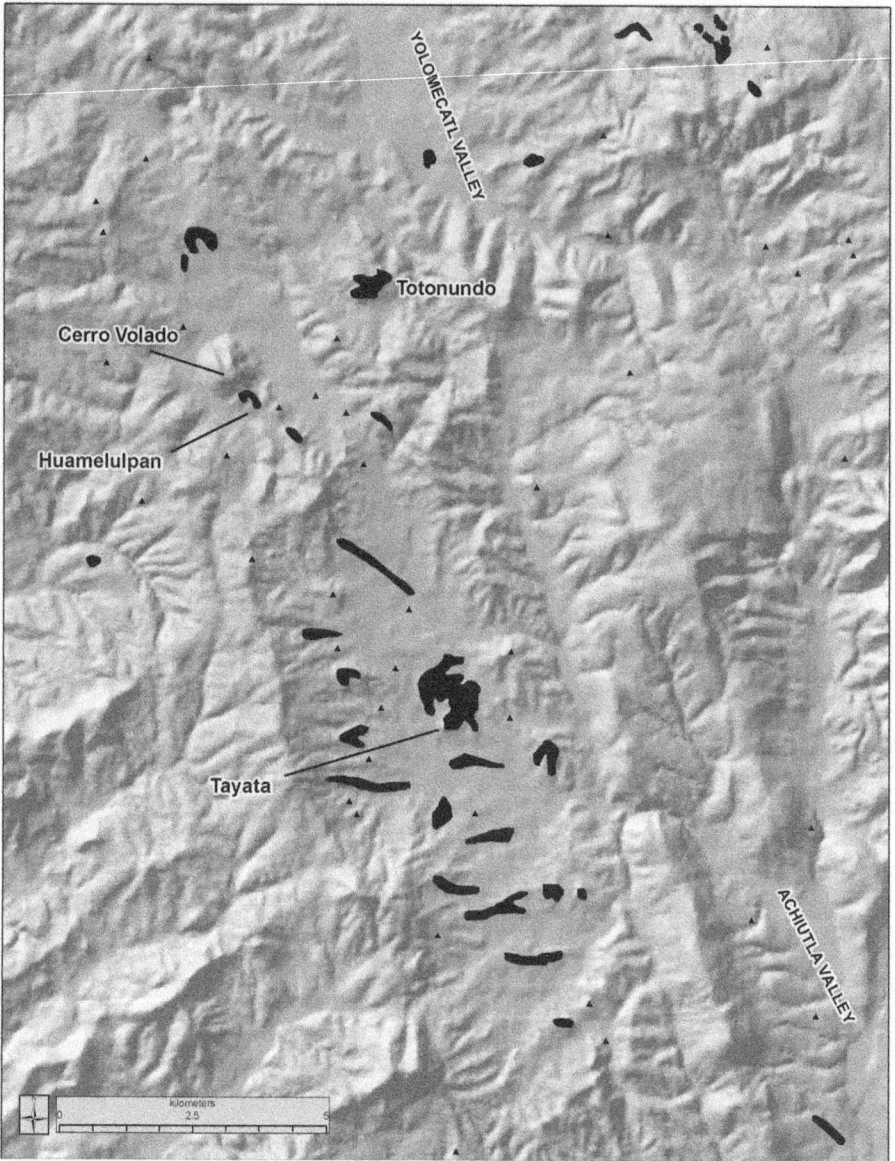

Figure 2.3. Map of Middle Formative settlement in the Tayata Valley.

The present evidence is ambiguous as to whether the expansion of Tayata and its neighboring superclusters was peaceful or not. Kowalewski and others, noting that superclusters grew from older sites and previously occupied valley pockets, argue that "political authority over core and subordinate clusters derived from precedence, not conquest."[42] This view is consistent with the regional survey data but is somewhat undercut by the Tayata excavations where human heads were used in ritual settings, and somewhat later deposits included decapitated bodies and likely human sacrifices.[43] Based on ethnohistorical analogies, these unfortunate individuals could have been captives taken in raids.[44] It is likewise the case that by the end of the Middle Formative, many core zones of occupation in the Mixteca Alta had moved to higher, more defensible ground.[45] Expansion into unoccupied lands could have been directed by powerful chiefs, to expand the subsistence base but also to defend the core territory from competitors. We cannot resolve this conundrum at present.

Mixteca Alta surveys for the Middle Formative suggest that regional population grew at least fivefold over the prior period, with major occupied clusters in Tamazulapan, Teposcolula, Tayata, Tlacotepec, and several subsectors of Nochixtlan. Kowalewski and others put the mid-range population estimate for the central Mixteca Alta survey area at 21,500.[46] This figure alone exceeds the comparable population estimate for the Valley of Oaxaca at the end of the Middle Formative, despite the central Mixteca Alta being a considerably smaller study area.[47] Adding the adjacent survey regions, including Coixtlahuaca, to the total, there may have been upwards of 40,000 persons living in the archaeologically documented parts of the Mixteca Alta. The Middle Formative Mixteca Alta was among the demographic core regions of Mesoamerica, comparable to the most populous occupied areas of Puebla and the Valley of Mexico.[48]

This is the first period for which there is relatively unambiguous evidence for the intensive agricultural features called *coo-yuu* terraces.[49] Many sites with exclusively Middle Formative occupations that are associated with these terrace systems are reasonably assigned to this period. As an example, several massive but extinct terrace systems were mapped at Tayata, an undertaking entirely out of proportion to the small size of later occupations of the site. It seems likely that Tayata's *coo-yuu* terraces were at least initiated during the Middle Formative. This is the kind of intensification one might expect in a landscape of competing polities, or what Flannery called, in reference to a later period in the Mixteca, "another classic example of a labor-intensive system which resulted from, and in turn supported, strongly centralized authority." Significantly, and again with an eye toward a somewhat later time period, "It is also probably a classic example of the way a relatively small state can intensify the productivity of its immediate sustaining area to the point where it has the manpower needed to exact tribute from weaker neighboring areas."[50] There are direct ethnographic parallels with the power-building strategies of pre-contact Hawaiian chiefs,[51] and in any event the presence of these agricultural features in the Mixteca helps us to understand the otherwise surprising demographic estimates compared to other Mesoamerican regions.

The site clusters and superclusters were hierarchically arranged, both with reference to a single large village but also with regard to public space and architecture. The larger sites could have two to four mounds, sometimes built over underlying platforms, and arranged around one or more plazas. It is perhaps significant that the larger sites often had more than one public area. This could represent more "corporate" kinds of sociopolitical organization,[52] but if one of the larger structures was at some remove from the residential areas, it may instead indicate a chief's or in later times a ruler's residence that was separated from the rest of the site. This is a pattern we see repeated again and again during Classic and Postclassic times in the Mixteca that presumably had earlier antecedents.[53]

Tayata had a Middle Formative plaza that was 90 meters long, with earthen mounds on either side of this space. The west mound, although mostly natural, was over 7 meters tall. The east mound upon excavation resembled the one-room temples from contemporary contexts in the Valley of Oaxaca.[54] The plaza space would be room enough for four thousand persons to stand together in approximate comfort, such that most residents of at least the core settlement cluster could attend public ceremonies. Gatherings of this dimension could be examples of the importance of public ceremonialism in pre-state societies, where institutional structures were not fully developed.[55] This scale of construction also lends some credence to the notion that social hierarchies in the Mixteca emerged from the ritual realm.[56]

Tayata and Other Excavated Sites

The Tayata excavations also revealed a second elite or ceremonial sector at some remove from the site center that consisted of an adobe-block pyramid 3 meters high built over a platform that was 1.25-meters high and at least 120 by 40 meters in surface area.[57] This was a distinct configuration, different from the other public areas and located in the most inaccessible part of the site. We believe this was a more private zone of ceremonialism, limited to the most elite members of the community, and possibly including the chiefly residence. Later construction in this area, both pre-Hispanic and modern, make it difficult to say anything more about the Middle Formative activities on this part of the site.

The pyramid in question was radiocarbon dated indirectly from a sample adhering to a Middle Formative potsherd from the building's interior, to

Figure 2.4. Partial remains of an adobe-block pyramid at Tayata, Middle Formative period.

around 560 B.C.E. That would place this building activity at a time just prior to, or roughly coincident with, the founding of Monte Albán in the Valley of Oaxaca. But the pyramid was by no means the only structure of interest in this part of the site. There was enough stone and earthen fill in the underlying platform to build a mound of 5 to 10 meters in height, depending on the structure's overall configuration.[58] This would be an impressive mound for any period, and it illustrates a key comparative point, given the ancient Mixtec penchant for platform-based architecture: that considerable labor went into building the platforms, less so on the mounds that sometimes sat atop them. The late pre-Hispanic/early Colonial capital at Yucundaa in Teposcolula was among the premier examples of platform building in urban design, as was Tayata's successor site at Huamelulpan, among many other examples.[59] This tradition of platform building, often in a rising series for the later pre-Hispanic periods, began at sites like Tayata during the Middle Formative.[60]

We have also excavated data from one of our secondary, or derived, settlement clusters at Yucunama. This 23-hectare village was likely subordinate to the Teposcolula supercluster centered on Loma Mina.[61] "Yucunama

Centro" dates to the Middle Formative and occupies nearly the entirety of a low hill supporting the present town of Yucunama. An INAH team headed by Raul Matadamas Díaz, working in 1989 and again in 1995–96, recovered the remains of a probable public building with numerous plaster floors and tamped-earth surfaces, masonry foundations, and more than thirty *pozo tronco-cónico* pits measuring up to 5 meters in depth and tapering from approximately 50 centimeters in diameter at the surface to about 2 meters at base.[62]

The one large structure at the site appears to be "public" rather than residential because of its size and because of the lack of *comales* (tortilla griddles), high frequencies of worn *ollas* (jars) or other cookware, *manos* and *metates* (grinding stones), or charred plant remains, animal bone, or other artifacts that customarily would be associated with domestic activity. These pits appear to have been constructed for ritual purposes, rather than for storage or waste disposal. Some contained extended, flexed, or secondary burials with few or no offerings. Others contained no burials or whole vessels; only fine soil and ash and pottery fragments dating to the late Middle Formative and the earliest stages of the Late Formative. Pits that have been encountered by citizens of the town in past years are said to have been large enough to house a small family. A few similar pits associated with domestic structures have been found at Yucuita and at other sites in the Valley of Oaxaca.

Present investigations suggest that the Mixteca as a whole was more populous, hierarchically complex, and interactive with other regions than formerly believed. Excavation data from Tayata have revealed intensive household-based craft production, including highly valued marine-shell ornaments, an indigenous gray-ware pottery tradition, obsidian-working and multiple obsidian source areas, making it quite clear that these village farmers were neither "backward hillbillies" nor were they isolated or markedly different from their Mesoamerican neighbors.[63] External contacts with the Valley Zapotec appear to have been the most significant, but goods entering the Mixteca were coming from virtually all points on the compass—whether marine shell or fish from the Pacific coast; obsidian from central Mexico, west Mexico, and Veracruz; or pottery trade wares. The Mixteca was both geographically speaking and in terms of actual exchange at the nexus of Gulf Coastal, central Mexican, and Pacific coastal exchange spheres. In this respect, the evidence for emerging social networks at Tayata and other Mixteca sites, especially for the relatively elite stratum, form one of the bases for projecting historically documented patterns into remote antiquity (see chapters 4 and 5). Where the settlement structure and architectural forms, as noted above, appear similar to later times and where specific cultural practices are found, such as the prehistoric cremation burials that are also depicted in codices, we become more confident in using native models derived from ethnohistorical sources.

We have nothing of substance to report from the Mixteca Baja at this time, although this vast subregion of the Mixteca remains underinvestigated. We would not be surprised to learn in the future of the existence of considerable Early and Middle Formative cultural materials. Meanwhile, the lower Río Verde Valley of the Mixteca Costa reveals a significant representation of Formative period settlement. Survey and excavation conducted by Arthur Joyce and his students are revealing early sites in the elevated areas bordering the river and at least one large center at Charco Redondo.[64] From evidence found at sites relating to the Middle Formative, it appears that early farmers were taking advantage of the rich alluvial soils in the lowlands, while simultaneously exploiting the rich coastal lagoons and surrounding localities for abundant plant, animal, and mineral resources. Although this coastal adaptation varies significantly from those of the highlands of central Oaxaca and the Mixteca Alta, there are many shared cultural features in architecture, burial forms, and pottery, which indicate important ties among all areas. We cannot, of course, infer the presence of Mixtec speakers at this early date, and so we defer further discussion of this important region until later in the volume.

The Olmec Question

The idea that the Gulf Coast Olmec were progenitors of all later Meso-american civilizations goes back many decades, originating at a time when very little was known about Formative Mesoamerica apart from ruins newly discovered in Veracruz and Tabasco.[65] The lack of comparable materials in Oaxaca led many archaeologists, including Alfonso Caso and Ignacio Bernal, to accept the Olmec as a precursor culture.[66] This view has persisted even though we know a lot more about the Mixtec, Zapotec, and other pre-urban Formative cultures of Oaxaca than Caso, Bernal, and their contemporaries did in the 1940s, 1950s, and 1960s. Still, to this day scholars disagree about whether Olmec/Gulf Coastal peoples were the "mother culture" or just one of several prominent groups arising together and being mutually influential during the Early Formative.[67]

We concur with Christopher Pool that little or no evidence exists for the unique transference of Olmec ideology and culture to other regions, whether via the movement of pottery or people, such that "Mesoamerican civilizations seem less the offspring of a single Mother Culture than the progeny of a promiscuous horde."[68] The alternative to the mother culture model is a form of competitive interaction, where growing complexity is catalyzed through exchanges among many coequal sites. We find it compelling that models of this kind aptly describe the nature of interaction among the Post-classic Mixtec, and evidently—based on our foregoing discussion—for earlier periods as well.

It is quite clear that there were important contacts and exchange rela-tionships existing among early village sites in the Mixteca and other regions of Mesoamerica.[69] We are also aware of the recent claims about Etlatongo and its purported ties to the Olmec site of San Lorenzo Tenochtitlan.[70] Yet those arguments, relating to the chemical origin of certain kinds of pottery, are reliant on a single line of inference and do not, in any event, explain how a particular repertoire of stylistic elements either reflect, cause, or otherwise influence the development of recipient societies.[71] On the contrary, the cumulative survey results from the Mixteca Alta suggest that this region, whether considered in tandem with the Valley of Oaxaca or not, constituted a demographic core within Mesoamerica. Based on the population figures cited above, one might as readily argue that the Mixtec were the mother culture rather than the reverse. We can also cite a range of excavated data, notably from Tayata, that show varied external trade relationships, nascent forms of craft activity, considerable internal continuity especially in pottery, and novel features such as the cremation of newly deceased but soon-to-be-venerated ancestors not shared by other cultures at this time.

All of these results, taken together, are suggestive of economic and political as well as ideological autonomy for the Mixtec of this time. The many preexisting forms of complexity that we have enumerated are impor-tant not only for understanding the Early Formative in Mesoamerica but also the later process of urbanization in the Mixteca that was roughly con-current with the foundation of Monte Albán.

THE URBAN REVOLUTION IN THE MIXTECA

Mesoamerican cities were extremely diverse, making it difficult to generalize about their origins and growth, but for the Mixteca several elements set the Late and Terminal Formative periods apart from all that came before (or the approximate time-span of 300 B.C.E. to 200 C.E.). These were, first and foremost, urbanism, the rise of the state, and a system of social stratification that would be recognizable to the protohistoric Mixtec.[72] Accompanying these transformational events were the beginnings of significant regional traditions, particularly as found in new survey data from the Mixteca Alta that have expanded quite considerably the known range of urban forms in Oaxaca.[73] Urban societies began to appear by the end of the Middle Formative, and their growth into urban states accelerated across many regions during the Late and Terminal Formative. This was a Mesoamerican-wide phenomenon, and much like the preceding transitions to sedentism and chiefly societies, it was a macroregional and interactive process.[74]

We view Mixtec urbanization as fundamentally autochthonous—that is, with the Mixtec cities originating where they are found. This implies, not incidentally, that there are historical processes of development that ought to be traced over time and that may be used for interpretive purposes. There is a second essential point to bear in mind, and that concerns variation. Mixtec cities were not all of a kind, and this was especially true in their initial "experimental" phase of development. This does not mean that we cannot understand the origins of the Mixtec urban tradition, only that we must adjust our thinking to deal with variation within regions as great as the variation we find among them. This approach recalls Joyce Marcus's observation "that the longer one attempts to devise a scheme for the ancient city, the more one is forced to ignore important 'exceptions.' The result is that the exceptions, as well as the variance they represent, go unexplained."[75] We believe that the nature of Mixtec urbanism cautions against this failing, and that in examining the variation among cities we find clues to their beginnings.

Yucuita/Cerro de las Flores

By the onset of "Ramos," or the early urban phase of the Mixteca Alta, important developments took place in and around Yucuita in the northern Nochixtlan Valley.[76] Yucuita was already a major "Cruz-era" chiefdom, but during the fourth century B.C.E. and continuing well into the Common Era, it was transformed into a complex urban center with several outlying dependencies (barrios) interspersed among highly productive farmlands.

Urban Yucuita was internally diversified, with blocks of apartmentlike structures containing several rooms arranged around bisecting streets, plazas, patios, a complex system of vaulted underground passageways and drains, smaller one- and two-room houses, and several raised platforms. These platforms—built to a massive scale—rather than the pyramids that are typical of other regions, were the predominant form of public building and were crowned with structures that undoubtedly figured in the ritual life of the community, but some probably also housed the community's political-religious leaders. As in later Classic and Postclassic times, it is often difficult to distinguish

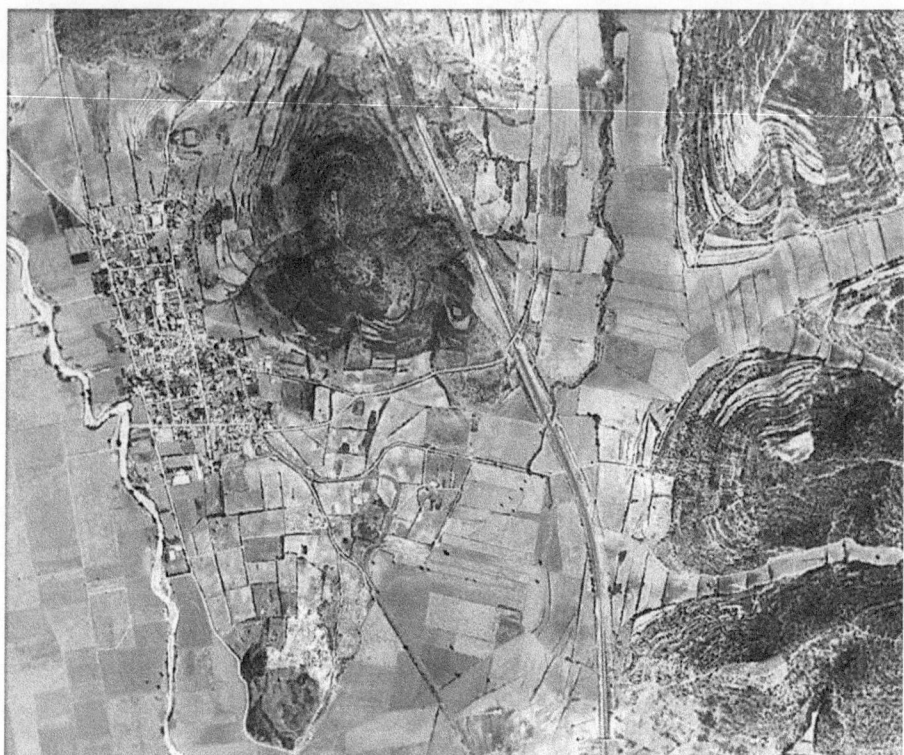

Figure 2.5. San Juan Yucuita and its hilltop archaeological site amid the broad expanse of the Nochixtlan Valley; a variety of terracing is visible on nearby hills. Google Earth photo.

between what may be purely ritualistic architecture and structures that may have served civic-political functions. Often they may have been one and the same. Burials were normally in stone or adobe-lined tombs, or cists, containing one or two individuals in extended position along with offerings of pottery vessels, stone tools, and shell or bone implements or ornaments. This manner of interment was markedly more formalized than the various "pit" burials of the earlier period.

Ramos-phase pottery was predominantly utilitarian, with vast quantities of plain tan (brown) conical or hemispherical bowls, large jars, or *ollas*, and flat-based bowls of tan ware decorated with red or black paint or wash, or a combination of both. Gray wares showing affinities with Monte Albán Late I and II in the Valley of Oaxaca are found in low frequencies in the area, indicating to us at least that contacts with the Valley Zapotec did not involve colonization or conquest; the presence of these wares is nonetheless important for establishing the precise timing of key events leading to urban states in various regions of Oaxaca.[77] Figurines are generally small and unremarkable, except that there seems to have been a fascination for unusual forms with extended bellies, in contorted poses, or appearing to have been intentionally mutilated, perhaps as "sacrifices."[78]

Yucuita, among the first, largest, and most complex settlements participating in the urban revolution in the Mixteca, was the linchpin, the primary integrative mechanism of a network of at least a dozen smaller, more homogeneous Late/Terminal Formative sites in the Nochixtlan Valley. Yucuita covered approximately 1.8 square kilometers in its core settlement alone, was heavily terraced and densely occupied, and based on architectural evidence of ceremonial-administrative buildings and at least three types of residential structures, would meet most or all criteria for prehistoric urban states. To the east along the Amatlan–Nochixtlan divide and to the west between Chachoapan and Yanhuitlan are at least six major terraced sites, covering from 10 to 20 hectares each, that undoubtedly were dependencies of Yucuita. This pattern of a core settlement surrounded by its several *barrios* and outlying dependencies was clearly derived in some fashion from the earlier settlement clusters and superclusters discussed for the preceding Middle Formative period. The Mixteca Alta tan-ware pottery tradition likewise was continuous, as was the platform-based monumental architecture and the presence of residential if not administrative subunits within the core settlement, all suggesting that the Mixtec urbanization grew from an indigenous design.

Huamelulpan, Monte Negro, and Other Mixtec Cities

We mention at this juncture the early urban development of Cerro Jazmín, a site that grew even larger in the Classic and Postclassic but participated in the initial Mixtec urbanization. One curious fact is its proximity to Yucuita, being located on a mountain southwest of Yanhuitlan and less than ten kilometers from Yucuita. That both sites were contemporary in their initial urban phases is not in doubt; neither is Cerro Jazmín's urban character.[79]

The Early Ramos or Late Formative occupation covers almost 80 hectares, including the top of the mountain and slopes on all sides covered in residential terraces. The mid-range population estimate is six thousand persons. Cerro Jazmín was, in effect, the urban agglomeration of the Middle Formative Xacañi polity and related sites in its cluster that extend into the north-central Yanhuitlan Valley. There were three separate groupings of public space—mounds on platforms, mounds surrounding plazas, and a staircase leading to a small mound and plaza group at the highest point on the mountain. Each

Figure 2.6. Cerro Jazmín and the eroded "moonscape" of the Yanhuitlan sector of the Nochixtlan Valley; the right-hand side of the frame is north. Google Earth photo.

of these areas of public construction was used in later periods, and although embellished, likely had their beginnings in Ramos times.

Cerro Jazmín's Formative occupation was short lived, confined largely to the Early Ramos or Mesoamerican Late Formative. It was likely an early competitor of Yucuita that could not sustain itself; whether it failed from external conflict, maintaining its urban momentum into a successful nascent state, or both, cannot be known without more intensive research at the site. Cerro Jazmín was in fact one of many Early Ramos hilltop centers that failed. This includes Monte Negro, discussed below, and yet another contemporary city south of Coixtlahuaca called Loma Sandage.[80] This perspective of a multiregional trend toward urbanism in the Mixteca complicates and undermines older notions of one-way influences emanating from the Valley of Oaxaca. Oaxaca's urban revolution consisted of a series of linked transformations involving, perhaps, a dozen or more urban and proto-urban sites.

Still other significant urban revolution sites are at Diquiyucu of Yucunama, Yucuncuu of Chalcatongo, Ñutandá of San Miguel el Grande, and Diquiyu at the transition point between the northern Mixteca Alta and the southern Mixteca Baja.[81] These unexcavated and partially investigated sites have civic-ceremonial centers with megalithic construction, carved stones as at Diquiyu, and numerous patios and residential terraces. They are usually situated in elevated areas, on mountains or ridges, above low-lying arable lands, and share the crowded, multifunction/multiple-nuclei pattern seen at Yucuita.

Monte Negro is located two kilometers southwest of Santiago Tilantongo, an imposing mountaintop center with dozens of impressive civic, ceremonial, and residential structures. We know a good deal about Monte Negro, an initial urban phase site that was the scene of pioneering research in the Mixteca Alta and has been described in detail.[82] As at Yucuita, there is a mixing of functions in the central area, with probable *barrio* components and subject settlements being clustered around the center. The surrounding regional political system is less impressive than at Yucuita, but this undoubtedly reflects what is perhaps the most interesting fact about the site—that Monte Negro was short lived and thus gives insight into the initial urban phase in the Mixteca. To understand what happened at the urban flashpoint, there can be no better place to look than Monte Negro.

Monte Negro dates to the onset of the Late Formative, or Early Ramos, in the Mixteca Alta—in other words, it was contemporary with the initial urbanization at Yucuita, Cerro Jazmín, Diquiyu, and other Mixteca cities, as well as Monte Albán Late I in the Valley of Oaxaca.[83] Although interpretations have been modified in recent years, the excavations at Monte Negro stand as a perpetual monument to Alfonso Caso, Jorge Acosta, and their associates and as a milestone in Mixteca archaeology. It was at Monte Negro and nearby Yucuñudahui that systematic archaeological research began in the Mixteca.[84] And, as noted above, the site continues to be a source of empirical as well as interpretive observations.

Burgoa reported the belief that Monte Negro was founded when "the first *señores* . . . came guided by their gods and penetrated these mountains and arrived in a rugged site which is between Achiutla and Tilantongo." Those first settlers "were dominated by a greater power and searched for a site which would aid them in their defense."[85] We might on present archaeological knowledge infer that the greater power in question was that of an expansionist Monte Albán. Monte Negro and its antecedent settlements showed two episodes of movement onto defensible hilltops, first at La Providencia in Late Cruz times and again with the Ramos urbanization at Monte Negro. The earlier sites are poorly preserved, but Monte Negro remains relatively untouched and shows the full scope of the urban transformation.

What is remarkable is how thoroughgoing that transformation was—from a thousand-year history of low-lying and more dispersed settlement to the mountaintop redoubt with its unique monumental plan, which appears to have its origins at the interface of the Middle/Late Formative. Virtually all prior sites near Tilantongo were abandoned. The new urban center was placed some 500 meters over the valley bottom, where an estimated thirty-five hundred to four thousand people resettled.[86] The site was terraced and covered nearly 80 hectares. Several enormous *coo-yuu* agricultural terraces were integrated within the urban plan and snake their way toward the valley floor. The area covered in *coo-yuu* nearly matches in size the occupied area of the site and gives further credence to Burgoa's observations of "mountains and *barrancas* . . . marked by stepped and terraced fields from top to bottom and looking like stone-edged stairways."[87] The architecture included columnar supports, patio groups, and temples—all diagnostic of Oaxaca-style administrative architecture—as well as buildings not seen elsewhere or for that matter ever again in Oaxaca.[88] Kowalewski and others comment that, despite the superficial similarities of Monte Negro's buildings to other sites, "the whole is like no other place."[89]

Monte Negro is an example of the importance of regional survey in the archaeology of Oaxaca. This was a site that despite having been thoroughly excavated at an early date has nonetheless remained mysterious and given rise to several widely reported and, as it happens, inaccurate conclusions about its origins. The site appeared to have come out of nowhere, but subsequent to regional surveys in the 1990s we now see the clear local antecedents to the site and are able to identify a process of development that this site has in common with many other early cities in Oaxaca. Monte Negro has emerged from the shadows and is now virtually the "type site" for Oaxaca's urban revolution.

Similar developments occurred well to the west of Monte Negro and the Nochixtlan Valley cities, including the rise of an urban capital at San Martín Huamelulpan.[90] The center lacks the extensive pre-urban foundations encountered at Yucuita but was nevertheless contemporaneous with the onset of urbanization at Yucuita and other Mixteca Alta sites. One does not have to venture far, however, to find the probable Formative antecedents for Huamelulpan at Tayata and sites in its settlement cluster.[91] Huamelulpan urbanized in the fourth century B.C.E. when the Tayata area was largely abandoned. That change represents several thousand persons who left places that were occupied continuously for more than a millennium. Tayata's Middle Formative central precinct was rebuilt with the same building layout and plaza size on Cerro Volado, Huamelulpan's highest point. This transition parallels the population movement and political replacement of San José Mogote by Monte

Figure 2.7. Remains of public buildings at Monte Negro.

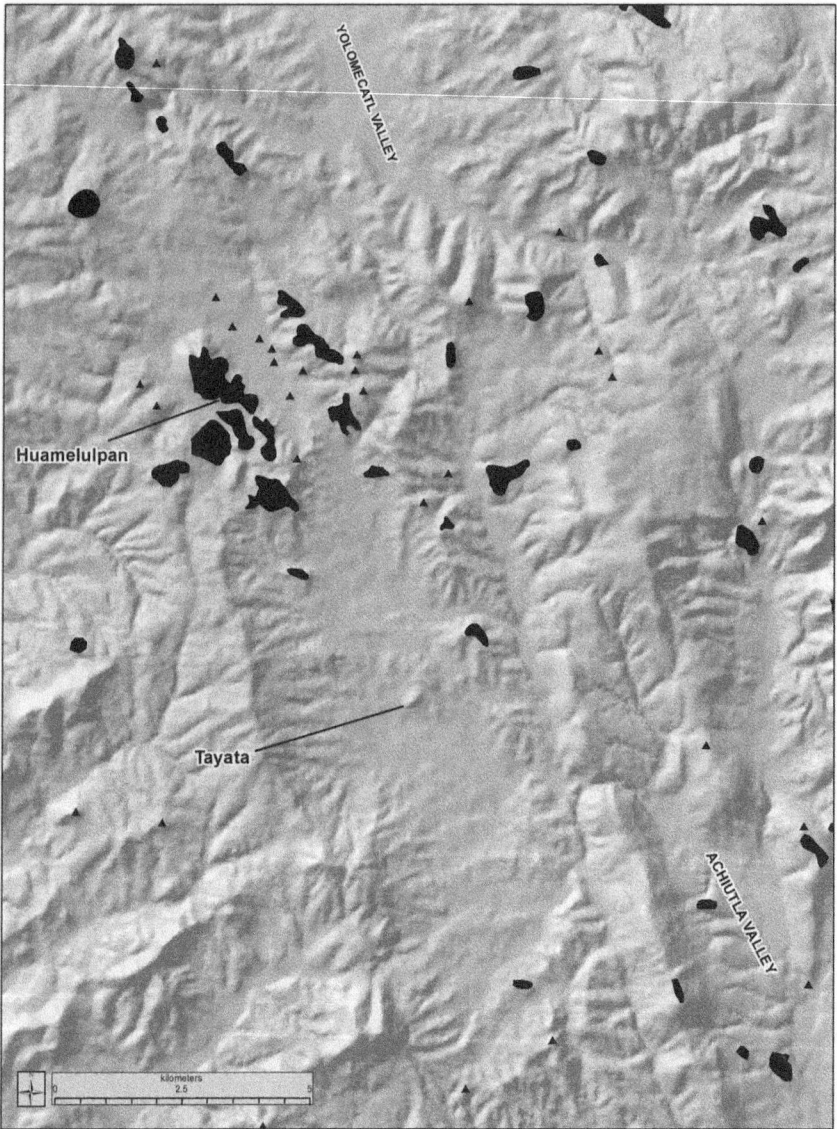

Figure 2.8. Map of Terminal Formative settlement in the Huamelulpan Valley.

Albán among the Valley Zapotec and, for that matter, the patterns of urbanization at Monte Negro, Cerro Jazmín, and other Mixtec cities.

Huamelulpan has a compact nucleus containing built-up plazas, some twenty surviving mounds, individual and apartmentlike housing complexes, and hundreds of residential and agricultural terraces. More than three hundred residential terraces are located on the slopes of Cerro Volado on the northern half of the site and along the hills extending southward from the hilltop, and vast stretches of *coo-yuu* agricultural terraces are found interspersed within the urban setting. Many of the residential terraces run for several hundred meters and, in effect, "wrap around" the hills. Although the ceremonial nucleus on the summit of Cerro Volado was smaller and less diversified than Yucuita, several other architectural complexes were dispersed across Huamelulpan— notably the Grupo de la Iglesia, composed of a truly massive series of descending platforms culminating in a ball court. Plazas and mounds sit atop the platforms, connected by monumental stairways. This was likely the administrative center of the city. The adjacent platforms northwest of the Colonial church terminate in monolithic cornerstones with inscribed hieroglyphs (discussed below). Both the platforms and their terminal cornerstones are characteristic Mixtec architectural forms.[92]

Among the innovations traced to this site was a large, well-constructed tomb with an accompanying tunnel entrance that was excavated by INAH archaeologists in 1990.[93] The tomb, which had been found and emptied of its contents in the 1930s, was covered by a mounded ceremonial complex, now reconstructed and accessible to visitors. A large stone figure called the "Huamelulpan monolith" that is displayed in the Museo Comunitario de San Martín Huamelulpan, is said to have been taken from the tomb.[94] Numerous other extended burials in adobe or stone-lined cists, altars associated with offerings, and an effective drainage system have been found in association with the Huamelulpan complex of plain and red- and black-painted tan-ware pottery. Gray wares that are usually associated with Monte Albán (especially the decorated varieties called "G.12") are present but occur in low frequencies— an observation true for both surveyed and excavated collections. Macroscopic and mineralogical examination suggests that many of these gray wares were in fact of local origin, a conclusion borne out in subsequent chemical studies of the clay fabrics.[95]

Huamelulpan was in a strategic location in the hydrological sense, often covered by clouds during the rainy season, drawing water and serving as the source of seasonal streams that run to the north toward Yolomecatl and to the south toward Tayata, Amoltepec, and Magdalena Peñasco. And since it could be seen as the source of moisture and fertility for the valley, it was most certainly of ideological importance. Its distinctive cone-shaped peak, moreover, is visible for miles around and is the basis for local creation stories about the site's origins. Urns showing Dzahui, the rain deity, were found with the Altar de los Cráneos and in elaborate tombs.[96] Other evidence of rituals involved

Figure 2.9. Cerro Volado/Huamelulpan, looking southeast over the valley and surrounding hills; the great cleft in the hilltop marks the inception of a *coo-yuu* terrace system that runs to the valley floor.

Figure 2.10. Surveyors examine one of the large residential terraces at Huamelulpan.

burned human remains, possibly from captive prisoners. Extending in all directions from Huamelulpan were numerous contemporary sites that doubtless served as components, or dependent settlements, of a Huamelulpan-centered regional state.[97] Huamelulpan's setting and ideological significance was associated with its political status at the top of the settlement hierarchy.

By Late Ramos or Terminal Formative times, only two of the original Mixteca Alta cities remained: Huamelulpan and Yucuita. Huamelulpan's urban core covered over two square kilometers and had a mean estimated population of 12,500 persons—comparable to Monte Albán's population at the time. Yucuita was built to a similar scale. But there were important differences in the administrative reach of the early Mixtec and Zapotec states. Monte Albán's territorial extent encompassed multiple valleys and ethnolinguistic groups, whereas the Mixtec capitals controlled only small territories.[98] Thus, two very different state-level societies emerged from the era of competitive chiefdoms, nascent states, and evident conflict that characterized Oaxaca when urbanism first began.

The Mixteca Baja and Costa

The Mixteca Baja and Mixteca Costa are insufficiently explored to draw firm conclusions on their status during this important transformational stage.

Figure 2.11. An expanse of *coo-yuu* terracing integrated within the urban plan at Huamelulpan.

Diquiyu, mentioned above, has its strongest cultural affiliations with the Mixteca Baja but has barely been explored and remains unsurveyed and unexcavated. Cerro de las Minas had a Late/Terminal Formative occupation, including considerable public building, but the site seems to have been more important later on. Most of the Mixteca Baja has never been surveyed, apart from reports focused on Classic and Epiclassic sites near Tequixtepec and Chazumba, so it is difficult to characterize the region as a whole (see chapter 3). Arthur Joyce and his students, on the other hand, are beginning to clarify developments in areas adjacent to the Río Verde and more generally along the Pacific coast of Oaxaca.[99] Surveys by Donald Brockington and associates and by Joyce indicate at least fifty-eight sites ranging in age from approximately 400 B.C.E. to 200/300 C.E. that were located between Pinotepa and Puerto Escondido.[100] Several of these sites are large and show considerable internal complexity.

As mentioned previously, significant coastal political centers were present since the Middle Formative, while the growth of San Francisco de Arriba (near Tututepec) during the Late Formative represents an initial, if as yet unexplained, step toward urbanism roughly coincident with similar changes in the Mixteca Alta. San Francisco de Arriba appears to have arisen from

Figure 2.12. The Grupo de la Iglesia at Huamelulpan, its pre-Hispanic platforms built to an enormous scale compared to the Colonial-era church.

local populations of smaller, somewhat scattered sites, being resettled on a terraced hilltop. The site eventually grew to nearly one square kilometer in size. Studies of this site in the 1950s by de Cicco and Brockington identified pottery similar to Monte Albán Late I/II, although Andrew Workinger, after mapping and excavating at the site, discounts links to the Valley Zapotec.[101] By the Terminal Formative, a new regional political center in the Lower Río Verde Valley was established at Río Viejo that was far larger and more monumental than any prior coastal center. Urbanism and the state were present on the coast by the time of Río Viejo's emergence. All of this is useful background to understanding the growth of the coastal empire of Tututepec during the Postclassic, although there is no evidence of a Mixtec presence on the coast prior to the eleventh century.

The Mixtec Urban Tradition

Urbanism in the Mixteca was widespread and varied to such an extent that study of "whole populations of cities" is now required. Viewing any one of these places in isolation—and that would include Monte Albán in the Valley of Oaxaca—is certain to be misleading.

Figure 2.13. The monolithic cornerstones at Huamelulpan, with hieroglyphs and lizard imagery. Photo by Josh Denmark.

What triggered these changes in the Mixteca, and urbanism more generally in Oaxaca? These events might be tied to Monte Albán's territorial expansion.[102] Urbanism in this context would represent a defense against external threats, and this reasoning may apply to other "sudden city" foundations in the ancient world, including Monte Albán, the Mesopotamian city of Uruk, and examples from classical Greece.[103] It also helps to explain the evident variation in urban forms in the early Mixteca, where cities were to some extent experimental.[104] Observations of this kind put the Mixtec urban tradition where it belongs—in a global comparative framework. The questions that arise are whether the first wave of urbanism in the Mixteca led directly to subsequent Classic and Postclassic developments, and whether we might use the ethnohistorical model to interpret it.

During the early urban period, the Mixteca's major centers shared a diversified urban core that served to integrate the cluster of surrounding communities. This is the "multiple nuclei" settlement pattern, identifiable to archaeologists with reference to focal architecture, their surrounding residential areas with a mix of household-based crafts and farming, and is especially apt for those instances where the site center is not obvious.[105] We liken these nuclei to *barrios* within the *cabecera*, after the ethnohistorical model for community structure.

Other trends are in force from the very onset of the urban period. A multitiered settlement system came into existence, or perhaps better said, became more elaborated and defined—and more to the point of identifying actual institutions, a diverse set of administrative hierarchies appeared. The range of building forms at sites like Monte Negro and Huamelulpan are consistent with expectations for functional differences in the administrative architecture of early states and are observed to descend down the settlement hierarchy.[106] There is as yet unrealized potential to identify specific structures with images from the codices and descriptions of political and ceremonial activities in other historical documentation, but it will require new excavations at the early cities with these objectives in mind.[107]

Other key traits of Mixtec urbanism should be mentioned. Populations moved from locations on the low piedmont to terraced hilltops. *Coo-yuu* terracing became an integral part of urban design. Platform building was emphasized. The new architectural programs dwarfed all prior forms of public building in the Mixteca. Subsectors of the urban core (the several nuclei) could be seen as *barrios* or residential wards, each of which was defined by its focal civic-ceremonial architecture. Within these wards a cross-section of society is found, integrated, perhaps, via their productive arrangements and the noble families in residence. Urban layout of this kind is consistently identifiable from site to site and more than slightly reminiscent of the ethnohistorical pattern. It gives some legitimacy to bringing ideological elements drawn from late pre-Hispanic and modern sources into the interpretive field.[108]

The Mixtec pattern of densely populated and agriculturally intensive, but territorially small, polities was established at this time and continued into the Postclassic period, suggesting that native forms of urbanism and statecraft, or what we call elsewhere the *yuhuitayu* or *cacicazgo*, endured over many centuries despite the occasional upheaval. Their variable configurations, in fact, could be one source of continuity over the long term. We might well call these "city states," but not overlook the importance of their dispersed rural settlement and productive arrangements, especially with regard to agriculture.[109] Given the regional configurations of the Mixtec kingdoms and the intensification of local agricultural production, the medieval ports of trade in Europe and the Mediterranean that come to mind when discussing city states are not the most apt analogies.

The Mixteca's ethnohistorical pattern of shifting alliances among relative equals might date from the period under discussion but becomes more fully convincing by the onset of Classic times, as described later on. We are left, at the present moment, with suggestions of the ethnohistorical community pattern and the institution of the *cacicazgo*, emerging here and there in Middle, Late, and Terminal Formative times, and await further discoveries that must come from archaeology.

WRITING AND CALENDAR

Mixtec writing constitutes one of the four major systems found in Mesoamerica, the other three being the Zapotec, Maya, and Culhua-Mexica, or Aztec.[110] The Mixtecs also possessed the Mesoamerican 260-day and 365-day calendar system.[111] Their year consisted of eighteen named months containing twenty named days and an additional five-day month (six days every fourth year). Years were further grouped into thirteen-year periods, which were regrouped into a fifty-two-year cycle. Birth dates, years, and the thirteen-year periods were associated with the fortunes of life and nature. The birth date controlled the fortune of the individual. Each person carried the birth date as a personal name throughout life. These dates are given as identifying glyphs in the Mixtec genealogical codices.

Although the calendar had obvious social and economic functions, it was also of highly substantial religious-mystical significance. Astrological priests trained from boyhood studied the movement of the heavenly bodies, kept track of time, maintained the calendar, and told fortunes. They were constantly consulted in all important undertakings and performed as close advisers to rulers and their families. Time, nature, life, and the spirit world were closely interrelated and were dutifully observed, maintained, and venerated in Mixtec ideology and religious practice. This description of Mixtec writing is derived from studies of the surviving pictographic manuscripts and other accounts from late pre-Hispanic and early Colonial times. The question that remains unanswered is how to connect the Mixteca's codex-based writing with its true antecedents.

We have only a fragmentary understanding of the origins and evolution of Mixtec writing. The earliest inscriptions are found on stone monuments from the early urban sites of Yucuita and Huamelulpan. The Yucuita stone, or Monument 1, discovered many decades ago on the eastern slopes of Cerro de las Flores is an unusual complex of undulations, swirls, floral-arboreal elements, and what are best described as vaguely toponymic devices, perhaps hills, and plants, presumably maize. The principal image may or may not refer to Dzahui, the rain deity. It is hard to tell. The lower portion of the monument is broken away and might conceivably have contained the calendrical devices

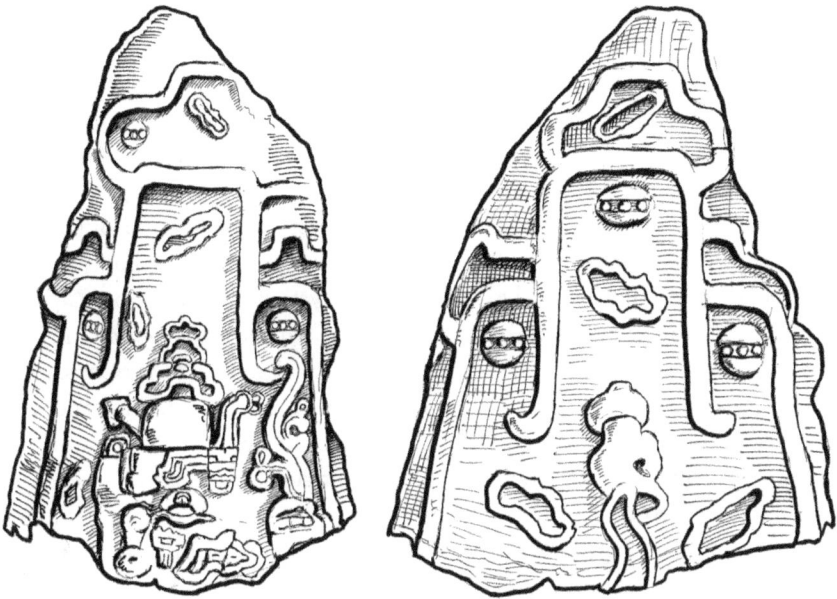

Figure 2.14. Monument 1 at Yucuita, both faces shown side by side. Drawing by Jason Poling.

one would expect to see. The hill signs, found on both sides of the stone, could be derived from similar-looking Zapotec versions.

The Yucuita stone carries several distinctive elements, but as "glyphs" they are rather ambiguous. An obvious rendition would be to consider the stone as a large symbolic and conceptual representation of a beautiful and bountiful place: Yucuita, Cerro de las Flores, Hill of Flowers. There appears to be an effort to integrate or incorporate several concepts and to reduce all to a "key symbol." If the key symbolic element is in fact Dzahui, then water, rain, abundance, and regeneration all come to mind. Iván Rivera, for example, likens the presence of Dzahui within the hill sign to being in a cave or inside the mountain, with mountains viewed as a source of water and fertility. Maize is still offered to an image of the rain deity in the Casa del Agua, a cave at San Juan Diquiyu.[112]

Two points should be made, however. First, we do not know that Postclassic and Colonial Yucuita was a place called Yucuita in prior centuries. Second, the discovery of the stone was fortuitous and not recovered in a systematic excavation. The presumption that this stone dates from Formative times is speculative. Excavations carried out by Vanderbilt University and INAH during several seasons between 1966 and 1990 failed to reveal any additional evidence of the Yucuita writing complex.[113]

A contemporaneous, but distinctive, notational configuration has been found at Huamelulpan, some forty kilometers west of Yucuita. As mentioned above, the carvings are found primarily on monumental cornerstones, a trait that endures in the Mixteca well into Classic times. Huamelulpan's glyphs depict realistic representations of identifiable beings, plants, and objects: an extended lizard, a stone knife, flower, monkey, cat, and human skull.[114] These glyphs are all readily identified using Caso's system for analyzing Zapotec writing.[115] The extended lizard, located on the southeast corner of the descending platforms that Caso and Gamio designated Building C, is of unknown significance; among the Zapotec, however, lizards can in some instances be earthly manifestations of lightning.[116] This would tie the "lizard stone," or those who commissioned it, to one of the principal supernatural forces and by implication to expressions of rulership.

A similar but smaller lizard has also been observed in a monumental context at Cerro Lagartija, a Formative site overlooking the towns of Santa Cruz and Santa Catarina Tayata, some six kilometers south of Huamelulpan. This shared lizard imagery, along with those developmental continuities already mentioned, furthers the case for sites in the Tayata Valley being linked to Huamelulpan during the transition to urbanism. Cerro Lagartija was also the reported origin for an out-of-context stone similar to the Huamelulpan monolith. This stone is currently housed in the Casa de Cultura, Santa Catarina Tayata. The Lagartija monolith could slightly predate or have been contemporary with its "twin" from Huamelulpan. Based on style, these stones likely date to late Monte Albán I times in the Valley of Oaxaca.[117]

Huamelulpan's glyphs are incorporated into calendrical inscriptions with bar-and-dot notation that are closely related to the Zapotec, or Monte Albán II, writing system.[118] This is somewhat surprising since the Postclassic Mixtec depicted the number 5 using five dots, rather than the bar. The glyphs are also all set in cartouches with numbers below, another Monte Albán II trait. Marcus nonetheless observes: "This does not in any sense imply that the site was Zapotec. It merely suggests that at the time the Mixteca did not have its own distinct writing system, separate from that of the Valley of Oaxaca."[119]

It was not until the Classic period that more extensive examples of writing appeared at Mixteca sites. These include carved stones associated with the remarkable cultural florescence in the Mixteca Baja called Ñuiñe, discussed in the next chapter. There are other examples, in other styles, at this time in the Mixteca Alta and Costa. We cannot, however, quite trace the line from the early Zapotec-influenced script to the various Classic period examples to the clearly indigenous codex-based writing of the Postclassic. Nothing more will be known about the origins of writing in the Mixteca until a greater number of systematic excavations are conducted and carved stone monuments are found in context.

3

THE PRE-HISPANIC
MIXTEC KINGDOM—*YUHUITAYU*

Oaxaca's Classic period, beginning during the third century, saw a second wave of widespread urbanism—with several new cities that were potential rivals of Monte Albán even within the Valley of Oaxaca. This "second wave urbanization" came after several of the original cities either collapsed or underwent significant reorganization. Huamelulpan reached its peak at this juncture and afterward, until the Postclassic period, lost most of its population. Monte Negro was already abandoned. Yucuita suffered a "hiatus" when public areas were burned and abandoned. Cerro de las Minas in the Baja and Río Viejo on the coast experienced similar episodes of political decline and depopulation. These changes left the Mixteca Alta and probably other regions with a fragmented settlement landscape by the onset of the Classic period, although the overall regional population was greater than before. We could therefore describe the Classic period as a "new beginning," albeit one derived from prior conditions.

Classic urbanism varied even within discrete subregions.[1] Variation could suggest greater political autonomy among centers than has sometimes been assumed, and sites probably occupied specialized economic roles within larger regional networks. The roughly equal-size centers throughout the Mixteca look much like the distribution and territorial extent of the Postclassic kingdoms. We therefore trace the origin of the *cacicazgo*, or small indigenous form of state known as *yuhuitayu* for the pre-Hispanic era, to the onset of the Classic period.[2]

The Classic period ended by C.E. 600 with the beginning of regional collapses similar in scope to what occurred at Monte Albán, Teotihuacan, and the Maya area during the Epiclassic (roughly 600 to 900). After 600 in Mesoamerica, the Classic period cities became unstable and in many cases collapsed spectacularly. Teotihuacan was in decline by the 600s (possibly as early as the 500s) and Maya cities were abandoned in waves during the 700s and 800s.[3] The final causes for these collapses remain in dispute, but this was not the first episode of decline or at least substantial reorganization.

The "second wave urbanization" left the original Oaxacan cities and their regions much altered. Monte Albán's transition into the Classic period, recognized in pottery as "Transición II/IIIa" was more than changing pottery styles; it also reflected new external relationships that had repercussions throughout Oaxaca.[4] All of the original Mixteca Alta cities declined or had already collapsed by this brief transitional phase. It seems something similar occurred in the Mixteca Baja and at the coastal urban center of Río Viejo.[5] This suggests that region-wide systemic problems were ultimate causes (limits to growth come to mind, but so do extremes of inequality), while short-term triggering events were more proximate.[6]

The rise of new centers during the Classic period was a situation latent with potential to upset the regional balance of power. Monte Albán was one of several large Oaxacan cities during the Classic, its political territory much reduced from Formative times.[7] We are not talking about one or a few but rather dozens of significant population centers, in all likelihood variously allied or in conflict, similar to the Postclassic situation. The transition into the Postclassic was a continuous process, chronologically and regionally speaking, and should not be reduced to the cessation of monumental building at Monte Albán or other notable Mesoamerican cities.[8] Teotihuacan, after all, remained a significant population center during the transitional Epiclassic period while competing city-states such as Xochicalco arose in nearby regions.[9] Maya populations, albeit much reduced, survived the collapse in the Petén Lakes region.[10] Elements of elite culture, such as writing on stone, ceased or changed considerably, but basic lifeways remained intact.

THE MIXTEC KINGDOM
DURING THE CLASSIC TO EPICLASSIC PERIOD

Since the time of Caso's work in the 1930s, research on the Classic period Mixtec (approximately 200 to 600, as discussed above) has been affected by a preoccupation with the influence, or outright political and cultural domination, of Monte Albán. Until recently, the emphasis on external relations has inhibited the effort to examine the rise of civilization *within* the area, to focus primarily upon the origins and development of Mixtec civilization per se and to place appropriate *secondary* emphasis on external influences or connections.[11] Much of this arises from Caso's Yucuñudahui excavations, described below, as well as the relative absence of archaeological research in the Mixteca prior to the 1960s. But old views die hard, and the perception remains. Present investigations have turned from this "externalism" characterized by excessive concern with Teotihuacan, Monte Albán, or in the Postclassic period with the Toltecs and Culhua-Mexica, toward increased concern for indigenous, autochthonous evolution. It is not that these external relations are lacking in importance. It is the misplaced emphasis on the outside actors and a secondary concern for Mixtec civilization itself that distorts the realities of development in the area.

The Classic period in the Mixteca saw the "breakout" of settlement into previously abandoned areas, overall growth in population, and a more urbanized and internally complex settlement landscape. We can refer to the central Mixteca Alta surveys by Balkansky, Stephen Kowalewski, and Laura Stiver Walsh for illustrative purposes, although these patterns were true for an even wider area. This central survey zone (encompassing Teposcolula, Tlaxiaco, and Tilantongo) grew in population over five times from the prior period, despite the Formative presence of Huamelulpan, and had a mid-range population estimate of 128,000. This is greater than the entire Valley of Oaxaca at this time. The largest site at Cerro Jazmín covered 229 hectares and had a mid-range population estimate of 17,000 persons—equivalent in population to Monte Albán in the Early Classic. Suffice to say that the central Mixteca Alta survey zone plus Nochixtlan constituted a demographic core within Mesoamerica and should not be overlooked in comparative studies of urbanism.

Rise of the Classic Cities and Hilltowns

After the third-century transition (and declines at Yucuita and Huamelulpan) there appeared a great profusion of sites in all areas of the Mixteca. Information combined from older and more recent surveys and excavations makes it clear that dozens of them easily qualify as urban.[12] These were small to medium-size sites (ranging from around 50 to 250 hectares) that formed concentrically around civic-ceremonial centers and crowned the summits of mountains and other high points in the Mixteca Alta and Baja. Their architectural plan, though relatively circumscribed, was monumental with great plazas, residential and agricultural terraces, platform building, palaces, ceremonial ball courts, and complex drainage systems. Exemplary of this pattern are Cerro de las Minas of Huajuapan; Cerro Encantado of Tlaxiaco; Cerro Jazmín of Nochixtlan; Ñucuiñe of Santa María Cuquila; Dzinicahua of San Mateo Peñasco; San Vicente Nuñu of Teposcolula and many other sites not mentioned or not yet fully explored. The Mixteca Costa was also heavily urbanized by this time and followed a similar trajectory when Río Viejo went into decline and a proliferation of smaller, probably competing Chatino centers emerged in the uplands of the Río Verde Valley.[13]

In the Mixtecas there was no primary center like Monte Albán or Teotihuacan. Instead, there were dozens of "mini-Monte Albáns," sometimes three or four simultaneously occupied centers in a given valley. The Nochixtlan Valley was occupied by Yucuñudahui, Cerro Jazmín, Etlatongo, and Jaltepec. The Tlaxiaco Valley held Cerro Encantado, Yucunitaca, El Tambor, Los Organos, and Cerro de la Virgen, all located concentrically adjacent to one another. The modern towns of San Pedro Yucunama, San Vicente Nuñu, and San Pedro y San Pablo Tequixtepec are flanked by Classic-period twin mountaintop centers. Although contrasting with settlement patterns in other areas of Mesoamerica, this arrangement is quite in keeping with the Mixteca political system of numerous interrelated small states, or *yuhuitayu*, so fundamentally characteristic of Postclassic times.

Nochixtlan Valley sites increased sixfold in the Classic period. Two of these—Yucuñudahui and Cerro Jazmín—were impressive mountaintop cities with clear residential and ritual-ceremonial precincts, extensive terracing, and internal street networks, as well as special activity areas, such as the great chert quarry at Yucuñudahui.[14] Half a dozen sites, including Etlatongo, Jaltepec, Topiltepec, and Tillo, were large and complex enough to deserve designation as quasi-urban towns. Some sixty additional sites are best called villages or hamlets. Yucuita was drastically reduced by this time, no longer a capital center but instead a dependency of a new capital, very probably Yucuñudahui. Developments were similarly impressive in the Teposcolula, Tamazulapan, and Huamelulpan valleys; in the Tlaxiaco, Cuquila, Chalcatongo, and Achiutla valleys; and in the Mixteca Baja from Silacayoapan north to Huajuapan, Huazolotitlan, and Tequixtepec. Each of these subregions was packed with strings of relatively compact but heavily-built sites on terraced hilltops.

The Classic period Mixteca had ties with other regions of Mesoamerica. There are obvious connections to the great city of Teotihuacan in the Valley of Mexico and to Monte Albán in the Valley of Oaxaca. These are manifest in the visible architecture and in pottery trade wares and apparent "imitations" of exotic cultural elements encountered at such centers as Yucuñudahui.[15]

Figure 3.1. Cerro Jazmín and eroded lands surrounding it in the Yanhuitlan sector of the Nochixtlan Valley.

Caso's discovery of Tomb 1 at Yucuñudahui is virtually unique—the structure contained burials, pottery, and mural art in the tradition of Monte Albán III, but to this day little else is known of Classic period art and writing in the Mixteca Alta. Exotic pottery styles, figurines, and architecture were present at, but by no means inundated, Classic period sites in the area. The basic local pottery wares were a persisting and evolving tan-ware tradition of local origins and the "fine orange" and "thin orange" tradition associated with the rise and enormous influence of Teotihuacan and the fine gray wares related to Monte Albán.[16] We cannot at the present juncture say more about shared styles, ideologies, or exchanges until more Mixteca sites of this period are excavated and discoveries like Caso's Tomb 1 put in a broader comparative context.

Warfare and Agriculture

Classic period sites in the Mixteca Alta and Baja continued to be located primarily in defendable locations. More sites were located at higher elevations than ever before. This was true even for Chatino sites on the coast. It was most certainly true for Monte Albán and Zapotec sites in the Valley of Oaxaca and nearby regions. Does this mean that defense was the primary motivation for

Figure 3.2. Yucuñudahui during the 1970 excavations by the VNVP, on a domestic terrace below the "Mound of the Rain God."

site placement? It is easy to postulate conflict as the reason that sites were located atop mountains, sites that were terraced and in some instances had wall-and-ditch fortifications. Much more difficult is explaining why the conflict occurred—who the conflicting parties were and what were their motivations, the intricacies of warfare strategy and tactics, and the effects on local societies and intergroup relations. Most arguments concerning warfare stop far short of satisfactory explanation. And, as with many things we discuss in this chapter, the lack of excavated sites makes our inferences even harder to come by.

One view is that Classic period Mixtec sites were placed as they are for ideological and religious, even aesthetic, reasons as well as for purposes of defense.[17] The sites themselves, perched on isolated mountain peaks, are something to behold. Their proximity to clouds, rain, and sky make them obvious locations for religious observances. Yet it is an undeniable fact that a significant number of Classic Mixtec sites have the remains of defensive walls. Many of the defensible sites are found on boundaries between competing polities. Shatter zones of little or no occupation separate the occupied valley pockets. Our colleague Laura Stiver Walsh has suggested that agricultural terracing was defensive in character, given their high and often forbidding locations far from more congenial planting surfaces.[18] Warfare might have been so endemic that communities could no longer protect themselves or their fields in the valley bottoms. It is rare, for example, to find small, isolated farmsteads on the valley bottoms despite their near ubiquity during Postclassic times. The debate between Mixtec "pacifists" and "warriors" has not been fully joined, so the matter remains open and much in need of systematic investigation.

Much has been written of Classic period warfare in the Mixteca emanating from Monte Albán, but those conclusions are doubtful. Monte Albán reached its greatest site size and monumentality during Classic and Epiclassic times, but it held a relatively small political territory compared to its earlier period of militaristic expansion. By this time the site had many potential competitors even within the Valley of Oaxaca that would have limited the site's administrative reach.[19] Scenarios involving the Mixtec culture hero Lord Eight Deer defeating Monte Albán overlords are especially offensive to reason. Eight Deer lived during the eleventh century. Monte Albán collapsed at least two hundred years before Eight Deer's epic conquests.

The likelihood of episodic political alliances among rival cities during the Classic, similar to the Postclassic situation, further complicates the matter. Market systems in any event were pervasive by the Classic period, moving goods and art styles within and among regions irrespective of shifting politics.[20] We do not, in short, require an expansionistic Monte Albán to explain the defensive character of Classic period Mixtec sites, or the presence of certain classes of pottery, but would rather look to the Mixteca's own internal dynamic. There were, quite obviously, considerable disruptions following the declines or collapses of Yucuita, Huamelulpan, and Río Viejo at the end of the Formative. Small polities filled the void left by those once-great centers.

Whether for defensive purposes, as a response to population pressure, or the less than optimal settlement locations (and probably all three), *coo-yuu* terracing was elaborated as a means of increasing agricultural production. A variant form of hillside terrace farming, the Mixtec *coo-yuu* (or *lama-bordo*) system of soil and water management was an apparently successful attempt to overcome the limited carrying capacity of the narrow valleys of the Mixteca.[21] Arable land was created by adapting normal channels of runoff to retain soils eroded from upper slopes as well as catching and retaining valuable moisture. These Mixteca terraces are similar to what geographers call "cross-channel" or "gully" terraces,[22] but built over time to enormous proportions with retaining walls one, two, and even three meters in height and that descend for hundreds of meters before spilling onto cultivated valley floors.

These terrace systems have persisted as a significant component of Mixteca agriculture from their inception, most likely in Formative times, to the present day. Their productivity supported the enormous population increases and occupation of the uplands during the Classic period. Hundreds of such terrace systems can be found throughout the Mixteca Alta and Baja from southern Puebla to Juxtlahuaca, Chicahuaxtla, Putla, and Ixtayutla, and they constitute some of the most productive lands in the entire region. This most fundamental of economic concerns was further elaborated in the Postclassic period, again underscoring the continuity of basic lifeways that crossed the Classic to Postclassic boundary.

Emergent Mixtec Native States/*Yuhuitayu*

The origin of the ethnohistorical Mixtec community/*ñuu*, its characteristic form of distributed urbanism consisting of core and outlying settlements, and in all probability its kingdoms, or *yuhuitayu*, is borne out through the regional settlement patterns, described above, and the excavations in the ceremonial precinct of a Classic period reoccupation at Tayata (more on this below). We are not entirely surprised to find these materials, or a settlement structure mirroring the protohistoric kingdoms. The senior author offered this same hypothesis more than twenty-five years ago when describing Las Flores sites from the Nochixtlan Valley in *The Cloud People*, while more recent evidence allows for a forceful reiteration of this model in the present.[23]

It is an inescapable fact that nearly every purported Classic period capital is located directly over or adjacent to the *cabeceras* of Postclassic and Early Colonial *yuhuitayu*. A simple overlay of Classic and Postclassic survey maps in every highland Mixtec region shows this pattern. The relatively even distribution of population and urbanism across subregions of the Mixteca (and now we speak primarily of the more extensively studied reaches of the Alta) likewise suggests a dispersion of political authority similar to the Postclassic. We have already given our reasons for doubting external control over the Mixteca Alta during Classic times.

The typical polity moreover consisted of one major hill town or urban center along with its several dependencies. The capitals themselves were sometimes architecturally complex but sometimes not; monumental architecture was in fact distributed quite widely among constituent sites of the small polities. Ceremonial areas could be spatially separate from the main residential areas. Sites within subregions or the "valley pockets" were clearly interdependent.

Intensive agricultural practices were ubiquitous. This patterning, again, looks much like the idealized settlement pattern for the community-kingdoms. And like the Postclassic kingdoms, there was significant variation in population, monumentality, site location and layout, and in prior and subsequent settlement histories. In short, it was precisely the kind of intensive, local adaptation in which sites and their polities might join or fracture, exchange goods or fight, or intermingle royal houses via marriage and child-rearing that was depicted in codices and described by eyewitnesses after the Spanish Conquest.

We also have excavated data from Tayata, a Classic reoccupation in the most isolated part of the site, consisting of platforms with mounded architecture, an *endeque*, or "soft stone," frieze that in all probability depicts a royal pair, and a steam bath replete with formal burials and child sacrifices.[24] It is important to realize that no significant residential activity dating to the Classic period occurred elsewhere on the site. The main residential area for this small polity—formed or reconstituted, perhaps, in the wake of Huamelulpan's decline —was the nearby hilltop of Cerro Lagartija and adjacent uplands around the modern Tayatas. During the Postclassic, royal residential zones as well as ceremonial areas were often segregated from the broader population. Yanhuitlan fit this pattern based on historical documentation. Tlacotepec and numerous other Postclassic *yuhuitayu* suggest this pattern in their archaeological settlement patterns. Tayata provides excavated confirmation of this pattern, as well as radiometric dates that place the origin of these practices in the third century. This is long before the royal dynasties mentioned in the codices, and long before the Epiclassic collapses. The Mixteca's protohistoric form of state was in place at least 1,200 years before the Spanish Conquest.

Classic and Epiclassic Writing Systems

The unfortunate grasping at straws resulting from the woeful lack of systematic archaeological excavation in the Mixteca continues into the Classic period. There is little reliable information from the Mixteca Alta that would shed light on the evolution of Mixtec writing. The area is light years behind the Valley of Oaxaca, central Mexico, and the Maya area in epigraphic studies. Tomb 1 at Yucuñudahui provides some information in the form of painted murals and some carved stone features. Both the painted forms and the stone carving relate to the Zapotec system, but at the same time there are obvious antecedents to design elements and content of the later Mixtec system. The Zapotec "presence" at Yucuñudahui (whether biological, iconographic, or both) could be nothing more than elite emulation or an especially auspicious marriage partner from the Valley of Oaxaca who was interred there.

Figure 3.3. Tomb 1 (Lápida 1) at Yucuñudahui, showing a mix of Zapotec and Mixtec styles; see the Zapotec bar-and-dot numeration below, the Mixtec "A-O" year sign above. Redrawn by Jason Poling from Caso 1938, figure 68.

Throughout the Mixteca Alta, most notably in and around Tlaxiaco, the Huamelulpan and Tayata Valley, Teposcolula, Yucunama, Chalcatongo, and Achiutla, dozens of stone images depicting Dzahui (a water-related supernatural) are found on sites and in surrounding fields. The surface finds are associated with Classic and Postclassic sites, and it is inferred that these forms were components of the ritual complex of these periods, but these out-of-context stones provide little help in dealing with the evolution of writing and calendrics.

An additional carved stone monument, removed from the badly looted site of Cerro Encantado,[25] in Tlaxiaco, has the peculiar combination of a glyphic cartouche surrounding what appear to have been intertwined serpents (possible Baja attributes). The inscription is obviously removed from a more extensive textual mural, so an adequate interpretation is not possible. The area of the site from which the monument was taken dates to the onset of the Classic period—timing that coincided with Huamelulpan's decline

Figure 3.4. Laura Stiver Walsh, looking for signs of Dzahui in San Vicente Nuñu.

and the growth of places such as Cerro Encantado that were becoming more autonomous.

The Tayata Project also reports an *endeque* frieze that likely depicted a marital pair, a find pertaining to a later reoccupation of the site. The stone appears to have been symmetrical, with matching elements on each end, although one of the marital pair is only presumptive—that section of the stone was scratched out in antiquity. That this was an alliance of some kind is suggested by the variant forms of place or hill sign that are linked to each of the personages.[26] The rectangular frame around the images, meanwhile, looks much like the Zapotec style of the time. Radiometric dates and stylistic comparisons all suggest that the stone and its context date to the onset of the Classic period, the time when Huamelulpan was going into decline. The chosen media and context of the Tayata frieze are different from the carved stones of both Huamelulpan and Cerro Encantado. This suggests that there was greater variety to Classic Mixtec iconography than we currently realize. This makes sense in a setting of newly emergent and competitive small polities and in localized efforts to establish ruling lineages.

Turning to the Mixteca Baja, specifically the area between Huajuapan de León and the Puebla border, there appears during the Classic and Epiclassic a distinctive writing style that Wigberto Jiménez-Moreno and John Paddock

Figure 3.5. The Tayata frieze made from cut *endeque* blocks and set into a rectangular frame; similar to the framing of carved stones at Classic-period Monte Albán.

called Ñuiñe. It is now apparent that this is a rich artistic-notational system, in some ways unique but in other ways related to the contemporary Zapotec and antecedent to the later Mixtec systems. Examination of the Ñuiñe style, especially carved stone monuments from San Pedro y San Pablo Tequixtepec, Chazumba, Miltepec, and Huajuapan, suggests a continuing evolution of Mixtec writing, perhaps beginning at Yucuita and then moving to Huamelulpan, to Cerro Encantado and Tayata, to Yucuñudahui, and finally, or concurrently, to the Ñuiñe. Sketchy, perhaps, but that is our best surmise based on present evidence. Why the Ñuiñe style is found extensively in the Mixteca Baja and not in the Alta is unclear, although survey in the central Mixteca Alta suggests large-scale abandonment by the later Classic. The picture will remain clouded until further excavation aimed at recovery and analysis of stone monuments is conducted, especially for the Nochixtlan Valley, where occupation was continuous throughout the Classic and Epiclassic.

Moving to the Mixteca Costa, numerous carved stone monuments have appeared fortuitously rather than as a result of systematic excavation.[27] While provenience can be assumed to relate rather closely to the places where the monuments were discovered, the lack of scientific controls makes dating problematical, especially for regions not yet formally surveyed. On stylistic grounds and on the basis of associated pottery complexes, the majority of inscriptions are believed to date to the Epiclassic (600 to 900) and Post-classic (after 900).

Urcid and Joyce report thirteen stone monuments from Río Viejo and nearby sites.[28] Río Viejo was once again an important site during the Epi-classic, and many of the monuments of this time depict elite persons, possibly rulers, wearing fancy attire, jaguar masks, headdresses and cloaks, and often carrying a hieroglyphic name following conventions of the 260-day ritual calendar. While the relationship to the Zapotec–Monte Albán tradition may be stronger on the coast than in the case of the Ñuiñe tradition of the Baja, there are still many features of the presumptively later monuments that relate closely to the Postclassic Mixtec tradition of the Alta. For example, many of the coastal monuments depict a deceased noble figure with arms crossed. This is a typical depiction found in the codices and on hundreds of small green stone amulets called *penates*. But we are getting ahead of ourselves.

Ñuiñe Art, Writing, and Culture

The Mixteca Baja consists of hilly but hotter, drier, and lower-elevation valleys than the Mixteca Alta, located in northwest Oaxaca, adjacent parts of Puebla and along Oaxaca's border with Guerrero. In the 1960s John Paddock salvaged a tomb at Cerro de las Minas (Huajuapan) with carved stones and other materials in the Classic to Epiclassic Ñuiñe art style of the Mixteca Baja.[29] Although this style has been described by several authors with further examples of the distinctive micaceous orange pottery, fired-clay figurine heads, large effigy urns, and writing, it remains enigmatic.

Ñuiñe art and culture is related to traditions in the Mixteca Alta, the Zapo-tec region, and central Mexico, but it has many distinctive elements. We are limited in that few antecedents are known for the region, and archaeologists have yet to apply themselves at sufficient regional scale to solve these problems.[30] Marc Winter's excavation of Cerro de las Minas is the most informative to date and includes an elite (probably royal) tomb, an effigy urn interred with the dead, and two carved stones each with a glyph, these being somewhat reminiscent of Tomb 1 at Yucuñudahui. Winter also excavated a number of houses that could represent a range of statuses.

The Ñuiñe art style is found on sites that are closely related architectur-ally and with respect to the pottery complexes to literally hundreds of sites in the Mixteca Alta. The site of Diquiyu,[31] situated on the interface of the

Figure 3.6. John Paddock during the 1960s, examining Postclassic murals in Mitla.

Alta and Baja, exemplifies this situation with obvious Formative, Classic, and Postclassic surface pottery similar to the Mixteca Alta but littered with broken basalt columns inscribed with Ñuiñe glyphs. We can think of few sites in the Mixteca with the potential to deliver more from a sustained research program than this one.

Present evidence indicates that Ñuiñe style is concentrated in a line running from Diquiyu to Tequixtepec with extensions into southern Puebla

Figure 3.7. Ñuiñe effigy urns from Paddock's excavations at Cerro de las Minas.

as far as Acatlan and Tepexi. Parts of Tamazulapan and Coixtlahuaca also have Ñuiñe materials.[32] These appear to be sharp boundaries, making Ñuiñe a relatively delimited phenomenon, but we suspect that future work will reveal considerable internal variation among sites in the region and a variety of external connections. Winter, for example, notes that a carved stone from San Juan Mixtepec was carved in "Ñuiñe provincial style." Iván Rivera, meanwhile, observes differences in the monumental layout of potential rival polities within the Baja.[33]

Glyphic conventions that apply to Ñuiñe sites include the distinctive round, but sometimes square, cartouche containing a day sign or other information, a place glyph in the form of a hill, and the bar and dot form of numerical notation. Caso's "Jaws of the Sky" motif is also present.[34] This motif is often found at Monte Albán and other Zapotec sites in tomb murals and carved stones dating to the Epiclassic period; it is associated with nobles, especially royal marriage scenes, and represents "the opening to an upper world where the deceased nobles lived; this opening allows communication and gift-giving between living nobles and their ancestors."[35] These examples of Epiclassic Zapotec writing were concerned primarily with marriage, descent, and legitimacy for rulership, a set of related concerns that were often

Figure 3.8. Stone XVIII from Tequixtepec. Redrawn by Jason Poling from VUPA 19, figure 36.

expressed in elaborate funerary monuments.[36] This pattern, too, would have echoes into the Postclassic with the almost maniacal genealogical concern found in the Mixtec codices. Ñuiñe writing is thus related to Zapotec, but that is where the comparative insights seem to end. Ñuiñe remains fundamentally *arte de la Mixteca Baja*, a notable variation from other Classic period forms and much in need of additional detailed study.[37]

These comparisons suggest that the northern Mixteca Baja experienced a florescence in lapidary art, that is, in stone carving with written script that is not evident elsewhere in the Mixteca. We know from regional survey data that by Epiclassic times a wave of abandonments depopulated many subregions or "valley pockets" of the Mixteca Alta, similar in extent to the localized abandonments during the era of incipient urbanization.[38] Outside of the Nochixtlan Valley, much of the Mixteca Alta may have experienced a hiatus in occupation. Yet we cannot resolve the meaning of these patterns, much less explain individual cases, without appropriate excavations and dated contexts from a far greater number of relevant Classic and Epiclassic sites.

The Tomb Murals at San Pedro Jaltepetongo

Ñuiñe was not the only enigmatic art style of its time. Some insights into the Mixtec writing system come from recent discoveries at San Pedro Jaltepetongo on the very eastern extremity of the Mixteca Alta, where the high mountains quickly give way to the Cañada de Cuicatlan some 700 meters below. In 1995, during roadwork, residents of Jaltepetongo found a tomb carved into the *endeque,* or *caliche* cap, underlying the town. Excavations by Raúl Matadamas of the Centro INAH Oaxaca brought to light a rectangular tomb, roughly 4 square meters by 1.5 meters in height, with walls and ceilings containing a fascinating complex of pictographic elements, related to the burial of the two individuals found in the tomb and to a variety of other concepts and ritualistic activities.[39]

It would be taking nothing away from Matadamas's forthcoming analysis to state that this is probably the most important epigraphic find to be made in the Mixteca in the seventy-five years since Caso's work at Monte Negro and Yucuñudahui. The painted scenes include mortuary rituals, fertility and calendrical symbols, and the image of Dzahui, the sacred "water-cloud-lightning-fertility" supernatural of the Mixtecs. There is clearly a mix of several styles, one Zapotec, one Mixtec, and a third new complex of elements that render the discovery unique. Although it is a single occurrence, this unique blend of writing styles does more than any work yet completed to clarify the relationship of Classic Zapotec-influenced writing and the Postclassic Mixtec system.

The Classic-Postclassic Transition

Several factors make it difficult to uniformly characterize Classic and Epiclassic writing among the Mixtec. The societal disruptions in the wake of the regional collapses then occurring undoubtedly "shuffled the deck." This was a period when new sets of regional elites were looking to establish their legitimacy to rule. Similar events occurred in the Valley of Oaxaca and bordering Zapotec regions.[40] Epigraphic boundaries overlapped, mainly, but not exclusively, from the penetration of Zapotec writing into the Mixteca Alta, Baja, and Costa. Further influences entered through Puebla and Veracruz, initially from Classic-period Teotihuacan, and later from El Tajín among other "meccas" of Epiclassic art and culture.

Our usual complaint applies as well, about there being so few excavations with intent to understand ancient written scripts (or, for that matter, transitional chronological phases).[41] Regardless of the cause, we are faced with a situation of considerable internal diversity in writing systems but too few reference points from reliable contexts. One fact about writing nonetheless seems certain despite the many crosscurrents: that by the Epiclassic if not before peoples throughout Oaxaca were effectively reading from their own hymnals. This seems as good a description as any for the Postclassic balkanization of Oaxaca, a process that was certainly ongoing since Classic times in the Mixteca.

The Postclassic Transition and the Historical *Yuhuitayu*

A cultural and artistic revolution occurred in the Mixteca between about 900 and the arrival of Europeans in the area in the 1520s. This was the "Golden Age" of the pre-Hispanic *señoríos*-states, of rulers and culture heroes like Lord Eight Deer, of the great convergence of philosophy, religion, politics, techno-logy, and aesthetic sensibility that produced the *arte mixteco* of the codices, polychrome pottery, delicately carved bone, the most impressive lapidary art and jewelry of Mesoamerica, and the still incompletely known mural art of the region. It was a dynamic time with great social, political, and economic movement and interaction, not only within the cities, towns, valleys, and subregions of the Mixteca, but among the Mixteca and other regions and ethnic groups of Mesoamerica. More than ever before, Mixtec culture and "nationality" are clearly identifiable, and they functioned in a truly inter-national arena.[42]

Postclassic Oaxaca saw the rise of the Mixtec kingdoms, called *cacicazgos*, *ñuu*, city-states, *señoríos*, and various other terms,[43] but in this book we use the Mixtec *yuhuitayu* for the pre-Hispanic era. Kevin Terraciano describes *yuhuitayu* as "both a place and a political arrangement created by dynastic alliances."[44] These political entities were, in effect, the combination through marriage, conquest, or inheritance of one or more *ñuu*, or local states, often shown in native pictorials with royal couples facing each other while seated on reed mats. It was a time of shifting alliances where ruling-class nobles "traded communities, gave away lands, and relocated populations like parti-cipants in a giant Monopoly game."[45] Warfare was endemic, but temporary military and marital alliances could unify multiple kingdoms.[46] Despite the transient nature of royal dynasties observed in the codices (not infrequently ending in captures, sacrifices, or assassinations), there was stability across the wider region, such that only the Spanish Conquest and subsequent Colo-nial period brought about their demise.

Prior to the modern era of research that began in the 1960s, it was com-monly believed that the Mixtecs invaded the Valley of Oaxaca, thus explaining the Mixtec presence in Zapotec towns at the time of the Conquest.[47] It is now clear that Mixtec expansion was an outcome of alliance-building strategies and intermarriage among royal dynasties, accompanied by persisting migra-tion from the Mixteca into the Valley of Oaxaca and further south, beginning in the thirteenth century and lasting into the sixteenth.[48] Archaeological exam-ples of these alliances and ethnically mixed situations include the Mixtec occupation at the base of Monte Albán; the identity of one or more of the

Figure 3.9. Mixtec polychrome "portrait" from excavations at Yucundaa–Pueblo Viejo de Teposcolula.

occupants of Tomb 7 at Monte Albán; and the fortress at Guiengola, on the Isthmus of Tehuantepec, scene of a protracted Mixtec-Zapotec military alliance against invading Culhua-Mexica armies.[49]

The Postclassic period offers opportunities for archaeohistorical approaches, but this potential cannot be fully realized until excavations "catch up" with the more detailed historical descriptions and something is done about the undifferentiated Postclassic chronology. The Postclassic runs from around 900 to 1521, albeit with few excavated contexts and even fewer radiocarbon dates. The divisions of the Postclassic proposed for other regions of Oaxaca, meanwhile, are idealized rather than demonstrated. On the other hand, historical documentation from late pre-Hispanic and early Colonial times is relatively abundant although containing its own limitations. Spanish sources are rich but full of gaps and biases that require constant professional interpretation and refinement by the ethnohistorian. Studies of native picture manuscripts (*códices* and *lienzos*) have produced enormously useful information and render the Mixteca virtually unique among Mesoamerican civilizations of the Postclassic period.[50] The conclusions drawn in this book would not have been possible without the marriage of these sources and methods.[51] Examples of this kind are discussed at the end of this chapter.[52]

Archaeological Settlement Surveys

For reasons that are not clear, the vast majority of the great mountaintop centers from earlier times were vacated and the residents moved down to the lower slopes, low hills, and along the edges of the alluvium, where valley lands meet the hillsides.[53] In those locations they formed their communities, large and small, but generally much less monumental than in the Classic period. An exception is Yucundaa–Pueblo Viejo de Teposcolula, which was constructed on a high hill overlooking the Teposcolula Valley, and although there are minor manifestations of Classic period settlement there, the Postclassic center is far greater in size and more complex than any of its antecedent sites.[54] Other nearly comparable examples of this pattern might be the Pueblos Viejos de Tamazulapan, Magdalena Peñasco, or Cerro Tonocahua of Santiago Huajolotitlan and sites in the Peñoles area. Few other exceptions can be cited from the surveyed areas of Nochixtlan, Tamazulapan, Teposcolula, Huamelulpan, Tlaxiaco-Chalcatongo, or the Mixteca Baja.[55]

Every region yet surveyed reached its pre-Hispanic peak in sites and estimated population during the Postclassic, occupations that have left a considerable imprint on the land even today: in terraced hillsides, many still being farmed, and in the locations of modern towns, nearly all having pre-Hispanic antecedents nearby. In many instances, notably the Teposcolula Valley, occupation was so dense that Postclassic occupations were nearly continuous, raising questions about the actual correspondence of archaeological sites as we typically define them with the native view of the settled landscape.

Several of the Postclassic *cabeceras* were very large indeed. Coixtlahuaca and its contiguous *barrios* covered at least 30 square kilometers. Teposcolula's core

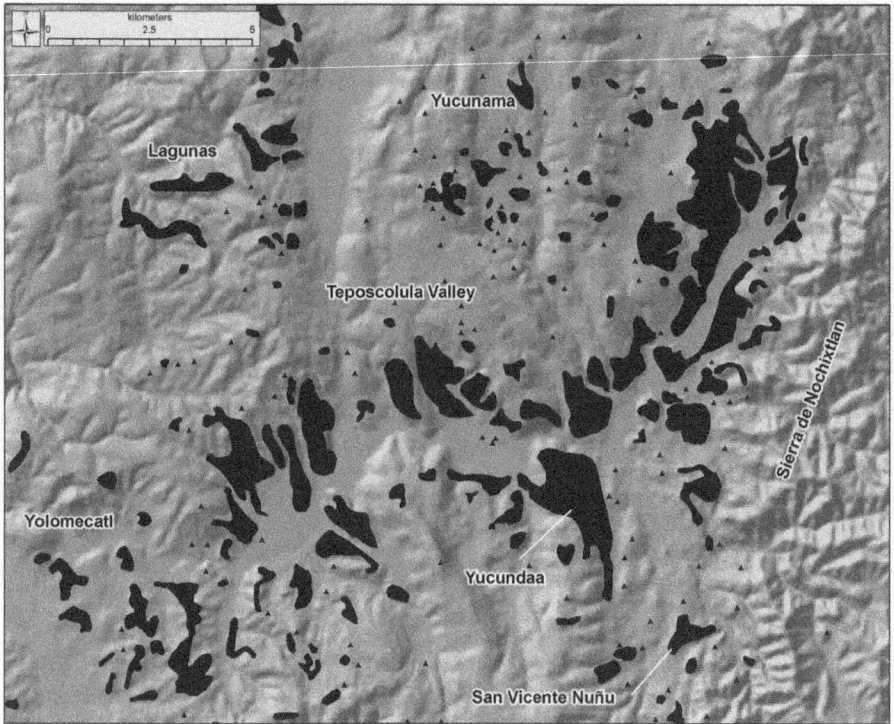

Figure 3.10. Map of Postclassic settlement in the Teposcolula Valley.

settlement cluster was nearly 25 square kilometers. Tilantongo and the sites in its immediate vicinity measured 9 square kilometers. Achiutla was nearly 8 square kilometers. Putla, very conservatively, its surrounding region not yet systematically surveyed, was 4 square kilometers. Yanhuitlan, though highly dispersed over a series of low hills, was at least 3 square kilometers in extent.[56]

Yanhuitlan was a typical case: the bulk of its residential population was probably located on the lower slopes of Cerro Jazmín and its immediate periphery, those sites along with the *cabecera* occupying an area exceeding 14 square kilometers, making this the largest core settlement in the Nochixtlan Valley.[57] The archaeological population estimate for Cerro Jazmín alone is 32,000. Yanhuitlan's *cabecera*, based on historical documentation, would have held at least 10,000 persons. We ask our readers to do the math themselves. These are some of the largest-order settlements in Postclassic Mesoamerica and rival estimates for other major urban agglomerations, among them the Culhua-Mexica capital at Tenochtitlan and the Mixteca Costa imperial seat at Tututepec.[58] What is meaningful in these instances, however, is not which site is the "biggest," but rather the continuum of size distributions and their placement over the landscape—it being the settlement clustering and regional hierarchies that reveal meaningful patterns, not the individual albeit occasionally spectacular cases.[59]

The archaeological settlement patterns raise questions about the means of sustenance for so many souls. Terrace retention agriculture, or Mixtec *coo-yuu*, underwent significant expansion in the Mixteca Alta and Baja as a solution to the problems of meeting basic subsistence needs, as well as demands from local rulers, and, in some *yuhuitayu*, providing surplus production in tribute to the Culhua-Mexica.

Burgoa, referring to the extent of cultivation near Tilantongo, observes that ". . . all the mountains and *barrancas* today are marked by stepped and terraced fields from top to bottom and looking like stone-edged stairways."[60] It is an apt description, and we know today that terracing of this kind is strongly correlated with Postclassic settlement, and especially sites sitting on or near the reddish soils of the Yanhuitlan Beds—deposits that are extensive, easily worked, and both fertile and "highly erodible."[61] It is impossible not to notice the extensive erosion in the Mixteca Alta today—clearly visible even in satellite photos—that is linked to the Yanhuitlan Beds, their extensive modification and use during pre-Hispanic times, and their abandonment subsequent to the Spanish Conquest. Abandoned terrace systems eventually fall apart, pulling whole sites down into the growing *arroyos* with them. This is one of the reasons, incidentally, that our site-area estimates for the Postclassic are an *undercount* of what was once actually in place.

Other factors affecting rates of erosion that Michael Kirkby[62] considered among the highest in the world are the recent centuries of sheep and goat grazing dating from the Conquest, and the fact that modern farmers typically dismantle terrace walls to create more planting surface. This is a short-term and ultimately self-defeating approach to the loss of fertile land. *Coo-yuu* terracing is still in operation in dozens of Mixteca Alta and Baja communities. The pre-Hispanic terrace system once fed hundreds of thousands of residents of the Mixteca Alta alone,[63] and it might do so again.

The Postclassic Mixtecs partook of their religious activity in older sites and ceremonial areas, less frequently within the core settlements themselves, as well as performing ritual observances at natural features—caves, springs, or impressive promontories—and constructed modest shrines within settlements. The central political-ceremonial areas of some of the Classic period centers, such as Yucuñudahui and Cerro Jazmín, were virtually abandoned. Only peripheral areas of these grand old cities were occupied, but the central

Figure 3.11. *Coo-yuu* terracing near Amatlan; the terraces flow down the hillsides like tributaries of a large river. Google Earth photo.

ritual precincts show clear signs of continued use, as though they were the scene of pilgrimages and more individualized offerings to ancient sacred places and forces.[64] Achiutla, among numerous similar examples, saw Postclassic ritual activity on the hilltop above its Pueblo Viejo and Colonial era convent even though its monumental structures, including a ball court, appear to have been built in earlier periods.[65] These practices left their mark on the present, as many of the late pre-Hispanic monuments and shrines, especially those situated on mountaintops, continue to be revisited by modern Mixtecos.

Warfare and the Culhua-Mexica

Depictions of warfare, capture, and conquest are abundant in the Postclassic codices, especially *Nuttall*, *Bodley*, *Colombino*, and to a lesser extent *Vindobonensis*.[66] Although fortifications or fighting from fortified positions are not often depicted, Burgoa leaves little doubt that such defenses were important, particularly along ethnic-political frontiers. Sosola, for instance, using natural

Figure 3.12. Achiutla, seen from atop the rising platforms of its pre-Hispanic *cabecera*, overlooking a modern cemetery, the sixteenth-century convent, and the surrounding valley.

high points and narrow passes, was a daunting obstacle "even for the great King Moctezuma . . . and through daring raids and skillful use of weapons and in the aftermath of their victories, their descendants multiplying across neighboring mountains, built walls along passes so their enemies could not enter."[67]

Clearly then, fortifications, whether man made or natural, were utilized during the Postclassic period. Sosola was situated along the Zapotec-Mixtec frontier, which may account to some extent for its defensive disposition. Mixtecs were fighting Mixtecs, however, as in the case of Eight Deer and other *señores* or rulers, and it is known from the documents that a conflictive relationship existed between Achiutla and Tilantongo in pre-Hispanic times, during the Colonial period, and for that matter until the present day.

It is not unreasonable to assume, then, that fortified sites might exist in this area, and in fact they do exist, but it is not always known which groups controlled the sites or may have joined forces there against external foes.

Warfare is well documented in the Postclassic Mixteca, but why then were the majority of Mixtec sites located in the valleys with no evident thought given to defense? Settlement patterns, likewise, show a clear reduction in "shatter zones," or the spaces between ñuu and yuhuitayu compared to earlier periods. Exceptions would be those sites with circumferential walls, or built-up passageways situated along the eastern borders of the Mixteca or as at Yucundaa–Pueblo Viejo de Teposcolula, in the heart of the Mixteca Alta, where Laura Stiver Walsh identified a massive wall (or monumental road) 2 kilometers long and surrounding the principal settlement. Several other structures measuring some 2 meters in height are possibly defensive barriers.[68] Survey data from the central Mixteca Alta yield only 15 of 843 Postclassic sites with fortifications, not counting the many sites situated in high, terraced, and naturally defensible locations.[69] This number could be many or few depending on your point of view. But it is nonetheless clear, and perhaps revealing, that these defensible sites clustered in certain zones, especially along boundaries where persistent conflict continues even to the present day.

Burgoa mentions various other conflictive engagements as well as fortified sites, including the "on again, off again" alliance between Zapotec Zaachila and Mixtec Achiutla to oppose the Culhua-Mexica.[70] We discuss this alliance in some detail in the next chapter. Achiutla was also reportedly at war with the coastal empire of Tututepec over a tribute obligation.

Burgoa gives an account of Achiutla's defenses and the ensuing battle: "They have in front of this town a very high hill, with a peak which ascends loftily almost to the region of the clouds, and it is crowned with a very extensive brick wall more than a stadium high. And it is told in their paintings of a historical nature, that they retired here to defend themselves from their enemies. . . . The enemy arrived and besieged the mountain, and looked for a route by which to scale it and come within fighting distance; and the battle was so bloody that afterward they counted the dead of both sides, and more than twenty-two thousand bodies were found."[71]

We now have survey data from Achiutla that supports this account.[72] There is a walled fortress on the ridge crest west of the Pueblo Viejo that dates from the Formative period urbanization at nearby Huamelulpan, but the site was reutilized during Postclassic times. The features consist of two circumferential walls and a ditch. One of the walls measures 3.5 meters in height. An abundance of projectile points was found on the steeply sloping surface below the walls. This was almost certainly the location for the battle between Achiutla and Tututepec. High hills near population centers were common as defensive redoubts in Postclassic Oaxaca, notably at the Mitla fortress.[73] Achiutla, it seems, beat back the invaders from Tututepec, but was no match for the armies of Montezuma II, being defeated in the Culhua-Mexica campaign of 1503–1504.[74]

One perplexing question is why, if the Mixtecs were such great fighters,[75] were numerous communities of the Mixteca Alta so easily conquered by the Mexicans?[76] This can probably be reduced to two major responses: the Culhua-Mexica, despite occasional setbacks, were known to have been formidable warriors; and the Mixtecs, more to the point, were never able to form a sustained alliance against the Mexicans.[77] The Mixtec, as with other peoples of Postclassic Oaxaca, were internally divided among rival polities where temporary alliances were just that—temporary—and individual dynastic considerations trumped national or ethnic identities.

The Mexican connection is interesting and worthy of further comment. It is clear from the historical record that many Mixtec *yuhuitayu* paid tribute to the Culhua-Mexica, but there is virtually no archaeological indication of a Culhua-Mexica administrative presence. Coixtlahuaca and a few other places have limited numbers of Aztec black-on-orange and Texcoco red potsherds recovered in excavations and surveys.[78] Tlaxiaco, for unknown reasons, has a relative abundance of these wares. But this could mean anything. Several dozen Postclassic sites reported by Arthur Joyce, Donald Brockington, and Scott O'Mack for the Mixteca Costa also show little obvious signs of external influences.[79] This was of course the area of the Tututepec Empire, which remained independent throughout the Postclassic period.[80] The Culhua-Mexica evidently drew off tribute where they could but otherwise left the Mixtec to direct their own affairs. The Mixtec, it seems, spent more time fighting each other than the armies of the Culhua-Mexica.

Postclassic Domestic Architecture

Household studies are now providing a richer knowledge of daily life during Postclassic times and of interrelations among the classes and their external connections. Archaeological survey and excavation at Chachoapan, Nicayuju, Yucuita, and Yucundaa–Pueblo Viejo de Teposcolula provide ample evidence of the form and positioning of various forms of dwellings. This information converges with descriptions from ethnohistorical sources such as the *Relaciones geográficas*. The best data on elite housing are from excavations at Yucundaa. The rulers resided in a rambling structure measuring at least 80 by 100 meters and consisting of numerous plazas, interconnected rooms, red and white stucco floors, mosaic-surfaced walls, drainage systems, multiple hearths, passageways, and stairways, with interiors and exteriors embellished with decorative discs and symbols reflecting royal status, friezes, painting, and low-relief stone carving.[81]

Adjacent to the royal palace at Yucundaa, the nobility occupied a series of closely spaced houses, much smaller and less elaborate than the royal palace, but well planned and constructed of the same sort of *endeque* stone blocks, with single or double patios, two to three rooms, hearths, and a drainage system. These noble-class structures are found on two platforms, each measuring approximately 20 meters east-west by 200 meters and elevated some 6 to 7 meters above the preexisting surface. Related elite structures have been found in Chachoapan, Nicayuju of San Juan Teposcolula, and in the southern elite administrative complex at Yucundaa. These structures vary significantly, some falling between the large royal residence type of architecture and the houses of the nobility, others between the nobility and houses of the commoners. Still other complexes, such as those at partially explored Postclassic Yucuita, combine elite and common-class elements in tightly grouped configurations rising up hillsides.

Postclassic commoner (*tay ñuu* or *tay yucu*) houses were composed of one, two, or occasionally three rooms grouped around a central plaza. Hearths might be located in the open patios or inside. These houses were made of adobe, stone, or *endeque* blocks, with stucco floors and (sometimes) lower walls. In poorer communities dwellings were composed of cane or slender poles covered with mud mixed with lime and roofed with coarse grass thatch. Houses of this kind are found in large numbers in the rolling hills and piedmont spurs of Yanhuitlan, Nochixtlan, Chachoapan, Tlaxiaco, Achiutla, Chalcatongo, and in the Pueblos Viejos de Teposcolula (Yucundaa), Tamazulapan, Coixtlahuaca, San Pedro Cántaros Coxcaltepec, and Santiago Huazolotitlan, and, in fact, everywhere Postclassic settlement has been described.

Exceptionally complete descriptions resulting from excavation of common-class houses at Yucundaa and a dwelling complex from Nicayuju have greatly clarified the residential dimension at these *cabecera* and *sujeto* sites in the Teposcolula Valley.[82] These were terrace-farmer households, with little indication that the residents were involved in significant craft production. One slight exception would be the existence of two or three obsidian-flaking workshops around common-class houses in Yucundaa, where the green, black, and gray obsidian was imported from multiple sources in central Mexico and reworked on site. Chipped and ground stone and other material indications of daily life are abundant, along with the ubiquitous broken pottery, the vast majority of domestic forms produced at Santo Domingo Tonaltepec some ten kilometers to the east of the city. Polychrome pottery and well-made miniature stone and bone ornaments and ritual symbols are indeed found in and around the Yucundaa houses but they tend to be fragmentary, with indications that they were salvaged from royal households where the commoners were required to perform labor services. All houses were modified through enlargement, repaving of stucco floors, addition of crude mosaic surfaces to walls, renovation or redirection of passageways, filling of pits, and relatively low frequencies of fancy pottery and obsidian.

One excavated household at Nicayuju contained a *temazcal*, or steam bath, but these were not found at Yucundaa. There is a distinct possibility, however, that the Nicayuju house may be elite rather than common class. Regardless, the growing range of variation now evident in residential building, along with the complementary nature of existing historical documentation, are providing a much fuller picture of Postclassic domestic life.[83]

Mixteca Fine Art: Polychrome Pottery

One of the most distinctive elements of the art and culture of the Mixtecs is polychrome pottery. Polychrome vessels, produced either primarily or exclusively in and around Cholula, Puebla, are decorated in "codex style" and hold considerable iconographic content.[84] John Pohl and Gilda Hernández review in detail the multiple artistic, symbolic, social, and political themes expressed in polychromes and see them as functioning within a broader set of alliances during the Postclassic, providing through shared iconography and ritual a means of promoting ties among the Mixtec as well as other ethnic groups.[85] Interestingly, although polychrome is most prevalent in elite areas and in excavations of noble houses, it was by no means restricted in its distribution—commoner houses also had access to polychrome, fragments of which are found at sites of all kinds throughout the Mixteca.[86]

No one doubts the importance of polychrome in late pre-Hispanic times. Although the center of gravity of its distribution is in the Mixteca Alta and Baja, polychrome is found all the way from the Valley of Mexico to Hidalgo, Puebla, Veracruz, the Valley of Oaxaca, the coast of Oaxaca, and on to Tehuantepec. Although it is under study by at least a dozen scholars focusing on style, symbol, artistic technique, and social and political implications, such matters as the exact place of production or the manner of distribution remain wide open. It is indeed an elite ware. It is probable that the basic thread of interregional distribution lay in exchanges of deluxe, highly symbolic items

Figure 3.13. Excavations of domestic architecture from Yucundaa–Pueblo Viejo de Teposcolula, a common-class residential complex on the eastern slopes of Cerro Yucundaa.

among ruling families in the various regions of Mesoamerica. A less exclusionary explanation might be that these highly valued wares circulated in the extensive market systems described for the early Spanish Colonial period, although this would likely have articulated in some fashion with the system of elite exchange that is more in keeping with the social, political, and economic patterns of Postclassic times.

Writing and Picture Manuscripts

Postclassic Mixtec writing is known primarily from a corpus of screen-fold books made of prepared deerskin.[87] The system is pictographic, at times quasi-phonetic, often in rebus style where representation of certain symbols may suggest or resemble intended words or phrases (e.g., in English, an eye, a hand saw, and a cloud being understood as "I saw a cloud"). These books and their texts are referred to in the modern literature as codices and were known to the ancient Mixtecs as *tonindeye* ("history of lineages") or *naandeye* ("remembrances of the past"). Among the most important are *Nuttall*, *Bodley*, and *Selden*, as well as *Vindobonensis* (or *Vienna*) and *Colombino-Becker*. These are named after collectors, scholars, or their present locations in museums and

Figure 3.14. Polychrome
pottery excavated from
Yucundaa–Pueblo Viejo
de Teposcolula.

libraries around the world. Their prehistoric antecedents are not entirely clear, but certain conventions are identifiable in the earlier Zapotec stone monuments as well as the Classic and Epiclassic carved stones of the Mixteca.[88]

The codices depict the places, landscapes, dates, names and figures of individuals performing varied acts, and celestial-spiritual beings with accompanying name, place, and date glyphs. The books combine dynastic history, personal history, the political and marital alliances of the ruling aristocracy, conquest warfare, native cartography, myth and ritual, astrology, and undoubtedly served as documents of entitlement and self-aggrandizement. Usually texts depict actual events, individuals, objects, and places together with mythological or supernatural elements. It is as though the celestial and the spiritual are brought down to earth, to everyday life, and there is a combining of the supernatural and natural worlds. That the codices contain "real history" was Alfonso Caso's major contribution, and the effort to extract historical information from the codices is the theme of nearly all current research.[89]

The codices consist of interrelated scenes separated by red guidelines and arranged either horizontally or vertically. They are read boustrophedon, or "zig-zag," style. The texts lack three-dimensionality, meaning that the scenes have a rather flat appearance, with movement being depicted right-left and up-down, not back-front. The background is white-tan. Fine black lines delineate scenes. Outlined figures are filled with painted elements. Prominent colors are reds, greens, blues, yellows, black, gray, and white, normally vividly rendered and sharply contrastive. The codices are sometimes described as cartoonlike, albeit with considerably different intent, or similar to modern storyboards, with the implication that they were not only read and consulted but also performed.[90]

Elements are presented in stylized or conventionalized pictures: glyphs with animal figures or objects with lineally linked dots. Skull with 11 linked dots = Eleven Death, a personal name; stylized hill with concavity or undulation at base, or a rectangular box often with step-fret decoration = place name; two individuals seated on a woven palm mat = marriage, or alliance; dart protruding from place glyph = conquest; white tied bundle = death; hand extended and pointing = to order, command, or relate; extended hand holding object = to offer; closed eyes = death; umbilical cord = birth; footprints = to travel; chevrons in linear series = to go to war; and so on. Scribes, specialized in the art of writing, were the "*huisi tacu* . . . whose craft is to write."[91]

Persons are identified by a compound name consisting of the calendar day of their birth and a personal name that may be connected to one's costume or headdress, an object held in the hand, or even a thin black line. Examples are Lady Eleven Water "Blue Jewel Bird"; Lord Eight Deer "Jaguar Claw"; Lady Six Monkey "Serpent Quechquemitl"; Lady Eleven Water "Blue Parrot"; Lord Eleven Wind "Bloody Jaguar"; and Lord Five Rain "Smoking Mountain." Herrera informs us that nobles were given personal names at the age of seven by a priest but does not explain why.[92] Clearly, however, some days and their calendrical names were viewed as being luckier than others, since certain combinations of day names and day numbers appeared more often than chance would dictate.[93]

Place names, or toponyms, consist of the principal element—a hill or mountain, a river, a rectangular structure, or a field plain—and a modifier that indicates the particular place. The list of modifying, or identifying elements is long: caves, springs, spiritual beings, smoke, plants and animals, fire, the ball court, celestial bodies, temples, houses, death bundles, and a variety of human, natural, and supernatural activities. Examples include "hill plus

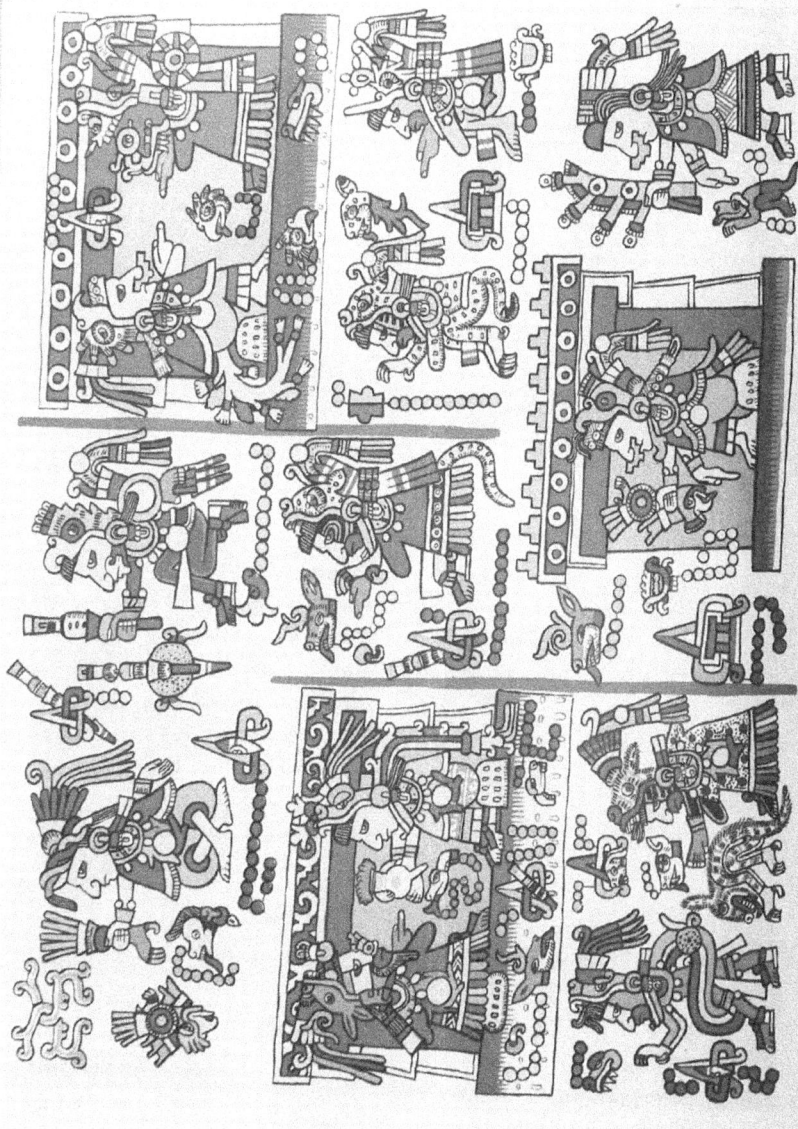

Figure 3.15. The Mixtec codices; at center left is the marriage of Lord Eight Deer to Lady Thirteen Serpent, who offers a frothy drink, either chocolate or *pulque*. *Codex Nuttall* 26, Nuttall 1902.

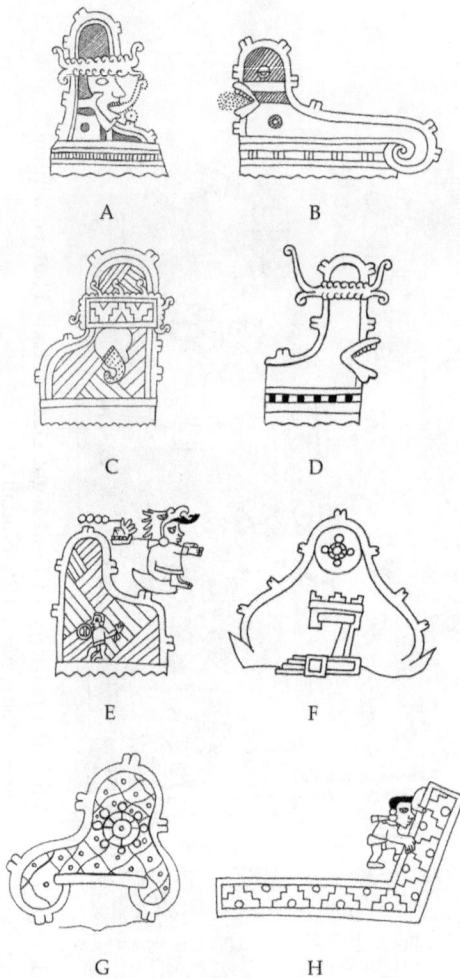

Figure 3.16. Place signs from Mixtec manuscripts; (A–D) variations of "Belching Mountain," or Magdalena Jaltepec; (E) Zahuatlan; (F) Tejupan; (G) Acatlan; and (H) Teozacoalco (redrawn by Jason Poling from figures 8.3, 8.6, and 8.9 in Flannery and Marcus 2003.

flower" or *Yucu ita* (Hill of Flowers); "house on black base" or *Ñuu tnoo* (Tilantongo, or Black Town); "hill plus distinctive plant-root" or *Yucu nama* (Hill of the Soap Root); "hill plus bean" or *Yucu nduchi* (Etlantongo, or Hill of Beans); "field plain with snake" or *Yodzo coo* (Coixtlahuaca, or Plain of Serpents). Many of these names come straight from the early grammars and dictionaries and from analyses of the codices and contact-era documentation by Alfonso Caso and Mary Elizabeth Smith, as well as from more recent analyses in conjunction with modern Mixteco place names. Of the hundreds of places named in the codices, most remain unknown.

A considerable variety of activities and events are depicted in the codices. The list of verbs—"to greet," "to run," "to offer," "to marry," "to fight," "to kill," "to sit," "to converse," "to negotiate," and so on—runs into the hundreds. Marriages, conferences, and alliances are shown by two individuals, almost always seated or kneeling, facing each other. People going to war are shown carrying darts, spear thrower or *macana* (double-sided, flint-edged sword), spear, or bow and arrow. Sorrow is shown with down-turned head and/or exaggerated tears exuding from reddened eyes. Capture or conquest is depicted by the appearance of a dart thrust into a toponym or holding a prisoner by the hair; sacrifice is graphically depicted as cutting and tearing out the heart of the victim, drawing blood from nose, ears or genitals as auto-sacrifice, presenting of bleeding animals, normally birds, or offering smoking incense from a *sahumador* or brazier. Many more examples could be given, but this conveys an idea of the types of activities depicted, and there is no substitute for consultation of the codices themselves.

Ethnohistory and Archaeology

Archaeological surveyors now know the approximate size and form of Postclassic kingdoms, but along with archaeologically inclined ethnohistorians they have also been impressed with the extraordinary variability of Mixtec *yuhuitayu*.[94] This variation has given us more than a few surprises. A good many places mentioned in documentary sources look less impressive on survey than expected; others, some little mentioned in the documents, had considerable populations and monumental zones. The great urban capital of Yucundaa–Pueblo Viejo de Teposcolula does not appear in the codices. Our information about the city comes from recent archaeological evidence and the slender early Colonial documentary record. After a century of research on Mixtec kingdoms, it is as though we had barely begun. An excellent framework has been established, but we are far from a complete understanding. These observations call for additional conjoined archaeological and ethnohistorical projects to understand the origins, growth, and variation of *yuhuitayu*. It is encouraging that good models for this procedure already exist.

Historical data on Tututepec of the Mixteca Costa and the culture hero Lord Eight Deer are a ready-made opportunity for convergent research.[95] Tututepec with its coastal resources, and weakness in the aftermath of the Epiclassic, was an attractive target for an ambitious royal upstart, and so it became entangled in a dynastic struggle originating in Tilantongo. Eight Deer took control of Tututepec and then embarked on a series of conquests, founding a coastal empire that lasted until the end of the pre-Hispanic era.

These actions for a brief time united highland and lowland *yuhuitayu* before Eight Deer was captured and sacrificed. Eight Deer's reign ended, so we are told, in the year 1063 when he would have been fifty-two years old, an age that coincidentally or not matches the span of the Mesoamerican calendar round.[96]

Archaeological survey has established Tututepec as a major demographic hub on the coast, its reported site size exceeding twenty square kilometers with an estimated fifteen thousand inhabitants. This puts Tututepec in the upper tier of Postclassic Mesoamerican cities. The core settlements of major highland *yuhuitayu* were comparable in scale and population size, although more limited in the extent of their political territories. Mixteca Alta and Baja centers consisted of high-density terraced sites with numerous subunits, perhaps corresponding to outlying *barrios* and *sujetos* that extended far into the countryside. Tututepec offers a lowland contrast, with settlement less dense but more or less continuous over a core zone tens of square kilometers in size (although similar to Coixtlahuaca), with a still larger political domain (achieved only intermittently, via alliances, in the highlands). The extent to which these differences reflect prior histories of occupation, ecological adaptation, or social organization awaits more extensive survey results from the coast and more intensive excavations of Postclassic sites in all parts of the Mixteca.

Significant recent contributions in convergent archaeohistorical research are the regional surveys of the central Mixteca Alta during the 1990s and the excavations at urban and rural sites pertaining to Yucundaa, the pre-Hispanic and early Colonial Pueblo Viejo de Teposcolula during the 2000s.[97] We now have the regional structure of one of the most highly urbanized settings in pre-Hispanic Mexico; the size, layout, and activities of noble and commoner households; and an archaeological perspective on the great transformation after Spanish contact (the site was not abandoned until 1550). We discuss these results further in subsequent chapters, but the project illustrates how research programs that were years in the making and involved sustained colla-borations among ethnohistorians and archaeologists have been and continue to be the way forward.

4

MIXTEC CULTURE
BEFORE THE CONQUEST

During centuries of residence in the mountains and valleys of western Oaxaca, the Mixtecs developed a unique way of life. Specialized social, economic, and political institutions and a corresponding worldview allowed a successful adaptation to the physical environment and facilitated the integration of Mixtec society while providing mechanisms for relating to other ethnic groups. The characteristic traits of Mixtec culture are most visible in the years just prior to Spanish contact and during the first century of Colonial rule—roughly the fifteenth and sixteenth centuries. This is also the point of convergence between purely archaeological information and what was for its time the ethnographic present.

The time of the late pre-Hispanic kingdoms was the Mixtec "Golden Age," and although there were several prior ages of considerable achievement, we know more about the late pre-Hispanic and contact period than earlier times. An understanding of ancient Mixtec culture logically begins with subsistence technology, adaptive strategies, and land tenure. We then proceed to social organization, government, and the economy. We end this chapter with religion, with reference to documents detailing the continuance of unquestionably pre-Hispanic practices and our own archaeological research on the topic.

LAND

On the eve of the Spanish Conquest, and since at least 1500 B.C.E., the Mixtecs were farmers. In the uplands they grew, and subsisted upon, a basic

Figure 4.1. *Coo-yuu* terracing near Yanhuitlan; the terrace was cut in half by the highway, but it once extended over four kilometers before reaching the valley floor.

dietary complex of corn, beans, and squash, with heavy supplementation from such domesticates as *maguey*, cactus, chili peppers, avocados, *chía* or amaranth, and *zapotes*. Although they derived the bulk of their diet from cultigens, they were also collectors of a great variety of wild plants, nuts, tubers, cacti, and fruits, which they utilized as food, for medicine, and for numerous practical and ceremonial functions.[1] In areas favorable for such crops, primarily in the lower and coastal areas extending from around Putla south to the Pacific, *cacao*, cotton, and peanuts were grown. Except for the dog and the turkey, domesticated animals were not important as food or as pack animals, but fish and wild game, such as birds, deer, cats, rodents, and a virtually endless list of insects, larvae, worms, and snakes were important in the Mixtec diet.

Throughout their history, the Mixtecs built their settlements in proximity to arable lands. The earliest sedentary communities were located on rises along rivers, especially at the confluence of streams where the best, most fertile farmlands were to be found. After urbanization, settlements were relocated to the higher hills and ridges but still adjacent to large stretches of well-watered bottomlands. This shift in settlement had implications for agricultural production, and among other things, accelerated an integrated process of intensification along with residential patterns and social institutions promoting maximal returns on agricultural production (see chapters 1–3).

At some point before the Postclassic, and possibly as early as the Middle Formative, the limited availability of arable valley lands led the Mixtecs to one of their greatest inventions, the *coo-yuu* system of agricultural terracing in otherwise unproductive gullies and areas of natural runoff and erosion. These vast terrace systems ascended the natural declivities along the margins of the valleys and served to greatly extend the area of available farmland. Once the major settlements were moved to higher ground—removed from, but still in easy walking distance to, farming and collecting lands and water sources— the *coo-yuu* terraces moved with them. This innovation and its later expansion fundamentally altered the productive capacity of the Mixteca's high, narrow valleys and led the Spanish chroniclers to refer to this region as "a land of milk and honey"—the Biblical reference not merely metaphorical but reflecting the intensively cultivated landscape.[2] Abandoned terrace systems are now a fixture of the Mixteca landscape, particularly in and around Yanhuitlan-Nochixtlan, Coixtlahuaca, Magdalena Peñasco, and Huamelulpan-Tayata, and the associated erosion puts the region's ecological underpinnings at risk.[3]

Throughout the long development of pre-Hispanic agriculture, the technology of farming, although dependent on centuries of domestication and adaptation, was basically simple *coa*, or digging-stick, cultivation. Although laborious and limited in potential, this system was adequate to meet the needs of an expanding population. On the eve of the Spanish Conquest, the Mixtecs were farming their lands with this simple technology, but deriving from their efforts a rich array of food products, sufficient to provide not only for subsistence but capable of producing a surplus that could be channeled into many uses. Our understanding of the ancient land base and basic subsistence thus connects with social structure, government, and broader economic and religious spheres that made each of these small kingdoms "agricultural powerhouses."[4]

As in other agricultural societies, Mixtec socioeconomic status was largely dependent on access to productive resources, especially agricultural land. The royal class and other nobility held private title to the most productive lands. These were the irrigable bottom lands and the fertile terraces of the Mixteca *coo-yoo* system. Property was held in estates, *yuhuitayu* (or, after the Conquest, *cacicazgos, señoríos,* or *principalazgos*), and transmitted from generation to generation along with royal and noble titles (*toniñe*).[5] Estates could also expand through marriage and through military conquest and annexation. Rulers controlled the most productive lands or at least held more of the productive lands than anyone else in a kingdom. At least some lands belonging to rulers

a

b

c

Figure 4.2. Erosion in the Mixteca Alta was photographed by Sherburne F. Cook in the 1930s and 1940s. This sequence comes from May and June of 1939, during a month-long trip on horseback with Robert J. Weitlaner: (a) incipient gully formation, see browse lines on trees; (b) sheet erosion near Santa María Nativitas, again see browse lines on trees; and (c) a fully developed system of *arroyos* on the road between San Cristóbal Suchixtlahuaca and Coixtlahuaca. Photos courtesy of Stanton A. Cook, used with permission.

were reallocated to nobles, often close relatives, to ensure continuing loyalty and service.

In many instances, however, *all* of the land of a given *ñuu* (town) or kingdom (*yuhuitayu*) belonged to the ruler. This, indeed, was the case in Tututepec in the Costa; Teposcolula, Achiutla, Chicahuaxtla, Cuquila, Ocotopec, and San Miguel Tequixtepec in the Mixteca Alta; and San Pedro y San Pablo Tequixtepec, Tonala, and Tecomaxtlahuaca in the Mixteca Baja.[6] Commoners were granted usufruct as long as they recognized and obeyed the ruler and paid tribute (*daha*) or worked the lands of the lord as serfs, (*tay situndayu*). In other communities, commoners appeared to "own" houses and agricultural plots but only with the permission and consent of the ruler, who might deny access to lands or banish individuals from a community. The implicit right of commoners to the lands which they worked became increasingly explicit during Colonial times, and the right of farmers to control their own lands has become a fixture of the modern Mexican political system.[7]

Rulers controlled important scarce resources like salt works, quarries of high-quality flint or precious stone, mines, fishing lagoons, and numerous forms of wildlife.[8] Many resources, however, were accessible to all residents of given communities or kingdoms. Wood, stone for building and for at least some types of tools and ornaments, adobe soils, clay for pottery, pigments, probably lime, at least more common minerals, small game animals, and the majority of wild plants must have been available to all. Each community had its lands, a collective holding for the use of the community as a whole.[9]

Although each region was capable of maintaining itself, local dietary complexes and regional economies were greatly enriched through trade with ecologically diverse areas near and far.[10] Also contributing to this enrichment were the products of numerous part-time specialists in pottery, stone working, metallurgy, weaving, skin working, and wood, bone, and shell carving, who existed in the various *ñuu* of the Mixteca. Mixtec civilization, in common with other advanced societies, depended on food production, and this pattern of accumulation and redistribution of agricultural surplus and wealth obviously depended on land and water and was finely articulated with available labor and technology.[11]

SOCIETY

Ancient Mixtec society was organized into three major social strata: the hereditary ruling class, *yya toniñe* or *yya tnuhu* (*casta linaje, caciques*); the hereditary

Figure 4.3. Farmer plowing with *yunta*, over an extensive *coo-yuu* terrace in Teposcolula. The surface area of multitiered terraces frequently equals or exceeds the sites they surround.

noble, or *tay toho* (*principal*) class; and a commoner, or plebian, class, *ñandahi* (also *dzaya dzana, tay yucu, tay sicaquai, nanday tay nuu, macehualli* or *macehuales*).[12] There were also groups of landless peasants and slaves that are discussed below.

The *yya toniñe*, the rulers, occupied positions of unusual power, wealth, influence, and responsibility. They held the largest and most productive agricultural lands, received tribute (*daha*) and labor services from subject populations, and benefited from services performed on the lands by the *tay situndayu*, or serfs. They monopolized certain scarce resources and production of desirable goods. They were entitled to wear exclusive costumes, jewelry, and ornamentation and to decorate their bodies in distinctive ways. *Yya toniñe* families ate special foods, used special forms of speech, and, normally in the company of the nobility, engaged in status-differentiating social activities, including royal hunts of deer, turkeys, and quail and special feasting, ceremonial, and social events such as weddings and funerals. The religious cult was sponsored by the *yya toniñe*, who played key roles in the ritual life of their communities.

Members of the Mixtec nobility occupied a position that was socially intermediate between the ruling caste and the commoners. Although less is known of *tay toho* than of the ruling *yya toniñe*, they are believed to have resided both in capital centers and in dependencies and to have organized themselves into extended families of a grandparental couple surrounded and supported by a cooperating cluster of their children and the children's families. Excavation of probable noble residences in Yucundaa-Teposcolula and Yucuita suggests that *tay toho* were privileged in terms of residence and patterns of consumption. Their houses were smaller and simpler than those of the royal caste but larger and better constructed than those of the commoners.[13] The Mixtec upper classes in general participated in extended, interregional social networks from birth to death. These extended spheres of interaction included marital and economic ties and various kinds of ceremonialism involving elite peers in the Mixteca and beyond.

The social life of the Mixtec common class was organized around the family and the *ñuu*.[14] Nearly all daily activities and associations occurred within this structure. Extensions of the social field occurred in marketing activities, when buyer and seller interacted in a regional and interregional economic network. A few individuals would be engaged in regional or long-distance trade or portage. Another form of extra-community interaction occurred in the round of ceremonial activities that took natives to shrines and activity areas in various parts of the Mixteca and beyond to the Valley of Oaxaca, to Puebla, and even to the Valley of Mexico. Outside the realm of economic and ceremonial activity, however, there was little to attract the commoner beyond the boundaries of the *ñuu*.

Commoners, for the most part, had to be content with their social position. Some degree of upward mobility might have been possible through the rare primary marriage between a common-class woman and a *tay toho* (*principal*). In such unions, however, women normally became secondary wives or concubines. Although they and their offspring possibly enjoyed heightened prestige and privilege, the documents are silent on native attitudes regarding such mating patterns, and little is known of the nature and frequency of aristocratic hypogamy. In at least some instances, commoners became serfs on royal lands, giving over their lives and services to aristocratic landlords and thereby descending into the *tay situndayu* status group. Again, the frequency with which this occurred is uncertain.

Other groups are identifiable, although they would not constitute a separate social class: the landless tenant farmers and slaves. The landless tenant farmers, or servants-laborers-serfs (*tay situndayu, terrazgueros*) existed in the larger and wealthier *yuhuitayu* (*señoríos, cacicazgos, estados,* or *reinos*) such as Yanhuitlan, Teposcolula, Tlaxiaco, Achiutla, and Tilantongo in the Mixteca Alta; Tecomaxtlahuaca and Tonala in the Baja; and Tututepec in the Costa.[15] It is quite likely that all *yuhuitayu* had anywhere from a few dozen to hundreds of *tay situndayu* who provided the rulers with a principal form of wealth and subsistence. This relationship of rulers to serfs would be the mechanism for moving large numbers of Mixtecs into the Costa after Eight Deer's take-over of Tututepec or into the Valley of Oaxaca after the short-lived Mixtec-Zapotec military alliance during the Postclassic (see chapter 3).

The final social category consisted of slaves—individuals captured in battle, born into the condition of slavery, purchased, or obtained in tribute. It seems likely that such individuals were not in all cases doomed to a life of servitude but could under certain circumstances raise their standing in society. In many instances, however, members of this lowest-status group would find themselves taking part in various ritual dramas, a bloody death awaiting them (see discussion of religion at the end of this chapter).

Suggestions that there may have been a class of traders (*tay cuica, merca-deres*) and wealthy people (*gente rica*) outside of the hereditary aristocracy are not substantiated by available documentation.[16] Although traders and men of wealth did exist in Mixtec society, differences in economic function or wealth do not seem to have led to formation of social aggregates beyond the major classes delineated above. Appropriate class membership was required to gain access to productive resources, which, in turn, set parameters on the allowable acquisition of wealth or attainment of economic advantage.

There is little indication that the Mixtecs had full-time professional classes of warriors, tradesmen, craftsmen, artisans, or curers.[17] Individuals involved in specialized activities also performed subsistence activities. The nearest approxi-mation to full-time specialization would be the priests who participated in the formal religious cult. Priestly functions notwithstanding, it is clear that a true division of labor did not develop to the level that it seriously affected the organization of society. Mixtec society was stratified, to be sure, but it is not possible to relate stratification to general patterns of specialization.

Royal Descent and Succession

Rules of royal succession were explicit and strict, and great care was taken to ensure legitimate transmission of title from individual to individual and from generation to generation. This process was ongoing at the time of the Spanish Conquest, and subsequent disputes among surviving nobles are a significant feature of the documentary record.[18] We refer briefly to issues of descent and succession here, discussing this matter at greater length in chapter 6.

Royal status was attained through direct descent from titled royal-class parents and ancestors. In a royal-caste marriage, one *tnuhu* (dynastic lineage, or *linaje*), or side of the family, might be emphasized or stressed, if it was advantageous to do so, to claim, validate, or sustain royal titles and inheritance. In other instances, both lines could be activated. Lineal depth and continuity of bloodline were of great importance to the ruling caste. Great importance was assigned to genealogy, the length and quality of the direct line of titled ancestors, and other principles of legitimate succession shown.

Royal patrimony could be affected, however, by failure to produce heirs, the death of an heir, assignment of titles from collateral kinship groups, and conquest. The "rules" of descent, therefore, were pragmatic, and subject to interpretation depending on the circumstances. On the basis of practices observed just after the Spanish Conquest, it seems safe to infer that there were instances when a lower-ranking *yya toniñe* or *tay toho* challenged the authority of the ruler to control and tax a subject community and to require personal services from its residents. If this individual could gain sufficient support and establish a claim, a "new" *yuhuitayu* (*toniñe* or *señorío*) might emerge. A *tay toho*-become-*yya toniñe* could demonstrate "direct descent" from former rulers by ignoring or elevating nonroyal-caste ancestors, and *tnuhu* (genealogies, or *linajes*) could be "cleansed," or "doctored," or omissions made to smooth out charters of entitlement.[19] Even the mighty ruling family of Tilantongo was accused of having engaged in such manipulation to further their own political agenda.[20]

Marital and Residence Patterns

Marriage for all classes was regulated by the custom of class endogamy. *Yya toniñe* married *yya toniñe*, *tay toho* married *tay toho*, and *ñandahi* married *ñandahi*. When noble males married common-class females, they were normally "secondary" wives. Community endogamy was customary among commoners. *Yya toniñe* and *tay toho*, on the other hand, acted in a much more extensive universe to find appropriate partners and to promote advantageous alliances for themselves and their children.[21] Caste endogamy was required of an individual who expected to inherit or retain royal title, property, and privilege, and only the offspring of such a caste marriage were considered eligible and legitimate heirs to titles (*toniñe*). Marriage between cousins was common in the royal caste, accounting for at least 15 percent of such marriages.

Figure 4.4. Royal nuptial bathing ritual (bottom); purification rites of this kind likely occurred prior to consummating the marriage (top). *Codex Nuttall* 19, Nuttall 1902.

Plural marriage was allowed in Mixtec society, but normally only the aristocracy practiced polygyny. High-ranking *yya toniñe* customarily had secondary wives or concubines because they could afford them and because it strengthened their ties of alliance with other groups and regions. In a polygynous marriage, however, only the offspring of the principal, or primary, wife could inherit titles from either royal-caste parent.

For the *yya toniñe*, residence was ambilocal. Following marriage, a royal couple might take up residence in a capital center held by either the man or the woman, or they might alternate residences between their holdings.[22] Normally these matters were decided at the time of marriage, when patterns of inheritance were delineated according to a complex set of principles, and through expediency.

Royal-caste families were large, usually consisting of a ruling couple, their children, their parents, their grandparents, and the couple's siblings. Often the family would be augmented by secondary wives and their children. These families lived in large, sumptuous "palace" complexes, or *aniñe* ("place of royalty") containing many elaborately decorated rooms, courtyards, shrines, drainage systems, tombs or burials, and furnished with an infinite complex of pottery, stone, metal, cloth, hide, bone, and wooden artifacts, and with furniture made of wood and decorated with painted and carved figures and with animal hides. Such residences are well illustrated in the pre-Hispanic codices, are described in the Colonial literature, and have been identified archaeologically in Chachoapan, Tejupan, and most impressively in Yucundaa-Teposcolula.[23]

Patrilocality was the preferred form of postmarital residence for commoners, with occasional residence with, or adjacent to, the bride's family. Both sets of parents usually resided in the *ñuu*, and a newly married couple could likely depend on the support of both families. Very little information exists on patterns of property inheritance among the commoner class, but inferences can be drawn from Colonial practices. Property was usually divided, greater proportions being assigned to the surviving spouse, and to older over younger children, and finally to sons, who were normally favored over daughters.

Although it is difficult to obtain reliable information on pre-Hispanic commoner family structure, it was likely similar to that of Colonial times. Nuclear families composed of parents and children were probably the customary form of domestic organization, with occasional inclusion of an elderly grandparent or siblings of the conjugal pair. Common-class houses in and around Yanhuitlan, Nochixtlan, Yucuita, and Chachoapan are small, one or two-celled structures capable of sheltering only a very few individuals.[24] We see examples of commoner residential compounds in the multiroom houses excavated at

Figure 4.5. The Casa de la Cacica, Teposcolula, a royal-palace complex with codex-style design elements (compare to prior image from *Codex Nuttall* and the following from *Codex Yanhuitlan*).

Nicayuju near San Juan Teposcolula.[25] These were probably extended-family dwellings, somewhat more elaborate than the instances just mentioned. Even among commoners, the range of dwelling types varied, possibly corresponding to the social divisions within the commoner class described above.

Corporate Groups

We cannot at present infer the presence of formal corporate groups in Mixtec society. Corporate lineages of the type found in many areas of North America, Africa, and Oceania were not a feature of Mixtec life. Institutions similar to the Culhua-Mexica *calpolli* have not been found in the Mixteca.[26] *Tnuhu*, or the royal *linaje* of Spanish Colonial times, referred to "lines of ancestors," males and/or females, and not to formal patri- or matrilineages. No evidence that lineage or clan organization or "corporateness" existed among commoners can be found in the kinship system, kinship terminology, or the Mixtec language. These groups might have been extinguished with the Conquest, but it is more likely they never existed. The closest approximation of the landholding corporate group would be the residential *barrios* and subject communities (*siqui*) extending outward from the capital centers, but we do not believe these were kin based. They were, rather, small-scale versions of the *ñuu*, with their own noble rulers and quite conceivably their own "gods."

GOVERNMENT

Mixtec kingdoms (*yuhuitayu*, *sina yya*, or *satoniñe yya*, and after the Conquest *señorío* or *cacicazgo*) were states with formally defined, hierarchically organized political offices.[27] These positions were filled by a supreme authority figure, *yya toniñe*, the ruler, and lower-ranking hereditary nobility, *tay toho*, who interacted directly and regularly with the ruler.[28] Rulers and nobles controlled positions of power and authority, the lands and resources of each *yuhuitayu*, the means of production and distribution of certain goods and services, and formal ceremonial institutions. They had the right to extract tribute (*daha*) and personal services from subject populations.[29] In return, subject peoples could expect protection, representation in external affairs, ceremonial sponsorship, usufruct title to agricultural and collecting lands of the state, and access to goods produced outside the state.

The great lords, furthermore, would adjudicate disputes among members of the nobility and offered appellate functions in cases involving commoners but settled in the first instance by lower-ranking nobles. The ruler also provided food and entertainment for the members of the nobility when they were in council. The administrative network radiating from a ruler included kinsmen, affines (in-laws), noble clients, and a small group of overseers, priests, merchants, artisans, and court retainers. In at least one instance, at Tilantongo, the ruler was aided by a permanent council of four members, one of which was designated chief councillor.[30] We must presume that other large *yuhuitayu* had similar standing advisory bodies. The delegation of authority was direct, from ruler to councillors, administrators, and specialists. The Mixtec system was pragmatic, however, and subject to given social and political circumstances. Rulers often utilized relatives in subsidiary roles, placing brothers, uncles, or cousins as representatives in subject communities, or employed them as advisers or administrators.

The graduated and extended delegation of authority characteristic of state bureaucracies was only minimally developed in the Mixteca. In comparison to the great classic states of European and Asian antiquity, *yuhuitayu* tended to be restricted geographically, demographically, and socially. They could be maintained without complex administrative hierarchies, standing armies, or a permanent police force. Individual states were potentially expandable through their capacity for alliance or conquest warfare but only to the extent that such acquisitions could be controlled through the existing political structure which emphasized direct ties of authority.

Political Expansion

The political capability to form large conquest states was well established by the eleventh century, as evidenced by the Tututepec Empire on the Pacific coast (see chapter 3).[31] The typical practice, however, was for political expansion via diplomatic subterfuge, marriage and inheritance, and more general forms of alliance making. A few examples illustrate these processes.

Just before the Spanish Conquest there was a military alliance between the Zapotec ruler of Teozapotlan (Zaachila) and a Mixtec ruler.[32] The Zapotec king wished to conquer the Tehuantepec area but lacked sufficient forces and organization to accomplish his goal. The Mixtecs were approached for aid. Certain concessions followed, including the right of the Mixtecs to occupy jointly the westernmost portion of the Valley of Oaxaca. A treaty was made, and the allies were able to conquer Tehuantepec. The Mixtecs, however, were dissatisfied with the outcome, grew angry, and turned against the Zapotecs. When the Zapotec ruler sent an ambassador to order the Mixtecs to leave the lands they were occupying in the valley, they killed the emissary and sent survivors of his party to inform their king that if he wanted the Mixtecs off the lands he must come personally and evict them.

The Mixtec response to their conflict with the Zapotecs was to consolidate their hold on the area between Teozapotlan and Guaxolotitlan (Huitzo); to settle in the southeast as far as Chichicapan; east to Huayapan, San Francisco, San Sebastián, and Santa Lucía; and as far south as San Martín Lachilaa and to move into the communities of Teozapotlan, San Raimundo, and San Pablo and to a high mountain between Santa Catarina and Santa Ana called Magdalena. They also settled in Cuilapan and founded Xoxocotlan in "the best site in the valley."[33] Clearly, the Mixtecs were in the habit of making alliances, even beyond ethnic boundaries, to the point of taking advantage of their allies to obtain additional living space and access to resources. This was not a new response for the Mixtecs. The codices contain ample evidence that such arrangements were being made since at least the eleventh century.

Conquest, whether via direct warfare or "voluntary submission," was widely practiced in the Mixteca and beyond in the Zapotec, Chatino, and Cuicatec areas among others. The *Relaciones geográficas* of 1579–81 make repeated reference to these intergroup conflicts and their resolution or

Figure 4.6. The Mixtec *cacique*, Nine House, sits before a throng of commoners in Yanhuitlan, with the royal palace in the background, mid–sixteenth century. Jiménez Moreno and Mateos Higuera 1940, plate II.

persistence in pre-Hispanic times. There were, of course, major conflicts between the Mixtecs and the armies of the Culhua-Mexica Empire. Among the more aggressive kingdoms were Tututepec, Tlaxiaco, Coixtlahuaca, and Tilantongo, but even the smaller states and communities were involved in warfare and raiding.

Fray Burgoa described the experience of Mixtec-speaking communities in and around Almoloyas, a high, rugged, desolate area on the eastern boundary between the Mixteca Alta and the Cuicateca Cañada. The Almoloyas environment was harsh and not sufficiently productive to support a large resident population. Within sight, but at lower elevation, the warm, well-watered Cañada produced fruits, tubers (*patatas*), chilis, tomatoes, cotton, probably some *cacao*, and abundant wildlife coveted by residents of Almoloyas and other Mixtecs from Jaltepetongo, Texcatitlan, Jocotipac, Apasco, and Ixtaltepec, but these communities lacked the organization and military power to take over the Cañada lands from the Cuicatecas.

Driven by hunger and "other vexations," the residents of Almoloyas were obliged to "appeal to Yanguitlan [Yanhuitlan], asking their favor, and protection, recapitulating and offering recognition of superiority and yearly fief, and accepting their condition of subjugation, they gave the Yanguiteco many people, and experienced *capitanes*, who moved out through the mountains subjugating all of the Cuicatecos . . . and from this point began the conservation of Almoloyas under the protection of the *señor* of Yanhuitlan, and left them with the obligation of sending him the fruits of the river valley and the animals which they hunted."[34]

The relationship between Yanhuitlan and its distant dependency of Almoloyas continued into Colonial times, being preserved in the organization of the *cacicazgo*, the *encomienda*, and the *doctrina* (religious province) of Yanhuitlan. Other Cuicatec towns near Huautla also came under control of Mixtec lords, and two of them, Tututepetongo and Tanatepec, continued under the administrative jurisdiction of Huautla during Spanish Colonial times.[35]

The linking of two or more kingdoms under the leadership of a ruling couple (both inheriting their patrimonies separately and in their own right) was a more characteristic form of expansion than was conquest warfare or voluntary submission. As early as the eleventh century, the ruler Eight Deer of Tilantongo held or controlled dozens of titles through combined inheritance, multiple marital alliances, and military conquest.[36] The states controlled by Eight Deer extended from the Pacific coast to the area of the modern Oaxaca-Puebla border, bridging the Costa, Alta, and Baja Mixtecas. Such aggregates were common in the Mixteca on the eve of the Conquest and persisted to the end of the Colonial period.[37]

Economy

Mixtecs were above all farmers. Some individuals practiced part-time specializations: painting, potting, flint and obsidian tool making, spinning and weaving, tailoring, sculpting, metal casting, basket making, feather work, trading, and so on, but everyone, except the aristocracy, engaged in basic subsistence activities.[38] Farming produced food and the surpluses that could be exchanged in the market system or drawn off as tribute. Full-time specialists were rare to absent, but regional and community specialization was present, and this stimulated active regional and interregional marketing and long-distance trade.

The most productive area of the Mixteca Alta was the Nochixtlan Valley. Good alluvial lands lay along the Yanhuitlan-Yucuita river system, and hillsides were made more productive by the *coo-yuu* method of runoff-irrigated terrace agriculture.[39] Maize, beans, and squash could be produced in any of the valley's thirty late pre-Hispanic communities, but the greatest quantities were produced in the fertile bottomlands rather than the less productive low hills, piedmonts, and higher slopes where many communities were situated.

Amatlan and San Pedro Cántaros Coxcaltepec, on the other hand, were high-elevation communities that could access pine and oak forests for wood, charcoal, resins, and other montane goods. High-quality chert could be quarried at Yucuñudahui. Excellent potters' clay and mineral pigments were available at Yucuita and Yanhuitlan. Coarse clays suitable for large cooking and storage vessels and *comales* were available on the eastern edge of the valley at San Miguel Adequez, at San Pedro Cántaros Coxcaltepec, and well upslope in the northern mountains at Santo Domingo Tonaltepec. Basalt for *manos* and *metates* could be obtained from outcroppings near Yanhuitlan and Pozoltepec or along streambeds in the vicinity of Yucuita and Coyotepec. Gold in small amounts was found in Jaltepec, but there is no evidence that the art of fine metalwork was practiced in the Nochixtlan Valley.[40]

Many desirable resources and products were unavailable in the Nochixtlan Valley and had to be obtained from outside through trade or tribute. Salt was imported, most likely from San Felipe Ixtapa, a dependency of Teposcolula; from Zapotitlan and Tehuacan in Puebla; and from the Mixteca Costa. Recent reconnaissance by the senior author in the area of Santiago Tamazola in the northwesternmost corner of the state of Oaxaca, most specifically at Santa María Salinas, revealed highly productive saltworks. A notable series of salt springs, channels, and evaporation terraces in clear and direct association with structures and pottery dating to the Classic period is still intensively utilized. This is a likely, heretofore unreported, source of salt for the Mixteca Baja and Alta in Classic and Postclassic times.

Many ancient lime kilns and heavy concentrations of convertible limestone exist in the Teposcolula area and in the borderlands between Tlaxiaco and Magdalena Peñasco, and it is assumed that these were primary sources for this indispensable product in pre-Hispanic times. Cotton and *cacao* came from the Mixteca Costa and from the Cañada to the east.

Modern Mixteca Alta communities, like Zahuatlan, Añuma, Zachio, and Jaltepec in the Nochixtlan Valley, and Yosondua and San Andrés Lagunas near Teposcolula specialize in the production of *petates, canastas, tenates,* and *sopladores,* but they must import raw palm from low-lying areas like Yutanduchi and Sindihui. Dozens of communities in the Coixtlahuaca-Tequixtepec-Teotongo area produce palm hats in great abundance. All of the raw palm must be imported from other areas. This undoubtedly represents persistence of ancient patterns of production and interregional exchange. Abundant graphic representations in the codices leave no doubt that this process was ongoing for centuries before the Conquest.

Other commodities, such as fish, shell, fruits, salt, obsidian, feathers, probably copper, and silver and gold, had to be imported from other areas of the Mixteca Alta, the Baja, the Costa, the Cañada, and beyond. Redundant production of maize, beans, and squash assured self-sufficiency in basic subsistence goods, but agricultural production was insufficient to meet all the needs of all the people. Local and long-distance exchange kept the economic system and the Mixtec way of life functioning.

Yanhuitlan, Tlaxiaco, Teposcolula, and Tilantongo integrated numerous *siqui,* or subject communities, that were specialized in terms of resources and/or production of certain goods. In fact, one of the primary functions of the central state seems to have been the integration of these specialized resources and products. This ensured a reasonable level of economic self-sufficiency and, at the same time, provided tribute for the ruling and noble aristocracy. Yanhuitlan maintained a huge periodic market in the subject community of Yucuita, and Yanhuitlan *yya toniñe, tay toho,* and *tay cuica,* or traders, engaged in local and interregional exchange.

The historical documentation of the sixteenth century, particularly the *Relaciones geográficas* of 1579–81 and materials from Teposcolula's judicial archive, indicate that markets and trading activities were conducted on an intensive level in Coixtlahuaca, Teposcolula, Tlaxiaco, Tamazulapan, and Tejupan in the Alta; at Putla, Huajuapan, and Acatlan in the Mixteca Baja; and in and around Tututepec, Jicayan, Pinoctecpan and Cacahuatepec in the Costa. Coixtlahuaca and Putla, in particular, have preserved major portions of vast civic-ceremonial and marketing centers that date to late pre-Hispanic times. The documents refer to smaller, possibly self-regulating, border markets, or *yahui* (also *yucuyahui, itnuyahui*), that were probably of major importance in the Postclassic exchange system.[41] Archaeological features, including ball courts and shrines, were often located away from populated centers at the edges of political territories.[42] These features could denote the locations of border markets.

Yanhuitlan traders traveled from market to market exchanging locally produced commodities for exotic goods. Archaeological remains provide ample supporting evidence of the existence of exchange relationships with other areas from Formative through Postclassic times.[43] Spindle whorls appear in quantity throughout the Nochixtlan Valley, in Teposcolula, Coixtlahuaca, and Tlaxiaco, indicating the importance of cotton textile production. Fish bones, shells, and sting-ray spines point directly to the Pacific Ocean.[44] Copper pins, axes, rings, and personal ornaments, jade objects, and at least nine varieties of obsidian were also imported into all the Mixtecas. Obsidian sourced from Mixteca archaeological sites originated in the great mines of Guadalupe Victoria, Otumba, Pachuca, and Zaragoza, among others.[45]

Although the vast majority of pottery vessels and figurines are of local origins, the not infrequent occurrence of such items from the Valley of Mexico and the Valley of Oaxaca among other regions indicate far-flung economic connections in Formative, Classic, and Postclassic times.[46] With respect to locally produced commodities, two natural resources, basalt and Yucuñu-dahui flint, were distributed extensively through the Mixteca Alta and into the Valley of Oaxaca. These were, of course, critical materials for the production of cutting and grinding implements, with only imported obsidian having comparable importance.

From the very beginning of village life in the Mixteca, pottery was a critical component in the material-cultural complex. Although reference has been made to importation of pottery from other areas, survey and controlled excavation of sites in the Mixteca Alta, Baja, and Costa, make it clear that 99 percent of the pottery recovered in good archaeological contexts was produced in the Mixteca.[47] As indicated previously, good clay sources are abundant in the region, and at least twenty towns continue production. Excavations

Figure 4.7. The Tlaxiaco weekly market in 2007 (a–b), showing vendors and their wares, including pottery made in Cuquila (photos by Ayla M. Amadio and Katherine South); and (c) the San Andrés Chicahuaxtla weekly market in 1990.

at Tayata revealed pottery-firing areas and local production of gray wares from 1000 B.C.E.[48]

Distinctive Mixteca polychrome pottery is, of course, found from the Gulf to the Pacific and from Puebla to Chiapas. The Nochixtlan Valley was an important locus for these wares, but they are even more plentiful in areas like Coixtlahuaca and Teposcolula. It is not yet possible to ascertain exactly where polychrome was produced, but it is clear that Nochixtlan, the Mixteca in general, and the surrounding areas were somehow involved in a distributional network that spread these wares over a huge area of south-central Mexico.[49] In this respect, it is quite probable that the multi-ethnic city of Cholula in central Puebla was a major producing and distributional center for Mixteca polychrome wares.

Exchange was of three major types: (1) open exchange by barter among producers, traders, and consumers; (2) monopolistic-entrepreneurial enterprises controlled by high-status *yya toniñe* and *tay toho*, involving such goods as salt, probably obsidian, fine clothing, jewelry and ornamentation, precious stones, fine feathers, possibly fine decorated pottery, and other exotic goods; and (3) a tribute system in which goods and services were extracted from subject populations by native rulers and then redistributed—to the ruling-caste family, to the nobility, to religious practitioners, to servants and part-time specialists in service to the ruler, to commoners on ceremonial occasions, and to serfs working the lands of the ruling elite.[50]

At the time of the Spanish Conquest, large quantities of tribute goods were channeled to the Culhua-Mexica Empire.[51] It is likely that conquest by the Culhua-Mexica resulted in further demands on tribute payers in addition to the customary requirements by the *yya toniñe*. There is no indication that the Mixteca and the Mixtecs were incapable of supplying both masters.

RELIGION

On the eve of the Spanish Conquest, ritual activity on an immense scale occurred at San Miguel Achiutla, Chalcatongo, Tilantongo, Yanhuitlan, Yucuita, Apoala, and Sosola.[52] These religious centers drew celebrants from all across the Mixteca and surrounding regions for ceremonies and to consult with resident priests. These larger centers as well as myriad natural places had a great attraction for the Mixtecs, figured in their mythology, served as important centers of ritual activity, and contributed to social integration among communities and kingdoms.

As a necessary preliminary to the study of Mixtec religion, it must be said that there are problems associated with the use of European concepts and verbal categories. Such an observation might be relegated to a long footnote, but it is of great importance to recognize the implied meanings of words such as *dios,* God, *demonio, diablo, ídolo, purgatorio,* priest, *sacerdote, papa,* and so on. In many instances these highly loaded concepts are not only inappropriate but convey absolutely wrong meanings and implications. There are also notable problems using Mixtec terms, many of which are not directly translatable and which must be approximated, rather than translated. That is why, in most instances, we do not translate either the Spanish or the Mixtec religious terminology but speak of concepts, acts, beliefs, or customs in behavioral terms, rather than by their "labels."

Any study of a culture not one's own is fraught with the same problems of cultural and linguistic translation. It is exceedingly difficult for a "foreigner," first to understand, and then to accurately describe, another culture. And speaking parenthetically, it is just as difficult to understand the more familiar religious traditions, such as Islam, Buddhism, Hinduism, Judaism, or Christianity. Any treatise on those religions will evoke virtually endless criticism and revisionism. We, as anthropologists, simply do the best we can in our studies and our inferences, and to convey our perceptions of the reality of Mixtec culture and history, and, in the present instance, of their religion, cosmogony, and worldview. If we do not do it, who will? We have waited for centuries. Should we wait longer?

Let us begin by saying that Mixtec religion is complex but not unfathomable.[53] It is basically animatistic, in that it is essentially a religion of forces and spirits, rather than elevated beings, "gods," or idols, with a strong emphasis on the forces of nature, the cyclic processes of life and death, the ability to influence nature and the spirit world through specific acts and observances, and a reverence for deceased ancestors. Mixtec religion emphasized a worshipful respect for the forces and features of nature, the spirit or essence of life (*ini*), and the mysteries of death, the afterlife, and the persisting relationship between the dead and the living.

Familiar elements of the Mixtec natural and cultural world were respected, venerated, and honored by offerings and sacrifice. Natural features, the land (*ñuhu*), mountains (*yucu*), caves (*cahua*), rivers (*yuta*), canyons (*duhua*), plants (*yutnu*), unusual stone formations (*yuu canu*), and the heavens (*andevui*) and heavenly bodies (*yya caa huiyu*) received special attention. Time (*quevui, huico*), motion (*yosoichi*), and the days of the week were equally charged with supernatural significance. Critical forces and elements of nature—water (*duta*), rain (Dzahui), clouds (*huico*), lightning (*sacuiñe tecuiye* or *sasaanduta tecuiye*), wind (*chi*), and fire (*ñuhu*)—took on special spiritual identities, as did certain animals of the Mixtec realm—cats (*ñana*), eagles (*yaha*), and serpents (*coo*). Occupying a place of special prominence were the spirits of deceased ancestors (*taynisiyo ñuu sindi*) of ruling lineages (*tnuhu* or *yaatnunundi*).

The omnipresent forces, elements, beings, events, and relations affecting people, culture, and nature were personified as spiritual things (*sasi ñuhu*) or *ñuhu* ("deities" or *dioses*) and could be represented by images (*naa ñuhu*), the inaccurately designated *ídolos* and *demonios* of Spanish Colonial times.[54] These elevated forces and spirits were known by various names. Xiton or Xitondocio was "god of the merchants." Dzahui, or "rain," was called the "*demonio* of water." Tizono or Tizones was the "heart of the *pueblo*." Toyna was known as "their own god" in Yanhuitlan. Yaguinzi was "air" or "wind." Yanacuu was "lizard" in Tejupan. Qhyosayo was simply *Dios* in Tilantongo. Guacusachi was the "principal *diablo* of Yanhuitlan." There were many others.[55]

In the Mixteca Baja, at Juxtlahuaca and Tecomaxtlahuaca, the principal religious elements were Cuaquisiqhi, Taadozo (associated with the sun, warfare, and human sacrifice), and Yocosituayuta (associated with fertility and offerings of rich plumage).[56] All major centers recognized and worshiped similar complexes of regional, even pan-Mesoamerican and local spirits, personified forces, and honored ancestors, particularly of the royal caste. Each community had its own patron, which was revered above the rest.

Many observances were of a general nature. Residents of Huautla and Jaltepetongo worshipped natural forces symbolized by stone and wooden images, offered birds and feathers, practiced autosacrifice, played instruments, danced, and held *borracheras* (ritualized intoxication).[57] The natives of Teozacoalco performed similar acts of piety but added sacrifices of human hearts, dogs, turkeys, and wild game.[58] The sacred stone and wooden figures standing in shrines in the highest ramparts (*peñas*) of Tamazola were said to have been "respected as lords and gods. They gave their priests copal to burn and turkeys and dogs in order that they be sacrificed to their idols . . . and they sacrificed adults and youths, flaying them alive and removing the heart and giving it to the priest for offering."[59]

Religious Practitioners

As indicated above, religious activities were directed by professional practitioners (*ñaha niñe, tay saque*), who were controlled by the native rulers. Religious

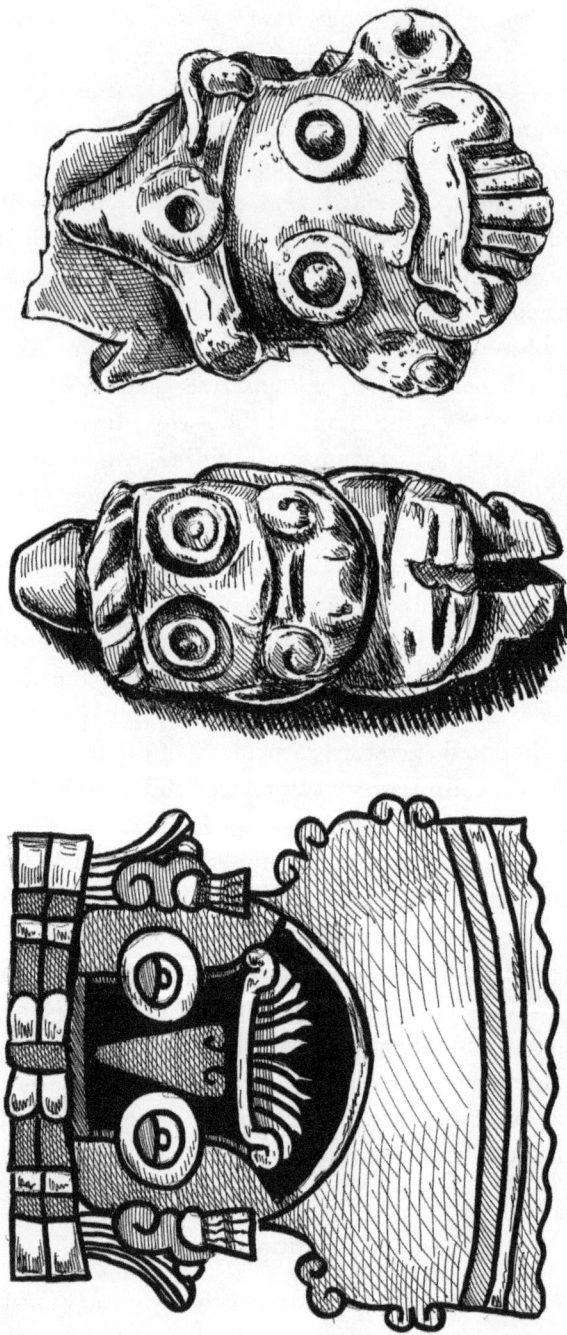

Figure 4.8. Dzahui, from *Codex Vindobonensis* 47 and artifacts depicting Dzahui (polished white–stone *penate*, part of a burned offering, and fragment from a pottery vessel found in a commoner house) from Yucundaa–Pueblo Viejo de Teposcolula. Redrawn by Jason Poling from Anders et al. 1992, with additional drawings by Poling.

activities for which the priests were responsible included fixed and movable feasts in and around ritual centers, prognostications, marriages, funerals and postfunerary observances, fertility rites in fields, and the training of boys and young men for priestly functions. It is also quite likely that the priests were the literate intelligentsia who maintained and interpreted calendrical-prognosticatory, ritual-ceremonial, and historical documents. These were the pictographic records now referred to as "codices," which give the Mixtecs a very special historical and cultural identity among ancient Mesoamerican peoples.

Once an individual entered formal training for the priesthood, usually around seven years of age, he was subject to numerous requirements and restrictions.[60] He was required to clean, maintain, and guard shrines, figures, and ritual paraphernalia; prepare offerings; learn rituals; and assist other priests in all sacrifices and activities. Once trained, the practitioner went into the service of a particular ruler, performing the necessary rituals, and continued in these functions for varying periods of time. Specific priestly acts consisted of leading and performing dances, singing, giving recitations, going into trances, receiving and presenting offerings (of *copal,* dogs, doves, quail, feathers, precious stones, prepared foods, tobacco, *pulque,* and clothing), and performing animal and human sacrifice and autosacrifice.

Priests exercised considerable power. The rulers consulted higher-ranking priests, as well as ones that had retired, on all matters of personal and public importance, and the priests' ability to influence opinion and political action was substantial.[61] It is clear, at least in early Colonial times, that each priest managed exclusively symbolic paraphernalia and ritual aspects of a single cult. Each priest thus seemed, or at least claimed, to have little knowledge of the activities of the other priests. Many priestly activities took place "in private," in remote areas, and sacred images were small and transportable, but this may reflect the need for secrecy in continuing native religious practices after the Conquest.

Persistence of Mixtec Traditional Religion in Spanish Colonial Times

In 1545 an unconverted native priest, Caxaa, "who was very old," and a recent practitioner, was called as a witness for the Holy Inquisition against the native ruler and two nobles of Yanhuitlan. Caxaa confessed that until four years previous, he and three other priests cared for "the idols of the said *pueblo,*" and that he had charge of "the god of water, which was called Zagui [Dzahui]."[62] He and the other priests resided "in the house of the *demonios* that is located in Tamaxcaltepeque."

The old priest went on at length regarding ancient native practices that survived in the Yanhuitlan area until at least 1540. With respect to the priests and their ritual paraphernalia, Caaxa reported that "all of them were in a large house where each priest had charge of his *diablo* and that they were in their own chamber and apartment . . . with one not knowing about the other [deities, priests, or ritual activities] and that the *cacique* [native ruler of Yanhuitlan] had a priest named Cagua."[63]

In response to questions concerning the form and manner of dealing with each "*demonio*" and the manner of sacrifice, Caaxa stated: "when there was no rain, he took out his *ídolo*" that was made of stone and with great reverence "kneeled before the *ídolo* and offered *copal*, feathers, and blood and said that he was sorry, that the natives were starving, and in order that the god of water [Dzahui] would cause it to rain" he promised to sacrifice doves, quail, dogs, parrots, and a person.

The priest then took water in a gourd vessel (*jícara*) and threw it over the offerings. He then "took a ball from this land which is called *ule* [or *hule*, natural latex rubber] which is a resin or gum from trees and tossed it on the ground so that it bounced and later burned the said ball and with that resin spread it on the *demonio* and later, made his sacrifice." Caaxa had called upon the *cacique* and Don Francisco to provide all the necessary items "and the person that was to be sacrificed." Afterwards, he returned the *demonio* to its place, adding that the *cacique* and Don Francisco "always had children [*muchachos*] on deposit for sacrifice."[64]

When asked how the sacrifices were performed, Caaxa replied, "he went to the highest mountain in the area and carried his *ídolo* and the person to be sacrificed and he placed the *ídolo* in a favorable place and gave copal smoke and spoke to the *ídolo* a while and later placed the child before [the *ídolo*] and sacrificed him." He added that older persons were not offered to this *demonio* of water, only children, and having been sacrificed "he removed the heart from the chest and placed it before the *ídolo* and thus it remained there for two days, or longer, and later he burned the heart and took the ashes and placed them with all that was to be sacrificed to the *ídolo* and kept it there."[65]

When asked how many persons he had sacrificed, Caaxa answered: "During the time he was a priest, he ordered killed, and killed, four children" when the rains were delayed.[66] When the old priest was asked how many persons had been sacrificed by the other native priests "he stated that he did not know because each priest is separate unto themselves and has charge of his *ídolo* and does not take part in other ceremonies, or speak of the others or what they do or have to do."[67]

Sickness and Death

Sickness and death, particularly in the case of the nobility, were also accompanied by important ritual and sacrifice. When the wife of Don Francisco of Yanhuitlan died around 1540, two priests named Coqua and Cocuyny cut part of the hair of the dead woman and attached certain stones and *chalchihuites* (precious stone figures), "and they offered them to the *demonio* and sacrificed many dove and quail and they fashioned a stone in the figure of the said dead woman and offered it to the *demonio*, and after all was done they carried her to be buried, and the said Francisco and all the others from the said house sacrificed [blood] from the ears, feasted and became inebriated."[68] These activities were verified by other eyewitnesses who testified in the Inquisition case. In other instances, as when Don Francisco had taken ill, "it was necessary to kill five or six Indians," these being slave boys of about ten years of age.[69]

With respect to archaeological findings, most persuasive is the association of a large burned offering with a burial of a woman, approximately thirty years of age, in the Postclassic/Early Colonial city of Yucundaa-Teposcolula. This probably "clandestine" very early Colonial period burial is associated with more than seventy thousand stone, bone, shell, and metal artifacts and thousands of charred bone, shell, and plant remains, all from the massive offering. The offering remains are found under, over, and surrounding the interred woman. Other burials in a Colonial cemetery are separate and seemingly unrelated to the burial-offering complex. The archaeological evidence parallels and coincides completely with testimony presented in the Inquisition case of the 1540s. It is hard to imagine a more convincing application of the "convergent methodology," which we apply and promote for the cultural history of the Mixteca.

There was little conscious conceptualization of the afterlife in Mixtec religion. Upon the death of an individual, the person obviously ceased to live, but the spirit or soul of the individual was not clearly defined as an entity but simply entered a different, but related, existence. Both inhumation burial and cremation were practiced. Burials might be made in the soil, or in the case of royalty and the nobility, the corpses were often placed in caves with offerings and rituals both at the time of burial and during anniversary celebrations in later years. Great attention was paid to deceased ancestors to the point of veneration, often, in the case of royalty, being remembered and celebrated both by their names in life and their death names.[70]

We have a compelling example of these practices in archaeological context. High-ranking persons, one female, the other probably male, were cremated and buried at Tayata around 1000 B.C.E.[71] This practice matches the cremation burial of a dog from the same context as well as the intentional burning of fired-clay human and animal figurines from nearby middens.[72] The practice of cremation was therefore widespread and extended across several conceptual categories, at least as archaeologists typically define them. It was also applied to relatively elite individuals at a time of emerging social-status distinctions. We cannot know for certain the intent behind these cremation burials, but they match depictions of ruling-class nobles being cremated in the codices.[73]

Sacred Places

First among the religious activity areas utilized by the Mixtecs was the home, with its altars and many distinctive, ritually expressive figures, offering vessels, sacrificial implements, and burial places. The pictographic manuscripts of the pre-Hispanic and Colonial periods and conventional Colonial documentation depict or describe religious acts taking place in and around dwelling places of the elite.[74] Figures, censors, braziers, offering vessels, and obsidian blades have been recovered in abundance in excavations of common-class, elite, and royal-class residences in Yucundaa-Teposcolula, Nicayuju, Chachoapan, Yanhuitlan, Yucuita, Nochixtlan, Huamelulpan, and Tayata.[75] These instruments of explicit religious practice are also found in abundance on the surface of Postclassic sites at Tlaxiaco, Teposcolula, Tamazulapan, Coixtlahuaca, Santiago Huajolotitlan, at San Miguel Achiutla, and at dozens of other contemporaneous sites. Except for variation in quality and quantity, complexes of these ritualistic devices were similar in wealthy and poor households as well as in ceremonial precincts.

In 1544–45 the aforementioned *cacique* and two *principales* of Yanhuitlan were said to have underground chambers, containing images, offering vessels, much ritual paraphernalia, and images of the ancestors of these nobles, specifically Don Francisco's father and mother.[76] Otherwise, temples (*huahi ñuhu*), shrines, and retreats were the primary loci of religious activity. These were situated in civic centers, in subject communities, in ritually significant places outside the population centers, in caves, at springs or along rivers, in groves, on rocky promontories, on mountaintops, or in abandoned ancient settlements. Residents of Peñoles, for example, made sacrifices and performed supplicatory rituals in a cave from which a stream issued.[77] Observances of this kind centered on fertility and communion with the forces and spirits of the underworld, and more directly to bargain for a special favor, water.

Native witnesses to the Holy Inquisition stated that Yanhuitlan had two principal *ídolos* of *piedra chuchuy* (precious stone), one a man, the other a woman. One was called Siquini and the other Xiv, among many others located in a high place or mountaintop along the road from Coixtlahuaca to Soyaltepec. It was also claimed that each time that water was needed, or because of illness of the *cacique* or *principales*, they performed sacrifices on the mountain range above Jaltepec called Dicuna. "They present their offerings of feathers, slaves, precious stones and mantles and other items to the *demonio*."[78] In a similar vein, a witness, Juan Neveda, testified that "in the *estancia* of Suchitepeque [Yucuita], which is subject to Yanhuitlan, they have a cave where the *tianguiz* [market] is held which they hold to be sacred, and which is customarily open and there are sacrifices and *ídolos* there to the present time [1544]."[79]

With respect to the special emphasis on caves in Mixtec religion, the Yucundaa-Teposcolula Project recently investigated an important component of the ancient city: a monumental elevated avenue that circles the central area of the site and passes at least a dozen cave entrances. In Yucundaa-Teposcolula, as well as in many other localities in the Mixteca, caves were considered entrances to the spiritual underworld, the source of life, fertility, water, and oftentimes served as the final repository for deceased ancestors.[80]

The entrances to most of the caves at Yucundaa-Teposcolula, or openings to the *inframundo* of the ancient Mixtecs, have been filled, apparently ordered closed as "temples of the *demonio*" by Spanish priests who arrived at the capital center around 1524 or 1525. The cave openings range in size from 2 or 3 meters to 20 meters wide, and many have leveled patio areas that may extend from 6 or 8 to 20 square meters. The causeway ranges from 5 to 10 meters in width, was probably between 3 and 5 meters high, and extends for approximately 2.5 kilometers around the upper third of the mountain. Although the causeway has obvious defensive potential, we hypothesize that its major function was to serve as a vast, monumental ceremonial complex incorporating dozens of important ritual activity areas.

Worldview and Cosmogony

The Mixtec universe operated in a regular, predictable, almost mechanistic fashion, as long as proper rituals, offerings, and sacrifices were performed and humankind was sufficiently respectful of nature and the spirit world. When rain failed or came late, propitiatory and supplicatory rituals were performed.

The supernatural realm was an extension of, and directly interrelated with, the natural world. It was regarded as a configuration of forces vital to the existence of man and nature, to be revered, honored, placated, manipulated, and controlled for the benefit of humanity. Major concerns were with natural forces, time, ancestors, fertility, and the continuity of life, all figuring prominently in Mixtec religion.[81]

There are good indications, as well, that noble ancestors were venerated. "It was said of Don Juan and Don Francisco of Yanhuitlan that they had *demonios* in their houses, and that among those belonging to them were [idolatrous images of] his father and mother, and about five years ago, more or less, when Fray Domingo learned of their existence, he ordered the burning of the *demonios* of Yanhuitlan."[82] Herrera describes rituals surrounding the death of a Mixtec ruler, including "women who were first made intoxicated and strangled in order that they might serve the *cacique* in the other world. . . . Honors were performed every year on the day of his birth and not on the day of death."[83]

Origin myths varied significantly among different Mixtec groups. The Mixtec people were variously described as having originated in the underworld, in a stream, from the roots of a tree, or to have come from the west or from the north.[84] The *Codex Vindobonensis* mentions the origins of the Mixtecs from the roots of a tree and with the intervention of a primordial couple and their offspring at Apoala.[85] This was followed by the foundation of the dynasties from the north (the Mixteca Baja, extending into Puebla), from the south (the general vicinity of Chalcatongo), the central region (surrounding Achiutla), the region of the Mountains of the Rain (to the east, and a mythical place of origin at Apoala), and from the west (an uncertain location). As discussed in detail by Maarten Jansen, all five foundations are introduced by the same set of establishment glyphs and construction of temples "of the eye," "of the bird," "of the vessel of blood," and "of cacao and blood."[86] The largest of these domains was the Mountains of the Rain, with seventy-one named places. This zone presumably included sites in the Yanhuitlan-Nochixtlan Valley and the surrounding dynastic core of the Postclassic Mixteca Alta.[87]

Although it was implied that various groups of Mixtecs may have had different origins and histories that could account for perceived cultural and linguistic differences, the origins of the universe and of humanity were less significant, or perhaps better said, conflated with dynastic origins and legitimacy. What counted in terms of religious belief was the maintenance of balance among nature, humanity, and supernatural forces through the performance of appropriate ritual. Mixtec religion was more activistic than intellectual or

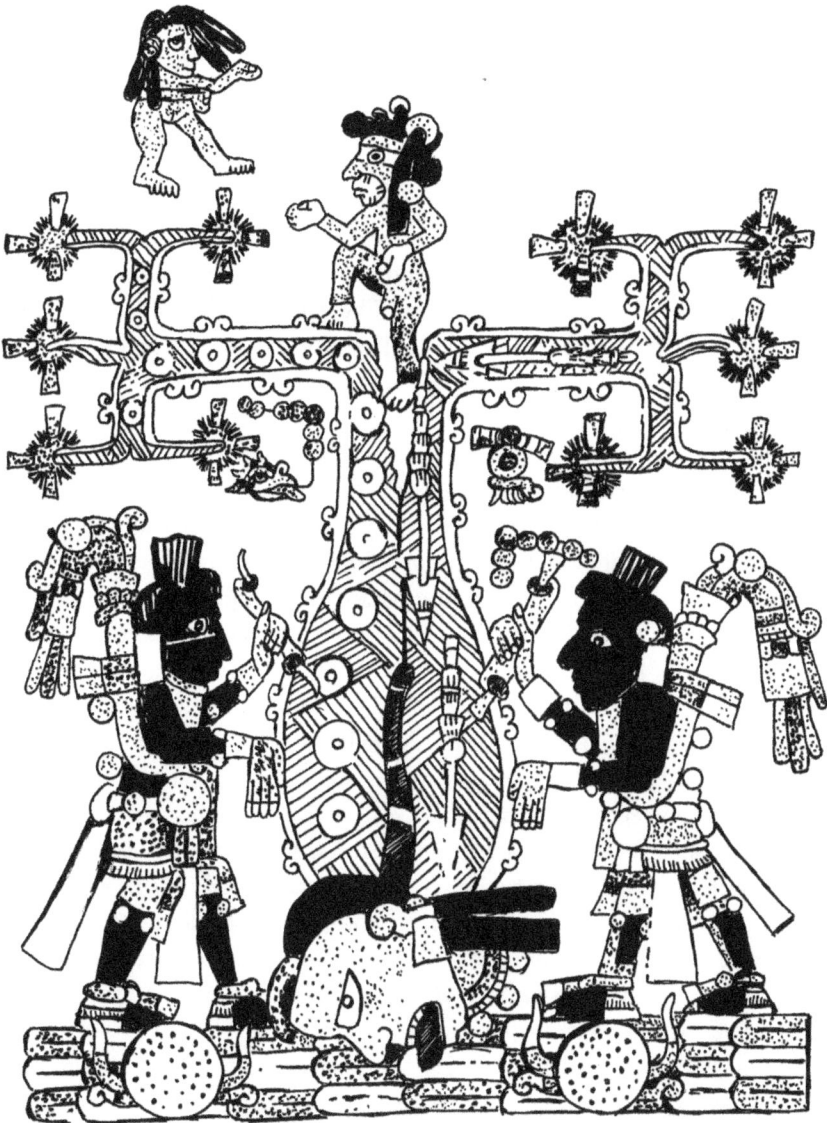

Figure 4.9. Tree birth at Apoala, showing the mythical origins of the ruling dynasties, *Codex Vindobonensis* 37. Redrawn by Jason Poling from Anders et al. 1992.

contemplative. Emphases were on the mechanistic or manipulative maintenance of life and universal relationships, not on morality or "proper" thought
and action. Ethics and morality, the exemplars and models of proper behavior
and interaction among humans, as might be found among Muslims, Christians,
or Hindus, were relatively insignificant in Mixtec religion. The models for

social interaction among supernatural beings, such as those described for the Culhua-Mexica deities such as Quetzalcoatl, Xipe Totec, Huitzilopotzli, Tlaloc, Ometecuhtli, or Coatlicue, are missing in Mixtec religion.[88] The powerful supernatural forces of heat from the sun, rain, wind, clouds, life and death, movements of the earth and heavenly bodies—although graphically symbolized, or "personified" as "beings," for example Dzahui, or Xipe— were not seen as sentient, anthropomorphized entities, that is, as gods. They were forces to be sensed, appeased, and to the extent possible, controlled through proper religious performance. The same can be said for revered ancestors, who were remembered, eulogized, and depicted graphically. They were honored and glorified, but there is no convincing evidence that they were deified.

This interpretation squares convincingly with the multiple lines of evidence available to the investigator. *Codex Borgia*, with its vivid depictions of identifiable spiritual beings and explicit acts associated with those representations, might be suggested as evidence contrary to this view. The fact of the matter is that, although involving Mixtec techniques and style or presentation, *Codex Borgia* is related to religious concepts and traditions of the central valleys of Mexico. It does not relate properly to Mixtec religion as it is represented in the Mixtec codices, in the documentation, or in its archaeological contexts. Manuel Hermann has skillfully considered the religious, as well as social, political, and economic content and implications of the Mixtec codices in his numerous recent publications in *Arqueología Mexicana*, and elsewhere.

Mixtec society was stratified, but there is no suggestion of a corresponding hierarchical principle in the supernatural universe. The spirits and forces of nature were individualistic and both complementary and redundant in function, rather than hierarchically ordered. And with the exception of the priests, whose behavior was quite circumscribed, there were no supernaturally derived social controls or guides to human behavior. In pre-Hispanic times, conduct was guided by social custom rather than religious precept. There were demands, however, that proper respect and observances be accorded the supernatural world. To violate these principles, to neglect the spiritual world, would lead to disaster.

PART TWO

THE MIXTECA
IN SPANISH COLONIAL
AND MODERN TIMES

5

THE GREAT TRANSFORMATION

One of history's greatest cultural confrontations began in the late fifteenth century with the European discovery and settlement of America. By 1519–20 the encounter between Spain and America had reached Mexico, and by the mid-1520s the Mixtecs and the Mixteca were fully involved in the convergence and amalgamation of two contrasting cultural traditions. This continued throughout the Colonial period and beyond.

The Spanish Conquest of Mexico did not end in 1521 with the sacking of Tenochtitlan but continued over subsequent decades through processes of native conversion, economic transformation, and European colonization. These more pervasive forms of conquest came with the legion of Spanish administrators, colonists, and clergy who followed in the paths of the *conquistadores*. They brought their muskets and cannon, their legal instruments, their animals and plants, new and devastating diseases, new technology and global markets, and of course the Holy Trinity. What emerged from this encounter by 1600 or so, after the Holy Inquisition, the plague years, and resettlement, was a hybrid society—no longer pre-Hispanic, but not Spanish either.

This was not the first "great transformation" for the peoples of Mesoamerica, but it was assuredly the most consequential, at least for the Mixtecs.[1] Let us first mention what did not happen. The Mixtec were not wiped out as a people. In contrast to Tenochtitlan or Cholula, their capital was not destroyed. Their culture, as well as the Mixtec people, survived in the mainstream of the Colonial culture of New Spain. By no means could they be cited as an example of "indigenous survival through isolation," as occurred only in the more remote regions of Mexico and Central America.[2] As in other areas, the Mixtec did not resist as much as accommodate and adapt.[3] The Mixtecs survived, and in some instances thrived, under drastically altered circumstances.

Relevant documents and archaeological materials are quite unambiguous in demonstrating that indigenous and intrusive elements and concepts coexisted. Eventually, as the sixteenth century progressed, composite forms and patterns owing to one or the other donor, or both, developed. By late Colonial times, virtually the entire indigenous cultural complex had been affected, but, simultaneously, nearly everything was traceable to pre-Conquest antecedents. What we expect to see, and in fact do see, are indigenous beliefs and cultural practices that "operate in a familiar manner under a Spanish-Christian overlay."[4]

The probable first contact between Mixtecs and Spaniards occurred even before the fall of the Culhua-Mexica Empire, but it is clear that within two to three years after that, Spaniards had arrived in the central Mixteca. Having penetrated the Mixtec domain, it is important to observe and analyze the means of colonization, these being largely nonviolent, bureaucratic, and biological (infectious diseases and new assemblages of plants and animals)— as well as economic and spiritual forms of "conquest."[5] Finally, it is essential to examine the changes evident in the post-Conquest archaeological record from the Late Postclassic and Early Colonial urban capital at Yucundaa-Teposcolula. The perspective of the Mixtec community in transition provides concrete, physical support for documentary materials showing the continuation of pre-Conquest native states and institutional structures long into the Colonial period.[6]

Apart from secular and Dominican priests, few Europeans visited the Mixteca until the middle to late 1530s, when effective minimal settlement was established. From this time forward, native technology, economy, social organization, government, and ideology underwent transformation, and the Mixteca and its people were increasingly incorporated into the Spanish Colonial realm, but without surrendering their identity.

CONQUEST AND COLONIZATION

On November 8, 1519, Hernán Cortés and his followers entered the island city of Tenochtitlan, the Culhua-Mexica capital, and sometime thereafter took its ruler, Montezuma II, into custody. Cortés then required the Mexican sovereign to provide information concerning the sources of tribute, especially gold, paid to him and the associated rulers of the Culhua-Mexica Empire by the myriad towns and provinces under their dominion. Montezuma responded by providing maps and native guides for expeditions of Spanish soldiers dispatched during succeeding months to various parts of the Mexican domain. One of these expeditions, led by Gonzalo de Umbría, penetrated the Mixteca Alta, visited the districts of Sosola and Tamazulapan, and brought back favorable reports concerning the settlements and resources of these areas.[7]

If we may assume that native trails followed the approximate route of modern roads through natural passes, it seems likely that Umbría proceeded through or close to Yanhuitlan on his way south. Any other route from Tamazulapan to Sosola would have required an arduous march through rugged country to the east of the Yanhuitlan-Nochixtlan Valley. This expedition was likely the first contact of Mixtecs and Spaniards, and the meeting seems to have been relatively peaceful and without notable incident.

Spaniards occupied Tenochtitlan until they withdrew on the evening of June 30, 1520, having suffered great loss of life during the Noche Triste (Night of Sorrows), when Culhua-Mexica warriors killed hundreds of *conquistadores* and their Tlaxcallan allies on the narrow causeways radiating out from the city. Cortés and his men escaped to Tlaxcalla.

Later in the summer of 1520, after further maneuvering and alliance-making with the natives, headquarters were established at Segura de la Frontera (Tepeaca) in southeastern Puebla, and it was from here that Cortés directed his Second Letter of Relation, dated October 30, 1520, to the Spanish Emperor Charles V.[8] At the time this account was written, Spanish soldiers had captured the city of Itzocan (Izúcar de Matamoros), an important place south of Cholula and the volcano Popocatepetl. Cortés's letter and other sources mention a visit to Itzocan by emissaries from eight of the towns under the province of Coixtlahuaca, who offered allegiance to the Spanish Crown and indicated that four other towns of the same area would soon do likewise.[9] It seems likely that Yanhuitlan, Teposcolula, Tlaxiaco, Tejupan, Achiutla, and other central Mixtecan towns and kingdoms would have been represented in this group.

Cortés was by this time already the de facto ruler of Mexico. The conqueror Bernal Díaz writes, "The chiefs of the captured towns sued for peace, and Sandoval [one of the Spanish captains] sent them to Cortés, who had by now achieved a great reputation among the Indians for bravery and fairness. Smallpox was spreading through the country, and many *Caciques* died. Consequently, various disputes as to the succession and ownership of property were brought to Cortés for settlement."[10]

While the Spanish forces were engaged in the final siege of Tenochtitlan, unrest among the natives of Oaxaca resulted in attacks on the Spaniards in

the Tepeaca area, in southern Puebla and northern Oaxaca, and this rebellious attitude prevailed for several months after the final defeat of the Mexicans
on August 13, 1521.[11]

In 1522 Pedro de Alvarado was dispatched with a sizeable force to restore
order and to impose effective Spanish dominion in southern Mexico. An
engagement was fought at Itzcuintepec with an entrenched force of Mixtecs.[12]
This force probably included Mixtec-speaking groups residing in and around
the Valley of Oaxaca. With the winning of this battle and a later encounter
on the Mixteca Costa at Tututepec, Alvarado achieved the final pacification
of the Mixtec and Zapotec peoples. By the end of 1522 or early 1523,
Spaniards had established control over the Mixteca and were never again
seriously challenged.

Early in the Colonial period, Spanish administrative entities known as
corregimientos and *alcaldías mayores* were installed in populous and strategic
zones of the Mixteca Alta, Baja, and Costa. Although Spanish administrative
practices and laws evolved in response to the circumstances and challenges
of colonization during the sixteenth century, the regional political units persisted as congeries of small or medium-sized communities and a few urban
capitals, the most important among these being Teposcolula, Yanhuitlan, Tlaxiaco,
Tejupan, Tamazulapan, and Coixtlahuaca in the Mixteca Alta; Acatlan, Huajuapan, Tonala, Tecomaxtlahuaca, and Putla in the Mixteca Baja; and Tututepec
and Jicayan in the Mixteca Costa. One large Mixtec-Zapotec center was
formed in the western Valley of Oaxaca in and around Cuilapan and a second
smaller multiethnic center in Huitzo (Huazolotitlan) in the northernmost
sector of the Valley of Oaxaca. The largest population concentrations lay in
the Mixteca Alta, and dozens of communities were incorporated into the
Provincia y Alcaldía Mayor of Teposcolula. This territory in the central Mixteca Alta was the economic power base for such important *conquistadores* as
Francisco de Las Casas, Tristán de Luna y Arellano, Gonzalo Sandoval, Luis
de Castilla, Martín Vásquez and his *mestizo* son Matías Vásquez Laynes, Francisco
Maldonado, Rodrigo de Segura, and others and was one of the most important centers of activity for the Dominican Order in New Spain.

Native Tribute and the Spanish *Encomienda*

Cortés and Crown officials hastened to exploit the labor and material resources
of the area, and between 1522 and 1535 dozens of *encomiendas* were assigned
to prominent *conquistadores*.[13] Although designed originally for application to
the West Indies as grants of labor services by a stated number of individuals,
in Mexico the *encomienda* underwent significant alteration. Here the Spaniards

found a native society using a system of tribute based upon periodic payments to the Culhua-Mexica rulers by subject communities. Consequently, Cortés and his governmental successors in Mexico made *encomienda* grants on the basis of *pueblo* units, or portions thereof, and authorized the payment of both tribute and labor service to *encomenderos*.

During the 1520s there was no limitation on the amount of tribute and labor an *encomendero* might require of a town assigned to him, or at least no such limits are stipulated in the laws of the time. This resulted in serious abuses, and Colonial officials, in accordance with royal directives, established, during the decades 1530–50, fixed periodic quotas of both tribute and labor. The tribute schedules called for payment in items of local production. In gold-producing areas the schedules often called for the payment of stated quantities of gold dust, strips or disks of gold, or gold jewelry; in other places the schedules called for payment of certain quantities of cotton textiles (*mantas, huipiles, camisas*, and so on) and/or agricultural products. Labor service might include the cultivation of fields and the assignment of natives as household servants.[14] A royal order of 1549 decreed the elimination of labor as part of the *encomienda* obligation. Henceforth, the *encomienda* became a system of tribute only for the benefit of designated conquerors and early colonists.[15] In so-called Crown towns, such as Teposcolula, tribute was assigned directly to the Spanish government rather than to individuals.

By 1565 standard annual payments in cash (*pesos de oro común*) and maize were established in most of central Mexico. This assessment was based on the number of *tributarios* (normally heads of families or adult single males and widows/widowers classed as half-tributaries) and the payment by each unit of one *peso* and a half *fanega* of maize (about fifty-five liters, but somewhat variable). In many towns, an additional assessment was also made of one or two *reales* per *tributario* for local community expenses. These assessments remained in force until the later decades of the sixteenth century, when new assessments had to be made because of population decline.

The Mixteca was rich both in resources and people, and some of the richest *encomiendas* in New Spain were awarded to the most powerful *conquistadores* and first settlers: Yanhuitlan, Tlaxiaco, Coixtlahuaca, Tecomaxtlahuaca, Tamazulapan, Tututepec, Achiutla, Chalcatongo, and Chicahuaxtla. Yanhuitlan was one of the largest and most important towns and *encomiendas* in the Mixteca.[16] In 1523 Cortés granted the community of Yanhuitlan to his cousin, Francisco de Las Casas, who subsequently achieved dubious fame after his sea expedition in 1524 to Honduras, where he participated in the assassination of Cristóbal de Olid, whom Cortés had sent to conquer that region.

In 1529, when Las Casas was absent in Spain, the First Royal Audiencia of Mexico revoked the grant and placed Yanhuitlan under direct royal jurisdiction. Las Casas promptly instituted legal proceedings to regain his title to the *encomienda*,[17] which was confirmed in 1537.[18] In later years he was frequently at odds with the church and offered little assistance to the Dominicans in their first efforts to establish a friary in Yanhuitlan.

At the death of Francisco de Las Casas in 1546, his son Gonzalo succeeded to the title of *encomendero*. The younger Las Casas was at first little better disposed toward the clergy than his father had been. By 1550, however, reconciliation occurred, and Gonzalo lent his active support to the concurrent ambitious building program of the Dominicans. In 1580 Gonzalo departed for Spain and left the *encomienda* in care of his son, Francisco II. The latter succeeded to the *encomienda* at the death of his father in 1591, and he remained as *encomendero* until at least 1622.[19]

The first record of a tribute assessment for Yanhuitlan dates from the early 1530s, when the town was temporarily a possession of the Crown and paid tribute to the royal treasury of New Spain. The schedule called for the payment of 120 *pesos, oro en polvo*, every eighty days, or 540 *pesos* each year. In addition, the Mixtecs had to provide food for the *corregidor* and the *alguacil*, these being local administrative functionaries.[20] This modest requirement, in terms of the large population of the community, may possibly be explained by the fact that during this early period, assessments for Crown towns were often less harsh than those of *encomienda* towns.

In 1548, two years after the death of Francisco de Las Casas, the tribute assessment for Yanhuitlan was revised. Required tribute and service were as follows: an annual payment of 782.5 *pesos* in *oro en polvo* and the cultivation and harvest for their *encomendero* of a field planted with fifteen *fanegas* of maize. Daily payments of four turkeys, two European hens, a small jar of honey, four hundred *cacao* beans, two cakes of beeswax, a bundle of sandalwood (tea), six hundred maize tortillas, thirty eggs, a half-*fanega* of maize, one plate each of salt, chili, and tomatoes, ten loads of firewood, and ten loads of fodder.[21] The daily assessment also included the services of ten Mixtecs in the *pueblo*.[22] The 1548 schedule represents a much heavier burden on the Mixtecs than that of the early 1530s. The annual gold payment had been increased by 45 percent. It would be difficult to calculate a money value for the daily payments in kind, but the Mixtecs must have regarded them as onerous and also as a veritable nuisance. In addition to payments in gold and in kind, natives were now required to give labor service in the *pueblo* and cultivate a field of wheat for the *encomendero*.

Yanhuitlan and its subject settlements had six thousand *tributarios* in 1565–70. On the basis of the standardized tribute assessment of the 1560s, the *encomendero* of Yanhuitlan would have received 6,000 *pesos* in cash and three thousand *fanegas* of maize worth 1,500 *pesos*,[23] or a total of 7,500 *pesos* annually. Although some Spaniards in New Spain enjoyed larger *encomienda* revenues, the *encomendero* of Yanhuitlan received a handsome annual income from this source on little or no investment. By comparison, the *corregidores* of Mixtec towns, as Crown officials, received salaries ranging from 200 to 600 *pesos* per year. Gonzalo de Las Casas would have been obliged, of course, to make fairly substantial payments in support of the missionary friars resident in Yanhuitlan and for his share (one-third, according to Colonial law) of the cost of building the massive church and friary under construction. But his *encomienda* revenue must have been augmented by income from other sources, such as the flourishing silk industry in which he was heavily involved.

Of course it was economically advantageous to an *encomendero* for his community to have as large a population as possible, for this was the basis upon which tribute was assessed and collected. As the population of Yanhuitlan declined, for example, so did the revenue of the *encomienda*. With a declining population, the Mixtecs were quick to complain of their inability to meet tribute assessments. It must have been of great concern to Gonzalo de Las Casas and his son Francisco to watch their main source of income decline steadily and drastically. A document of 1596 records the number of *tributarios* as 2,475.[24] The gross *encomienda* income would at that time have amounted to only 3,862.5 *pesos*, plus the maize contribution, or about one-half of what it had been in the peak years of 1565–70.

Other powerful *encomenderos* of the sixteenth and seventeenth centuries were Francisco Maldonado, Tristán de Luna y Arellano, and Carlos de Luna y Arellano, who held Chalcatongo, Tecomastlahuaca, Cuquila, Ocotepec, and other *pueblos*, and Matías Vásquez Laynez and the family Andrada Moctezuma, who held Tlaxiaco and several other pueblos in the Mixteca and in central Mexico. Gonzalo Sandoval and Luis de Castilla succeeded Hernán Cortés and Pedro de Alvarado at Tututepec. The activities of these individuals and their families are well documented in the collections recovered from the judicial archives in Teposcolula and now housed in the Archivo Histórico del Poder Judicial del Estado de Oaxaca, in the Archivo General de la Nación, Mexico City, and in the Archivo General de Indias, Seville.[25]

Silk, Cochineal, and Sheep

The money economy of larger communities like Yanhuitlan, Teposcolula, and Tlaxiaco in the sixteenth century was basically dependent upon three industries. Because of ample water and fertile lands, it was possible to conduct extensive general agriculture throughout the valleys and terraced hillsides surrounding those towns. There was continued cultivation of the pre-Conquest crops of beans, maize, chili, and squash, but new industries were introduced with considerable success by the Europeans. Cereal grains, mainly wheat and oats, were very important additions to the agricultural complex. The principal sources of income, however, were silk, cochineal, and sheep.

Sometime after 1531, Hernán Cortés, who had experimented with sericulture in other parts of the New World, gave some seed worms to María de Aguilar, his cousin and the wife of Francisco de Las Casas. These silkworms produced about one pound of eggs, and from this began the great Mixtecan silk industry, of which Yanhuitlan became the principal center.[26] Other important silk production centers were Teposcolula, where the site of the probable original *casa de seda* has been identified some two kilometers south of the city; Tejupan; Tamazulapan; and San Mateo Peñasco. This takes on added significance when it is known that the Mixteca Alta was the most important silk-producing area of New Spain for about half a century.[27] From the 1530s to 1580, the period of the great silk boom, Yanhuitlan and almost every corner of the Mixteca Alta were devoted to silk culture. Mixtecan silk was known in Europe, and although silk production declined in the rest of New Spain after 1555, it remained of the utmost importance in the Mixteca until late in the sixteenth century.[28]

Much of the success of the silk venture, of course, is attributable to the Dominican friars, among them Domingo de Santa María and Francisco Marín, who instructed the Mixtecs and promoted sericulture throughout the region.[29] Silk was of such great importance and interest that the second *encomendero* of Yanhuitlan, Gonzalo de Las Casas, wrote an extensive treatise on raising silk, the first of its kind in the Spanish language. It was printed in 1581 under the title *Arte para criar seda.*[30]

By 1580 sericulture in Nochixtlan and Yanhuitlan had become the main "cash producing industry."[31] By the 1590s, however, annual silk production in the Mixteca was in steady decline. The exhaustion of the labor supply through the great plague of 1575–85, competition from the China trade, and the excessive demands of the clergy and civil officials contributed to the demise of the industry, and with its termination the Mixteca was deprived of its most important economic asset.[32] Silk, probably more than any other single enterprise, had brought the Mixteca Alta a level of prosperity that would not again be attained.

Silver was the leading export of New Spain in 1600. Ranking next to silver, according to Raymond Lee, was cochineal.[33] By the end of the sixteenth century some 250,000 to 300,000 pounds of *grana* (dried cochineal that produced a unique crimson dye) valued at 500,000 to 600,000 *pesos* moved annually through Veracruz en route to European cloth makers.[34] A native Mexican dye had in the span of eighty years become "one of the most important New World exports to the Old World."[35]

The raising of the tiny insect *Coccus cacti*, or *Dactylopius coccus*, of which some seventy thousand were required to produce a pound of *grana*, was generalized throughout the Mixteca, but at least three communities of the Mixteca Alta figured most prominently in the industry: These towns were Tamazulapan, Nochixtlan, and Yanhuitlan.[36]

Gonzalo Gómez de Cervantes, writing at the close of the sixteenth century, mentions the Mixteca Alta as an important *grana* center and states that the Spaniards had greatly increased pre-Conquest production.[37] The *Codex Mendoza* shows that the Culhua-Mexica Empire acquired eighty-five bags of cochineal from its tributaries in the Mixteca Alta. Although production figures are imprecise, it is clear that the cultivation of the microscopic dye-producing insects continued to play a major role in contributing to the prosperity of numerous Mixteca communities during the sixteenth century.

Of great importance to Mixteca economy was sheep raising (actually both sheep and goats). Miranda indicated that there were, in all, some three hundred thousand sheep in the Mixteca, and that of sixty-one registered flocks, forty-four were in the Mixteca Alta and seven in the Baja.[38] It is estimated that there were well over two hundred thousand sheep in the Alta late in the sixteenth century. The principal centers were Coixtlahuaca, Nochixtlan, Tejupan, Teposcolula, Tlaxiaco, and Yanhuitlan. There were also communal herds of sheep that ranged far and wide throughout the Mixteca. Although positive benefits derived from herding may have been somewhat offset by what Miranda calls "the irrational and immoderate raising of sheep" and destruction and impoverishment of tillable lands by erosion, the immediate positive economic implications for the Mixteca were great.[39] The large communal, church, and individually owned flocks contributed thousands of *pesos* annually to the wealth of the owners, and the wool produced from the flocks fed a vast textile industry that extended from the Mixteca to greater Oaxaca, Puebla, and central Mexico.

Sheep and goat herding continues to this day (Burgoa remarked that all manner of European livestock was in evidence around Yanhuitlan in the seventeenth century, with sheep and goats massively outnumbering cattle and horses).[40] Although the loss of arable land due to erosion, caused in part by grazing of flocks of sheep, continues to the present, the herds are far smaller and fewer in number than in Colonial times, and better controls are in place. As a result, erosion is far less pronounced today than in earlier times, and there are concerted efforts to repair, resuscitate, and rejuvenate heavily eroded lands and put them back into production.

The Church

The missionary program in the Mixtec and Zapotec areas of New Spain was carried on mainly by members of the Dominican Order. The first Dominicans, a group of twelve friars, arrived on the North American continent in 1526. Death soon claimed five, and four others left the colony of New Spain within a short time. In 1528 twenty-four new missionaries arrived, and with these reinforcements the order was able to embark upon a wide-ranging missionary effort in central and southern Mexico. The Dominican corps of missionaries was steadily enlarged by new contingents, which arrived in 1535 and in later years, and also by the admission of new members who took their vows in Mexico. By the mid-sixteenth century the Dominicans were the second largest missionary group—second only to the Franciscans—in New Spain.

Until very recently, the study of missionary activity in the Mixteca had focused on Yanhuitlan. Clearly this was an extremely important center, and the religious activities which took place there were of great consequence. In many ways, however, this is a reflection of the type and quantity of documentary evidence that has been preserved.[41] But Yanhuitlan has also contributed to something of a distortion of the reality of religious activity in the region. Other important centers of religious activity and conversion, such as Teposcolula, Tamazulapan, Tlaxiaco, Achiutla, Tilantongo, and—in the Valley of Oaxaca—Cuilapan are far less known.

Subsequent to recent archaeological investigations at Yucundaa-Teposcolula, it is becoming quite evident that the Dominicans arrived there very early, probably in the late 1520s, and constructed a church and a religious residence, beginning possibly as early as 1530 and continuing until 1550 when the church and the city were abandoned and relocated to San Pedro y San Pablo Teposcolula in the valley bottomlands to the west.[42]

The Iglesia Vieja and religious residence at Yucundaa-Teposcolula represent the oldest extant religious architecture in the Mixteca, and very likely in all of Oaxaca. With the exception of the briefest mention of the Dominican presence there in the Inquisitorial proceedings of 1544–45, and two or three somewhat ambiguous drawings in the *Códice de Yanhuitlan*, there is virtually no conventional historical documentation relating to these developments. This being the case, it could be said that, in effect, the material remains at Yucundaa-Teposcolula stand as the best and most valuable "documentation" so far available on this earliest of Dominican enterprises in Teposcolula and the Mixteca. These findings also prompt us to redouble our efforts to search for additional documentation and to proceed with archaeological investigation in order to greatly augment our present knowledge of early Colonial religious activity.

During these early years, the Dominicans took active measures to combat and eradicate the continuing practice of native religion in the Mixteca, most notably in Yanhuitlan, especially by prominent Mixtec officials of the *pueblo*. It is apparent, however, that in these activities and in other phases of their missionary effort, they encountered opposition from Francisco de Las Casas, the *encomendero* of Yanhuitlan. Because of the hostility of the native officials and the *encomendero*, in 1541 the Dominican provincial, Fray Pedro Delgado, instructed Fray Domingo de Santa María, who, as it happens, authored a grammar of the Mixtec language, to transfer his friary from Yanhuitlan to Teposcolula.[43]

From 1541 to 1547 the mission at Yanhuitlan was administered by secular clergy.[44] It was during this same period that Don Francisco and Don Juan, governors of the *pueblo*, and Don Domingo, the acting *cacique*, were subjected to Inquisitorial process on charges of the continuing practice of native religion.

The Dominicans returned to Yanhuitlan in 1546–47 and had permanent charge of the mission thereafter. Coinciding with the return of the Dominicans was the succession of Gonzalo de Las Casas to the title of *encomendero*, and it appears that Gonzalo eventually gave more active and positive support to the missionary program than had been true with his father and predecessor, Francisco de Las Casas. During the years following 1547, the Dominicans established such a wide measure of influence in local affairs that a Spanish resident of Yanhuitlan, Alonso Caballero, was prompted to send a lengthy complaint concerning their activities to the visitor-general of New Spain. This document, dated 1563, describes the Dominicans as the directing force in community affairs and accuses them of using their position for economic exploitation of the Mixtecs. Some of the charges made by Caballero were that the Dominicans were forcing the Mixtecs to work long hours in the stone quarries for little or no pay, assessing fines for missing Mass or fiestas, carrying on monopolies in certain commodities, charging excessive prices for goods and services, and conspiring with the *caciques* to exploit the Mixtecs.[45]

The Dominican foundation at Yanhuitlan served a large population and ranked high among the great convents of New Spain during the Colonial period. Around 1550 the construction of the massive church and friary, which today dominate the landscape at Yanhuitlan, was initiated. This monumental example of sixteenth-century church architecture, in the opinion of George Kubler, cannot antedate 1550 and was, in all probability, begun that same year.[46] Construction continued for about twenty-five years, and Burgoa writes that the project required the services of more than six thousand Mixtecs, working in shifts of six hundred, to carry stone, water, and lime, in addition to a considerable staff of skilled workers and artisans.[47] It is evident that the building of the structure placed a heavy burden on the labor force and natural resources of the area. Indeed, it was in part such exploitation of native labor that prompted Alonso Caballero to make his criticism of the Dominican Order in Yanhuitlan.

It is commonly believed that the Yanhuitlan convent was built over a pre-Hispanic structure. Excavations conducted in the late 1960s did, indeed, reveal the existence of an earlier, pre-Hispanic structure under the church-convent, but since these contexts and relationships between the Colonial and Late Postclassic structures have been virtually destroyed and unrecorded in hasty architectural "restoration" between 2010 and 2012, this important historical information may be lost forever. The ancient platform, upon which the church and convent rest, was vastly expanded under the direction of the Dominicans.[48] Burgoa implies that the base was a creation of the friars, and he speaks of the problems involved in its construction.[49] The entire edifice was completed around 1580 after the introduction by Gonzalo de Las Casas, in the later stages of building, of an Italian architect. The Italian and the great religious artist, Andrés de Concha, applied the finishing touches to the masterpiece.[50] Despite the ravages suffered during the War of Independence and the Mexican Revolution, when the church was employed as a fortress, much of its majestic beauty has been preserved to the present day.

Responses to Spanish Control

Owing to the sense of relief among natives at the overthrow of the Culhua-Mexica Empire, some accomplished diplomacy by Hernán Cortés and his collaborators, and the persisting good fortune that followed the Spaniards in their American venture, little resistance was encountered in northern Oaxaca, in the Mixtecas Alta and Baja, the Mazateca-Cuicateca, or in the Valley of

Oaxaca. Shortly after the relatively quick victory by the colonists, however, the *cacique* of Tututepec, Coaxintecuhtli, his son, Ixtac Quiautzin (later baptized with the given name of Pedro de Alvarado, in honor of the Spanish *conquistador*), and the people of Tututepec rebelled.[51]

Although they fought ferociously, they were finally defeated; Tututepec was sacked, with thousands of *pesos* in gold and other goods extracted by Pedro de Alvarado and a later series of *encomenderos*, including Hernán Cortés, Gonzalo de Salazar, Luis de Castilla, Tristán de Luna y Arellano, and others. The ruling *cacique* was murdered by the Alvarado forces, and the people were generally brutalized and exploited. After this time, except for one or two highly localized *tumultos*, little in the way of organized resistance developed in and around Tututepec or, for that matter, on the entire Pacific coast from Guerrero to Tehuantepec during the sixteenth and seventeenth centuries. Natives were far more likely to quarrel among themselves over boundaries, *cacicazgos*, resources, or subject communities seeking independence from their *cabeceras*, than they were to openly or violently resist Spanish domination.[52]

The story at Teposcolula was quite different from that of Tututepec. A few Spaniards arrived in Teposcolula around 1524–25, and an early *corregimiento* was established there in 1527. In 1528–29 the Dominicans established a church and monastery, or *casa religiosa*, at the site of Yucundaa-Teposcolula. This pre-Hispanic city and political capital occupied some 289 hectares along a high ridge two kilometers southeast of present-day San Pedro y San Pablo Teposcolula, at elevations ranging from 2,200 to 2,400 meters. While there is virtually no historical documentation relating to the first two decades of the Colonial period at Yucundaa-Teposcolula, five seasons of archaeological research at the site reveals a dramatic transformation of Mixtec culture during the period 1527 to 1550. What is special about Teposcolula, however, is that the transition was achieved without violence or notable social upheaval.[53] Although there is no evidence of violent confrontation, there was a horrific decimation of the native population of Yucundaa-Teposcolula attributable to the epidemics of the 1530s to 1550. In 1550 the city was abandoned—with no signs of active resistance—and the people as well as church and civic administration were shifted to San Pedro y San Pablo Teposcolula on the valley floor.

In the Mixteca during the 1530s, the response to mistreatment from the Spaniards was to flee rather than fight.[54] In 1535, confronted by exorbitant tribute assessments and excessive labor demands by the *encomendero* Francisco Solís, the population of Tamazulapan, following their *cacique* Don Hernando, abandoned the community and went into hiding in the high, distant mountains.[55] Later, following a change of *encomenderos*, the natives returned to find that lands which they claimed were occupied by settlers from the neighboring communities of Coixtlahuaca and Tequecistepec (Tequixtepec). Tamazulapan and its *cacique* brought suit in Mexico City before the Royal Audiencia, but the case was decided in favor of the invading towns.

The Tamazulapan case, which began with a demonstration of native resistance "by flight" from Spanish domination, evolved into a conflict among three native communities and their *caciques*, a conflict that was resolved through the newly introduced legal system and not through violent confrontation. This is only one of hundreds of such native versus native disturbances that occurred in the Mixteca over the three centuries of Spanish colonization. Complaints, when they arose, were not against the Spanish or their Colonial system. On the contrary, natives used the legal institutions in their search for solutions and justice, rather than resort to violence.[56]

During the sixteenth century, when *alborotos* and *tumultos* occurred in the Mixteca, they were limited to a single *pueblo*, of short duration, and only infrequently were they directed toward Spanish officials, but more frequently toward their own indigenous authorities.[57] In general, it can be said the Spanish domination of the Mixteca was rather easily accepted.

The Mixteca was quickly conquered and hispanized in the sixteenth century. The Spanish instituted an effective multilevel system of government, and with little resistance the Dominicans converted the Mixtecs, built massive religious structures in their midst, and introduced Spanish civilization. Although the Mixtecs readily embraced Catholicism, European technology, and the Spanish Colonial political and economic systems, they did not give up their language and retained much of their traditional worldview and culture. The Mixtecs did not become homogenized into a pan-Colonial peasant culture but remained distinct from Nahuas, Zapotecs, and the other native peoples of Mexico.

Mixtec communities were left standing, and their identities were further validated through the granting of legal titles, territorial delineation, and through subsequent adjudication by Spanish courts. Whether those claims were verified or moderated, the existence of the system of litigation and the building of in-group morale reinforced the identity of the community as opposed to other such communities. The courts furnished a stage for acting out a highly symbolic drama of community identity formation that went far beyond the often quite minimal economic values of disputed lands, boundaries, and resources. The multilevel system of government reinforced the identity and autonomy of these communities while simultaneously linking individual communities into the ascending system of Colonial government. These Colonial predispositions help in understanding native communities in the present and, for that matter, explain the continuance of *pleitos* of various kinds that in many instances date from Colonial times.

THE TRANSFORMATION OF MIXTEC SOCIETY

The transformation of native society under Spanish rule was neither uniform nor pervasive. Family organization, kinship reckoning, marriage, and patterns of socialization underwent little modification. The four-level class system of rulers (*caciques* or *yya tnuhu*), nobility (*principales* or *tay toho*), commoners (*gente común, tay yucu, tay ñuu, macehuales*), and tenant farmers (*tay situ ndayu*) and servants of pre-Hispanic times persisted but was substantially modified. The system expanded to include Spanish bureaucrats, clergy, merchants, and three or four status groups of aristocratic, common, itinerant and indigent Spaniards, as well as *criollo* and *mestizo* civilians residing in the Mixteca. To this could be added members of the Spanish military and a relatively small group of African slaves. The resulting social system consisted of an amalgamation of Mixtecs, Europeans, and persons of mixed ancestry, and a contingent of slaves and their "pure" and intermixed descendants.

It is both an oversimplification and a distortion of reality to conceive of the social system as an ethnic-political dyad of Colonials led by Spanish-born *peninsulares* and a subservient underclass of natives and Africans. Some Mixtecs—rulers and *principales*—ranked on a par with European bureaucrats or clergy and above certain Spanish civilians, military, and indigents. Even in the case of the common class, the intent of Spanish law and policy was to deal evenhandedly with natives and to protect them from abuse. There is no evidence in the thousands of criminal and civil cases processed by the magisterial court in Teposcolula that Mixtecs were treated either more or less fairly than were Spaniards, *mestizos*, and others. Offenses and abuses committed against Mixtecs were met with punishment, as were acts committed by Mixtecs against Europeans. In civil and criminal matters, natives, as well as Europeans, were advised of allegations and options and, in serious cases, were represented by counsel.

The social mechanisms linking pre-Hispanic Mixtec families into communities, communities into kingdoms, and kingdoms into regional and interregional networks persisted into Colonial times. There were, however, modifications. Common-class marriage tended to be regulated by requirements of community endogamy. That is to say, a marriage partner would be selected from among unrelated, or distantly related, members of one's own village. Intercommunity marriage, on the other hand, was customary among the nobility. Inter-kingdom and interregional marriages continued among members of the ruling class throughout the Colonial period, thereby preserving traditional inter-polity and interregional social and political ties.

The marketing complex continued to serve as a basis of social contact for members of the common class, as well as an institution of economic interaction. Colonial documentation indicates substantial movement among communities such as Yanhuitlan, Nochixtlan, Tamazulapan, Coixtlahuaca, Teposcolula, Tlaxiaco, Juxtlahuaca, Huajuapan, towns in the Mixteca Costa and in Puebla. This movement took place not only on market days, but also in order to visit with relatives, engage in ritual activities, transact business outside the periodic market, or for such services as curing, smithing, or conversion of raw resources.

Relations among members of different communities were not always harmonious. Many of the sixteenth-century criminal cases recorded in the Teposcolula Judicial Archive involve disputes, thefts, and violent interaction among persons coming together on market day or in the transaction of business in administrative centers. The incidence of conflict between individuals from different communities, however, was not by any means as great as it was within communities. On the other hand, intergroup conflict was most often between communities and was not organized along class or ethnic lines, that is, native Mixtec versus European. Such "revolutionary" or class-based struggles simply were not a significant aspect of life in the Colonial Mixteca.

Kinship and Community

Several sixteenth-century sources support inferences about mid-century native population, community organization, and household composition. These sources include the *Suma de visitas* of 1547–48, the *Libro de tasaciones* of 1531–1600, the *Relación del Obispado de Oaxaca* of the 1570s, and the *Relaciones geográficas* of 1579–81.[58] Although the types of data vary from community to community and through time, certain conclusions can be drawn concerning basic Hispano-Mixtec social, demographic, and settlement patterns that were established by 1550.

Average household size in 1547–48 ranged from 3.2 persons in Teposcolula and Tilantongo to 4.5 persons in Achiutla and an unusually high 8.6 persons in Yucuañe. Figures for eleven major towns in the Mixteca yield a combined average for the area of 4.84 individuals per household. The addition of the "under three years of age" component would likely place the true average at just over 5 individuals per household. No appreciable differences in household size are noted for the more urbanized *cabeceras* as opposed to their *sujetos*. People resided in compact settlements, as they had in pre-Hispanic times, rather than being dispersed about the countryside in isolated homesteads.

A census list dating from 1746 provides useful information on the number of families residing in Mixtec communities in later Colonial times. Although the figures are useful for determining the numbers of Mixtec and non-Mixtec families, it is difficult to correlate or compare the 1547–48 and 1746 data, since the census criteria were different and community composition was variable, making it difficult to determine whether or not the Apoala, Achiutla, or Teozacoalco of 1547 were structured the same in 1746 or precisely how they differed. One clear trend was the drastic decrease in the number of families and, therefore, the total population; another notable trend was the substantial presence of non-Mixtec families in the provincial *cabeceras* and larger communities.

Colonial kinship, marriage, and residence patterns varied from class to class, but little change in intra- or interclass relations occurred from 1520 to 1820. For native commoners there was notable continuity in bilateral kinship reckoning (through both the paternal and maternal lines) and patterns of inheritance, community endogamy, ambilocal postmarital residence, and preference for nuclear or limited extended-family household organization.

In the traditional patterns of inheritance for rulers (*yya tnuhu* or *caciques*), estates of parents might be joined and passed on to a single heir as a conjoined—but not combined—estate, or parents' estates might be held separate and passed on to either of two children. In a family with several children, lesser or non *cacicazgo* land and movable property could be joined, but individual *cacicazgos* were viewed as indivisible. Marriage was a requirement for succession to title, but *cacicazgos* were held individually by the contracting parties. Residence was ambilocal, *cacique* couples maintaining multiple residences and settling at whichever locality they deemed most advantageous. Although the Spanish administrative and judicial system imposed a male bias on the system of inheritance, women as well as men inherited *cacicazgos* throughout the Colonial period. *Cacicas* of such places as Tututepec, Nochixtlan, Tejupan, Tlaxiaco, Achiutla, and Teposcolula were among the wealthiest and most influential people in Oaxaca.[59]

Native population declined precipitously between 1540 and the first quarter of the seventeenth century, but no perceptible alteration in settlement patterns or social organization occurred between the 1540s and late Colonial times. The basic Colonial pattern had been established by 1550, and neither population fluctuation nor economic change appears to have had much effect on settlement, family organization or size, kinship reckoning, marriage, postmarital residence, or intergroup relations. Analysis of nine-teenth-century data, in fact, suggests strongly that these patterns persisted through Colonial and into Republican times.

Settlement, Social Class, and Ethnicity

Mixtec communities served as the stage upon which Colonial social life was enacted. The small *pueblos* and *estancias* were socially and economically homogeneous settlements occupied almost exclusively by Mixtecs. A large group of commoners and a very few *principales*—perhaps only a single family—constituted the population of the outlying settlements.

Social diversification and stratification were most evident in the capital centers, or *cabeceras*. Situated in the central precinct, with its plaza, church, administrative offices, and principal places of business, were the highest-status Mixtecs, the *cacique* and wealthier *principales*, and upper-status Spanish businessmen and administrators and their families. Attached to each of these households were a few Mixtec servants and, quite often, African slaves. The friars usually resided in a *casa religiosa*, or monastery, but many also owned houses in the central precinct of the larger centers and/or agricultural lands or livestock *estancias* in the countryside.

Lying adjacent to the central precinct of large communities, such as Teposcolula, Yanhuitlan, Coixtlahuaca, or Tlaxiaco, was a zone populated by a few Spanish or *mestizo* tradesmen, artisans, and skilled laborers, and several Mixtec *principales*. Here also were Mixtec commoners of relatively advanced social status. Some were attached to business enterprises in the center; others functioned as mediators or brokers between higher-ranking Mixtecs and Spaniards and the Mixtec common class.

Although many Mixtecs resided in the capital centers, the mass of Mixtec commoners resided in the *barrios* and in the outlying *estancias*. All of the *estancias* or *sujetos* of such important centers as Yanhuitlan, Teposcolula, Tlaxiaco, Nochi-xtlan, Chalcatongo or Achiutla were engaged in full-time farming in sur-rounding fields. Some residents also performed services for higher-status Spaniards, *mestizos*, or Mixtecs or were engaged in the production of textiles, clothing, baskets, candles, wood or metal items, pottery, and other consum-able goods. Still others processed plant and animal resources or carried on commercial activities. Blacksmiths, butchers, cobblers, leather workers, brick makers, and traders and others populated the countryside. Many commoners made their living by a combination of these pursuits. The relatively small numbers of *mestizos* living in Mixtec communities tended to follow pursuits closely associated with the Mixtec sector or were involved in shopkeeping, trading, mining, or animal husbandry. All subject communities owed tribute and services to the *cabecera* of the community and to their *cacique*.

Social differences were clearly related to differences in wealth and access to productive resources. The names of wealthy and influential Spanish families appear repeatedly in the notarial records from the late sixteenth century to the end of the Colonial period. They were involved in countless transactions in land, slaves, livestock, mines, raw and processed goods, loans and mortgages, wills and inventories. Recorded transfers of property found in Teposcolula attest to the great wealth and the extensive economic interests and holdings of many Spanish residents of the Mixteca.

The estates of the sixteenth-century Mixtec *caciques* of Yanhuitlan, Teposcolula, Tlaxiaco, Nochixtlan, and Tejupan were valued at hundreds of thousands of *pesos*, as befitted their social station, political power, and economic importance. Although the status of the *caciques* declined after 1600, they continued to possess great wealth and power to the end of the Colonial period. Their wealth in goods, lands, privileges, and services was exceeded by no one, even affluent Spaniards. Between 1665 and 1725, Teposcolula *caciques* Francisco Pimentel y Guzmán and his son and successor, Agustín Carlos Pimentel y Guzmán, controlled vast estates. They held farmlands, grazing lands, houses, and livestock; made large donations to religious foundations; and regularly rented and sold properties.

The Mixteca *cacique* families of Guzmán, Mendoza, Pimentel, Velasco, Villagómez, Alvarado, and Arellano constituted a native landed gentry from the sixteenth century until the end of the Colonial period, and as revealed through the meticulous studies of John Monaghan, the influence, vast holdings, and complex legal maneuvering of many of these families continued long after Independence. Other *cacique* families, although less wealthy and influential than those mentioned above, were well to do in comparison with Mixtecs or less affluent Spaniards and *mestizos*. About three hundred cases involving *cacique* families in the Archivo Histórico del Poder Judicial del Estado de Oaxaca and hundreds more in the Archivo General de la Nación reveal a vast, tangled skein of land and property suits, claims to title, inheritance and succession matters, grants of licenses and privileges, rentals and sales of property, loans and mortgages, dealings in goods and livestock, and trade and other business enterprises.

Estates of common-class Mixtecs contrast markedly with those belonging to Spaniards and *caciques*. Examination of many wills in Mixteco and in Spanish reveal individual holdings, as well as patterns of inheritance. Most Mixtecs left only a simple house, a few furnishings and personal items, such as clothing or kitchen utensils, a small piece of land, and perhaps an animal or two. Some, however, such as María Sihueyo of Yanhuitlan and Domingo Ramos of Yucuita, left money, tools, clothing, feathers, and larger animals. Although common Mixtecs were treated fairly before the law, it is undeniable that their economic circumstances were less than ideal. They were caught up in a pervasive system of economic and social inequality that had existed in pre-Hispanic times and persisted through the Colonial period into the modern era.

An active traffic in African slaves was carried on in the Mixteca throughout the Colonial period. Spanish civilians, merchants, officials, and priests, as well as aristocratic Mixtecs, bought, sold, and held slaves. Slave activity is well documented in the Teposcolula Judicial Archive by hundreds of sales contracts, most especially notable during the period 1563 to 1750. Slaves also figured in dowries and heritable estates. Africans were more numerous in the lowland areas of the Mixteca Costa, in Cuicatlan-Teotitlan, and in other warmer areas, where they were utilized in sugar production. Oaxaca City was a major center for slave trading, and most blacks in the Mixteca came into the area and left it with traders or owners with primary residence in the city.

The Colonial social system was characterized by a high level of direct interaction between Mixtecs and Spanish administrators, religious leaders, merchants, traders, miners, *encomenderos*, travelers, and residents. Social status corresponded with economic function. Spanish merchants and clergymen served a vital role in the integration of the native economic system into the international system, and even from the Mixtec perspective, they became a necessary component of Mixtec society. The radical extension of native economy and the articulation of local regions and societies into the broader world would not have occurred without this mediation.

Although the impact of Spanish settlement and policy on the Mixteca was great, traditional patterns of social intercourse among native populations were not seriously altered. What was new was the social confrontation with a politically dominant group of foreigners. Surprisingly, however, the biethnic hierarchical structure characterizing Spanish-Indian relations elsewhere in Spanish America did not develop in the Mixteca. The persistence of, and toleration for, many traditional Mixtecs to participate in the broader economy, and the genuine efforts of the Dominicans and most administrators to protect the rights of Mixtecs and frequently to intervene on their behalf, promoted successful interethnic adaptation. A reasonably effective administrative-judicial system also provided a means for resolving conflicts that otherwise might have culminated in violence or in the formation of pervasive opposition between the two groups.

Exhaustive review of massive documentation in the local, state, and national archives of Mexico render it abundantly clear that the often idealized peasant revolution was never a feature of Mixtec Colonial society. Minor uprisings occurred occasionally, but organized political revolts or social movements did not. The organization and, from all indications, the attitude and motivation were lacking—conflicts developed horizontally between adjoining communities, not hierarchically between socially stratified status groups. Native political movements or religious revitalization known to result from disadvantageous circumstances in other areas of the world did not develop in the Mixteca. The need to rise and throw off the yoke of Spanish authority either was not widely felt or was not effectively articulated by a charismatic native spokesman. By the end of the sixteenth century, the Mixtecs were part of Colonial society.

THE MIXTEC COMMUNITY UNDER SPANISH INFLUENCE

Initial contact between native peoples and Europeans occurred in the 1520s. Effective penetration by Spanish administrative officials, *encomenderos*, and Catholic priests did not begin until the second half of the decade, when important changes began to occur.

In an effort to bring about more effective subjugation, administration, exploitation, and Christianization of the Mixtec, Spanish authorities introduced several changes in the patterns of native settlement. These processes were set in motion after 1530 and continued in operation during the remainder of the sixteenth century. Some settlements were relocated, others remained in aboriginal locations, and others were congregated into larger collectivities. After about 1580 there was a solidification of settlement that was to remain in effect until recent times.

The civic-ceremonial center remained the pivotal component of the community, but as new construction was instituted under Spanish auspices, a rectangular grid, or checkerboard arrangement of intersecting streets and building alignments, was introduced. A civic-religious plaza was placed at the center of the settlement, and streets emerged in four directions from the plaza. Probably there was an increasing concentration of settlement in the center as a result of the new alignment. In the fringes of settlement, as in the modern *cabecera*, buildings tended to occupy a rather random distribution peripheral to the rectangular plan of the central core.

Colonial Yucundaa-Teposcolula represents a major early effort to introduce Spanish urban planning to the Mixteca and to New Spain. The Spanish plan of an urban nucleus was superimposed on the traditional city plan. This involved the placement of a church and monastery on the eastern side of a town plaza, a spacious plaza or *atrio* immediately to the south in front of the church complex, retention of the pre-Hispanic royal palace complex on the western side of the plaza, the rededication of the ancient civic-ceremonial complex on the far north of the plaza, and the modification of an existing royal-class structure to serve as the locus of the newly introduced native governmental council, or *cabildo*. These new Spanish-influenced structures and related developments are described in the various publications of the Alfredo Harp Helú Yucundaa Archaeological Project and remain under intensive investigation.[60]

The form and function of hamlets were little affected by the Spanish occupation. They were allowed to retain the random cluster arrangement of pre-Conquest times. Indeed, this is a pattern that is seen in the *ranchos* of the modern Mixtec *municipio*. Little or no effort was made by Spanish officials to realign the hamlets. The community center, or *cabecera*, rather than the dependencies, figured in plans for reorganization. The attention of the population of the hamlets continued to be focused on the community center, where were located the market, the mission and the clergy, Spanish administrative and judicial authority, and the traditional native ruler who continued to be recognized and to perform his role much as he had before the Conquest. Tribute and labor services continued to be delivered to the center as in pre-Conquest times.

In various instances, ceremonial precincts were moved from locations adjacent to the civic center into the center itself. In actual practice the ancient ceremonial center was abandoned and was replaced by the Catholic mission. The ceremonial unit and the civic and commercial units were combined into a central plaza complex which has characterized the *cabecera* throughout the Spanish and Mexican national period to the present time.

With the arrival of the Spaniards, the church and civic offices were placed at the center of the town. The palace, *ayuntamiento*, and civic offices were positioned on one or another side of the great central plaza, with the main church and associated buildings taking up position on the opposite side. All was integrated into a civic-religious plaza complex that persists everywhere in Mexico and is the pattern in modern Jaltepec, Nochixtlan, Yanhuitlan, Teposcolula, Tamazulapan, Tlaxiaco, Chachoapan, Yucuita, Tejupan, and Coixtlahuaca, and in dozens of other communities in the Mixteca.

The civic-religious plaza with an enveloping residential zone is unquestionably the modal pattern of the modern *cabecera* of the Mixteca Alta. The subject *ranchos*, quite naturally, are well removed from the center itself. Under the Spaniards, ceremonial religion was made convenient by the placement of the church, the most impressive piece of architecture on the horizon, in the midst of the population center. Wherever possible, small chapels were constructed in outlying spots, possibly to coincide with ancient shrines or temples. These can yet be seen in a number of locations throughout the Mixteca Alta and Baja (with notable examples at Tilantongo, Nochixtlan, Yanhuitlan, and Huajuapan). The result of one such attempt to "rechristen" an old religious center may be in evidence at Tilantongo, where the friars sought to take advantage of the "good will" reposing in an ancient religious center. Modern Mitla in the Valley of Oaxaca affords something of a parallel example, where the church occupies a seat directly over and among ancient ceremonial structures, while the population and civic center is well removed from the church.

Community lands continued to be utilized for agriculture, for hunting, and for collecting. For the first time, however, community lands were devoted to the herding and grazing of livestock, particularly sheep and goats. New crops, increased requirements for production of native and European crops, livestock, minerals, cochineal dyestuff, and silk, and the introduction of superior iron tools, technology, and animal power allowed a far more effective realization of the productive potential of community lands. The result was an unprecedented economic florescence in the Mixteca Alta around the middle of the sixteenth century.

Archaeological survey and early Colonial documentation indicate that numerous major communities of that time were in the locations they presently occupy, or nearly so. There were down-slope relocations of many communities, such as Nochixtlan and Teposcolula, and the *cabecera*, or central precinct, of Yanhuitlan, Yucuita, Chachoapan, Santiago Huajolotitlan, San Pedro y San Pablo Tequixtepec, San Pedro Cántaros Coxcaltepec, and many others, but these were sites directly adjacent to aboriginal locations. Other communities— like Tututepec on the Mixteca Costa, Tilantongo, Cuquila, sixteenth-century Achiutla, Coixtlahuaca (with considerable realignment), Tejupan (also with realignment), Yolomecatl, San Juan Teposcolula, San Jerónimo Sosola, and so on—remained in their aboriginal locations.

Serious efforts at concentration (*congregación*) of native settlements in the Mixteca Alta began at mid-century and were reintensified in the 1590s. These attempts were made primarily for the benefit of the clergy and for greater ease of administration, and in numerous cases to relocate towns closer to water sources. Because of complaints registered with the vice-regal authorities and the reticence of the small communities, the majority of such recommended moves were never consummated. Such communities as Yucuita, Huautla, and Coyotepec in the vicinity of Nochixtlan and a number of communities in the vicinity of Yanhuitlan and Teposcolula apparently won permanent stays of congregation orders.

In 1599 there was a massive attempt to congregate communities in and around Tlaxiaco and San Mateo Peñasco of the Mixteca Alta.[61] Clearly, the small communities in general were not eager to move, but if a move was necessary, they had clear preferences where they wished to go. Those in the area east of Tlaxiaco and north of Chalcatongo, for example, wanted to be congregated at San Mateo Peñasco with its good lands, climate, and waters. Other areas were not acceptable, and the Spaniards resisted the urge to go against native wishes and did not force the issue, especially for communities lying far away from the *cabecera*.

Subsequent to recent survey and observation in and around Tlaxiaco, it is virtually a certainty that this is a congregated community made up of perhaps a dozen surrounding smaller communities.[62] Tlaxiaco is located in a narrow but fertile valley watered by a year-round river. Archaeological survey of the town center reveals no significant Postclassic remains, whereas in the surrounding area there are numerous sites containing Postclassic remains and, usually, a very few European-style ceramics. Once the great Dominican church-monastery was constructed, it appears that every effort was made to draw the native population of the surrounding countryside into the center. Probably these resettlements occurred between 1550 and 1580 and apparently were accomplished with little resistance or conflict. Recent salvage excavations by INAH in the vicinity of the church, near the town center, turned up post-Conquest burials of Mixtec nobles, who wore brass buttons on their coats and had other indications of an early Colonial date.

In contrast to Tlaxiaco, the communities of Guadalupe Tixá, San Miguel Tixá, San Felipe Ixtapa, Santo Tomás Tecolotitlan, and Santa Catarina Delgado are five small communities within a few minutes' walk of each other and located on a system of hills and lower slopes approximately five kilometers west of San Pedro y San Pablo Teposcolula. The settlements sit astride the major ancient, and present-day, routes from Teposcolula to Tlaxiaco and beyond and from Teposcolula north to Tamazulapan and Huajuapan and south to Achiutla, Chalcatongo, and, ultimately, to the Mixteca Costa. These currently occupied sites are in their aboriginal locations. The cluster looks very much like Tlaxiaco would have appeared had it not been congregated.

In the aftermath of the Spanish occupation of the Mixteca Alta, the traditional community center underwent realignment; the ceremonial precinct was combined with the civic and commercial center and relocated as part of the pivotal plaza complex, and new crops, new industries, and more effective technology brought about a notable upturn in native economy at mid-century. Social and political ties, traditional means of production and consumption of most consumer goods, many basic technologies, diet, basic family organization, and concepts regarding the nature of existence represent continuities in traditional Mixtec culture. These served to dampen the effectiveness of external influences on the total society and to impede the processes of acculturation.

The high degree of social interaction between the hamlets and the center seems not to have diminished in the least as a result of the Spanish Conquest, and except for the changes already mentioned, the sixteenth-century community, in slightly altered form, exists today in the modern Mixtec *municipio*. The old native rulers, the regular clergy, the tribute and labor service systems, and the flourishing economy of the middle and late sixteenth century have disappeared, but the post-Conquest community that has been described remains a major organizing influence in Mixtec life.

6

The Colonial Mixtec Kingdom-*Cacicazgo*

Pre-Hispanic *cacicazgos*—for which we prefer the Mixtec term *yuhuitayu* to denote the institutional form as it existed prior to Spanish contact—were small states operating within a universe of otherwise similar small states. Colonial *cacicazgos*, in contrast, were semi-independent polities deriving from pre-Hispanic antecedents but modified so as to be compatible with Spanish Colonial government, religious institutions and objectives, and new economic demands. As a formal institution, the *cacicazgo* persisted well into the 1700s and provided the organizational template for Spanish administrative activity. Our sources of information now derive almost entirely from post-Hispanic documentary materials, most of these written in Spanish but some being complementary sources written in Mixteco.[1]

During post-Conquest times, frequent conflicts arose over *cacicazgos*—oftentimes concerning matters of royal succession, but in other cases taking the form of boundary disputes among *cacicazgos* or claims for autonomy by former subject communities. Many of these conflicts found their way to the Spanish courts and now constitute a valuable segment of the legal documentation preserved in Mexican and Spanish archives.[2] Examination of this material reveals the principal features of the royal institution in the Mixteca, and the rights, obligations, and prerogatives of *caciques*; their sources of wealth, status, and heritable properties; the rules for and actual means of royal succession; and information on the two best-documented *cacicazgos*: Yanhuitlan and the combined kingdom of Teposcolula-Tututepec. We end this chapter with consideration of Colonial-era women who were recognized as legitimate *cacicas* in their own right, as well as being significant regional entrepreneurs and power brokers.

Before considering the native system of governance, it is necessary to review the Spanish end of the political equation. Colonial government as adapted to the Mixteca incorporated both European and native customs.[3] Spanish objectives were to be achieved, but local communities also had to be governed. By the last quarter of the sixteenth century, local, regional, and crown levels of government were effectively articulated, and a broad spectrum of judicial, administrative, and economic needs were being met. Once in place, this multilevel system was little changed for the remainder of the Colonial period, and it provided the foundation for state and local governance in modern Mexico.

THE SPANISH COLONIAL SYSTEM

The multilevel Colonial system included the imperial government (the Crown), the Colonial Virreinato (vice-regency)-Audiencia of New Spain, the political provinces (*alcaldías mayores* and *corregimientos*) of the Mixteca, and local community governments (*cacicazgos, cabildos, repúblicas,* and *ayuntamientos*). The nature of political institutions at the imperial (Corona y Consejo de las Indias) and Colonial levels (Virreinato y Audiencia Real) are authoritatively treated by several Latin-American historians.[4] Government and legal institutions at the local level, however, have received less attention, although these were the levels where most Mixtecs encountered Spanish administration.[5]

The Spanish Crown, although obviously committed to the economic exploitation and ideological conversion of native peoples, was also concerned with governing them well and seeing to their welfare. In the effort to control the Mixtec natives with as little disruption as possible and yet to accomplish imperial objectives, certain aspects of traditional government were tolerated and even encouraged. In the former empires of the Culhua-Mexica[6] and the Purepecha,[7] the largest, most complex, and highly evolved of native Mexican political systems, the power and positions of the ruling caste were curtailed, and Spanish institutions and administrators were substituted. In the Mixteca, however, many elements of traditional native government endured. *Caciques* continued to be recognized and supported as the highest-ranking social and political figures in their domains, and they continued to maintain traditional prerogatives and to exercise the powers of government long after the Conquest. We therefore begin our discussion of Spanish Colonial government at the local level and then work our way up the administrative hierarchy.

Governance in the Provinces

Mixtec local or community government derived from an ancient indigenous base. As noted above, *caciques, principales*, and a few functionaries of noble or common status continued to perform political roles during the early Colonial period. While exercising authority over local populations, the leaders were simultaneously incorporated into the Spanish political and economic systems through government, tribute and labor service, *encomienda*, religious conversion and administration, and production and commerce.[8]

During the sixteenth century, the *gobernador* of the typical native community was either the *cacique* or a higher-ranking *principal* (native nobility).[9] The other four or five highest offices were also held by important *principales*. The formal council and a group of *pasados* (older nobles serving in an advisory capacity) were referred to as the *república* of a community. This corporation served as the effective government of the larger communities and was recognized as the official representative body in both internal and external affairs.[10]

By 1550, however, the Spanish-style *cabildo* (town council) had been introduced to most Mixtec communities and was becoming the main institution of local government in Mexico. During the sixteenth and seventeenth centuries, key positions in *cabildos* were occupied by *caciques* and *principales*. It was not until the eighteenth century that commoners were regularly elected to office. At the same time, *caciques* became less active in politics and devoted more attention to retaining their traditional standing, prerogatives, and personal estates.

Mixtec *cabildos* were popularly elected councils composed of a *gobernador* (responsible for the natives, the peace of the jurisdiction, the supervision of religious functions, and the collection of tribute); two *alcaldes* (who would adjudicate minor infractions and disputes, but in the dependencies they were analogous to the *gobernadores*); three to four *regidores* (councilmen); the *alguacil mayor* (chief of police); a *mayordomo* (overseer of community property, public works, and mandatory community labor, or *tequio*); an *escribano* (court clerk or notary public); and a varying number of minor functionaries and persons on hand to keep the peace.

The *cabildo* was the lowest official level of native government recognized by the Crown. Interference from *alcaldes mayores, corregidores, encomenderos*, and church officials in local affairs was loudly protested before viceregal or

Audiencia officials, and although not entirely prevented, vigorously discouraged and penalized. Once established in the sixteenth century, the *cabildo* continued as the primary organ of local government until the end of the Colonial period and survives as the modern *ayuntamiento* of hundreds of Mixteca communities.

Governance by Crown Authorities

From early Colonial times to the final decade of the eighteenth century, the effective mechanism of royal civil government at the regional or provincial level was the *alcaldía mayor* or *corregimiento*. *Alcaldes mayores* and *corregidores* stood next in line in the political chain of command from the viceroy and the Audiencia of New Spain. They were the chief executive and judicial officers in the Colonial provinces.[11] Although the powers of Spanish magistrates were not always clearly defined, in general they had broad authority to intervene in local matters not explicitly prohibited by the Crown or viceregal authorities. Besides political and judicial functions, they were responsible for the care, protection, and good treatment of native peoples. Such broadly defined authority allowed and encouraged intervention in nearly every facet of native life.

In the Mixteca, *alcaldes mayores* tended to have authority over larger territories, or *provincias*, as well as capital centers, or *cabeceras*, while the functions of *corregidores* were focused on a single community. When Teposcolula and Yanhuitlan provinces were combined in the final decades of the sixteenth century, for example, the *alcalde mayor* governed from and resided in Teposcolula, while the administration of law and government in Yanhuitlan was delegated to a *teniente,* or lieutenant of the *alcalde mayor.* Teposcolula's *alcalde mayor* also had civil and criminal jurisdiction over Yanhuitlan and at least fifty other communities in the province of Teposcolula, many of which, including Tejupan, Tilantongo, Nochixtlan, and Soyaltepec, had their own *corregidores*.

The Colonial magistrates were powerful but by no means despotic or totally self-serving. Mixtecs and Spaniards were quick to lodge complaints with viceregal officials whenever magistrates stepped out of line or became abusive in their personal or official activities. Additionally, *alcaldes mayores* and *corregidores* were subject to judicial review, or *residencia*, at the termination of their tours of duty and could be prosecuted for crimes committed while they were in office. Such mechanisms, coupled with a personal sense of propriety, morality, and responsibility found in most magistrates, served as guides to administrative behavior and as checks on the boundaries of permissible action. Some magistrates were well liked, and in several cases subject communities petitioned the crown for extensions of tenure or reappointment.

In 1786 the reformative *intendencia* system was introduced to New Spain.[12] Oaxaca became one of twelve *intendencias* in the colony, and an *intendente* (or *gobernador intendente*) was appointed to head the new political entity. The *intendencia* was subdivided into *partidos* (more formalized versions of the old *provincias*) and headed by *subdelegados* occupying the offices and performing the functions of the old *alcaldes mayores*. Although this innovation introduced an additional level of government to the traditional system, there was little discernible alteration in the operation of the magisterial office. Traditional political institutions, legal procedures, and processes of administrative action, implementation, and enforcement as they affected Mixtec communities remained stable until the end of the Colonial period.

Parapolitical Activity

During the Colonial period, political activities were conducted through formal offices and channels of government (*cabildo, alcaldía mayor,* and *virreinato-audiencia*), but individuals who were not officially involved in government also played active political roles. Clearly the *caciques,* the direct descendants and heirs of the Mixtec ruling families of pre-Hispanic times, whether or not serving as governors, influenced decisions of the *cabildo*. Elected officials would come and go, but the *cacique* ruled for life. *Caciques* also served as effective power brokers between Colonial and provincial authorities, *encomenderos,* and the clergy, on the one hand, and native communities, on the other.[13]

Also working effectively in the background were the *principales,* the traditional nobility. *Principales* not only were consulted but insisted on participation in political matters and were included as signatories to official acts of the *cabildo*, petitions to the Crown, and litigation involving their communities. Among other things, they comprised the recruitment pool from which functionaries were chosen, and it is clear that they possessed substantial power in influencing decisions and in directing the governance of Mixtec communities.

In the Spanish-native form of *cabildo* government, women had no official political roles. But it would be misleading to conclude that women were not involved in politics. They most assuredly were. It is quite clear that high-status *cacicas* were consulted in the decision-making process, that they directly influenced the *cabildos*, and that they were skilled in political manipulation. Since they were mothers to sons who would eventually be important political figures, they had a significant role in shaping the thinking of future decision-makers and in positioning them to advantage (as discussed below).

The Spanish clergy are another group often observed in the political background, educating natives in the means of gaining access to the Colonial political-legal system. Spanish clergy taught natives to utilize the system for such ends as resolution of persisting conflicts; relief from excessive taxation or labor requirements; protection from abuses by Spanish officials, clergy, military, or civilians; regulation of economic activities; and civil and criminal justice. Friars were often called to testify in important cases involving Mixtecs or Mixtecs and Spaniards.[14] The friars were generally respected by both Spaniards and natives, and their participation was highly valued. Their role in decision making and native government and in promoting the development and utilization of the multilevel political-judicial system should not be underestimated.

The Kingdom-*Cacicazgo*

The Mixtec kingdom-*cacicazgo*, an institution whose development we trace over a period of some 1,500 years, was further elaborated after the Spanish Conquest. It was in the initial decades of the Colonial period that native concepts and customs were articulated with Spanish expectations and objectives, adding new layers onto the previously discussed *ñuu*, *yuhuitayu*, and the Spanish-influenced *cacicazgo*.

We should make a few clear distinctions at the outset. First, the Colonial *cacicazgo* was not synonymous with the community. The community was a territorial, demographic, and administrative unit composed of a center (*cabecera*), lands devoted to farming and collecting, ceremonial spaces, and in most instances one or more subsidiary settlements (*sujetos*) and, of course, their residents. The *cacicazgo* was related to a given territory and its settlement or settlements, but included the combined duties, prerogatives, services, goods and properties, and the prestige, power, and influence derived from and pertaining to the title and position of native ruler-*cacique*.

Second, recent investigations reveal that communities were customarily considered by residents, by *caciques*, and by the nobility to *belong* to the *cacique*. That is to say, the community was a component of the *cacicazgo*. The *cacique* owned the community, and the residents had the privilege of working the *cacicazgo* lands and to engage in ritual and economic activities sponsored by the rulers. This seems quite clear in the sixteenth and seventeenth centuries in such polities as Yanhuitlan, Teposcolula, Coixtlahuaca, Tejupan, and Tututepec, but this sort of suzerainty persisted in some instances until the 1700s.

Third, the *cacicazgo* was a changing, fluent, expanding, and contracting entity, marked by accretion and attrition and functional adjustments over time. The content of a *cacicazgo* was shaped and conditioned by the personality of the *cacique* in interaction with a massive commoner class that the leader sought to exploit; the local nobility, which lent support and through which the *cacique* ruled; the rulers of other kingdoms; and the fortunes of marriage between holders of separate *cacicazgos*. After the Conquest, the Spanish Colonial system of governance and the new economic orientations provided new dimensions to the institution.

The Royal Patrimony

In 1580 legal proceedings were conducted to validate Don Gabriel de Guzmán's title as *cacique* of Yanhuitlan, his right to receive labor service and tribute from the native Mixtecs of his *cacicazgo*, and the legitimacy of his claims to specific pieces of land as part of his *cacique* patrimony.[15] Sixteen witnesses, most of them of advanced age, were summoned to give testimony in response to an interrogatory of twelve questions that set forth the points Don Gabriel wished to establish. Several of the questions dealt with his direct descent from pre-Conquest and early post-Conquest rulers of the *cacicazgo*, the regency of his uncle during his minority, and his marriage to a woman of *cacique* rank. Other questions considered significant components of the *cacicazgo*.

Question 10 concerned the prerogatives and authority of the *caciques*. As was customary in such *probanzas* (proofs), testimony of the sixteen witnesses was purely in the affirmative. The response of Domingo Lopez, aged seventy, a native from Yanhuitlan, was typical:

> . . . the witness stated that it is certain and well known, as declared in the question, that in the time of the infidelity of the Indians, the natives of this *pueblo* of Yanhuitlan and its subjects recognized their *caciques* and *señores* in every way and served and respected them in everything, providing them with personal services, working fields for the sustenance of their houses, and gave them great quantities of clothing, precious stones, precious feathers from Guatemala, fowl, and all that they asked and commanded as *señores absolutos* of the said *pueblo* and its province, until the arrival of the Spaniards. Since that time the *señores* and *caciques* have been presented with an assessment of what they could receive, and the present witness has seen that for this reason the *caciques* are in great need.[16]

Witness responses clearly indicate that recognition of the *caciques* as *señores absolutos* and unquestioning obedience to them constituted a fundamental feature of pre-Conquest Yanhuitlan. Question 10 also compares the labor services and tributes in kind that pre-Conquest and Colonial *caciques* of Yanhuitlan received from the natives of the *cacicazgo*. The labor obligation included personal services for the *cacique's* household and the cultivation of fields for his sustenance and support. The interrogatory specifically mentions clothing, precious stones, Guatemala feathers (probably quetzal plumage), and fowl as items of tribute. After the Conquest these sources of *cacique* income were progressively reduced.

Subsequent questions took this general complaint further, regarding the post-Conquest reductions in labor service, and for our purposes serves to illustrate a significant feature of aboriginal custom. The declaration made by Domingo de Guzmán, aged sixty-seven, is illustrative, referencing Don Gabriel's grandparents, "who in their time had in the patrimony of the said *señorío* many *barrios* with Indians for domestic service. But when the Spaniards came to this New Spain, they removed these from the said *caciques*, and from others, and registered them so that they would pay tribute like the rest of the people, notwithstanding the fact, as the witness had always seen, that the said *barrios* and the Indians belonging to them were known to belong to the said patrimony." The witness further stated that "with the pestilences and mortalities" subsequent to the Conquest there were now many fewer natives available for household duties.[17]

The 1580 testimony shows that the *barrios* of Yanhuitlan were pre-Hispanic in origin and represent a native concept. *Barrio* is of course a Spanish term. The corresponding term in Mixtec would be *siqui*, *siña*, and *dzini* as subunits of the municipality.[18] The concept was native, but under the Spanish occupation there must have been significant alteration. Employing an equation of 4 people per *casado*, or tributary unit (the original question referenced 309 *casados*), would amount to 1,236 people residing in fourteen *barrios* that were said to be for the exclusive personal service of the *cacique* of Yanhuitlan in Colonial times. The number of such individuals probably exceeded 2,000 in pre-Conquest times. These several hundred individuals dedicated to his personal service constituted a part of the royal patrimony.

Caciques were often at odds with Spanish officials wanting to place these individuals on the tribute rolls. Don Gabriel claimed that the natives of the fourteen *barrios* listed in his memorial should not be subject to the labor and tribute assessments imposed by the Spaniards on the rest of the *pueblo* population.

Similar claims for exemption from post-Conquest assessments of tribute and labor service were made by *caciques* for Mixtecs serving as tenant farmers (called *terrazgueros*) on lands of their *cacicazgo* patrimony. They sought to justify such exemption on the ground that the *terrazgueros* had not been subject to tribute in pre-Conquest times. These claims were resisted by royal officials and *encomenderos* for the obvious reason that tribute exemption would naturally reduce the number of tributary units in Crown and *encomienda* towns.

These kinds of disputes further underscore the fact that certain properties and rights to labor service could not be legally alienated by a *cacique*, explaining in part the application of the term *mayorazgo* (entailed estate) to describe the Colonial *cacicazgos*. It should be noted that a *cacique* might acquire personal property in land, livestock, and other goods apart from *cacicazgo* property, which could be sold or donated or bequeathed by final testament. Entrepreneurial activity was certainly a *cacique* prerogative, as is shown below.

Yanhuitlan

During the legal proceedings of 1580, Don Gabriel filed a long list of real estate to which he claimed title as part of the royal patrimony of his *cacicazgo*. This list included "... the large houses, where the *alcalde mayor* formerly lived ... the new arched houses made for Don Gabriel de Guzmán ... lands and fields belonging to the *cacicazgo* [among them] a field called 'Yodozooconuu.' Another field called 'Yuchadzaa.' Another field called 'Saayuugh.'" This list of fields (*sementeras*) located within the *cabecera* numbered 46 in all. Numerous other fields were located in more distant *estancias* of Yanhuitlan and the distinct *pueblos* of Apoala, Patla Ixtlauaca (Yodocono), Etlatongo, and Notzixtlan (Nochixtlan), numbering 102 in all. The testimony in the 1580 *probanza* affirmed Don Gabriel's title as *cacique* and his personal dominion over all lands named in the document.[19]

At the time of succession of Francisco de Guzmán as *cacique* of Yanhuitlan in 1591, a *memoria* of lands pertaining to the *cacicazgo* was executed at the direction of Spanish officials.[20] This account differed considerably from that of 1580. Thirty-five plots of land were claimed in and around Yanhuitlan, and twelve in the *estancia* of Tecomatlan. The *memoria* also listed thirty tracts in other communities: Etlatongo, Tonaltepec, Tlaxila, Apoala, and Tecondeye. Regardless of how one construes the documentation and changing extent of *cacique* holdings, the *cacicazgo* of Yanhuitlan in the last years of the sixteenth century was very large. It is likewise certain that most of these holdings remained in *cacique* hands until the late 1700s, when there was considerable erosion of *cacicazgo* lands as communities like Tecomatlan made good their claims over pieces of the old patrimony.[21]

Teposcolula

The Teposcolula *cacicazgo* of the 1560s was comparable to Yanhuitlan in importance, in lands, houses and resources, movable property, privilege, and in the prestige and power of its *caciques*. In 1569 the *cacicazgo* was transferred from Don Felipe de Austria to Doña Catalina de Peralta and her husband, Diego de Mendoza, *cacique* of Tamazulapan.[22] It was at this time that the most complete listing of *cacicazgo* lands and houses can be reconstructed. All of the following properties were transferred between November 8 and 18, 1569: "a house of many rooms and halls in the *cabecera* of Teposcolula in front of the monastery," along with five other houses in this vicinity, one of which must be the Casa de la Cacica, which is partially preserved to this day. These houses together constituted the *tecpan*, or royal compound, of the *caciques*. Acts of possession included placing *petates* (palm mats) and chairs upon which Doña Catalina and Don Diego sat in the main room of each house, opening and closing doors and windows, unlocking and locking doors, ejecting people, and throwing out clothing and personal items from the houses.

The list of royal properties being transferred from Don Felipe to Doña Catalina and Don Diego is immensely long, and only representative portions are given here. The listing includes "a great field where maize is planted in the plain of San Pablo of this said *pueblo* of Tepozcolula, across from the monastery where the river passes that is called in the *misteca* language Ytonocuyoo . . ." and continues in this manner before mentioning that these lands pertained to the *cacicazgo* "for twelve lives of *caciques*" or perhaps six hundred years.[23] There is further reference to other lands in the *estancias* of Teposcolula, to the *maceguales* and *naturales* (Mixtec commoners) who worked those lands and the produce given in tribute, the names of the lands in Mixteco and still other lands whose names were unknown to the witness, and lands once belonging to Tilantongo and Tlaxiaco but now pertaining to Teposcolula. And last, the list included many orchards of fruit trees from Spain with their precise locations and place names. This 1569 *probanza* and act of possession is particular in its details and includes information of considerable interest to students of the Mixteca, and not least to the modern residents of Teposcolula, who in some instances are direct descendants of persons mentioned in the document.

Tututepec

In 1550, when Ana Sosa was confirmed as successor to her husband Pedro de Alvarado as *cacica* of Tututepec, she had vast holdings.[24] She held twelve subject communities, meaning that she owned the lands and was entitled to exact tribute and personal services from the residents of those properties (*estancias*). She also possessed thirty-one orchards, or *huertas*, of *cacao*; great stretches of farming and grazing lands; highly productive saltworks; *lagunas* rich in fish, game, and shellfish; and numerous houses, including the *tecpan*, or palace complex. Doña Ana's holdings made her the largest landowner in the Mixteca Costa in the middle to late sixteenth century. Before her death, Doña Ana ceded the Tututepec *cacicazgo* to her son, Don Melchior, and by well-established principles of royal succession the title eventually went in 1657 to Don Francisco Pimentel y Guzmán (governor and *cacique* of Teposcolula).[25] It is difficult to imagine that any set of properties held by native *caciques* in New Spain could have exceeded those of the Teposcolula-Tututepec combined *cacicazgos*, but this collectivity grew even larger in the eighteenth century under Don Agustín Pimentel y Guzmán.

Movable Goods

In addition to the lands that comprised the major part of the properties of their *cacicazgos*, the *caciques* of Yanhuitlan, Teposcolula, and Tututepec possessed movable goods of substantial value inherited or acquired during their years of office (some of this being *cacicazgo* property, but other items were personal acquisitions). A few examples illustrate the general pattern.

At his death in 1591, Don Gabriel de Guzmán, *cacique* of Yanhuitlan, left in movable goods fifteen hundred sheep, three horses, great quantities of worked gold and silver, precious stones, items of clothing, art and religious objects, knives, cups, plates, and other items. In his last will and testament he directed that the bulk of this property was to be sold at auction and that the proceeds, after adjustment of his debts, were to be divided equally among his heirs.[26] The total complex represents a body of merchandise that moved from a fully native inventory at the Conquest to one increasingly composed of European goods. The conversion of goods to money represents a further alteration in the material composition of the *cacicazgo*.

The last will and testament of Felipe Osorio, *cacique* of Teposcolula, written in 1563, reveals something of the movable wealth possessed by the *caciques*.[27] Don Felipe's possessions included several varieties of cotton cloth (*mantas*); three horses; various and numerous jewels, jewelry, and bells made of jade, copper, silver, and gold; feathers and other items of cloth and clothing featuring exotic plumage; boxes filled with fancy petticoats, cloth, service items from Spain, and silk; clothing with silver buttons; velvet and felt hats; jewels adorned with pearls, and so on—the list totals more than a hundred separate entries that frequently reference multiple items.

On the Mixteca Costa, Don Pedro de Alvarado, "Señor Natural" of Tututepec, had many movable possessions along with his vast holdings of property. In his *memoria* of 1550, the year of his death, many items were enumerated,[28] among them strings of precious stones and shell beads; strings of turquoise, pearl, and gold; gold earplugs; silver bells; various jewels; and a fancy mirror from Spain, among many other things listed. All of these goods passed to Don Pedro's widow, Doña Ana Sosa, in 1550, together with other jewelry, precious bird plumage, huge quantities of cotton *huipiles* and other textiles, livestock, and stores of products from his fields, saltworks, lagunas, and *huertas*, and the land, labor, and tribute holdings described above. Few if any native women of her time in Oaxaca if not all of New Spain possessed greater wealth or earning potential.

Cacique Privileges

The *cacique*, standing at the very pinnacle of native society, was accorded privileges that no other person of native birth, or even most Spaniards, could ever expect.[29] From the time of the first Christian *caciques* of Yanhuitlan until the end of the Colonial period, all were granted the rank of "Don," a title reserved in sixteenth-century Spain for the *hidalgo* or noble class. During the last quarter of the sixteenth century, Don Gabriel de Guzmán was given a permit to raise or have in his possession enormous quantities of livestock, especially sheep and horses.[30] He also wore a Spanish riding habit and bore firearms, all of which were indicative of highest rank. These privileges could be gained only by specific viceregal order in the sixteenth century.[31] Through permission of the viceroy, Don Gabriel also engaged in the profitable merchandising of European as well as native goods in Yanhuitlan.[32] The latter privilege gave him an important source of income and afforded considerable economic advantage over other merchants in the community.

Don Gabriel was without question the most influential native of Yanhuitlan, and probably the entire Mixteca, during the Spanish sixteenth century. Of comparable standing were native rulers such as Francisco de Mendoza and Felipe de Austria of Tilantongo; Pedro Osorio and Catalina de Peralta of Teposcolula and their seventeenth- and eighteenth-century successors; Francisco Saavedra and María Saavedra of Tlaxiaco and Achiutla; Pedro de Alvarado and Ana Sosa of Tututepec; Diego de Mendoza of Tamazulapan; and, in the seventeenth century, Jerónimo, Pedro, and Juana de Lara of Tejupan and Cuilapan. We turn now to the means by which these individuals came to power.

ROYAL SUCCESSION

Royal succession among the Mixtec, both before and after the Spanish Conquest, was guided by a number of traditional principles. Mixtec ruling families

were acutely aware of linear continuity and made every effort to pre-
serve the ancient tradition of succession in a direct line by carefully recording and remembering their genealogies and by vigorously defending their
ancient rights.

   In matters of succession, legitimacy was dependent upon the recognized
and legitimate marriage of the parents, both being of ruler-*cacique* rank and
caste, and the child being the recognized and legitimate offspring of the
parents. Herrera mentions these requirements and their essential implications: "For succession to the *Señorío*, the *Señor* had to marry a woman of his
own caste; the children of these inherited. . . . If the principal wife had no
children, the bastards could not inherit."[33] These were ancient customs that
persisted during the sixteenth century, confirmed by testimony in succession
cases at Yanhuitlan,[34] Teposcolula,[35] Tejupan,[36] and Tlazultepec (Tlacotepec)[37]
in the Mixteca Alta; Mixtepec,[38] Tecomastlahuaca, Juxtlahuaca, Ayusuchqui-
lacala, and Putla in the Mixteca Baja;[39] and Tututepec in the Mixteca Costa.[40]

   The manner of succession in the Mixteca was thus determined on the
basis of direct descent, that is, descent in the most direct and legitimate fashion
possible from former native rulers. This was a specific requirement in all cases
of royal succession. Without exception in the sixteenth century, any person,
male or female, seeking to exercise the role of ruler-*cacique* had to be of
ruling rank and caste. One acquired this condition only by being the son or
daughter of a father and mother who were both of ruling rank and caste. One's
bloodline had to contain an uninterrupted series of royal-caste ancestors. This
was a closed social universe that could be legally penetrated only by birth.

   After the Conquest, a Mixtec ruler might seek to confirm traditional
privilege through a series of legal confrontations, petitions, and official orders.
This customary action and the fortunate preservation of the record make it
possible to observe patterns of succession in the Colonial period. We focus
on Yanhuitlan as a well-documented example of the kingdom-*cacicazgo* in the
sixteenth century, but for a fuller understanding of the complexities of royal
succession, materials from Teposcolula and other communities are considered.

Succession at Yanhuitlan

Namahu and Cauaco were the native rulers of Yanhuitlan at the time of the
Conquest.[41] At present, we do not know who preceded them. We can find no
connection between either of these individuals and the Lord Three Monkey
whom Herrera states was killed by the Mexicans in 1506,[42] nor is there a clear
picture of the relationship between a Lord Nine House mentioned prominently in the *Códice de Yanhuitlan*[43] to either Namahu or Cauaco. The only

good documentary evidence for the existence of Nine House comes from a 1582 record that states that a Nahui Calci (a corruption of "Nine House") was once lord of all the Mixteca.[44] Caso translates Namahu as "Eight Death" and Cauaco as "One Flower." A Lord Eight Death "Tiger-Fire Serpent" appears in the *Codex Bodley* as the husband of Lady One Flower "Tiger Quechquemitl." They ruled a place shown as Feather Carpet–Jawbone–Arrow Beak. Caso believes this to be Yanhuitlan.[45]

Lord Eight Death was son of the third king of the Fourth Dynasty of Tilantongo, a person called Ten Rain "Tlaloc-Sun." Caso equates Ten Rain of the *Codex Bodley* with Xico, listed in the 1580 litigation as the father of Namahu.[46] The brother of Eight Death, a man named Yacqua, or Four Deer, was ruler of Tilantongo at the Spanish Conquest. Eight Death (Namahu) and Four Deer (Yac Qua) are the last persons to appear on the obverse of *Codex Bodley*, and Caso states that these individuals were still alive in 1533.[47] Accordinging to currently available sources, Namahu, probably a younger son, left Tilantongo in pre-Conquest times and became *cacique* of Yanhuitlan at the time of his marriage to Cauaco, who was in line for the title as a direct descendent of the rulers of Yanhuitlan.

Namahu and Cauaco ruled Yanhuitlan at the time of the Conquest but were not baptized. Cauaco survived her husband and continued to be *cacica* of Yanhuitlan until her death. Witnesses stated in 1580 that they had known both Namahu and Cauaco and they remembered Cauaco as being alive about fifty years prior to 1580.[48] In a lawsuit brought in the 1530s by the first *encomendero* of Yanhuitlan, Francisco de Las Casas, there was reference to the "Señora of Yanhuitlan," who had been visited by Juan Peleaz de Berrio, *alcalde mayor* of Antequera (Oaxaca City) in 1529.[49] Although not mentioned by name, the "Señora" most probably was Cauaco.

Namahu and Cauaco, married in accordance with native law, had five legitimate children. The oldest was María de Cocuahu.[50] María de Cocuahu (Two House) is shown in *Codex Bodley* as being the daughter of the rulers of Yanhuitlan.[51] There were four other children. Three of them became rulers at Coixtlahuaca, Tezoatlan, and Tiltepec. A fourth son, whose subsequent history is unclear, was identified by Caso as Seven Monkey "Tiger-Torch."[52]

At the death of Cauaco, her daughter Doña María succeeded as ruler of Yanhuitlan. Doña María married Diego Nuqh, or Six Motion, *cacique* of Chachoapan-Tamazola, around 1530.[53] María and Diego were recognized as *caciques* of Yanhuitlan and Tamazola-Chachoapan for a period of ten to twelve years. The couple spent most of their married life in Tamazola, where their two sons were born. As was customary in the Mixteca Alta, the older son,

Don Matías de Velasco, was reared in the town he was to inherit, in this case Tamazola. Don Gabriel de Guzmán, the younger son, was taken to be raised in Yanhuitlan.[54]

María probably died in the early 1540s. Since a half-brother to Gabriel and Matías appeared prominently at Tecomatlan, an *estancia* of Yanhuitlan, around 1580,[55] it is assumed that Diego Nuqh survived María, remarried, and produced a third son, Diego de Guzmán. Don Gabriel was too young to assume the title of *cacique* of Yanhuitlan at the death of his mother, so the leading *principales* of the region designated Don Domingo de Guzmán, brother of Doña María, to serve as *cacique*-regent until Gabriel reached a responsible age.

It was during his regency that Don Domingo was brought before the Inquisition for alleged practices of idolatry, human sacrifice, and polygyny.[56] Statements in the Inquisitorial proceedings of 1544–45 indicate that Domingo (born in 1510) had been converted by the first wave of Dominican missionaries coming into the area in 1529. According to the testimony of the witnesses, however, Don Domingo, Don Francisco, and Don Juan, all high-ranking nobles from Yanhuitlan, after having been baptized as Christians, reverted to paganism with sufficient enthusiasm to be brought to the attention of the missionary clergy (see chapter 4 for a detailed description of this proceeding).

Domingo spent a year in prison but avoided conviction and was recognized as *cacique*-regent until 1558. During this period, he also occupied the position of governor of Yanhuitlan. This was to establish a precedent for the two *caciques* who were to succeed him during the sixteenth century. As stated previously, the two offices were separate and distinct, but the governorship ensured the *cacique* of important additional powers and greatly affected the performance and nature of the role of the native ruler in Colonial times. Domingo died on, or shortly after, September 22, 1558, and without children.[57]

As had been intended by his parents, as provided by custom, and as designated in the will of Don Domingo, Don Gabriel succeeded to the title of *cacique* of Yanhuitlan as the "son of Doña María Cocuahu and the grandson of Namahu and Cauaco."[58] Don Gabriel was approximately twenty-two years old at the death of Domingo and was of sufficient age to assume the title. Gabriel followed his uncle as governor, probably through election by the *principales* who gathered at the making of Domingo's will. Gabriel was confirmed both in the office of governor and as *cacique* in a viceregal order of December 17, 1559.[59]

Don Gabriel ruled as *cacique* and governor until 1591. He was an exemplary Christian, spoke Spanish, wore the clothing of a Spaniard, was known "throughout New Spain," and was said to be as honest, righteous, and intelligent a man as any Spaniard.[60] During the thirty-three years of his reign, Don Gabriel rose to great power and wealth and was clearly the most influential man in his community in all phases of native life. Don Gabriel left a great estate to his heirs at his death, having acquired the *cacicazgos* of Achiutla and Tlaxiaco through his marriage to Isabel de Rojas, daughter and heiress of the *cacique* of Achiutla.[61]

While on his deathbed in August 1591, Don Gabriel dictated his will. By its terms, the *cacicazgo* of Yanhuitlan was left to his only son, Francisco de Guzmán.[62] The will provided that if Francisco died without issue, the *cacicazgo* was to pass first to Gabriel's oldest daughter, María de Guzmán, and then to her children, heirs, or successors by *linea recta*. Thus Don Gabriel took measures to ensure legitimate inheritance of the *cacicazgo* by means of direct succession, a tradition that had been observed in Yanhuitlan for more than six hundred years.[63] Gabriel stated in the closing portion of his will that he had done this to avoid the litigation and differences that might arise, having been aware of lawsuits over succession in other *cacicazgos*.[64] On September 13, 1591, Don Francisco de Guzmán was given formal possession of Yanhuitlan, actions confirmed by a subsequent viceregal decree, and held title until his own death in 1629.

On May 15, 1629, Baltazar de Velasco y Guzmán was confirmed as *cacique* of Yanhuitlan. He succeeded to the title by virtue of being named heir in Francisco's *testamento* of September 22, 1626, and because Baltazar was Francisco's nephew and nearest direct descendant.[65] In company of the governor and *cabildo* of Yanhuitlan and the *alcalde mayor* of Teposcolula-Yanhuitlan, Baltazar was taken to the *cacique's* palace, where the *alcalde mayor* "took the hand of the said Don Baltazar de Velasco y Guzmán, and they passed through the patios of the said *tecpan*, entering its rooms and parlors, and as an act of possession opened and closed the doors, clearing out the said governor, *alcaldes*, *regidores* and other persons and performing other acts of possession, which was done quietly and peacefully and without contradiction."[66] The succession to title was confirmed subsequently by the Spanish viceroy in Mexico City.

The next successor to the Yanhuitlan title was Francisco Pimentel y Guzmán, the legitimate heir and son of Baltazar de Velasco y Guzmán. Francisco was *cacique* of Teposcolula and Yanhuitlan in 1653, but his domain extended far beyond these two communities and included Tututepec on the Mixteca Costa.[67] Francisco's father, Don Baltazar, had acquired Tututepec at the death of his brother's son, who had failed to produce an heir.

The next step in the history of succession at Yanhuitlan is somewhat unusual. On June 25, 1669, Don Francisco Pimentel y Guzmán relinquished title to his daughter, Doña María Pimentel y Guzmán, "whom I have loved dearly," and who was married to Don Diego de Villagómez y Guzmán, *cacique* of Silacayoapan and Acatlan in the Mixteca Baja, "who has served me well, and I relinquish [title] to my said children and to their heirs and successors."[68] Possession of Yanhuitlan and its *tecpan* was granted to Doña María and Don Diego on July 9, 1669. Until the end of the Colonial period, Yanhuitlan was linked to Silacayoapan and Acatlan and several other *cacicazgos* in the northern Mixteca Baja, and the families Villagómez, Pimentel, and Guzmán remained in control of these important holdings until well after Mexican Independence.

Succession at Teposcolula

Pedro Osorio, the *cacique* of Teposcolula and Tejupan, died on July 2, 1566. Although the record is quite sketchy, it is virtually certain that he was the son and heir of the pre-Hispanic rulers of Teposcolula, known only by the Nahuatl titles of Tecpateutl and Ozomasuchitl.[69] Pedro Osorio died without sons. After Don Pedro's death, Felipe de Austria presented himself before Alcalde Mayor Francisco Morales Batidor of Teposcolula in an attempt to claim the vacant title. In such cases of failure of the male line at Teposcolula, Felipe claimed, he was entitled to succeed to the title by virtue of being the son of Juan de Mendoza, *cacique* of Tilantongo. Felipe maintained that Pedro Osorio had nephews and nieces, but no male children, and that the title should not go to them but to a son of the *cacique* of Tilantongo. The ruling lineage of Tilantongo was said to be the superior one and might claim such vacant titles in the Mixteca.

The actual justification for Tilantongo's claim has never been fully clarified, but the pretentions of the Tilantongo family are reiterated several times in the Colonial documentation, and there is absolutely no doubt that the lineage is of great importance in the codices, particularly *Codex Nuttall* and *Codex Bodley*.[70] This may have been true, or it may simply be an artifact of fortuitous preservation of the Tilantongo picture manuscripts, while similar devices for Yanhuitlan, Teposcolula, Tlaxiaco, or Coixtlahuaca did not survive. Tilantongo and its surrounds were small, and although densely populated, lacked the monumentality one finds among several of its contemporaries, notably Achiutla and Teposcolula.[71] It could be that the principal ruling line resided in an unremarkable retreat if it was considered superior for religious-philosophical reasons, or by simple virtue of being older and more established. Yanhuitlan, Teposcolula, Chalcatongo, and Coixtlahuaca nonetheless appear to have contained far greater natural and agricultural resources. Achiutla,

Apoala, and Sosola meanwhile appear to have been mythically and ritualistically more important than Tilantongo. The mystery continues.

Felipe de Austria had the good sense to marry Inés Osorio, daughter of Pedro Osorio.[72] On July 5, 1566, there was a hearing before the *alcalde mayor* of Teposcolula. Pedro's widow (and Inés's mother), María de Zárate, was present and claimed that the *caciques* of Teposcolula were also of the Tilantongo lineage. Juan de Mendoza, the Tilantongo *cacique*, was said to be a close relative of María de Zárate. Still, in his will of 29 June 1566, Pedro, who was both *cacique* and *gobernador* of Teposcolula, ceded the *cacicazgo* of Teposcolula to Felipe de Austria. Felipe, who was elected as governor, then became *cacique*.

In the course of the legal proceedings relating to the succession, it was mentioned that Inés, Felipe's wife, was dead.[73] It also developed that there was another claimant, Doña Catalina de Peralta. On August 30, 1566, Diego de Mendoza, *cacique* and governor of Tamazulapan, acting through power of attorney on behalf of his wife, Catalina, claimed that she was the daughter of Doña María (a sister of Pedro Osorio) and granddaughter of Tecpateutl and Ozomasuchitl. Felipe de Austria's attorney claimed that Catalina de Peralta was only a transversal relative of Pedro Osorio and, in another place, that she and her husband were simply *indios macehuales* and ineligible to succeed to the title. The overwhelming, and ineffectively refuted evidence, however, supported Catalina's claim, and she was recognized in 1569 and ruled Teposcolula until her death around 1600.[74]

Doña Catalina and Diego de Mendoza had no surviving children. Around 1600 the title at Teposcolula fell to Baltazar de Velasco y Guzmán, the aforementioned *cacique* of Yanhuitlan and Catalina's cousin. Through inheritance and marriage, Baltazar eventually ruled Teposcolula, Yanhuitlan, Tilantongo, Tututepec, and Tezoatlan. Baltazar's son, Francisco Pimentel y Guzmán, succeeded to all of his father's titles around 1640. He married Lucia de Orozco y Cortés. In 1669, Francisco ceded the *cacicazgo* of Yanhuitlan to his daughter María Pimentel y Guzmán and his son-in-law Diego de Villagómez. At the time of Francisco's death, in 1685, his wife, Lucia, succeeded to the title of *cacica* and *tutora* of the couple's children. After a period of skilled management of *cacicazgo* resources by Lucia, their daughter married the *cacique* of Achiutla and their son, Agustín Carlos Pimentel y Guzmán y Alvarado, succeeded to the title in 1704.

Agustín Carlos was among the most entrepreneurial of all Mixtec *caciques*, and he married Lucia Ramírez de León, *cacica* of the Villa of Etla. After their death in 1736, their daughter, Juana Faustina Pimentel Alvarado Ramírez

de León, succeeded to the titles of Teposcolula, Tilantongo, Tututepec, Jamiltepec, Tezoatlan, the Villa of Etla, and other *cacicazgos* of the Mixteca Costa
and Baja.[75] Prior to succession, Juana Faustina married Don Martín Carlos
de Villagómez y Guzmán, "*cacique principal* of the *cabeceras* of Silacaioapa,
Acatlan, Petlalsingo, Yanhuitlan, and their subject *pueblos*."[76] The combined
holdings and economic power of these two individuals took on astounding
proportions, extending from southern Puebla to the Pacific and from the
Oaxaca-Guerrero border to the Valley of Oaxaca.

Other Sixteenth-Century Cases

There is repeated evidence that in Yanhuitlan direct succession was an inflexible requirement from the 1000s to 1629[77] and that it remained important
throughout the Colonial period.[78] This pattern was preserved at Tejupan[79]
and Teposcolula[80] until the late eighteenth century. Caso has shown direct
succession for Tilantongo from 692 (although subsequently revised to the 900s)
until the end of the sixteenth century.[81] Direct lineal succession was present
in Chachoapan-Tamazola until well into the seventeenth century.[82] In other
communities, there is good evidence that the requirement of direct descent
from pre-Conquest native rulers was observed in Atoyaquillo,[83] Tamazulapan,[84] the two Mitlatongos,[85] Teozacoalco,[86] and Tequixtepec.[87]

Common ancestry and marriage were involved in every kingdom-
cacicazgo in the Mixteca Alta. When two individuals married, they became in
effect a "joint person" in the legal terminology of sixteenth-century New
Spain. A husband often appealed a case in the name of his wife where she
had succeeded to the title by birthright and he had married in from outside. "Joint person" cases were entered by the *cacique* husbands of the *cacicas*
at Teposcolula in 1566–69,[88] at Tlazultepec in 1597,[89] and at numerous other
localities throughout Colonial and into Republican times. The children of each
union, of course, had rights to all titles and possessions joined in their parents.

The general rule of succession for "disenfranchised" individuals, whether
by accident of birth order or failure to marry into a *cacicazgo*, was assignment
to subservient positions under a sibling ruler as lords of *sujetos* within the
kingdoms. In time they lost their ruling-caste identity and became simply
members of the hereditary nobility. In many cases, however, such individuals
attempted to establish their own dynasties, a practice that could account for
the appearance of new kingdoms throughout Mixtec history. Don Gabriel de
Guzmán of Yanhuitlan brought a half-brother to live in the *estancia* of Tecomatlan, where he was regarded as a privileged noble. Eventually this person,

Diego de Guzmán, attempted to establish a dynasty in Tecomatlan. His attempts were vigorously contested, but by the end of the seventeenth century his descendents had succeeded in gaining recognition as *caciques* from an increasingly more tolerant Spanish administration.[90]

Spanish Influence on Succession

While most of the rules of succession in the Mixteca Alta had their origins in native custom, some reflected acculturative influences derived from Europe. From around 1550, Spanish concepts of *mayorazgo* (entailed estates) and inheritance seem to have had considerable effect on native succession. In particular, transverse succession seems to have been affected by the end of the sixteenth century by the European concept of primogeniture: sons, regardless of age relative to a sister or sisters, would inherit the *cacicazgo*, and older sons would inherit before their younger brothers.

We know, however, that early in the century Doña María Cocuahu inherited the *cacicazgo* of Yanhuitlan before her brother, Don Domingo de Guzmán, and that the mother of the children, Cauaco, was mentioned frequently as Señora of the community without reference to the father, Namahu. Domingo de Guzmán came to power only as a regent in favor of his nephew, Don Gabriel de Guzmán. Doña María received title from her mother, and inheritance in this fashion is stressed in later claims to the Yanhuitlan title. Thus, in ancient times, an effort may have been made to keep certain titles in the female line and others in the male line. But more important was the practice of awarding the kingdom of one parent, probably the father, to the eldest child and that of the mother to a younger child. The latter seems to have been the case in the succession of Don Gabriel de Guzmán to Yanhuitlan and of his older brother to Chachoapan-Tamazola.

It is difficult to derive an inflexible principle from the above, except that there was a tendency for a title residing in female hands to remain in female hands in succeeding generations, for an older son to inherit title from his father, and for the younger son to receive title from his mother. While we do not know the rules of priority between a female and her brothers, we do know that there were cases where a woman received title and her brothers were sent outside to marry *cacicas* of other communities. This is precisely what occurred at Yanhuitlan in the case of María Cocuahu and her brothers. Marriage, of course, furnished a convenient escape, and the efforts of *caciques* to negotiate advantageous marriages for their children can be read between the documented lines.

Archaeological Implications

What can we make of these patterns of succession, and what purpose might they have served? The pattern of *cacicazgo* growth throughout the Colonial period is typified by cyclical acquisition, aggregation, fusion, and concentration on the one hand, and by forces of dispersal, division, and fission on the other. This had the net effect of distributing power widely across the region, preventing excess concentration of wealth and authority in one or a few families. Examples to the contrary were short lived or the product of Colonial-era epidemics that created unanticipated opportunities for the acquisition of titles, infectious diseases having decimated royals and commoners alike. This meant that individual *cacicazgos* might undergo flux and periods of changing fortunes, but perhaps counterintuitively brought long-term stability to the region as a whole.

This pattern, and the dynamics underlying it, could explain some of the phase-to-phase and period-to-period changes in regional settlement patterns, where entire "valley pockets" surrounding one or more polities might empty in favor of others in adjacent areas. Human labor was the essential productive "technology" in pre-Hispanic times, and moving whole populations closer to the seat of power, or in conjunction with the movement of a royal individual as part of a marital alliance, may have been a common practice. It would also help explain the persistent continuities in observed material and cultural practices, despite episodes of abandonment over large swaths of the Mixteca in certain prehistoric periods. A few core regions such as Nochixtlan appear never to have been abandoned en masse and would therefore retain the traditions and principal features of the *cacicazgo*, despite shuffling their dynastic alliances.

COLONIAL *CACICAS*

During the sixteenth century, the vast majority of communities in the Mixteca fell into one or another of some fifty *cacicazgos*.[91] Ruling caste couples, widows, widowers, and orphaned children assisted by guardians held legal titles to power, property, and privilege in these polities. Women and men succeeded to title through inheritance by direct descent from a line of royal-caste ancestors, by abdication of preceding rulers, and by marriage. Women, in effect, became consorts of their *cacique* husbands when they married. Likewise, when *cacicas* married men from other communities, the women were recognized as the true and legitimate holders of their own *cacicazgos*, and their husbands were entitled to privileges only by virtue of their relationship to their wives. Legitimate offspring of *cacicas* inherited titles held by their mothers as well as those of their fathers. Mixteca *cacicas* were involved in frequent lawsuits to protect their rights and privileges, and through these cases and the special awards, grants, permits, and protections granted by Crown officials, we know a great deal about certain royal women in the Mixteca.

Cacicas owned the best houses in their *cacicazgos* and the most fertile irrigable lands, orchards, saltworks, mineral deposits, grazing lands, and herds of sheep and goats as well as horses, cattle, mules, and *burros*. Rarely, and only in major centers like Yanhuitlan and Teposcolula, did anyone, Spaniard or native, possess greater wealth or prestige. *Cacicas* wore the finest clothes; had abundant jewelry, furniture, and works of art; and were carried on palanquins when on extended journeys. The natives provided them with tribute and personal services in their houses and fields. *Cacicas* gave lavishly to the church, and they occupied places of honor at mass and in fiestas and were buried in the nave of the principal church of their *cacicazgos*. In every way the *cacicas* stood at the pinnacle of native society and occupied a position comparable to high-status Spaniards, even *encomenderos* or Dominican priors. Mixteca *cacica* status equaled or exceeded that of the *ladina-mestiza* (racially mixed, Hispanicized) daughters and granddaughters of Montezuma, such as Isabel de Montezuma, who held *encomiendas* in the Mixteca, most notably in Tlaxiaco.[92]

The "golden age" of the Mixteca *cacica* was the period from around 1550 to 1620. Strong native traditions and favorable Spanish laws and institutions, including those put in place by the Dominicans, reinforced the status and power of the traditional native rulers. After the middle 1600s, patterns of direct lineal succession were weakened by failure to produce children, by death of direct successors, or through usurpation. Population growth following the disastrous declines of the sixteenth and early seventeenth centuries also put pressure on agricultural and other resources. Especially desirable, of course, were the highly productive lands that had traditionally been held by the native lords. Spanish courts and administrators, however, continued to recognize the institution of the Spanish *mayorazgo* or *cacicazgo* as it applied to the caste of Mixtec *señores naturales*, and they insisted on legal demonstration of direct lineal succession and right to title throughout the Colonial period.

Ultimately the role, power, position, and wealth of the *cacicas* eroded. But there was variation in the pattern, and in many instances we see strong persistence of the *cacicazgo* until the time of Mexican Independence in the 1820s. Mixteca *cacicas* continued to occupy positions of importance well into the mid-nineteenth century, particularly in the Huajuapan-Acatlan area of the northern Mixteca Baja, and their property and financial holdings formed the basis for family estates into the twentieth century.[93] Three exemplars of sixteenth-century "cacicadom" in the Mixteca were Ana Sosa of Tututepec, Catalina de Peralta of Teposcolula, and María Saavedra of Tlaxiaco-Achiutla.

Ana Sosa of Tututepec

Tututepec, as already discussed, was the seat of a pre-Hispanic conquest state on the Mixteca Costa that dominated the region from the Isthmus of Tehuantepec to the borderlands between Oaxaca and the present state of Guerrero.[94] It was the scene of fierce battles between the Mixtecs and the Spanish forces under Pedro de Alvarado in 1522, and it was recognized by natives and Spaniards alike as one of the richest areas of New Spain. After the death of the *señor natural* of Tututepec, the title fell to a son who took the name Pedro de Alvarado. The *cacica* was Ana Sosa, who, upon the death of Pedro, around 1550, became *cacica de la Provincia de Tututepec*. She was confirmed or reconfirmed as *cacica* in 1554, in 1559, and again in 1561 and occupied that position, asserting her authority and defending her entitlements through the courts, until the son of Pedro and Ana, Melchior de Alvarado, succeeded to the title around 1570.[95]

Ana Sosa had vast holdings. She possessed twelve *estancias*; thirty-one *huertas* (orchards or groves) of *cacao*; great stretches of farming and grazing lands; highly productive saltworks; lagoons rich in fish, game, and shellfish; and numerous houses, including the *tecpan*, or palace complex, in Tututepec. She also held valuable movable property in the form of gold, silver, jade, coral, and turquoise jewelry and necklaces, precious bird plumage, vast quantities of cotton *huipiles* (blouses) and skirts and other textiles, livestock, and stores of products from her fields and other resources. Her holdings on the Mixteca Costa clearly exceeded those of Don Tristán de Luna y Arellano, the powerful Spanish *encomendero* in the region during the mid- to late sixteenth century. Only the estate of Hernán Cortés in the Valley of Oaxaca and in Tehuantepec would have exceeded that of Ana Sosa.

Catalina de Peralta of Teposcolula

Catalina de Peralta succeeded to the royal title at Teposcolula in 1569.[96] She acquired the *cacicazgo* after a long court battle with Felipe de Austria of Tilantongo. Felipe was the widower of the daughter of the deceased *cacique* of Teposcolula and claimed further that when the *cacique* line at Teposcolula was terminated, as occurred when the *cacique* Pedro Osorio died on July 2, 1566, without living children, the title would fall to a son of the *cacique* of Tilan-tongo. Catalina, as noted above, was able to substantiate her claim to the title as the daughter of Pedro Osorio's sister and the *cacique*-caste relative nearest her uncle. She further reinforced her claim by demonstrating that she was the granddaughter of the pre-Hispanic rulers of Teposcolula, Tecpateutl (Tecpan-tecuhtli) and Ozomasuchitl.

Teposcolula was the Spanish administrative capital of the Mixteca and an important *cacicazgo* both before and after the Spanish Conquest. The legally declared value of the goods (*bienes*), houses, jewels, lands, and orchards was "six thousand pesos of gold and much more," an enormous sum for the sixteenth century.[97] Among the properties that Catalina inherited were five dwellings, including the *cacique*'s palace in the royal compound of Tepos-colula. Catalina received twenty parcels of the most highly productive salt mine in the central Mixteca and two large orchards of apples, pears, peaches, and oranges. Substantial returns were realized through rental of these proper-ties to Spaniards, to wealthier natives, and to the Dominican and Jesuit orders of the Mixteca, Oaxaca, and Puebla. She also acquired large quantities of jewelry (much of it pre-Hispanic in origin), fine textiles, silverware, furniture, and *huipiles*, skirts, and other clothing by way of inheritance and acquisition.[98] Although she was forced into extensive litigation, she successfully defended her title to Teposcolula until her death.

María Saavedra of Tlaxiaco

In 1573 a youthful María Saavedra succeeded to the *cacicazgos* of Achiutla and Tlaxiaco, two of the largest and wealthiest of native patrimonies in the Mixteca. She received title at the death of her father, Don Felipe Saavedra, who inherited Tlaxiaco from his grandfather, Cuzcaquautli (One Eagle) and his father, Francisco de Maldonado.[99] Proper succession in the royal lineage was of utmost importance to Mixtec *cacique* families, and Felipe had directed in his will of November 15, 1573, that his daughter should marry the son of his sister, Doña Isabel de Rojas of the *cacique* family of Tlaxiaco-Achiutla. This propitious marriage would constitute a firm alliance and ensure legitimate succession and control by members of the ruling lineage.

In addition to numerous lands, houses, and entitlements to life-long tribute and services from the subject populations of her *cacicazgos*, Doña María also inherited movable property from Don Felipe.[100] Included in the inventory of goods were fifty-four silver *flores*, along with spoons, pitchers, necklaces, censors, miscellaneous items of silver and beaded jewelry, religious images, capes, books, decorated *cocos* (dried coconuts), magnets, large quantities of textiles, trunks, a large herd of sheep, pack mules, and even a silver pick ("with which I cleaned my ears") and a pair of eyeglasses. As with all Mixteca *cacicas*, she also received vast quantities of *huipiles* and skirts, most of them lavishly decorated with woven designs, *tochimite* (rabbit fur), and bird plumage.

In real property, María inherited the extensive lands of the *cacicazgo* of Tlaxiaco, which included many *huertas* of fruits trees, nine large *milpas* (fields) located in the most productive lands of the region, and unspecified stretches of grazing and resource-producing and -collecting lands. This was clearly the largest and most valuable configuration of real estate owned by any individual in the province of Tlaxiaco in the middle to late sixteenth century. She held enough property in 1581 that she was able to donate and sell some of her more valuable lands to the Dominican monastery of Tlaxiaco.[101]

In 1587 María Saavedra, in compliance with her father's instructions, was married to Francisco de Guzmán, son of the *cacique* of Yanhuitlan, Gabriel de Guzmán, and Doña Isabel de Rojas of Tlaxiaco-Achiutla.[102] As previously implied, María and Francisco's marriage was between first cousins, a common practice among members of the endogamous Mixtec *cacique* caste in Colonial and earlier times. In celebration of María's marriage, the natives of Tlaxiaco were ordered to spin numerous *fardos* (large bundles) of cotton cloth and to provide numerous other services.[103] Viceroy Villamanrique, after noting "the said Doña María is the greatest *cacica* that there is in all of this Mixteca," affirmed that "it has always been customary among them in that province that when the children of the *señores* married, the natives aided the recently married couple with cotton yarn and clothing and other things."[104] The direct line of *señores naturales* of Tlaxiaco ended with the death of María in the mid-1590s.

Cacicas and *Cacicazgos*

The several cases cited above are representative of consistently recurring patterns in the Mixteca during the Colonial period. *Cacicazgos* varied in size and composition, and some *cacicas* were much more wealthy, prestigious, and influential than others. The rules of succession and the *cacica* lifestyle, however, were the same everywhere. All of the *cacicas* of the Mixteca were, after all, members of the same endogamous caste and all were related through marriage and kinship. They were of course key players in the alliance system linking *cacicazgos*. The *cacicazgo* system brought cohesion and stability to the region more effectively than any other native or Spanish institution.

Mixteca *cacicas* were equal in rank to their brothers and husbands and succeeded to titles in their own right. They held wealth and property and were regarded with great deference by natives and Spaniards alike. *Cacicas* were active and influential in pre-Hispanic times and played an important role in the formation of Colonial Mixtec society. Our focus on royal-caste women reflects social class biases in the documents as well as our interests in the *cacicazgo* as an institution. But students of the Mixteca and the Mixtecos should be aware that the activities of women of all socioeconomic classes are revealed through their participation in civil and criminal matters handled through the Spanish courts, administrative branches of government, and ecclesiastical offices, myriad examples of which are found in Colonial archives.

7

THE WAR OF INDEPENDENCE
AND THE CENTURY THAT FOLLOWED

The political-administrative system of New Spain was a multilevel configuration that began with the Royal Crown and the Council of the Indies in Spain and passed directly to the viceroy and Royal Audiencia of Mexico, then on to provincial administrators—the *alcaldes mayores* and *corregidores*—before terminating at the local, or community, level of *cabildos* and *ayuntamientos*.[1] Although somewhat flawed by bureaucratic inefficiency and a slow pace of reform, it worked reasonably effectively for three hundred years and served, after the Colonial period, as the basis for local-level government in Oaxaca and elsewhere in Mexico until the present day.

THE BIRTH AND EARLY LIFE OF A NEW NATION

As discussed in the last chapter, from the beginning of Colonial times until the 1780s the native communities of New Spain were organized into *provincias* consisting of multiple communities. These farming settlements had their own governments but also fell under the control of the *alcalde mayor* or *corregidor* of their region. They operated concurrently within the Colonial administrative hierarchy, with the Catholic clergy, and with a traditional body of *caciques*, *principales*, elders, and Spanish administrators and merchants.

Between 1786 and 1789 Oaxaca, together with the rest of New Spain, was reorganized through the installation of the *intendencia* system.[2] New Spain was divided into twelve *intendencias* and three large military districts, each governed by an *intendente*, who functioned as the principal administrative and judicial authority in each division and was directly responsible to the viceroy and the Audiencia of Mexico. The Intendencia of Oaxaca was divided into a central zone comprised of the capital of Antequera (Oaxaca de Juárez or Oaxaca City) and twenty *subdelegaciones* or *partidos*, including Teposcolula, Huajuapan, and Jamiltepec in the Mixteca. In 1804 Oaxaca was the fourth largest *intendencia* of New Spain, with a population of 528,860, the vast majority of whom were natives residing in the more than nine hundred surrounding communities.

This chapter covers the transition into an independent Mexico and the changing economic fortunes of local Mixtec communities as the nineteenth century wore on.[3] Mixtec *caciques* persisted, despite being stripped of their traditional powers by new national and state constitutions during the 1820s. The "ex-*caciques*," as they were often called, nonetheless retained considerable standing in their communities and simply transitioned into advantageous positions as wealthy landowners.[4] Over time, however, their wealth and prerogatives continued to erode, and by century's end most *cacique* lands had reverted back to their communities. The term *cacique*, as used today throughout the Mixteca, refers to a person of relative wealth, power, and influence but bears no relationship to actual descent from the Mixtec kings.

The War of Independence

Around 1812, political dissidence was affecting the Colonial status of Oaxaca, especially in the Mixteca. On January 11, 1812, royalist forces in Yanhuitlan were attacked, but on the fifteenth the insurgents abandoned the area and retreated north to Cuautla, where they united with the forces of José María Morelos. Morelos was the former parish priest and student of Miguel Hidalgo who led the insurrection after Hidalgo's capture and execution the preceding summer.[5] Later, in November of 1812, the Morelos army (composed largely of natives and *mestizos*) marched southward from Tehuacan and captured Oaxaca City. In May of 1813, however, Spanish forces regained control of the province and survived attempts by the insurgents to capture Huajuapan, Tlaxiaco, Silacayoapan, and other Mixteca communities. Morelos was eventually captured and executed. A military stalemate ensued, with royalists in control of the capital but with various guerrilla bands loose in the provinces.

By 1820 it was clear that Spain, suffering political turmoil at home, could no longer control the colony, and in June of 1821 Antonio de León, operating from Tezoatlan in the Mixteca Baja declared the independence of Oaxaca from Spain. On July 10 León entered Oaxaca City and assumed control of the province. The War of Independence in Oaxaca was over.

The capture of Oaxaca by rebel forces was rapid and relatively easy. Spanish political domination had ended, but most Colonial political institutions continued with little or no change. This was the case with the *intendencia-subdelegación-ayuntamiento* governmental system, which persisted. Although political nomenclature changed, political and legal procedures continued as before Independence. Civil and criminal cases, conflicts over land, boundaries, and resources were handled as they had been during the Colonial period.

At the local level, *ayuntamientos* continued to be elected and operated as before. In the Valley of Oaxaca, the title "governor" was replaced by *alcalde primero*, while the larger communities of the Mixteca continued the positions of *gobernador* and the form and functions of the *ayuntamientos*. On November 25, 1821, for example, the community of Tidaa in the Partido de Teposcolula, elected a *gobernador*, two *alcaldes*, four *regidores*, one *escribano*, two judges, four *topiles* and a *mayordomo* of the community, two *fiscales*, and two *topiles* of the church, all of them elected by a plurality of votes to serve their terms during 1822. Similar elections were held throughout the Mixteca, in such towns as San Andrés Lagunas on November 2, 1821, and San Juan Teposcolula on December 2, 1821.[6] Except for minor, mostly rhetorical, innovations, the functionaries and their positions remained unchanged from Colonial times in the various regions of Oaxaca, including the Mixteca.

The Mexican Empire

Mexican Independence under the *criollo* military officer Agustín de Iturbide was established in 1821,[7] and before long the *intendencias* were converted to *provincias*. But the office of *intendente*, as well as its major administrative functions, continued as during Colonial times.

Although the official title of the chief official for Oaxaca was *jefe político de la Provincia de Oaxaca*, or *jefe,* the designation *intendente* continued in use. For the first time, Oaxaca communities participated in elections for state and national representatives to provisional assemblies (*asambleas*). From these beginnings there evolved the Congreso Nacional, the Congreso Estatal, and the beginning of true representative government in Oaxaca. At this time, the first Tribunal Superior de Justicia was formed in Oaxaca.

Under Iturbide's short administration as Emperor Agustín I, directives were sent out to provincial and local levels of government and justice to continue functioning much as they had during Colonial times. There were to

be no changes in offices, functions, or in relations between local, intermediate, and provisional levels of government. The most visible change was the
design of official letterheads used in government communications.

The Federal Republic

Antonio de León maintained control of Oaxaca during Iturbide's reign, but
when Iturbide dissolved the Constituent Convention (a body of constitutional
oversight and reform) in October of 1822—making himself in effect dictator
of Mexico—problems reemerged in Oaxaca. León issued a declaration against
the Empire, and on June 9, 1823, he and Nicolás Bravo directed the recovery
of Oaxaca from the imperial government.[8] Oaxaca was declared "Estado Libre
y Soberano," and a provisional junta was established, as well as the basis for
a new state and local government. The continuity of public order and of
the government was thereby assured. By this time Iturbide was in exile and
eventually shot to death by firing squad, following an ill-advised return to
Mexico. By October of 1824 there was a new constitution and Mexico was a
federal republic of nineteen states modeled after the United States of America.[9]

During the critical period of 1823–24, local governments were notified
of the overthrow of the Iturbide regime and that the area was reorganized
under the provisional control of the *jefe político de la Provincia de Oaxaca*. The
establishment of the provisional junta and election of *diputados* for a Congreso
Estatal were also announced. On July 6, 1823, members of the new congress
decreed that all civil, military, and political authorities in the state continue
in their assigned duties. The Oaxaca state government also advised the political
dependencies of the region that all orders, laws, and regulations in effect at that
time were to continue permanently. The province of Oaxaca was declared
to be loyal to the provisional government in Mexico City. Twenty *partidos
políticos* arising from the old *subdelegaciones* of the Intendencia de Oaxaca were
created. The capital district included Oaxaca City and its nearby dependencies.
Other *partidos* included Nochixtlan, Teposcolula, Huajuapan, Juxtlahuaca,
Jamiltepec, Chontales, Quiechapan, Teotitlan del Valle, Villa Alta, Teotitlan del
Camino, Zimatlan, Teococuilco, Miahuatlan, and Ixtepeji.

It is important to note that once these forms and functions were established in Oaxaca, the system of state and local government has continued
through the vicissitudes of the multiple changes of government during the
nineteenth century, the dictatorship of Porfirio Díaz at the end of the century
and during the early 1900s, the Mexican Revolution, and the period of modernization that has continued until the present. The governor, state legislature, court
system, local *ayuntamientos* with their governors, *regidores, alcaldes*, secretaries,

treasurers, and police, as well as the commissioners of communal properties, have persisted. Myriad new committees for migrants or schools, welfare organizations, and special interest groups have indeed proliferated, but the basic form of government has remained the same. What is most notable, however, is the alteration in the official role and influence of the ancient rulers, or *caciques*, so important in pre-Hispanic and Colonial times in the Mixteca. We turn now to consider the nineteenth-century history of this important group of traditional leaders.

MIXTEC *CACIQUES* AND EX-*CACIQUES*

The institution of the *cacicazgo* persisted strongly in the Mixteca not only into the later Colonial period, but well beyond 1821 and into Republican times. As late as the 1880s, *caciques* and *cacicas*, customarily called "ex-*caciques*," remained socially and economically active and important and continued to control vast land resources and wealth. Although the overt political power and traditional privileges of the *caciques* declined during later Colonial times, their wealth, economic power, and social status remained essentially intact. "Poor" *caciques*, as well as wealthy and influential ones, were normally treated with deference and distinguished from the general population. Some lost their lands and privileges and drifted into the general rural population of the Mixteca, but many, perhaps most, stood clearly apart. They were *caciques* or ex-*caciques* and continued to have a special place in society.

What did it mean to be a Mixtec *cacique* in the mid-nineteenth century? Clearly the ancient privileges of personal service and tribute were curtailed, even outlawed by the Mexican Constitution of 1824. As in the Colonial period, when *caciques* were sharply sanctioned when they attempted to claim privileges not expressly granted them by viceregal decree, such attempts, when reported to provincial officials, were normally quashed. Also greatly reduced were the nearly automatic rights of the *caciques* to the highest political offices in their communities. Natives of lesser rank, the *principales* and *macehuales*, moved strongly into these positions as early as the mid-seventeenth century but more commonly in the eighteenth century and later. It was no longer automatic that the *cacique* would have the privilege (or responsibility) of filling these formal leadership positions in the native communities.

Often, even late in Colonial and into Republican times, community and *cacique* were synonymous, unified, and—legally and in the minds of the people— one and the same. Francisco de Jesús Velasco and the community of San Andrés Lagunas in their long land suit with the adjoining community of San Pedro

Yucunama is instructive.[10] This conflict lasted from 1797 until 1936, when it was resolved through presidential action. In the portion of the case running from 1800 to 1801, *cacique* and community were united—there being no distinction between community lands and those belonging to the *cacicazgo*. The *cacique* (Francisco de Jesús, actually representing his wife, the *cacica* Clara Sebastiana de Esquivel, and acting as joint legal person with her) and the community were represented by one attorney and depended on the same surveyors to measure their holdings. In 1863, however, the case was quite different. The father-son *caciques*, Don Bonifacio Pimentel y Guzmán and "Fulano" Pimentel sold their lands for 800 *pesos*. The town, through its attorney, responded, indicating that these were community lands and could not be sold. The courts, however, denied the authenticity of the community's claim and decided in favor of the ex-*caciques*.[11]

In late Colonial times, during the struggle for independence, and in early Republican times, the meaning of the term *cacique* was undergoing transformation. Strong-willed "self-aggrandizers" who were not of the traditional *cacique* class began to act as *caudillos* in their communities, stirring up unrest and seizing opportunities to benefit from it. The legitimate native aristocracy, the ex-*caciques*, content to function as a landed aristocracy, retreated into the background in terms of local leadership, and others moved in to fill the resulting political vacuum. The *caciques*, in the sense of the traditional "natural" or "native lords" (*señores naturales*) were not the pushers, the *egoistas*, who seized power in the communities and developed into the class of ruthless petty dictators that survived the Reforma of the mid-nineteenth century and the Mexican Revolution of the 1910s and 1920s to appear and reappear throughout central and southern Mexico until modern times. Although traditional *caciques* did sometimes behave in an autocratic or high-handed fashion, they were quickly brought into line by the social pressure of their coequals, the people themselves, and by the threat and application of Colonial law. The *caciquismo* of modern Mexico has virtually nothing to do with the traditional institution of the *cacicazgo*, or the *señores naturales* of pre-Hispanic and Spanish Colonial times.

Ex-*caciques* and Their Lands

The best indicator of the privileged condition of the nineteenth-century *caciques* and ex-*caciques* was their control of land. In 1816 Clara Sebastiana de Esquivel was *cacica* of Santa Ana Tepejillo and El Rosario in southern Puebla; Santos Reyes, Suchiquilasala, Santiago Tilapa, San Juan de las Piñas, Santa Catarina Martir, all in the area of Juxtlahuaca near the boundary with the

State of Guerrero; and Santiago de las Plumas and San Francisco Teopam near Coixtlahuaca.[12] These titles were consistently reconfirmed by decisions of the *alcaldes mayores* and the Royal Audiencia.

Even more noteworthy was the estate held by Bonifacio Antonio de Pimentel y Guzmán around 1863. The daughter of Clara Sebastiana, Andrea María Guadalupe, married Hípolito José de Pimentel y Guzmán, *cacique* of Tilantongo, Teposcolula, and Tututepec. Their son, Don Bonifacio, inherited all of the *cacicazgos* of his maternal grandmother, Clara Sebastiana, plus San Miguel Ixtlan, Puebla, from Francisco de Jesús de Velasco, his grandfather and husband of Clara Sebastiana. Additionally, as son and legitimate heir of Hípolito José, he became *cacique* of the three richest and most important of all the Mixtec *cacicazgos*: Santiago Tilantongo, San Pedro y Pablo Teposcolula, and the Villa de Tututepec. Although in constant litigation over his vast holdings, Don Bonifacio retained rights to the great majority of this estate until his death.

Later in the nineteenth century, we gain insights into what eventually occurred with many of these holdings. By the 1880s *cacicazgo* lands were not only rentable but could be bought and sold like other private lands. On September 8, 1876, Bonifacio's widow, Doña Petra Rafaela Esquivel, sold *cacicazgo* lands in the community of Teopam, near Coixtlahuaca, to five individuals from the nearby community of Magdalena Jicotlan.[13] The community of Teopam attempted to claim these lands but experienced strong resistance. "The lands occupied by Teopam are not theirs," wrote Roque Jacinto Cruz of Magdalena Jicotlan to the governor of Oaxaca on May 2, 1892. "They belonged to a *cacicazgo* whose last owner was Don Bonifacio Pimentel, husband of Doña Petra Rafaela Esquivel, who, with the death of this *Señor* and of their son Don Francisco Tomás Pimentel, was exclusive owner of these lands, and being such, she sold them to me and to four others from my town." The transfer of property took place before the judge of first instance in Tlaxiaco, where Doña Petra resided, and the sales price was a very substantial 1,500 *pesos*. Teopam protested the sale, and a long suit ensued between the purchasers and the community. By 1903 the matter remained pending, with neither the courts nor the governor of Oaxaca making a decision.

For reasons that are not entirely clear, the residential base for Mixtec *caciques* in later Colonial times shifted from places like Tututepec, Yanhuitlan, Teposcolula, Tamazulapan, Nochixtlan, or Tilantongo north to northern Oaxaca, around Huajuapan, and southernmost Puebla, in and around Acatlan, Petlacingo, Chila, and Tepejillo. They continued to hold *cacicazgos* as far south as the Pacific coast, and in the central and far western Mixteca, but resided in the northern communities where most, if not all of them, possessed estates.

All through the Colonial period, residents of northern Oaxaca focused more on the cities to the north—Puebla, Tehuacan, Veracruz, and Mexico City—than Antequera/Oaxaca City in the south. Political and economic power was centered in the north. These were places of residence for the social elite and the scene of important religious activities. The northern Mixteca fell into the Bishopric of Tlaxcala, and the headquarters of the Dominican Order was in Puebla. European manufactured goods and foods which were in demand by the native elite came from the north. Oaxaca City was less important and more difficult to reach than the cities to the north.

As *cacique* families began to focus more on business, education, religious careers, and living more like *ladinos* and less like native Mixtecos, and depending less on traditional tribute and services and rents, they looked toward Tehuacan, Puebla, and Mexico City. These connections are clearly indicated in the contracts for real estate, for goods and services, and for donations, for example, to Jesuit and Dominican foundations in Puebla, for the borrowing and lending of money, and as alternative places of residence for *cacique* families.[14] In those areas lay opportunity, social and economic connections, and better access to political and religious institutions. Residing in the Huajuapan-Acatlan area placed the *caciques* more advantageously than if they were in communities further removed from these important Colonial and Republican power bases.

Still, the most persistent component of the ancient and Colonial *cacicazgo* was ownership of land. Land holdings, primarily farm and grazing properties, were so vast in many cases that it is nearly impossible to calculate the total estates held by the wealthier *caciques*. Holdings of individuals with one or two of the smaller *cacicazgos* might range from a hundred to several hundred hectares, but even these were customarily the most productive lands, many of them irrigated or irrigable and capable of producing more than one crop per year. Other *cacicazgos*, however, grew to enormous proportions. Bonifacio Pimentel, who held thirteen *cacicazgos*, several of them large and rich in resources, controlled literally thousands of hectares of highly productive property extending from southern Puebla all the way to the shores of the Pacific Ocean.[15] In addition to lands, the *caciques* normally possessed sumptuous living quarters in the *cabecera* of one of their *cacicazgos* and other houses, stables, commercial buildings, corrals, orchards, grist mills, saltworks, fishing lagoons, and other types of real and movable property.

In the case of *cacicazgo* lands, particularly the larger and more important estates, like Teposcolula, Tututepec, or Tilantongo, the ancient institution of serfdom was perpetuated by nineteenth-century *caciques*. *Terrazgueros* occupied *cacicazgo* lands, almost always the best lands in the region, and planted and harvested crops, the majority of which went to the *caciques*, but the remainder was reserved for the serfs. As in early Colonial times, many landless families preferred to work the productive lands belonging to the *cacique* rather than marginal, nonproductive communal lands acquired as residents of a given *pueblo*.[16] Around 1825 there was litigation between the aforementioned *cacique* Bonifacio Pimentel y Velasco and the community of Magdalena Jicotlan over *cacicazgo* lands in Teopam.[17] Numerous witnesses testified that ". . . the said lands had always been utilized by the children and neighbors of San Francisco Tlacotepec and Santiago Plumas as *terrasgueros* of the *cacique*." The principle was established through litigation and decisions of the Royal Audiencia in Mexico City in 1718, and reconfirmed in 1750–51, 1806, and 1809, and later by the Republican courts in 1825 and 1863. Both Magdalena Jicotlan and Teopam pressed claims until late in the nineteenth century.[18] Both towns were frustrated by the Pimentels' negotiations to sell lands to private parties.

As was true in Colonial times, the *caciques* of the Republican period continued to rent out their estates to Spaniards, *mestizos*, and Indians and to the religious orders, such as the Companía de Jesús (the Jesuits) or the Dominicans.[19] Normally these lands were used for grazing of livestock, some of the herds of sheep and goats amounting to thirty, forty, or fifty thousand head. These great herds, called *haciendas volantes*, ranged over a vast domain between Tehuacan, Puebla, and the Pacific coast, and the proprietors depended on the *caciques* and the communities of the Mixteca for rental of appropriate grazing lands. With understandable modification, this institution has persisted into the contemporary period.[20]

While many *cacicazgo* lands were utilized for grazing, the *caciques* often reserved the right to continue farming and collecting natural resources from these lands for their own use or donated the privilege of doing so to their *pueblos*. In late Colonial times and throughout the nineteenth century, the donation of lands to communities or the sale or rental of lands to individuals or communities fomented virulent and protracted land suits between *caciques* and the *pueblos*. Both appealed to tradition and custom and attempted to underscore their claims with documentation and through litigation.

Through their attorneys, the communities claimed titles by virtue of de facto use-possession, as a traditional privilege, or, in the aftermath of the rhetoric and activities of the Independence movement, there was an emphasis on the rights of natives to take over lands within their communities or in contested areas in adjoining communities. This was especially the case in areas of northern Oaxaca and southern Puebla visited by José María Morelos in 1811–12. In numerous cases, for example in San Martín Zacatepeque and in San Pedro y San Pablo Tequixtepec, natives invaded *cacicazgo* lands and attempted to claim them permanently.

For their part, the *caciques* refused to accept the loss of their lands. In 1817 Mariano Francisco Villagómez, *cacique* of Tequixtepec, Camotlan, Nochixtlan, Suchitepec, Miltepeque, and "others of the jurisdiction of Huajuapan," asked the *alcalde mayor* of Huajuapan for "restitution of lands that were taken and given to the *naturales* of the *pueblo* of Miquistlahuaca by Father Morelos in the year 1812."[21] The courts decided in favor of the *cacique* Mariano Francisco, and his titles, said to date from 1744, were reconfirmed. In 1818 the *cacique* of San Martín Zacatepeque complained bitterly of the "despotism of the natives" in the loss of *cacicazgo* lands in the Insurrection of 1811 and sought full restoration and damages in the amount of 245 silver *pesos*.[22] The *caciques* of Tequixtepec and adjoining communities fought for decades to recover full possession of lands seized or otherwise appropriated through actions of the native populace.[23]

Mixtec *caciques* claimed traditional rights, and normally they could more readily validate their claims through documentation and the force of judicial decisions. Both sides alleged usurpation, deceit, and bribery, and a willing contingent of lawyers stood at hand to formulate arguments, to manipulate and to promote claims in the district, state, and national courts, and of course to profit from the discord. These ambiguities provided a basis for two centuries of land disputes, open warfare between communities, and protracted litigation that sorely taxed the administrative and judicial capacity of the Mexican states and nation from Independence to the present day.

The Last Kings and Queens of the Mixteca

As the end of the nineteenth century approached, the ex-*caciques* moved into the background. They seem to have disappeared from the small towns and the rural countryside. They show up less and less frequently in litigation, being displaced for the most part by communities fighting and litigating over scarce lands and natural resources. They appear simply as Don Manuel Villagómez, Don Francisco Alvarado, Hilaria Mendoza, or Doña Teresa Andrada.[24] Clearly it had become unpopular to be regarded as a native aristocrat. The referential *cacique* or "ex-*cacique*" dropped from use, except in derogatory contexts or where demanded by legal process or with reference to precedence. Many *cacicazgos* were sold off, donated to *pueblos*, lost through litigation, or usurped. *Cacique* families appear to have simply given up, exhausted from generations of litigation, eroded privileges, and outright "takings" or annexations.

Descendants of *caciques* drifted into the social network of larger communities like Huajuapan, Puebla, or Tehuacan. The traditional designation of "Indian," "*mestizo*," and "Spaniard" was generally dropped from official communication and litigation. Intermarriage blurred the racial and social distinctions that were so important in Colonial times. As John Monaghan has shown through in-depth studies of nineteenth-century *caciques*, members of these families appear in the documents as merchants with commercial enterprises in and among the communities of Oaxaca and Puebla, as litigators or lawyers, priests and nuns, or political functionaries.[25] Some high-born members of *cacique* lineages even disappeared into the ranks of the common class of town and country. Women, sometimes unmarried and often widows, attempted to defend titles to land, buildings, and natural resources. When well represented, they often won their suits. In other cases, it was difficult to find final resolutions, or the claimants simply gave up or donated title to communities. Of course, many *caciques* died without issue, or their children died before reaching maturity.

Most *cacique* families nonetheless persisted through the nineteenth and twentieth centuries, and today the descendants of the ancient royal families of the Mixteca still reside in Huajuapan, Oaxaca, Tehuacan, Puebla, Mexico City, and even in the United States, many not knowing, others not caring, that they are descended from Mixtec kings.

The Mixtec Economy in the Nineteenth Century

Regional economies based on agriculture, household-based craft production, and plaza-market (*tianguis*) marketing remain features of rural Mexican culture whose origins extend deeply into antiquity. Analysis of archaeological materials and historical reconstructions of Otomanguean and Uto-Aztecan languages provide ample evidence of the existence of craft specialization, local and long-distance trade, and local marketing since the Formative period in Mesoamerica. Traditionally, basic subsistence was derived from maize-beans-squash agriculture, with variable dietary supplementation from other regionally adapted cultigens, wild plant and animal foods, and, especially after the Spanish Conquest, small quantities of meat from domesticated stock. Necessities and luxuries beyond subsistence had to be satisfied through agricultural surpluses, sale of livestock, or through specialized occupational activities.

The Mixteca produced at least 90 percent of its basic subsistence goods in the nineteenth and early twentieth centuries (the period under discussion runs from the War of Independence to the Mexican Revolution). This would include its agricultural products and livestock; vegetables and fruits; cotton and woolen textiles; leather goods; lumber and wood products; pitch pine and charcoal; most essential metal products; its coffee and its inebriating *pulque, mezcal* and *aguardiente;* brick and adobe; bread and tortillas; rope and hemp-fiber products; slaked lime; and sugar-*panela.* The regional market system integrated clusters of interdependent farming communities into a virtually self-sufficient economic system and provided collection points for goods destined for outside markets and as a conduit for imported items. This exchange system endured from the onset of the Colonial period through the nineteenth century, and it persists throughout the Mixtecas as strongly today as it did decades, even centuries, ago.

The existence of an unusually good corpus of documentation from late Colonial times through the nineteenth century allows observation of the regional economic system as it has evolved in the Mixteca since the War of Independence. Special attention is focused on agriculture and livestock production, specialized household/community industries, and the circulation of people and commodities through the traditional *tianguis* and fixed-locus *tienda* distributional network. The Mixteca's system of production and exchange as it was constituted during this period served to meet the economic needs of an entire region with virtually no dependence on the Mexican national or broader world economy. This was just as well, for especially in the 1820s the Mexican national economy was in tatters following the protracted struggle for independence. Governmental coffers were empty, wealthy Spaniards had fled, and trade with the mother country ceased. What followed were decades of political instability until the Porfiriato (1876–1910). This was the period of "Order and Progress" during the dictatorship of the *mestizo* general with Mixtec antecedents, Porfirio Díaz, whose rule brought rapid economic growth along with political repression.[26] This nineteenth-century background is important for understanding the modern era and its effects on the Mixteca that we discuss in the last chapter of this book.

In economic terms, the most adequately studied area for the post-Independence era is the Mixteca Alta, consisting of the modern districts of Teposcolula, Tlaxiaco, Nochixtlan, and Coixtlahuaca. The Mixteca Alta in general is mountainous, with narrow, steep-sided valleys being dominated by surrounding peaks and ridges that are difficult to farm. Extensive open plains simply do not exist, and only limited stretches of undulating valley lands are available. Farmlands are essentially small plots scattered across low hills, along piedmont and mountain slopes, and up the *arroyos* or gullies where the ancient *coo-yuu* terracing system makes additional space available for farming. Lands used for farming and/or grazing range in altitude from 1,300 to 2,500 meters, but all four of the districts mentioned above extend from higher and cooler lands to lower, warmer elevations.

The existence of the trade-market system made it feasible for such commodities as cotton or palm fiber produced in the lower elevations to be utilized in palm-weaving and cloth-making industries in the higher-elevation areas where those commodities were not produced. Fruits, nuts, and animal products moved actively throughout the Mixteca, provisioning a way of life that went far beyond basic subsistence. Such regional or subregional interdependence has existed since ancient and Colonial times through the nineteenth century, and it continues until the present. This pattern of "ecological complementarity" in the Mixteca, seemingly an adaptive strategy to offset agricultural risk, is discussed in prior works by Spores, Rodolfo Pastor, and John Monaghan.[27] The movement of workers among these sometimes distant lands is yet another precursor of the labor migration that is so characteristic of the present day.[28]

The Era of Regional Independence in the Mixteca

During the 1820s, the Mixteca had a nearly self-sufficient economic system. Although the communities themselves were virtually independent with respect to satisfaction of most basic daily needs through production of maize, beans, squash, and other food crops, communities also had wild and domesticated plants and animals, lumber, and firewood but differed significantly in natural resources, manufactured products, and specialized services. Each community occupied a special niche in a multiregional economic network.

There is notable variation in geography, resources, and population density among the three Mixtecas (more fruits and wild plants in some areas than others; variability in quality and quantity of lands, rainfall, and water availability; and so on), but in terms of general economic activities there is quite substantial similarity from region to region. If any area may be said to be "typical" or representative, however, it would be the central Mixteca Alta. In the early years of Independence this would be the area that was divided into three political *partidos* corresponding to the three largest subregions of the Mixteca Alta: Teposcolula, Nochixtlan, and Tlaxiaco. Although all communities depended on agriculture and livestock production, they were diversified in social, political, and economic composition. A moderately complex network of interdependent settlement existed in the 1820s: semi-urban, internally diversified *villas*; specialized, quasi-diversified *pueblos*; and unspecialized agricultural settlements. The typical population of these communities ranged in size from fifty to twenty-five hundred, with the *villas* tending toward the higher end of the range.

For present purposes, five communities (Teposcolula, Tamazulapan, Yanhuitlan, Nochixtlan, and Tlaxiaco) were semi-urban, internally diversified *villas*. Ninety-three communities were specialized or quasi-diversified. There were seventy-nine unspecialized and socioeconomically undiversified farming communities. The last category includes communities dedicated to agriculture but without significant economic or occupational specialization. Although the *villas* would not be considered "urban" in the modern sense, they were large for the time and the region, relatively complex socially, and "open" in terms of connections with other communities and with other areas by way of emigration-immigration, marital exogamy, and long-distance economic exchanges.[29]

These semi-urban communities were economically and occupationally diversified when compared to other Mixtec communities. Dozens of specialties, small industries (*industrias pequeñas*), and businesses served complementary economic functions in the *villas*, and the largest concentration of population, wealth, and wealthy families were found in these places. These centers performed necessary economic and political functions not only for themselves but for the other communities within their subregions and for the greater Mixteca in general.

These *villas*, as well as the specialized smaller communities, required basic food resources from the unspecialized agricultural communities and from the shops (*tiendas*), the plaza-markets (*tianguis*) and the occupational specializations of the *villas*. The unspecialized communities required the services and the products of the specialized communities and the *villas*. The last mentioned, by way of the great periodic markets and *ferias* and through a multilevel political system, provided facilities and connections with the larger political and economic networks of Oaxaca, of Mexico, and ultimately the world. This last point, however, requires some qualification. External connections available through the *villas* were generally limited to high-status consumable goods with no evident impact on the basic economy.

From the social standpoint, the *villas* were stratified among a wealthy class, a middle class with moderate, but sufficient, resources, and poor families making up the vast majority of the population. The unspecialized and specialized communities were much more homogeneous in their social structure and more endogamous in their marriage patterns, although their population reflected a tendency to migrate within the Mixteca, but generally not far beyond. The majority of the specialized and unspecialized communities had fewer than five hundred inhabitants, although some compared favorably in population with the more complex *villas*.

Spanish was the most important language in the *villas*, with a variable representation of Mixtec speakers, from a high proportion (Tlaxiaco), to a medium presence (Nochixtlan), to a small proportion (Tamazulapan). Although Spanish was spoken in the majority of specialized and unspecialized *pueblos*, Mixtec was clearly the dominant language, although Trique was more important in Chicahuaxtla and the surrounding area, and both Chocho and Mixtec were spoken in Coixtlahuaca and environs.

All of the Mixteca communities, large, small, simple or complex, depended on agriculture and to a greater or lesser extent on livestock herding. In most but by no means all circumstances, they produced sufficient quantities of maize, beans, and squash for their own use and also variable quantities of other cultivated plants. They also took advantage of available wild plants and animals and natural resources (stone, lime, basalt, clays, coloring substances, and so on) for their basic subsistence and, in the case of surplus, for market exchange.

Some of the outlying *pueblos* had very few lands and resources and sometimes produced insufficient food supplies to maintain themselves. Production in all of the communities varied greatly from year to year, frequently to the point of inadequacy. Many of these communities attempted to compensate for their insufficiency with other products derived from local cottage industries (the *industrias pequeñas*), such as pottery; baskets and mats (*petates*); wooden furniture or tools; rope, twine, matting, and clothing made from *ixtli* fiber; firewood or carbon; woven cloth; woolen, cotton or silk thread and yarn; or cochineal (*grana* or *cochinilla*). Other communities placed greater emphasis on interregional commerce as an occupational specialization. Survival in difficult times or when production was limited for lack of productive lands or technology often meant dependence on these industries and specializations.[30]

Marketing and External Connections

The great regional markets at Tlaxiaco, Yanhuitlan, and Teposcolula were vital for distribution of basic raw materials and locally produced goods and livestock, as well as goods imported from other areas. The fixed-locus shops of these communities enriched the traditional markets, above all by providing exotic items and goods imported from other regions. The markets, the shops, and the different specialists were concentrated in the *villas*, and people residing in the communities came to these integrative centers to buy and sell their products and livestock and to obtain services from resident specialists.

The regional markets of the Mixteca were interrelated among themselves and with other markets that were comparatively more informal and located in the less-complex communities of the region. They were also connected with the other *villas* and cities of adjacent areas: Oaxaca, Putla, Pinotepa-Jamiltepec, Juxtlahuaca-Tecomaxtlahuaca, Silacayoapan, Huajuapan, Teotitlan del Camino, and Cuicatlan. The unifying mechanisms were none other than the clients who circulated among the market centers, but perhaps more significant were the merchants and pack-train operators who carried goods among the various centers.[31]

Within the Mixteca Alta, native producers sold or exchanged raw goods or the products that they had manufactured themselves. For example, the potters of Cuquila, Santo Domingo Tonaltepec, Santa Catarina Adequez, or San Pedro Cántaros Coxcaltepec; the fabricators of hats, palm-leaf mats (*petates*) and baskets (*tenates*) of Sachio, Teotongo, Zahuatlan, Coixtlahuaca, Yutanduchi or San Sebastián Nicananduta; the *maguey* fiber (*ixtli*) from Los Peñones, Tamazola, or Sotula; and the fruit and vegetable cultivators of low-lying *pueblos* like Los Peñascos and Atoyaquillo, all carried their own products to the largest market centers. In other words, the producers distributed their goods directly to the consumers through the system of markets or to numerous intermediaries who worked in and between markets.

The circulation within the Mixteca was concentrated primarily on food products: maize, beans, squash, and, in lesser quantities, wheat flour, fruits, chilis, garlic, cabbage, radishes, tomatoes, onions, carrots, and at least some locally produced salt. Other items circulating through the system were beef, mutton, chickens and turkeys, wool, hides, some cotton, some sugar, firewood, carbon, *pulque*, lime, *mezcal*, hand-woven wool and cotton products, clothing, sandals and shoes, *ixtli* products, pottery, some basic metal implements for home use, and various other products of the artisans residing in the *villas*. Given the availability of these goods and services, there was little need to look beyond the region or the regional market system to satisfy basic daily needs.

Information from the customs (*aduana* and *alcabalas*) offices in Huajuapan nonetheless reflects the existence of constant importation, primarily from Puebla and Veracruz, of several products: sugar and sugar cake (*panela*); cocoa or chocolate (*cacao*); shrimp and fish; distilled spirits (*aguardiente*); cotton; soap; thread, yarn, ribbon and other sewing supplies; paper; clothing; metal and metal objects; and other manufactured goods.[32] The most voluminous exports that passed through Huajuapan customs were livestock (primarily sheep and goats), dried meat, animal fat, and modest amounts of cochineal (*grana*).

Other goods, such as wheat flour, which was produced in the Mixteca Alta, was exported to various destinations, primarily to the cities of Oaxaca, Puebla, and Tehuacan. Many Mixteca products passed through Puebla to other areas of central Mexico, such as Mexico City. This was true also for many goods that simply passed through the Mixteca on their way to destinations beyond the region. As in pre-Hispanic times, there was considerable interregional commerce within the state of Oaxaca. The registries of the customs offices in Oaxaca and Tehuantepec reveal that it was primarily raw materials, salt, dried fish and shrimp, *añil* (indigo), and *cacao* that were sent from the Isthmus to the Mixteca.[33] *Mezcal*, the distilled and highly intoxicating beverage produced from the *agave* or *maguey* plant, was the most frequent export from Oaxaca City to the Mixteca. Commerce between the Mixteca Alta and the Mixteca Costa was very active. Various communities in the *partidos* of Tlaxiaco and Nochixtlan, such as Santiago Nuyoo, Pueblo de Los Reyes, Itundujia, Los Peñascos, San Andrés Chicahuaxtla, Yanhuitlan, and Tlaxiaco, were actively involved in this commerce. Salt, *cacao*, fish and shrimp, and cotton moved from the Costa to the Mixteca Alta, and wheat flour and maize passed in the opposite direction.[34] Clearly, a well-developed system of interregional commerce was in operation in and around the Mixteca Alta during the Independence era.

Manufactured goods that entered from outside the area, originating primarily in Puebla and Veracruz (European and North American as well as Mexican products) were available in the stores and shops of the *villas*, but the great majority of those goods passed *through* the Mixteca on their way to Oaxaca City, Guerrero, and Chiapas rather than being consumed *within* the Mixteca. Externally produced goods were destined, above all, for the wealthier residents of the *villas* of Teposcolula, Yanhuitlan, Tamazulapan, Nochixtlan, and Tlaxiaco, but they appear to have had only slight effects on the general pattern of consumption or on the economic activities of the majority of Mixteca communities.

There were few exports from the Mixteca Alta. Sheep, goats, and a few cattle, salted meat, wool, animal fat, cured hides, and flour were the most important products being sent to other areas. Of secondary importance was silk and cochineal, which was produced in small quantities in the decade of the 1820s. Income from these sales went principally to the wealthiest entrepreneurs of the *villas* and into the hands of outside merchants involved in capitalistic enterprise.[35]

Based on available data, there is little evidence to contradict the existence of a basically self-sufficient regional economy in the early years of Independence or to suggest that the internal economy of the Mixteca was significantly affected by external commerce. Although imported goods were desired by elite consumers in the Mixteca to enhance their status in the eyes of their peers, these products could hardly be seen as essential components of the economy. The system would have functioned and survived quite well without the infusion of external goods. It is to be noted, moreover, that the majority of the commodities that entered the area came from adjacent regions: the Mixteca Baja, the Mixteca Costa, the Cañada de Cuicatlan, or the Valley of Oaxaca. "The extras" were obtained solely by the few who could afford them; these were the wealthiest individuals residing in the *villas*, the store owners, the owners of the most productive lands, and the highest-ranking functionaries. The Mixteca's relatively few conspicuous consumers could have managed quite well without the luxury goods.

The 1890s

Mexico was by this time undergoing rapid economic modernization, internal integration via new communications technologies and the railroads, along with considerable capital investment and trade with the United States and Europe. This was also the period of heightened European stylistic influences, in the arts, architecture, and elite culture. The Mixteca saw the rise of a modern aristocratic class, especially in Tlaxiaco, whose reputation by the 1890s as the "Little Paris" of Mexico is still visible in the now dilapidated theater and other buildings near its town square. This period was brief and had only a limited impact on the economic activities and fortunes of the general population. The Mixteca, by and large, remained an agrarian, autonomous society despite the volume of exchange goods passing through the region.

Major crops produced in the Mixteca during the 1890s were maize, wheat, barley, and beans. All communities in the districts of Nochixtlan (sixty-five), Tlaxiaco (sixty-five), Teposcolula (sixty-five), and Coixtlahuaca (nineteen) produced maize. Among other major crops, wheat was produced in thirty-one communities of Nochixtlan, in thirty-three communities of Tlaxiaco, and in all communities of Teposcolula and Coixtlahuaca. Barley and beans were produced in much the same proportions.[36]

In addition to the major crops indicated above, others were tomatoes, chilis, avocados, peas and vetch, broad beans, lentils, sugar cane, fruits (lime, mango, banana, *zapote*, orange), *maguey*, alfalfa, olives, coffee, tobacco, and palm. With the exception of *maguey*, which was raised throughout the Mixteca highlands, these crops were produced in only a few of the geographically suitable communities, within the more humid and hotter valley pockets, among them Tlaxila and Sindihui in the district of Nochixtlan, and San Miguel el Grande, Hacienda La Concepción, Yucuañe, Teita, Itundujia, and San Mateo Peñasco in the district of Tlaxiaco.

Sheep and goats (*ganado menor*) were raised in nearly all communities, with the largest and commercially most important herds being found in the district of Nochixtlan. Cattle, chickens, turkeys, pigs, horses, *burros*, and mules were also raised, but in relatively small quantities. Sheep and goats figured prominently in the economy of the region both in terms of providing meat and raw wool for the important weaving industry within the Mixteca and as a primary resource for exportation of live animals, meat, or wool sent to the surrounding regions and as far as Puebla and Mexico City. *Ganado menor*, together with maize and wheat, were the primary exports from the region in the 1890s, much as they had been in the 1820s.[37] The slaughter of cattle and hogs (*ganado mayor*) was a relatively significant factor in the economy of such centers as Nochixtlan, Tamazulapan, Yanhuitlan, and Tlaxiaco. Nowhere in the Mixteca Alta, however, did the raising of *ganado mayor* equal the importance of sheep and goats or take on the economic significance of cattle, horses, and pigs in other areas of Oaxaca and Mexico.

The Mixteca economy of the nineteenth century emphasized several features or tendencies:

1. a strong local-regional ecological interdependency;
2. agricultural production via basic technology;
3. combined subsistence production and production for market;
4. relatively low output of a narrow range of items;
5. emphasis on the family as the primary unit of production;
6. intraregional differentiation and specialization;
7. integration via the market system.

The market system furnished a controlled but open forum for exchange, whereby families of even the lowest socioeconomic status gained access to the general economy by producing and marketing agricultural commodities, raw and processed resources, and cottage-manufactured goods (cloth, *sarapes*, candles, bread, and shoes), as well as through small amounts of cash earned in labor activities—including small factories or on the farms, plantations, and *ranchos* of Veracruz, the Mixteca Costa, or the Cañada, and in converting those sources of production and income to consumables. As in other peasant societies, marketplaces and market transactions of produce and resources were common, but nonmarket transactions (such as gift exchange or ritual investment) were relatively infrequent and involved far smaller quantities of goods and resources than those which passed through the regional markets of Nochixtlan, Teposcolula, Tlaxiaco, and Coixtlahuaca.

The market thus served a critical economic function for the Mixteca, just as it had in prior times, but it also figured prominently in the municipal budgets of the sponsoring *cabeceras*. The prominence of the market with respect to the financial support of the communities is revealed in the *cortes de caja y presupuestos* of Mixteca communities. As shown in the accounts for Nochixtlan, Teposcolula, Tamazulapan, Tlaxiaco, and other Mixteca Alta market centers, market receipts made up at least half of total municipal revenues.[38]

As is the case of other peasant market systems,[39] villages and towns within the Mixteca were integrated internally and then linked to other settlements by common language, religion, government, social arrangements (marriage, kinship, *compadrazgo*), geographical contiguity, and through the market system. The Mixteca, moreover, was linked—although far less significantly than in modern times—to the greater Mexican society and culture by social, political, religious, linguistic, and economic ties. In other words, Mixtec families simultaneously participated in interrelated local, regional, and national systems but with overwhelming emphasis first on their own communities and secondly on the Mixteca region. Clearly, this was true of economic activity, but consultation of sources utilized in the present study make it clear that economic activity was more intensified at the regional level, that is within the Mixteca, than it was with the larger national system.[40]

Moreover, although there was significant demographic and economic growth in the Mixteca from the 1820s to the 1890s, we see that the relative independence and integrity of the Mixteca economy was well established early in the nineteenth century, and despite far-reaching political changes, remained remarkably stable in these respects until 1900.[41] But changes, or at least long-term trends, nonetheless occurred between the War of Independence and the last decade of the nineteenth century. So what were they?

Discernable demographic and economic changes in the Mixteca between the 1820s and 1890s are enumerated as follows:

1. increased population in all districts;[42]
2. increased intra- and interregional mobility;
3. increased specialization and/or specialized production;
4. increased diversification of production and occupations;

5. increased agricultural production;

6. increased craft and resource production.

These changes did little to alter the function or form of the traditional economy or the market system, which in the 1890s continued to integrate the Mixteca economically and to allow the region a virtually independent existence from the rest of the nation. In the 1890s, as in the 1820s, the Mixteca continued to be largely self-sufficient economically, with only minor economic interaction with other areas, primarily in nonessential (at least for the average person) or supplementary goods.

"Closed" versus "Open" Communities

It has been suggested that a characteristic feature of peasant life in Mexico and in other areas of the world is the "closed corporate community." Such settlements are inclined to be endogamous, to exclude outsiders, and "to limit the flow of outside goods and ideas into the community."[43] Not in the demographic or in the economic sense, however, can we conclude that the late nineteenth-century communities of the Mixteca were either "closed" or economically or demographically self-sufficient (not to be confused with the foregoing comments on the relative isolation of the wider region). By 1890—actually well before this time—any demands beyond basic subsistence in the smaller communities depended upon the regional exchange network which circulated diverse resources, products, and services among the various communities. Larger, more diversified *cabecera communities* also depended on the market network for basic foodstuffs and resources.

Centers like Nochixtlan, Teposcolula, and Tlaxiaco were occupationally more diversified than the smaller communities that depended on the special production and services of the *cabeceras* and the special integrative functions served by the periodic markets held in those places. The *cabeceras*, in turn, were dependent on both the raw goods and the individual specializations of the smaller communities. Focusing on the region as a whole, one can observe a kind of organic opposition and solidarity engendered by the complementary interaction of farming communities, those with one, two, or three specialized productive activities and the larger, diversified *cabeceras* or *villas*.

In consideration of the system of production and distribution, it is useful to consider briefly the demographic aspects of the "closed" community and its logical obverse, the "open" community. Possible indicators of the relative permeability of individual communities might be the number of individuals, relative to total population, moving into the community from other places;

or the number of individuals absenting themselves (*ausentes*) or emigrating from the community on a long-term basis.

Of sixty communities in the district of Nochixtlan in 1890, thirty-four communities, or 57 percent, had from 0 to 1.7 percent of their populations originating from other places. It seems reasonable to conclude that such communities may be classified as "closed" with respect to demographic penetration. On the other hand, twenty-one, or 35 percent of the communities, had between 1.8 and 14% of their inhabitants originating from other places. Given the influx of residents from other places, those twenty-one communities may be classified as "open." Although data on five communities (8 percent) was inadequate to make a secure determination, we may reasonably conclude that both relatively closed and open communities coexisted in the region.[44]

Relative numbers of individuals absenting themselves from communities for various periods of time varies significantly.[45] The figures relating to absences in the various district capitals of the Mixteca—and for Oaxaca as a whole—are as follows:

Nochixtlan: 3.64% (population: 42,799; absent: 1,558)
Teposcolula: 3% (population: 32,268; absent: 970)
Tlaxiaco: 3.65% (population: 66,181; absent: 2,420)
Coixtlahuaca: 5.63% (population: 17,823; absent: 1,005)
State of Oaxaca: 3% (population: 794,424; absent: 23,828)

The relative numbers of absences for the Mixteca are basically the same as those for the state of Oaxaca as a whole: the notable exception is Coixtlahuaca, which remains the poorest and most underpopulated of the Mixteca districts and which has been one of the primary providers of seasonal labor in the Cañada and Veracruz. Principal migration destinations in the 1890s were contiguous communities within the district or in adjacent districts; Oaxaca City; Puebla City; Orizaba in Veracruz; the Cañada; and Mexico City.[46]

The levels of emigration might bring into question the relative capacity of the Mixteca to support its population. Clearly there was seasonal migration to the plantations and *fincas* of Veracruz, the Cañada, and the Mixteca Costa. Relative to other regions of Oaxaca, these figures are not unusual. Certainly they are far below modern levels of emigration from the Mixteca. As in all economies, even in those of relatively high self-sufficiency as the Mixteca, migrants are perpetually seeking economic opportunities outside their home regions. This would be the case particularly in difficult times, as reported in Tlaxiaco in 1892.[47]

Although district economies were significantly integrated through weekly markets and commercial enterprises in the *cabeceras*, individuals within the districts had access to goods and services in centers of neighboring districts. Residents of the Coixtlahuaca region traded in Tamazulapan, Teposcolula, Nochixtlan, and even in Huajuapan, the Cañada, and Teotitlan. Consumers and traders frequently patronized not only markets in their own districts but those of neighboring districts. Itinerant merchants (*regatones*) also circulated goods among market centers and among villages that did not have their own regular marketplace. Market areas[48] in the four districts could, and did, extend beyond a single major periodic marketplace or subregion. Goods from Tlaxiaco, for example, were distributed not only through the district but well beyond to Teposcolula, Putla, and other communities in the Mixteca Baja. Likewise, consumers and traders from these surrounding areas and beyond (Huajuapan, Puebla City, and Oaxaca City) came to Tlaxiaco to buy and sell. A very similar pattern was reported for the Tlaxiaco market during the 1950s and increasingly so from the 1960s to the present day.[49]

Occupationally diversified centers, like Tlaxiaco, Teposcolula, Nochixtlan, Yanhuitlan, or Tamazulapan, individually or collectively, served to integrate numerous unspecialized agricultural communities and to link these communities to the larger Mexican economy. In economic terms, it is clear that these were not "closed communities." None could have developed beyond the bare subsistence level without open interaction with surrounding communities and regions. Some could not even have sustained themselves without such revenue-producing specializations as pottery making (as at Santo Domingo Tonaltepec or Cuquila), carbon making (at various localities), basketry (as at Zachio), or weaving (as in the Tayatas). In fact, those communities were most often situated in marginal agricultural lands with few exploitable resources. It is nonetheless evident that survival and a decent quality of life did not require connections far beyond the Mixteca itself.

8

NEW BEGINNINGS IN THE MIXTECA AND BEYOND

It is well known that the Mixteca and Oaxaca in general have for centuries been areas of intense local affiliation and identification. The region in general is also one of the most conflictive areas in North America, with a pattern and frequency of intercommunity conflict that is virtually unmatched anywhere on the continent. These intercommunity conflicts, which date from pre-Hispanic times, are well documented for the Colonial period, gathered momentum in the nineteenth century, and have actually intensified since 1900. Their continuance in the contemporary period has attracted considerable anthropological interest. John Paddock and other scholars have raised deep questions about the nature of conflict, not just its ostensible causes but also the circumstances that make some communities conflict averse, or "antiviolent."[1] Intercommunity conflict has been a critical component of life in the Mixteca for generations such that any comprehensive discussion of modern culture in the region requires that conflict receive special attention.

Since pre-Hispanic times, Mixtecs have been strongly attached to their individual communities. They think of themselves first and foremost as residents of a given *pueblo* far more than belonging to a political district, ethnic group, state, or nation.[2] Carol Nagengast and Michael Kearney put the matter succinctly: the Mixteca is an area where "the primary political opposition is between villages, and ethnicity is not salient."[3] Miguel Bartolomé and Alicia Barabas make similar remarks with respect to Oaxaca in general, saying that "this tendency between autonomy and intercommunity conflict is found even among communities pertaining to the same ethnicity."[4] They also find themselves in agreement with Julio de la Fuente, who called these groups "small enemy republics."[5]

Although it is tempting to discuss the causes and consequences of intergroup conflict in the Mixteca, such a discussion would require a book-length treatise unto itself, and our present concerns are better focused on ethnicity and the recent history of regional coalitions. Subsequently, we turn to the modern economy and patterns of migration, before drawing some concluding observations regarding the Mixtecs and the Mixteca. Our perspective on these several interrelated topics is one of "convergence" among methods, aims, and subject matter, and of the past as being an ever-present force now and for the future of the Mixteca and in all things relating to the Mixtec.

REGIONAL COALITIONS AND ETHNICITY

There have been several attempts to form local and regional coalitions in the Mixteca since 1900. During the incessant intercommunity conflicts from Colonial and even earlier times, it was relatively common for two communities to form temporary alliances against another community or communities. We have seen these in the Mixteca in the case of Achiutla joining with its bitter enemy Tilantongo against Yucuañe, or Atlatlauca joining with Tlaxiaco against San Miguel el Grande. These alliances were fragile, short lived, and normally addressed a single issue, that of coinciding interests of individual communities to protect or extend boundaries or simply to settle a score. From either an ideological or structural perspective, none of these arrangements involved larger ethnic, ideological, or interclass confrontation.

Other coalitional efforts of a military or protectionist sort arose out of the instability and hostilities of the revolutionary period and its immediate aftermath (1910s and 1920s). These were also organized ad hoc under external threat and with little or no enduring structure. In response to persisting hostilities after the Mexican Revolution, the governor of Oaxaca authorized the establishment of community militias, or Defensas Sociales. The *ayuntamientos* organized within their jurisdictions "groups of citizens that possess their own arms who with sufficient spontaneity present themselves where necessary for public security."[6] These locally focused associations soon became a problem, however, as they developed into uncontrolled vigilante groups and involved themselves in intercommunity warfare and otherwise exacerbated conflict, and they had to be forcibly disarmed by federal troops.

More persisting in structure and function perhaps were organizations that emerged on a regional level during the 1920s and 1930s with respect to land redistribution and/or labor issues. These organizations inspired by the reformist rhetoric and legislation of the post-Revolution period, were organized essentially around single issues or in an effort to gain specific concessions or objectives. One such group that organized in the early 1930s in Mexico City was the Agrupación Socialista Orientadora Mixteca "Tlaxiaco" (ASOMT). This was an organization made up of approximately one hundred Tlaxiaco natives, most of them professionals or skilled workers, and their families, resident in Mexico City.[7] Their slogan was "Mutual Protection. United, We Shall Overcome." In 1935 the group raised funds for construction of the Mercado Juárez in Tlaxiaco and for school construction. Although ASOMT, technically, was a coalition—and an apparently successful one— the activities and the interests of the group were directed almost exclusively to Tlaxiaco and civic improvement, rather than toward Mixtecs in general or the greater Mixteca.

Another, more specifically focused group, organizing in the 1930s, was the Liga de Resistencia de Arrieros Socialistas de la Mixteca (LRASM), with its headquarters in Tlaxiaco.[8] The group coordinated its efforts with La Liga Socialista de Arrieros de Nochixtlan, since their interests and work space often coincided (*arrieros* are muleteers). The objectives of the groups were to promote and protect the interests of a large number of pack-train operators and workers, then the backbone of the transportation system in the Mixteca. The group was often involved in disputes over rates and salaries, violations of federal work laws, contracts, and other conflicts, particularly with merchants in Tlaxiaco.[9] These professional, rather than community-based, organizations continued to operate into the 1950s, when mineral production declined in the area, roads were completed, and automotive transportation largely replaced animal conveyance. While they were in existence, the carriers' coalitions were usually effective in their negotiations with local merchants and producers. Their demands did not extend beyond their specific endeavor, however, and there was no broader ethnic or ideological articulation. They did, however, maintain broader alliances with such regional, state, and national organizations as the Confederación de Ligas Socialistas de Oaxaca and the Unión Revolucionaria de Campesinos.

Manuel Hernández Hernández and the CPMO

The most notable effort at coalition came in November of 1951 with the formation of the Coalición de los Pueblos Mixtecos Oaxaqueños (CPMO). This was a group organized by educated professionals, politicians, bureaucrats, and teachers born in the Mixteca but residing in Mexico City or dividing their time between the Mixteca and Mexico City. The president, principal founder, and guiding figure in this coalition was Dr. Manuel Hernández Hernández, the Mixteca's most prominent leader, sometime legislator, sometime bureaucrat, but full-time political and social activist. The central executive committee of the organization included prominent educators, lawyers, representatives from medicine, education, law, and the sciences. The technical consultant for the group was Alfonso Caso, who was director of the Instituto Nacional Indigenista (INI).

A devastating earthquake struck the Mixteca on May 24, 1959. Dr. Hernández Hernández, who was simultaneously *diputado federal* for the districts of Teposcolula, Tlaxiaco, and Nochixtlan and president of the CPMO, quickly reconnoitered the area, assessed damage, processed information from local authorities and residents, and made two reports to Adolfo López Mateos, the president of the Republic (1958–1964).[10] Extensive damage had been caused by the earthquake, and Hernández Hernández described the problems and asked the Mexican president to intervene with relevant agencies to provide relief. In effect, Hernández Hernández acted as facilitator-mediator for the individual communities by processing and delineating their demands to higher authorities. The relationship of community to facilitator, then, was of a dyadic nature—there was no hint of a pan-Mixteca interest and effort.

Earlier in 1959, Hernández Hernández had intervened on behalf of fourteen of the largest communities in the Mixteca Alta, seeking to mediate their demands to the Comisión Federal de Electricidad for dam construction and electrification.[11] Each community presented its own demands to the government agency with notification to Hernández Hernández, who collated and endorsed the demands and promoted the interests of the communities with the appropriate bureau and officials. Once again, these were individualized requests for assistance rather than collective action.

In 1975 Hernández Hernández, as president of the CPMO, intervened in requests presented by at least fifty-five communities in the districts of Nochixtlan, Tlaxiaco, Teposcolula, Coixtlahuaca, Silacayoapan, Huajuapan, and Jamiltepec.[12] He intervened on behalf of specific communities with the Secretaría de Obras Públicas, Director General of Electrification in the States, C.F.E., Secretaría de Salubridad y Asistencia, the governor of the state, and numerous other state and federal agencies. Demands involved schools, health care delivery and hospitals, highway and bridge construction, potable water and irrigation works, schools, electrification, telephones, sanitation, and public health. Although requests were grouped, each community's demands were presented individually.

Hernández Hernández was a tireless worker, constantly negotiating on behalf of Mixteca communities with Caso and INI, the Secretarías de Salubridad y Asistencia, Educación Pública, Recursos Hidraulicos, the governor of Oaxaca, judicial authorities at the federal and state level, and with unions and other coalitions. Hernández Hernández, employing the CPMO as his operational base, was in a very real sense the major broker between the Mixteca and state and federal government. He was unusually adept at working the political network of the nation to bring about significant change throughout the Mixteca. Given the enormous problems faced by the Mixteca during Mexico's economic modernization, his achievements border on the truly heroic.

The focus of Hernández Hernández and the CPMO was always on the region, the Mixteca, but more specifically on its individual communities. Never was there an explicit appeal to Mixtec ethos or ethnicity, no rebellious intent, no call to organize and fight the oppression of the state or the privileged class. Nowhere in the report in the *Labores de la Coalición* of 1964–65, for example, do we find mention of any long-range plan for the Mixteca or Mixtecs. This is also true for the 1970–71 and 1975 reports of the activities of Hernández Hernández and the CPMO. Community demands were closely monitored and promoted. He served as an effective gatekeeper in the presentation of demands, as the key figure in the informational feedback loop, and as a primary facilitator in the delivery of services to the region. Demands centered around resolution of conflict, land entitlement, resettlement and migration, public education, acquisition of potable water systems, irrigation and erosion, electrification, roads and bridges, extension and repair of telephone systems, health centers and delivery, distribution of *productos de primera necesidad*, administration of justice for native Mixtecos, protection of resources, and general development and advancement of the region.

In all of Hernández Hernández's activities until the 1980s, we may observe a long series of mediated dyadic relationships between community and higher-level agencies or between communities and an interested constituency, normally residents of a particular community, such as "Tlaxiaqueños Resident in Mexico City" or "Asociación Unificadora Coixtlahuaquense," for promoting the general welfare of the community, intervention with public officials or agencies, funds, specific crises, or for multiple objectives of particular communities. There is no pooling of effort or interests, no marshaling of group support on a regional level, no sacrifice of local interests and objectives on behalf of the region as a whole, and no sense of ethnic unity.

Grupo de Tlaxiaqueños Radicados en el Valle de México, A.C. (TRVM), an apparent successor to the CPMO, was established in the early 1980s.

According to their charter, it is a group made up of individuals born in Tlaxiaco and living in the Valley of Mexico.[13] Their objectives are to represent the general interests of Tlaxiaqueños; to study questions affecting administrative activities in Tlaxiaco; to act as a consultative body with respect to various civic and administrative activities; to exercise the right of petition to state and federal authorities in administrative, legal, and economic matters; and to act as a commission of arbitration and mediation with respect to internal differences of Tlaxiaqueños located in the Valley of Mexico and the *municipio* in Oaxaca.

Between 1982 and 1985 the TRVM was involved in fund raising for construction and repair of public buildings in Tlaxiaco and celebration of important events in Tlaxiaco or involving Tlaxiaqueños, such as those honoring Hector Ramírez Bolaños, better known as RAM, the great newspaper caricaturist; the creation of a nursery in Tlaxiaco; celebration of the Tlaxiaco centennial in 1984; and creation of a cultural and promotional film about Tlaxiaco.[14] During the existence of the coalition, concerns shifted somewhat from basic services (water, health, electrification, telephones, and intercommunity conflicts) to construction, community boosterism, administrative matters, and political, ceremonial, and symbolic endeavors. Consistently, however, the group was always community oriented. Ethnicity or the Mixteca as a whole were never important issues.

The Trique Movement

Although the matter has yet to be studied in depth, it is quite evident that a concept of ethnic unification may be emerging among the Trique (or Triqui), a very strong cultural and linguistic enclave within the Mixteca. Although the region—which spans portions of three districts, Tlaxiaco, Putla, and Juxtlahuaca—has for generations been torn by intergroup violence, there is growing recognition of a common Trique ethnicity and language. There are signs that Triques are organizing on a supracommunity level. This is one of the most conflictive areas in all of Oaxaca—and that is saying a lot—and most of the conflict takes place among Trique communities. The militant Movimiento de Unificación de Lucha Triqui (MULT) was formed in 1981.[15] The organization was created with the help of the Coalición Obrera Campesina Estudiantil del Istmo (COCEI), and it is unclear whether this development represented a grassroots political movement or was an externally initiated movement arising out of the nationally pervasive student and teacher movement, the critical economic situation of the early 1980s, and growing national awareness of the plight of indigenous peoples. The movement seems to have met with some limited success by calling attention to conditions in the Mixteca and by affecting elections.

Marcos Sandoval of San Andrés Chicahuastla emerged as an effective leader and mediator on the intercommunity level. He made serious efforts to mediate and resolve intercommunity conflicts and to raise Trique ethnic awareness. He and members of his family have sponsored the development of a weavers' guild in San Andrés that includes women from San Andrés and surrounding *ranchos*, but this remains a basically San Andrés coalition. Until medical disabilities and advancing age conspired to limit his activities, Don Marcos regularly intervened in local conflicts while simultaneously being involved in indigenous affairs at the national level. Neither he nor others, however, have succeeded in bringing social and political cohesion to the Triques. Much of the organization and the raising of Trique ethnic consciousness is the result of influences by political activists or teachers, but it is equally clear that the Triques themselves, Marcos Sandoval Jr. among them, have been instrumental in both the initiation and leadership of their own ethnic movement. Thoroughgoing anthropological study of the Trique movement should be a high priority for current and future students of the Mixteca.

Mixtec Ethnicity

According to Fredrik Barth, "ethnic groups are categories of ascription and identification by the actors themselves,"[16] and designate, either wholly or in part, groups that are biologically self perpetuating; share fundamental cultural values; make up a field of communication and interaction; and have a membership that identifies itself and is recognized by others as different from other categories of the same order. For these criteria to be relevant to the Mixteca, either now or in the past, "ethnic group" is best equated with village, *pueblo*, or community rather than with a nation or people. Even Triques, although affiliated through such movements as MULT, still identify strongly with particular communities, such as San Andrés Chicahuaxtla or San Juan Copala.

Although references to Mixtecs, Triques, Chochos, Amuzgos, or other sociolinguistic collectivities are widely employed, it is still the *pueblo* that is most meaningful to residents of the Mixteca. Activists, scholars, writers, and politicians find these terms convenient, but for modern "Mixtecos," and, in the sense of Barth's definition, the relevant "ethnic group" and point of reference is the *pueblo*. All modern ethnologists working in the Mixteca, from Tecomastlahuaca to Cuquila, Nuyoo, Coixtlahuaca, Tilantongo, Jicayan, Tlaxiaco, Mixtepec, or Nicananduta, focus intensively, and nearly exclusively, on the particular *pueblo*, not on a broader ethnic agglomeration. Beyond the community the concept of a broader, regional ethnicity has little relevance or practical application for the Mixteca.

Crises, common interests and needs, charismatic leadership, and external threats have not brought communities together in the region, at least not in modern times. Any such tendencies are impeded by a long-standing enmity between communities, a pervasive ethos of limited good—that is, political and economic resources are limited, and there is never enough to meet the demands of all communities—resulting in a kind of community *egoismo* and a seeming inability to organize beyond the local level. To date, ethnicity has not played a significant role in the coalitional equation or in hundreds of conflict cases, the presentation of demands, or statements of public interest. The external conflicts that Bartolomé and Barabas[17] suggest to be the critical factor in the circumstantial agglutination of communities and the formation of ethnopolitical movements simply have not occurred or have not occurred with sufficient force in the modern Mixteca to induce supracommunal regional organization or ideological unification.

So, what would induce amalgamation, or give a sense of common identity and purpose, a sense of "We have something in common. We are Mixtecs!" This concept is most relevant and operative when Mixtec migrants leave their home communities, move outside to the *colonias* that they have established in Tehuantepec, Mexico City, Ensenada, Southern California, Fresno, Chicago, or in Woodburn, Oregon. This linking on the basis of regional or ethnic identity seems to occur when Mixtecs feel threatened, alone, defenseless, and disenfranchised. The traditional community support group is missing. This results in a grasping for an identity, for collateral and moral support beyond the traditional family, *compadrazgo*, and community level.[18]

The concept of "ethnicity," in the sense of social identity, ethnic pride or strong, even militant, identification with a particular ethnic group, emerged strongly in the United States in the 1960s with the Black Pride/Power movements, the Chicano movement, Native American activism, and so on. It was also at this time that anthropologists began paying attention to the concept and began explicit studies of "ethnicity." In the 1970s and 1980s, ethnicity became a subject of attention for Latin Americanist scholars, particularly with respect to groups that have suffered obvious oppression and were without an effective voice or representation. Anthropologists, in effect, took it upon themselves to speak for these groups, to attempt to represent their interests, and to plead their cause, as well as to define, describe, and analyze the concept and the reality of ethnicity.[19] An additional point worth stressing is that there is a strong temptation on our part, as anthropologist-spokespersons for the groups that we work with, to infer a social identity, when they themselves may not be conscious of their own ethnicity. Or their concept of ethnic identity may differ substantially from the one which we may assign to them. The extension of this point is that we do not believe that there is now, or ever has been, an ethos of Mixtec ethnicity among the populations resident in the Mixteca of Oaxaca. There is identification with the Mixteca region, but far stronger is the identification with community. Douglas Butterworth, Carlos Orellana, and others have found this to be true even among migrants who had established themselves in Mexico City.[20]

Soy Mixteco means "I am from the Mixteca," and sometimes "I speak Mixteco," but it does not mean that one is culturally or ethnically Mixtec. One would call attention to oneself in this way only when speaking of a cognitive opposition to Zapotecs, Chinantecs, North Americans, and so on. Mixtecs residing in the Mixteca do not dwell on Mixtec culture or being identified with other Mixtec speakers, and they voice no particular pride in being Mixtec. The extent to which notions of ethnicity or "common cause" might change in response to economic conditions and the current Mixtec diaspora across North America is difficult to predict, but it has not happened in the past.

MODERN MIXTECA ECONOMICS

We mentioned in the preceding chapter that the Mixteca's regional market-exchange system of the 1890s met 90 percent or more of the economic needs of the area. As a result, there was little need to reach beyond the regional system for basic commodities and services. Tailored dresses, shirts and trousers, satin ribbon, olive oil, wine, jewelry, and porcelain produced in Europe, Mexico City, or Puebla had their place on the shelves of the larger stores of the *villas* and may have been considered "necessities" by a privileged few, but they were simply incidental to the larger economy of the region. National economic stability and Porfiriato-era industrialization contributed little to the integration of the Mixteca into the larger economic domain. Exchanges with the national system were limited; some maize, wheat, livestock, meat, hides, and wool were exported, but little was demanded from the outside. It is perhaps not surprising that there is strong persistence of many traditional economic patterns, especially through the 1950s, and some until the present day.[21]

The Mixteca's system of production and distribution had attained a high level of independence with respect to the rest of Mexico by the end of the nineteenth century, but with the dramatic upheavals of the Mexican Revolution, the influences of migration, the extension of national highways and motor transport to the area, the intrusion of foreign markets and products and "created needs," and poorly conceived national economic policies, economic autonomy has been sacrificed. With twentieth-century modernization we observe "mutually reinforcing changes that work in the same direction to change more or less self-sufficient village economies and societies into inter-acting sectors of national economy, culture, and polity."[22] To some extent these changes have improved educational opportunities and economic pros-pects for the majority of citizens in the Mixteca (more so, however, for Spanish-speaking individuals), but at the price of greater dependence on the vicissitudes of the national and global economy. Whether this trend is reversible remains to be seen.

There is virtually no formal study of the economy of the Mixteca during the first half of the twentieth century, and only a few incidental studies in later years. It is useful to be guided by baseline studies conducted in the Mixteca in the 1940s and 1950s, again in the 1970s, and by the authors' nearly constant observation of production, marketing, and migration activity in the Mixteca since the 1960s.[23] De la Peña's studies of the 1940s emphasized geo-graphy, resources, and production activities; the lack of, and the need for, infrastructural development; shortage of productive lands; and inadequate or antiquated technology. There was a major emphasis on the impoverishment of the area; the denigration of cottage industries, such as palm weaving, pottery, and rustic woodworking, as being basically nonproductive, nonlucrative activi-ties; and the exploitation of human labor and natural resources by greedy businessmen in Tehuacan, Puebla, and Mexico City. The major recommen-dation to come from this policy-oriented study of the Mixteca was emigra-tion on a grand scale. There was little hope for a satisfying life in the Mixteca, and constructive recommendations or solutions were not offered.

Alejandro Marroquín and a small group of students concentrated efforts on a study of the periodic market of Tlaxiaco. Although there are illumi-nating descriptions of market activities, occupational specializations, and moni-toring of the origins and destinations of market clients and the flow of products through the plaza, the emphasis was on systemic failure—the failure of Tlaxiaco to develop an industrial base, criticism of the dependence on exchange for profit rather than productive activities in the *cabecera*, and, once again, the exploitation of marketing activities by a privileged group of entre-preneurs. There was virtually no consideration of the historic development of the market, which has operated in Tlaxiaco since the mid-sixteenth century, and probably since pre-Hispanic times. Neither was concern shown for the economically integrative functions which the market served for a huge area of the Mixteca or for the important relationships between fixed-locus businesses in Tlaxiaco, itinerant trade, and the weekly plaza.[24]

The third significant study is John Warner's detailed consideration of the Nochixtlan Valley market system in the early 1970s. Warner described in detail not only the physical aspects of the Nochixtlan market, as well as those of Jaltepec, Teposcolula, Tamazulapan, and Coixtlahuaca, but focused on the flow of goods and people through the markets, the activities of numerous *regatones* who ranged widely in cyclical fashion from market to market within the area and between the Mixteca and critical capital markets in Mexico City, Puebla, Tehuacan, and Oaxaca. The study, richly authenticated by a massive photographic collection, stands today, forty years later, as the best available source of reliable description and statistics on the modern Mixteca economy. Warner emphasized the strength of the Mixteca market system, and unlike the more pessimistic Moisés de la Peña and Marroquín, predicted not only survival of the system but even greater future growth beyond the level of the 1970s. Viewing the system as it functions in the present, it is abundantly clear that Warner's predictions were right. Markets in such centers as Nochixtlan, Huajuapan, Tlaxiaco, Tamazulapan, Jicayan, Pinotepa, and Putla are thriving as never before.

Several other studies conducted primarily in the 1970s and 1980s have focused primarily on production activities and economic demography, some being community-based studies, others depending heavily on the official Mexican censuses of 1970, 1980, 1990, and so on. All studies point to a general economic deterioration in the communities; the inadequacies of cottage industries like palm weaving, textiles, woodworking, and pottery; the failure of economic self-reliance; the increasing reliance on migration either as an escape from poverty or as an essential component to the maintenance of life in the communities; and the increasing dependency on governmental social and economic supports. These studies are either too preliminary or simply fail to take into account recent trends in the communities toward visible improvement in the general standard of living.

Economic Globalization

Levels of independence-dependence shifted significantly in the 1950s with the extension of a highway system into the area. Mass-produced goods were introduced, and preferences shifted in favor of "city goods." Local industries declined in importance as buyers opted for the plastics of Mexico City; the blankets, blouses, shirts, dresses, and trousers of Puebla; the shoes and leather goods of Tehuacan; the metal goods of Monterrey; the glazed pottery of

Guanajuato or Puebla; the canned goods from all over the Republic; and the vegetables and fruits of Puebla, Veracruz, and the Isthmus of Tehuantepec. Losing favor were the products of local household industries: baskets, *petates*, pottery, hand-wrought iron, leather garments, harnesses and saddles, shoes, boots, cotton clothing, woolen garments and covers, and wooden tools and containers.

Resulting from the "modernizing" extension of highways from central Mexico to Huajuapan, Nochixtlan, Tlaxiaco, and to Putla and gradually beyond, was the transformation of the Mixteca from an integrated and essentially independent market system to a system organically dependent on, and captive to, the national-international marketing system. What did remain intact, however, was the traditional *tianguis* (plaza market), which not only survived the coming of the highways but which functions today much as it did before the 1950s. Although product mix has changed markedly in recent decades, these markets continue to link dozens of farming communities, some of them with specialized household industries, into distributional constellations and to serve as collecting points for goods being imported from or exported to other regions.

It is unlikely at this point in history that there can be a shift in the Mixteca economy from the current trend toward broader economic involvement. Undoubtedly, most observers would agree that such involvement is both necessary and desirable. Unfortunately, modernization is inevitably coupled with increasing external dependence and lessening regional self-sufficiency. If the Mixteca is to survive as a cultural, social, and economic entity, however, ways must be found that are both innovative and retroactive. There must also be an examination of the economic potentialities of the area, the needs and desires of the people, and the requirements of national and international market systems. Practical solutions should be sought that borrow from the past, yet function realistically in the present and are adaptive for the future.

It is suggested that potent alternatives to the current socioeconomic situation may be found by reviving and readapting nineteenth-century microindustrial production to the realities of the present and the anticipated demands of the future. We are, in fact, advocating a return to something resembling the economic system in operation in the Mixteca at the close of the nineteenth century and that we described in the last chapter. At the same time, it must be said that the region is beyond the point of no return. It is irrevocably linked to the Mexican national economy and beyond. Electricity, roads, schools, and potable water systems have been extended into the Mixteca largely through action of the federal government. Remittances sent home from migrant workers have become essential components of household and municipal incomes. These trends are likely to continue.

Mixtecs cannot be denied the cell phones, satellite dishes, four-wheel drives, PCs and iPads, and other consumer goods that they have grown to expect as basic needs. Their way of life will be far more secure, however, if there is a resuscitation of the nineteenth-century economic system with modifications and restructuring to meet secondary as well as primary needs and a backing away from the creeping dependency on a national and inter-national economy that is, after all, based on profit and the exploitation of market participants. Mixtecs are certainly capable of producing the maize-beans-squash-chili-wheat, the bread and tortillas, the meat and poultry, the cloth, garments, bed covers, lumber, furniture, hides-leather-shoes, felt hats, and baskets-mats-bags that they produced so effectively in the nineteenth century and in some instances until very recently.

Despite a relatively stable population and the intrusion of external markets, production in all of these areas in Tlaxiaco is well above what it was a decade ago, and clearly it is substantially above late-nineteenth-century levels. Although comparable evidence is not available, similar spot growth is present in Nochi-xtlan, Putla, Tamazulapan, and Huajuapan. The more persistent trend, however, is the relative growth of commercial enterprise, retail outlets for externally produced clothing; electrical appliances, radios, and televisions; hardware; construction materials; and so on. Thus, while there are indications that localized production of certain items continues strongly, the clearest indications are that the penetration of the external market, economic exploitation, and dependency of the Mixteca on the national-international market has never been greater. The situation is further exacerbated by the exodus of migrants who contribute to the external labor force and abandon any possibilities of building the Mixteca's productive base. This includes, not incidentally, the agri-cultural base and a local, reliable, and sustainable means of food security.

Recent economic advances in the Mixteca are made possible primarily from reinvestment of funds derived from labor and other economic activities in Mexico City, Puebla, Oaxaca, and especially northwest Mexico–Baja Cali-fornia, the United States, and Canada. The most visible manifestation of this economic "turnaround" is evident in the greatly increased building activity and accumulation-consolidation of property by migrants in such "migratory towns" as San Sebastián Nicananduta, Chilapa de Díaz, Coixtlahuaca, San Juan Mixtepec, San Pedro Yucunama, Tejupan, Juxtlahuaca, Huazolotitlan, and Nochixtlan. This new capitalization is also highly evident in larger market centers like Tlaxiaco, Putla, Pinotepa, Teposcolula, Tamazulapan, Huajuapan, and in Acatlan, Puebla, where increased building, land acquisition, and entrepreneurial activity result both from migrant investment and a general upsurge in production-distribution and extension of federal and state agencies and services to the regional capitals. Huajuapan, for example, has grown from a modest population of around thirty-five thousand in 1970 to over a hundred thousand inhabitants today and is known as Oaxaca's "northern capital."

These hopeful developments are not to be taken as an indication of the achievement of an economic miracle in the Mixteca. They simply provide strong evidence that economic conditions have improved vastly in the region since the 1950s. The economic collapse that came with the end of the Porfiriato and the disruptions of the revolutionary period, a collapse that in some instances led to food scarcity and starvation, has moved beyond living memory. That the Mixteca survived that implosion had much to do with its relative productive autonomy. That circumstance has assuredly changed. In the present-day context, the Mixteca is far from finding a balance between global integration and economic self-sufficiency. To the extent that such a balance is achieved could well determine the fate of the Mixtec in their native land.

The Great Mixtec Diaspora

The roots of migration lie deep within the Mixtec population of Oaxaca. By the fourteenth and fifteenth centuries, two to three hundred years before the Spanish Conquest—and probably earlier—Mixtecs, feeling the pressure of population growth in an area of limited arable lands and resources, coupled with a desire to exploit the fertile lands to the east, were moving into the rich lands of the Valley of Oaxaca. Their presence was strongly manifested along the western edges of the valley, in Huitzo, Etla, Cuilapan, Xoxocotlan and Zaachila, but historical and archaeological evidence indicates a Mixtec presence far to the east, around Mitla, Tlacolula, and Matatlan, even as far east and southeast as the Isthmus of Tehuantepec.[25] Others were being attracted to the area of central Puebla and either voluntarily or forcibly arriving in the Valley of Mexico. The evidence of Mixtec influence and authorship of Culhua-Mexica art and craftsmanship is so strong as to leave little doubt of their actual presence in and around Tenochtitlan.[26]

During the Colonial period, Mixtecs were on the move. They were fully involved in trading expeditions to Tehuantepec, Guatemala, Guerrero, Puebla, Veracruz, Mexico, and Guadalajara. They migrated seasonally to Veracruz, Puebla, the Cuicatec Cañada, and the coastal areas of Oaxaca and Guerrero, where they worked Spanish *fincas*, *haciendas*, and mines, and as laborers on royal roads, fortifications, and port facilities in such widely separated areas as Veracruz, Acapulco, and Zacatecas.[27] While these movements occurred constantly and involved significant numbers, there is little indication of permanent removal of populations from the Mixteca to other areas of New Spain. Throughout the post-Independence nineteenth century, the Mixtecs, except for seasonal migration to Puebla, Veracruz, and other parts of Oaxaca, were not assimilated into other areas or cultures. They very much stayed at home. In the twentieth century, however, this was to change drastically, as the Mixtecs wandered far beyond the Mixteca in their continuing quest for survival and betterment.

Migration before and after the Mexican Revolution

From the early 1900s until mid-century, the migration of Mixtecs to the north, particularly to the border and beyond in the American Southwest, was generally as individuals, in some cases families, but there was little recognition of ethnic identity, of belonging to Mixtec society or an organization of Mixtecos. An individual migrates. A brother follows. Then a nephew comes. The process was sporadic, intermittent, and without formal associations, agencies, or sodalities. Eventually, as the gates to migration opened, Mixtecs went to the more familiar, albeit less lucrative, Mexican northwest: Sinaloa, Sonora, and Baja California until there were literally thousands of them in that quadrant of the country. With a foothold, a strong presence in northwest Mexico, the next logical step was to continue into the United States, first to California, Arizona, and Texas, but quickly well beyond the southwestern United States.[28]

What began as a trickle in the early twentieth century eventually became an inundation by the 1960s and later. This grand south-to-north movement continues unabated until the present day and extends from Oaxaca to central Mexico; the greater northwest of Mexico, including the vast Mexican-American border zone; and on into the contiguous United States, Canada, and Alaska. Until mid-century, however, there was little or no systematic study of the migratory process, with most information on Mixtec migration or transnational association being anecdotal and, for the most part, unrecorded. Although noted by investigators such as Manuel Gamio, Gonzalo Aguirre Beltrán, Manuel Hernández Hernández, and Douglas Butterworth, major anthropological-sociological attention was directed to the Mixtec community, and to ethnohistorical and archaeological studies focused on the Mixteca itself. Significant advances were made between 1970 and 2010 when research turned more fully toward those Mixtecs who had settled outside of the homeland

and were living and working as well as migrating between Oaxaca and cities to the north.[29]

The reasons for emigration from the Mixteca to the north are in some cases clear and in others perhaps more obscure. The obvious primary cause would be economic necessity. Although figuring prominently in the history of Mexico and generally seen as a force of progressive change, the Great Revolution of the early twentieth century had a devastating effect on the Mixteca countryside. No one living there was unaffected by the war. Until a few years ago, old-timers spoke of the "good old days" of the Porfiriato, when everyone knew what to expect, life was dependable, and people had what they needed to survive. The Mexican Revolution, however, was devastating. Anarchy prevailed, with groups of *bandidos* riding into town one day, robbing and burning, and the next day another group doing the same. It was a time of eating rats, snakes, worms, insects, leaves, and wild roots, of boiling up corn cobs, in order to survive. The "time of misery" lasted from around 1915 until a semblance of peace was attained in the late 1920s. There were many Mixtecs who vowed never to repeat those experiences. Those who had been involved in the *golondrina* (literally, a swallow or other small migratory bird) seasonal migration to Veracruz, Tehuantepec, and Puebla moved permanently to those areas. Reluctantly perhaps, others went to the larger cities like Puebla and Mexico City. Some stayed, establishing *colonias*.

Migratory trends continued through the 1920s and persisted until the present, but as time passed the paths of migration extended further and further north, to the Mexico-U.S. frontier, to Baja California, to Texas, Arizona, California, and beyond. This great march north, like a swift-flowing human river, once set in motion gained increasing momentum and has remained a fixture of Mixtec life to the present. Never again can the Mixteca or the Mixtecs be seen in isolation, holed up in the mountains and valleys of western and northwest Oaxaca and southern Puebla. They are caught up in a vast "transnational community," living their "trans-border lives," and quickly assimilating to the new cultures of the north, adapting as they have adapted for thousands of years to the varied landscapes and climates of North America and to the cultures and peoples that occupy those lands.

As an example of early migration to the United States, the case of an individual from the Tlaxiaco area can be mentioned. Otilio Sánchez was from San Miguel el Grande, but feeling the devastation of the Great Revolution and the ongoing warfare with neighboring Chalcatongo, and in response to the attraction of opportunities in the United States, he left his home community,

journeyed north, crossed the frontier at Tijuana in the mid-1930s, and settled in the San Isidro area near San Diego. Having left a wife and child
behind in San Miguel, he lost little time in finding work in the fields and
factories of the area and in establishing a new family in the north. Given the
great difficulties of communication and travel at the time, Otilio developed
a double life, maintaining his new family in California, with infrequent
returns to San Miguel to see his primary wife and a daughter, assist in labor
and maintenance of the household, and provide at least some financial support,
before returning to California, where he eventually died. His first wife never
left the Mixteca, but his daughter migrated to Mexico City, then married
and lived in the northern United States. His granddaughter was highly educated and became a professional musician, performed internationally, and
became widely recognized as a spokesperson for the Mixtec people, especially Mixtec women. There are many such personal histories relating to the
continuing expansion and adaptation of Mixtecs and their descendants over
the last century, and as presented in the incisive works of Butterworth, Kearney,
Edinger, Colby, Stephen, Velasco Ortiz, Cornelius and associates, and others.

Braceros, *Golondrinas*, and Migrant Identities

Many others followed migratory pioneers such as Otilio in search of a better
life in the north, slowly and sporadically in the 1930s, increasingly, as temporary
laborers, under the U.S.-Mexico Bracero (hired hand) Program from the early
1940s until 1964, with migration rising to massive proportions in the 1970s
and persisting to the present. The Bracero Program arose from an agreement
between Franklin Roosevelt and the Mexican president, Ávila Camacho, to
bring contract laborers into the United States during the Second World War.[30]
By the time the program was terminated, upwards of four million Mexicans
had crossed the border. Once the program came to an end, the *braceros* and
their families quickly learned how to get themselves across the border and
how to adapt to the new environment. In prolonged conversations with about
two dozen *braceros* and "ex-*braceros*" in the community of San Juan Yucuita
(Nochixtlan), it was clear that each individual went to the United States on
a contractual basis, all expecting to return to their home communities after
periods ranging from a few months to two years. It was only later that many
of those same individuals and their relatives migrated with the expectation of
residing permanently in the United States. One of those individuals, Gilberto
Cruz Ramos, by 1966 had made fourteen trips to the United States. By 2010,
including sons, daughters, grandchildren and great grandchildren, sons and

daughters-in-law, nieces and nephews, well over a hundred *familiares* of Don Gilberto had made a successful adaptation to residence and a permanent life in Nashville, Tennessee.

Residents of the community of San Jerónimo Nicananduta in the Mixteca Alta, as described in commendable detail by Catherine Colby, have worked out a successful adaptation whereby two groups of men and women are permanent *golondrina* migrant workers, one in the United States and the other in Canada.[31] They consistently remit funds to their families in Nicananduta and have become the primary source of support for the governance, general community improvement, and sponsorship of its major ritual-ceremonial activities. The investment in the community is visibly reflected in the expanded, modernized *norteamericano* style of domestic and commercial architecture, and in clothing, cars, and trucks. In some cases, as with the pioneer Otilio, some of the male migrants have formed two families, one in Nicananduta and the other in the north. At least some of the migrants invite their wives and children from the north to visit Nicananduta, so they "can know their sisters and brothers."[32]

In the 1980s "hometown associations" formed along the Mexico-U.S. border, in Mexico City, in the fields of Sonora and Sinaloa and in the San Quintín Valley of Baja California Norte, and then spread to Tijuana and on into California. Gradually, the associations grew to include not just Mixtecs but eventually Mixtecs, Zapotecs, Triques, and Mixes of Oaxaca. In the north these associations shared a common identity as "Oaxacan indigenous people straddling two nation states."[33] This change in the identity of Mixtec migrants in California was first pointed out by Michael Kearney and Carol Nangengast, but it was not until the late 1990s that there was systematic study of the relationship between collective agency—such as these new associations—"and the process of reconstituting migrant ethnic identity."[34]

By the mid-1990s, fourteen Oaxacan indigenous migrant organizations, mainly of Mixtec origin, had formed along the Mexico-California border and were registered as functioning binational organizations. In September of 1994 the largest and most inclusive such organization, the Frente Indígena Oaxaqueño Binacional (FIOB), had formed, and the organization included not only hundreds of participants from the cities along the border but also government officials from Mexico City and California, activists, academics, and students. By 2000–2001 Laura Velasco Ortiz found twenty-two such organizations, including FIOB in the area, such that some sixty thousand farm workers were registered in San Quintín, most of them Mixtecs, with their numbers rising to a hundred thousand depending on the agricultural season.[35]

It was abundantly clear that by the early 2000s the Mixtecs were the largest group of indigenous migrants in the Mexico-U.S. border zone. Velasco Ortiz nonetheless observes that "after almost two decades of mass migration to this region, it had become evident that their hometown roots, and their sense of ethnic identity as Zapotecos, Mixtecos, and so on, still exercised a powerful influence on their patterns of association."[36] In terms of general adaptation the sense of being Mixtecs, Zapotecs, or Triques, or just as indigenous Oaxaqueños, was a source of solidarity. Having noted those circumstances, it is vital to recognize that with the recent upsurge in migration and settlement along the border, a new transnational identity had formed and migrants saw themselves as "binational indigenous Oaxaqueños."

Velasco Ortiz expertly describes how ethnic identity changes under conditions of international migration and convincingly demonstrates the processes contributing to the emergence of organizations and their leaders as collective and individual agents of change. Curiously, perhaps, the Mixtecs thus managed two major achievements in the mid- to late twentieth century: in their migrations northward they retained their local "hometown" identities while simultaneously developing a whole new "binational ethnic identity." And they subsequently carried this orientation with them to new destinations in California, the American Southwest, the Pacific Northwest, and even to Chicago and the area of Carbondale, Illinois, where the junior author resides, and elsewhere in the United States.[37]

Emergence of a Transnational Culture

As the level and penetration of migration have risen, it is essential to point out that there has been a corresponding increase among certain individuals and groups in the United States to oppose the incorporation of Mexican migrants.[38] Code words such as "illegal" or "alien" or "undocumented" are repeatedly heard in conversation, in regional and national newspapers, and most especially on rabble-rousing talk-radio and cable news programs. An additional, equally pernicious element embedded in coded expressions is that any Mexican, Guatemalan, or Central American, frequently fully documented or citizens by birth or naturalization, is stereotyped and branded thus and suffers from the prejudice associated with the expressions.

Having referenced the "bad side" of the recipient society, one must hasten to add that Mesoamerican migrants, Mixtecs most prominently among them, are considered to be hard-working and dependable, and they make up a significant proportion of the work force associated with seasonal agriculture, food processing, wine producing, home and garden maintenance, restaurant operation, auto and machine repair, and construction. Many have opened their own businesses, and quite successfully so. This is abundantly obvious in the Oregon communities of the home territory of the senior author, places like Gresham, Hillsboro, Portland, Salem, Keiser, Woodburn, Eugene, Newport–Lincoln City, Madras-Redmond-Bend, and elsewhere.[39] Washington State, and quite obviously California and the greater Southwest, Nashville, Atlanta, Chicago, and many other areas, even Washington, D.C., and New York City, reflect comparable successes. It is difficult to imagine vineyards/wineries or fruit and vegetable production of the western and southeastern United States or Canada without the involvement of Mixtecs and their Oaxacan neighbors. They also figure prominently in the labor/management cadres of major manufacturing concerns and service/maintenance providers, in leisure and recreation industries, and as entrepreneurs and operators of significant commercial enterprises throughout North America. The contribution of Mixtecs to United States commerce, industry, and services has been great, especially when considering their relative numbers and the hardships they face in entering and remaining in their adopted country. Their successes, moreover, are directly reflected in the Mixteca itself, through the financial reinvestment and technological applications resulting from their experiences abroad.

Despite concerted official efforts to turn back the tide of migration, the flow of Mixtecs to the United States and Canada has persisted. Their adaptation to life in the north has been highly successful, and the economic, social, and ideological effects on countless communities and families throughout the Mixtecas have been monumental. The studies of Michael Kearney and associates, Steven Edinger, Federico Besserer, and Lynn Stephen have produced some of the most graphic and intimate descriptions of the successes and failures of these resettled individuals, their adaptations as families, their transnational associations, and the effect of migration on home communities back in the Mixteca. These anthropological participant-observers, along with Laura Velasco Ortiz, Catherine Colby, and many others, have, in fact, indicated that Mixtecs throughout northwest Mexico, the Mexico-U.S. border, and the entire western United States have become part of a vibrant new transnational culture.[40]

This movement to north of the Mexican frontier is both related to and in contrast to the ages-old dispersal of the Mixtecs and their culture from the Mixteca Alta and Baja to the Pacific coast, the Valley of Oaxaca, Puebla, and eventually all the way to the Valley of Mexico, at least some of this movement taking place by the eleventh century, perhaps earlier. Throughout this process, however, the Mixtecs retained their identity, and through their social and political institutions they developed relations with Zapotecs, Chochona,

Ixcatecos, Triques, Chatinos, Tlapanecos, Cuicatecos, Nahuas, and, eventually, with Europeans and Africans. We view these successive migrations as an adaptive strategy that intentionally or not has contributed to the Mixtecs' long-term cultural survival.[41]

It is remarkable that, as of this moment, Mixtecs continue to adapt to modern circumstances by once again working out relationships among the groups of the component towns and villages of the native region, even at a distant remove from the Mixteca, and perhaps even more impressively with Zapotecs, Triques, Mixes, and other ethnic groups of Oaxaca, and, of course, with the ethnic congeries of North America. As a result, they are undergoing rapid integration into the nations of the United States and Canada, and certainly in a new and special way as a widely scattered ethnic group in their native Mexico. Moreover, the mark and effects of these recent migrations are starkly evident in the Mixteca. It is, however, abundantly clear that the Mixteca is a special place with a special identity, a way of life that began to take shape more than thirty-five hundred years ago and that thrives and continues to evolve to the present time.

Past, Present, and Future of Mixtec Studies

In the preceding pages an attempt has been made to collect, organize, and utilize several types of source materials and through them to observe a developing culture and its major adaptations and transformations over three and a half millennia. The senior author has published two earlier volumes in English with an aim toward comprehensive coverage, but reanalysis and revision of old materials, acquisition of new historical materials, a virtual revolution in archaeological survey and excavation, and the appearance of new anthropological studies of all kinds have made it both feasible and desirable to prepare the present volume. This convergent methodology stresses the integration of archaeology, linguistics, history, and ethnology, and it is the only approach that can lead to an understanding of the unfolding history of Mixtec civilization.

The story began with the prehistory of the Mixteca. This is a construct based on inferences drawn from archaeological evidence. Archaeology has its strengths. How else could the facts, continuities, and transformations of prehistoric cultures be known without examination of ancient cultural remains and studies of past environments? Archaeology emphasizes its scientific objectives, methodology, and procedures. But archaeology is as much art as science. Science dominates archaeology in its goals of systematic research design, the formation and delineation of theoretical propositions, careful strategic planning, precise techniques of recovery, preparation of materials, and meticulous recording. In the game of science as practiced by the archaeologist, however, a good deal of faith is involved—faith that the archaeologist has been reasonably objective, careful, and honest. It is virtually impossible to replicate an archaeologist's excavation. Normally the context of discovery is destroyed in the process of recovery and study. Where sufficient numbers of comparative studies are available, patterns emerge and begin to form an interpretive context. But we are limited in our ability to use an approach of this kind, there being so few comparative archaeological studies available for the Mixteca. The regional surveys discussed in this volume are an example of this approach, but how many excavations offer a genuine one-to-one comparison? We just do not have them (yet) in sufficient abundance in the Mixteca.

We emphasized the value of the historical document that may be reduced to raw ethnographic data and incorporated into a reconstruction of culture either *in* or *through* time. The document is the key to all. The better and more abundant the documentation, the better the archaeologist may follow and describe the development of individual cultures over extended periods of time. Conscious or not, archaeologists operate with a model of what they know, often very superficially, of the Culhua-Mexica of Bernardino de Sahagún or the Yucatec Maya of Diego de Landa. Absent the documentation, archaeologists must base their reconstructions on what they discern from material remains and modern comparative ethnology or from "models" drawn from just about anywhere in the world of something roughly comparable.

The archeological record is highly fragmentary. It lacks the necessary detail to flesh out a cultural complex or a totally reliable long-range history of development. Some archaeologists like to excavate ceremonial centers and clean out tombs, but they find domestic architecture mundane, boring, or just incidental to what is happening "downtown." Others reverse the preference. Hopefully, they will work at the same sites. With respect to ethnographic materials, trying to infer the past from the present, even in the conservative rural societies of Mexico, is a risky procedure, and unless done carefully and authoritatively, is likely to produce distortions of past reality. Done properly, with several independent and complementary sources of information, it can transform our views of prehistoric life.

The historical record is full of gaps and can be a quagmire of misconception, prejudice, and exaggeration. But the ethnohistorian, if doing a proper job, is alert to these problems and takes them into consideration. The real strength of ethnohistory, however, is the potential for replication inherent in documentary research. The document is there. It is available. Inferences drawn by one researcher can be reexamined by another. That, in some ways, is closer to science than what we do as archaeologists. Where archaeologists have specific documentation from the sixteenth century on, as in Mexico, they are doing less than their best if they fail to utilize the available record to the utmost in attempting to discover what actually happened in the past. How spare and distorted would be our vision of Tenochtitlan, the Templo Mayor, or the rather unimpressive piles of stone at Tula, Hidalgo, without Sahagún, Durán, Bernal Díaz, Cortés, Motolinía, Herrera y Tordesillas, Tezozomoc, or the *Codex Mendoza*?

Several significant features of Mixtec culture have been observed as they were conditioned by temporal and historical factors. These range in magnitude from a total cultural tradition (Mixtec culture) or the generalized features of native government in Mexico (the *cacicazgo*) to the population profile, religious practices, economy, sociopolitical organization, and communal structure of specific localities like Yanhuitlan, Teposcolula, and Tututepec, and the content and function of the ruling institution and its changing complexes of goods, privileges, services, and properties. An attempt has been made to consider a specific role, that of *cacique*-ruler, during the Colonial period and to make certain judgments as to the personalities and modes of performance of the individual occupants of that role-complex.

It is now possible to more adequately realize the potential and limits of the historical document as an ethnographic device. It can be specific in its content; it allows the anthropologist to follow the history and cultural development of a society, and in the case of Colonial Mexico a single community or even a particular role can be observed. The document records what would inevitably be lost. The reliability of written records can be scrutinized by careful collation and comparison with other forms of evidence, and the raw data—that is, the documentation—can be subjected to repeated examination and reevaluation.

The writers of sixteenth-century documents were not trained ethnologists, and they could not foresee the interests of twenty-first-century anthropologists. Consequently there are limitations to the use of such records, particularly in the study of social and community organization. Unfortunately, there are no treatises on the Mixtecs that are comparable to those of Sahagún for the Culhua-Mexica, Landa for the Mayans, or Fray Pablo Beaumont for the Tarascans. Available documents often record hints and suggestions on many aspects of Mixtec life, but it is sometimes quite difficult to find sufficient material to complete the picture of a particular cultural element. Despite these limitations, unpublished archival documentation contains more specific cultural data than one might suspect. For the anthropologist the major obstacle to the use of this documentation is the laborious process of gleaning information that was considered useful to Spanish administrators from a mass of verbiage and legal formulary and converting it to pertinent ethnographic data. This task calls for considerable patience, but the effort yields significant rewards.

Retrospective evaluation of the long-range development of culture in the Mixteca prompts the question of whether the Mixtec pattern at the time of the Spanish Conquest had fulfilled its potential. The Mixtecs were farmers who hunted and gathered to supplement their diet. Agriculture was intensive and irrigation, particularly *coo-yuu* water and soil management, was practiced where feasible. Production of exploitable surplus was possible. When practicable, people settled in the valleys, but they located their settlements in such a way as to not take valuable farmlands out of service. The most densely populated areas shifted over time, and apart from the great centers of the Yanhuitlan-Nochixtlan Valley, usually had one or more phases of limited to absent habitation. Historical factors, not always visible to the archaeologist, would seem to explain these varied evolutionary trajectories as much as geographical and environmental realities. The land, then, provided sustenance, but it also imposed restrictions and influenced to a considerable degree the evolution of Mixtec culture. There were no great open plains, but Mixtecs adapted to their surroundings. They developed urban civilization and the state in spite of relative limitations. The growth and expansion of Mixtec culture knew limitations that could be overcome by technological innovation and through more refined political, economic, and social institutions and an integrative religion. The Mixtecs developed a great civilization, a true variant of the Mesoamerican pattern. They were not Teotihuacanos, or imitators of the Zapotecs of Monte Albán, or Mayans, Toltecs, or Nahuas. They were something else, something quite special.

This was a culture of small things: small valleys, small cities, towns and villages, great art in miniature and a specialized system of writing on animal skin, native paper, bone and stone, and on murals. Even the political system consisted of a vast network of small states, dialectical provinces and complementary zones of production and commerce. Each was ruled by an autocratic ruler assisted by a body of noble retainers, priests, advisers, and assistants. These rulers were closely related, but despite references to supreme authorities at Coixtlahuaca, Achiutla, or Tilantongo, there is little evidence of unified control of the Mixtecas by one great lord. The Tilantongo ruling family, it was claimed, was "the most honored" of the Mixtec lineages, and to emphasize a relational tie with the rulers of Tilantongo served to reinforce and validate claims to royal title and privilege in other communities. Yet these claims to consanguineal priorities did not translate into supreme political power being invested in Tilantongo. Each little state was a discrete entity, and affiliations between states shifted from generation to generation depending on circumstances of marriage, inheritance, conquest, treaty, and as necessity dictated. Sometimes this form of geopolitics did not work well. Despite the external threat of the Culhua-Mexica during the 1400s and early 1500s, this congeries of small states could not be brought into an effective political alliance, and several of the Mixtec *yuhuitayu* were forced into tributary relationships.

The key to development and to survival over thirty-five hundred years of sedentary life has been creativity and adaptation. The first settlers came to the area in small numbers, set up their villages, planted their *milpas*, and laid the foundation for the future. By Formative times, as population grew, technology improved, production increased, and exchange intensified, social, political, and more esoteric forms of knowledge proliferated, and the culture became more complex. Chiefdoms emerged, as at Tayata. States formed, as at Huamelulpan, Monte Negro, Yucuita, and eventually many other places. Urban life developed as a critical component in a new hierarchy of settlement and governance. Religion became more formalized and public, and it unified this emerging culture as much as language, writing, and the arts. By the second urban climax, in Classic times, connections with other regions were strong, and the Valley of Oaxaca, adjacent areas of Tehuacan and Puebla, and most certainly the Valley of Mexico served as a notable stimulant to this growing complexity. Urbanism spread across the Mixtecas, as the region participated in the Classic-period florescence of Mesoamerica.

The Postclassic period was a time of political, artistic, and ideological renaissance. Populations grew. Alliances, markets, and other social networks expanded. The evident wealth and stability of the region, at least after 1200 or so, was unmatched compared to any prior phase. As we move into the protohistoric era, the small states continued to evolve, as at Yucundaa-Teposcolula, Tilantongo, Achiutla, Yanhuitlan, Tututepec, and others too numerous to mention. The books that the Mixtecs wrote, and all of the historical, archaeological, and ethnological evidence gathered to date elucidate the existence of this great interacting network of autonomous kingdoms, coexisting, intermarrying, entering into treaties, trading, and even fighting, but all highly evolved and interdependent. The institution of the *cacicazgo, señorío mixteco,* or *yuhuitayu ñudzahui,* was so strong, in fact, and so useful to the Spanish conquerors, that it persisted from the pre-Conquest years until far into the Colonial period and, in attenuated form, into the nineteenth century.

Although an enormous complex of new elements was introduced to the Mixteca during the Colonial period, Mixtec culture and ideology was not simply eliminated. As the architectural historian Barry Kiracofe has demonstrated, many native elements were integrated into the symbolism of Colonial buildings and religious institutions in the Mixteca,[42] and pages could be devoted to other elements, like the *coo-yuu* system of terrace farming, the *huipil*, the *coa*, and the native curing complex that have survived unto the present day. Mixtec culture did not die during the Spanish Conquest, the Colonial period, or the upheavals of the nineteenth and twentieth century. It exists today, in the Mixtecas, all over Mexico, and wherever Mixtecs have gone in their "great diaspora." Many have left the Mixteca, but their hearts, their sentiments, their thoughts return home: the song says, "Que lejos estoy de la tierra donde he nacido. Que nostalgia invade mi pensamiento."[43]

The final word has been written on none of the subjects treated in this book. We have made an effort to present a description of a prominent Mesoamerican culture and to analyze some of its more significant institutions as they appeared in pre-Hispanic times and during the Colonial period. We have made an effort in this last chapter to bring the study of Mixtec civilization into the present. The book is designed to serve as a stepping-stone to further study. It is hoped that the definition of problems and procedures and the demonstration of the convergent method will serve to stimulate new inquiry into the cultural development of the Mixtec people and other cultures of Oaxaca and Mexico. We fully intend to undertake further investigations to supplement and test the findings set forth on these pages, and to encourage and facilitate similar efforts by our Oaxacanist colleagues, young and old.

Abbreviations Used in
Notes and Bibliography

AGEO	Archivo General del Poder Ejecutivo del Estado de Oaxaca
AGI	Archivo General de Indias, Seville, Spain
AGN	Archivo General de la Nación, Mexico City
AJT	Archivo del Juzgado de Teposcolula, Oaxaca
AMT	Archivo del Municipio de Teposcolula, Oaxaca
APJO	Archivo Histórico del Poder Judicial del Estado de Oaxaca
ARMT	Archivo Regional de la Mixteca del Municipio de Tlaxiaco
CIESAS	Centro de Investigaciones y Estudios Superiores en Antropología Social
CMASPP	Central Mixteca Alta Settlement Pattern Project
CONACULTA	Consejo Nacional para la Cultura y las Artes
FCE	Fondo de Cultura Económica
HHYP	Alfredo Harp Helú Yucundaa Archaeological Project
INAH	Instituto Nacional de Antropología e Historia
INI	Instituto Nacional Indigenista
MAFP	Mixteca Alta Formative Project
RMEH	*Revista Mexicana de Estudios Históricos*

SEP	Secretaría de Educación Pública
UNAM	Universidad Nacional Autónoma de México
VNVP	Vanderbilt University Nochixtlan Valley Project
VUPA	Vanderbilt University Publications in Anthropology

Notes

1. Marcus 2003a [1983]; Spores 1965.

2. Flannery and Marcus 2003 [1983].

3. Caso 1941, 1958a, demonstrates his methods; see Marcus 1976, Paddock 1966, Redmond 1983, and Spores 1967 for "second and third generation" examples in the Caso tradition. This approach is now so pervasive in Oaxaca that it is almost beside the point to offer further citations, but see works discussed in Balkansky 2012.

4. We are discussing, in effect, derived versions of the direct-historical method and the conjunctive approach.

5. Steward 1942, 337.

6. Spores 1967, 3–29.

7. What does this mean in practice? Publication of results in monograph form is a good start. Providing sufficient empirical detail so that others are able to reanalyze your results is even better.

8. Blanton et al. 1999; Flannery and Marcus 2003 [1983]; Kirkby 1972; Marcus and Flannery 1996; and Spores 1972, 1974a, 1974b, and as summarized in 1984.

9. See detailed consideration of the ethnohistoric approach in Spores 1973.

10. Smith and Hopkins 2003 [1983]; West 1964.

11. Palerm and Wolf 1957.

12. The Mixteca sections of Flannery and Marcus 2003 [1983] offer much of interest on the environmental background and cultural geography of the Mixtecas as well as providing a broad comparative treatment consistent with our objectives.

13. Dahlgren de Jordán 1954.

14. Ibid.

15. Ibid.; and see Spores 1967, 1984, passim.

16. Spores 1984, 80–84.

17. Spores 2003a [1983].

18. See additional locations found on survey in Kowalewski et al. 2009, 387–94 and passim.

19. Balkansky and Croissier 2009; Spores 1972; and Winter 1984.

20. Ahern 1993; Lackey 1991.

21. Dahlgren de Jordán 1954; Kirkby 1972.

22. Caso 1969.

23. Fernández de Miranda et al. 1959; Longacre and Millon 1961; and Swadesh 1967.

24. Nicholas A. Hopkins 1984; Josserand, Winter, and Hopkins 1984; and see Marcus 2003a [1983].

25. Josserand, Jansen, and Romero 1984, 151–54.

26. Ibid., 154.

27. Ibid., 162–63.

28. Bruce Byland is innovative in this regard, but there has been little follow-up from other surveyors and anthropologists, perhaps owing to the need for new linguistic analyses that archaeologists are ill equipped to undertake. But the point is that such integrative research can and should be done.

29. But see Byland 1984; Byland and Pohl 1994; and Pohl's discussion of alliance corridors and their relation to linguistic boundaries in his introduction to Williams 2009.

30. Paddock 2003 [1983]; and chapter 3, this volume.

31. Joyce et al. 2004; Spores 1993; and chapter 3, this volume.

32. Spores 1967; Redmond and Spencer 1994.

33. Spores 1984, 64–96.

34. Spores 1967, 90–188.

35. This effort began in Spores 1967, 90–104, with further modifications in Spores 2003b [1983] and 1984, 48–57.

36. Dahlgren de Jordán 1954; Spores 1967; and Jiménez Moreno and Mateos Higuera 1940.

37. Spores 1964; and see Gibson 1964 for central Mexico.

38. Burgoa 1989 [1674], passim; and chapters 3 and 4, this volume.

39. Kirkby 1972; Spores 1969.

40. Balkansky 1998a; Spores 2003c–d [1983].

41. Balkansky 1998a; see a similar configuration at Monte Negro in Balkansky et al. 2004, figures 1 and 8; and aerial photographs in Bernal 1992, 114.

42. Kowalewski et al. 2009, 347; also Balkansky 2006a.

43. See Cowgill 2004; Sanders and Webster 1988; and Michael E. Smith 1989, 2009.

44. Palerm and Wolf 1957.

45. Balkansky 1998a; Marcus 1983.

46. Spores 1998.

CHAPTER 2

1. Bernal 1965 and Paddock 1966 summarize the early decades of research. The VNVP that began in 1966 was designed to find the archaeological origins of the Mixtec kingdoms and establish a pottery typology/chronology for the Mixteca Alta; see Spores 1969, 1972, and 1974a.

2. The Formative of the Mixteca Alta is summarized in Balkansky 1998a, 1998b, 2012, and Spores 2001, 2007, 2008. Extensive bibliographies follow. Stephen A. Kowalewski's regional survey in Coixtlahuaca will become essential once it is published, as will Verónica Pérez Rodríguez's mapping project at Cerro Jazmín. The Formative of the Mixteca Baja is summarized in Winter 1994a, 2005; and the Mixteca Costa—although this era predates an actual Mixtec presence—in Joyce 2010. The regional surveys that form an essential underpinning of our knowledge of the Mixteca are listed sequentially in Balkansky 2002, table 2.1, 87–93, and discussed in Balkansky 1999, 2006b, and Kowalewski 2008.

3. The Tayata excavations and the MAFP are ongoing as of this writing, but the most recent overviews are Balkansky et al. 2008, Balkansky et al. 2009.

4. Blanton et al. 1999, Flannery and Marcus 2003 [1983], and Marcus and Flannery 1996 are the best places to start for comparative treatments of Valley Zapotec archaeology. Balkansky 2012 and Joyce 2010 summarize the most recent sources.

5. Balkansky 1998b, 1999.

6. Spores 1984, 13–18; Flannery and Spores 2003 [1983].

7. Flannery 1986; MacNeish 1964; and MacNeish et al. 1972.

8. This period begins where the Pleistocene ends and is characterized by dispersed groups of mobile hunters and gatherers, initial experimentation with plant domestication, and ends with the transition to sedentary life.

9. Kowalewski et al. 2009, 285–87.

10. Garvin 1994, 250–52.

11. Kowalewski et al. 2009, 287.

12. Finsten et al. 1989; Flannery 1986.

13. Lorenzo 1958a.

14. Flannery and Spores 2003 [1983].

15. As is customary in archaeological research programs, significant periods of regional cultural development are named. Several broad but still provisional periods

are recognized for the Mixteca Alta: Cruz (Early and Middle Formative), Ramos (Late and Terminal Formative), Las Flores (Classic), Natividad (Postclassic), and Convento (Early Colonial). Still others have been designated for the Mixteca Baja and Costa. In this book we omit these names except in specific instances, such as Ñuiñe in the Mixteca Baja, where the term carries more meaning than just chronology, or where we find it necessary to avoid ambiguity.

16. Pool 2007.

17. Winter et al. 1984.

18. Marcus and Flannery 1996, 93–110, refer to the loss of village autonomy as a key indicator of chiefdom formation. This process could occur through warfare, or the budding-off of daughter sites and settlement clusters into adjacent valley pockets. This latter process seems to characterize the Mixteca Alta settlement data for the Early and Middle Formative—see Kowalewski et al. 2009, 293—although these processes need not be mutually exclusive.

19. Carneiro 1981; Spencer and Redmond 2004.

20. Clark 2004; Grove 1981; and Love 2007.

21. Balkansky 1998a; Balkansky et al. 2000, 2008, 2009; Blomster 2004; Kowalewski et al. 2009, 287–95, 334–35; Spores 1996a, 2003f–g [1983]; Stiver 2001; and Zárate Morán 1987.

22. Joyce 2010.

23. Winter 1994a.

24. The radiocarbon dates in this volume are uncalibrated in order to facilitate comparison with prior publications from Oaxaca that generally use uncalibrated dates, e.g., Drennan 2003 [1983].

25. Spores 2003f [1983], and 1984, 18–23.

26. Drennan 1976; Flannery and Marcus 1994; and MacNeish et al. 1970. We refrain from using the Mixteca chronologies more than is minimally necessary to avoid confusing readers, especially when comparing results from several regions. It is nonetheless instructive that Zárate Morán 1987 aligns his subdivided Cruz phases with the Valley of Oaxaca sequence.

27. Byland 1980; Brockington and Long 1974; de Cicco and Brockington 1956; Finsten 1996; Joyce 1991; and Spores 1996a.

28. Essential comparative material from the Valley of Oaxaca is found in Blanton et al. 1999; Flannery 1976; Flannery and Marcus 1994; Flannery and Marcus 2003 (1983); Flannery and Marcus 2005; and Marcus and Flannery 1996.

29. This would still be Early Cruz, following Spores 1972, 2003f–g [1983], but is sometimes referred to as "Middle Cruz" or "Cruz B" in more recent surveys and excavations and is otherwise coincident with the San José Phase in the Valley of Oaxaca.

30. Blomster 2004, 66; Kowalewski et al. 2009, 30–31 and Figure 2.2; and Spores 2003g [1983].

31. Duncan et al. 2008; prehistoric cremations were not generally reduced to ash, since the sustained temperatures one finds in modern crematoriums were not possible.

32. Marcus 1992a, 332–38, and 1998a, 183.

33. Meissner et al. 2012 and MAFP.

34. Marcus and Flannery 2000.

35. Kowalewski et al. 2009, 83–85, Figure 3.1; Stiver 2001.

36. Balkansky will revise this figure in future publications based on intensive-site surveys of Tayata during 2003 and 2009, but this anticipated change does not affect the general character of the settlement patterns described in this chapter.

37. Balkansky et al. 2000; Plunket 1983, table 3; and Spores 1972. Other settlement clusters occur near Etlatongo, Tilantongo, and Yanhuitlan.

38. Kowalewski et al. 2009, 289. This is a relatively conservative, mid-range estimate assuming ten to twenty-five persons per hectare. Balkansky 2002, 31–32, and Kowalewski et al. 2009, 24–25, discuss the rationale behind pre-Hispanic population estimates. These methods are derived from the Basin of Mexico surveys, although being somewhat updated with each successive long-term field project; but see key foundational statements in Sanders 1965, Parsons 1971.

39. Balkansky 2006b.

40. Kowalewski et al. 2009, 290–95, 334–37.

41. Ibid., 293.

42. Ibid.

43. Duncan et al. 2008 and MAFP.

44. Marcus 1992a, 373–87. Redmond 1983 provides extensive comparative documentation on Zapotec warfare. Gaxiola González 1984, 51–52, reports decapitated human heads at Tayata's successor site, Huamelulpan.

45. Balkansky et al. 2004.

46. Kowalewski et al. 2009, 290, table 7.3.

47. Kowalewski et al. 1989, 90. The CMASPP covered approximately 1,600 square kilometers, 400 of which were in the sparsely inhabited Sierra de Nochixtlan. The Valley of Oaxaca Settlement Pattern Project covered 2,150 square kilometers and had no comparable empty zones. The Mixteca Alta was densely occupied at this time.

48. Charlotte A. Smith 2002 summarizes the accessible population estimates for all surveyed regions in highland Mesoamerica. The central Oaxacan demographic core clearly extends from the central Mixteca Alta and Nochixtlan Valley into the Valley of Oaxaca, especially in the Etla region and the cluster of sites near San José Mogote.

49. These terrace systems are also called *lama bordo*, Spores 1969; see chapter 1, this volume.

50. Flannery 2003a [1983], 331.

51. Earle 1997.

52. Blanton 1998.

53. See chapter 3 on the Classic and Postclassic. Secondary sites during the Middle Formative usually had only one mound. Other kinds of "ground-hugging" paved surfaces and platforms are not always visible on surface survey and so are undercounted. Results from the Mixteca's limited number of excavated sites suggest there are many features of interest reflecting social distinctions that we cannot see on the surface, although surface survey is the only systematic way to find the appropriate sites and make informed decisions about excavation.

54. Marcus and Flannery 2004.

55. Marcus 1974.

56. Spores 1976, 2003h [1983].

57. Modern uranium mining destroyed much of this zone, making it impossible to know its original size and organization.

58. This estimate is based on reviewing the structure summaries from Kowalewski et al. 1989, appendix VIII. The platform itself, based on test pits in several locations and observation of areas exposed from modern mining operations, as well as radiometric dates, dates from the Middle Formative. In prehistoric times it would have been larger than measured, but at least half of the original structure was sheared off by bulldozers.

59. Gaxiola González 1984, 1986; Spores and Robles García 2007.

60. This excavated result is consistent with our survey data suggesting that public construction began in earnest during the Middle Formative; see Kowalewski et al. 2009, passim. Given the emphasis on platform building in the Mixteca it is misleading to compare mound volumes from the Mixteca with the Valley of Oaxaca and then draw conclusions about relative administrative complexity. The Mixtec were dedicated platform builders, the Zapotec more inclined toward mounds. Surveyors tend to overlook the platforms by lumping them together with residential terraces, which they otherwise resemble.

61. Kowalewski et al. 2009, 84–85, 292; Stiver 2001.

62. Matadamas Díaz 1989, 1996. Spores and Balkansky worked on the Yucunama excavations during 1995 and 1996, and this memorable experience is reflected in our remarks.

63. Amadio 2010; Balkansky and Croissier 2009; and Bedard and Balkansky n.d. on the obsidian source data from Tayata. Blomster 2004, 94–95, discusses the obsidian source data from Etlatongo. Stephen Whittington also has an obsidian-sourcing study from Cerro del Fortín, a site with an Early Formative component near Teozacoalco (personal communication 2010).

64. Joyce 2010.

65. Coe 1965; Covarrubias 1944; and Stirling 1965.

66. Bernal 1969.

67. Diehl 2004 and Flannery and Marcus 2000 are good representatives for the two main factions; see also Clark 2007, Grove 1997, and Love 2007 among others for

further background. Balkansky has also involved himself in these debates; see Flannery et al. 2005.

68. Pool 2007, 300.

69. Winter 1984. On the question of the Olmec, Winter 1994b suggests that Gulf Coast peoples invaded Oaxaca, and although this argument is quite speculative it shows that a range of ideas remain under consideration.

70. Blomster et al. 2005.

71. Sharer 2007.

72. States, after Flannery 1972, have distinct administrative hierarchies and administrative specialization as an evolutionary response for managing information flows. One of their primary functions, after Spencer 2010, is territorial control, including organized warfare. If these are indeed fundamental characteristics of early states, we would expect to see changes in civic-ceremonial architecture, especially in the functional diversity of building forms, when states were forming, and these entities should have the capacity for political expansion. All of these traits are demonstrably true for the Mixteca's Postclassic *yuhuitayu* and for a considerable period before.

The point at which the Mixteca Alta's Cruz phase villagers began moving onto terraced hilltops marks the onset of Early Ramos, a relatively brief transitional phase (Late Formative). Early Ramos centers were urban, or on the threshold of urbanism; see Spores 2003c [1983]. Urban states are clearly in place by the Late Ramos (Terminal Formative); see Balkansky 1998a and Balkansky et al. 2004. We assume, but cannot at present demonstrate, that this sequence encompassed the as yet unexplored areas of the Mixteca Alta and Baja. There could be a dozen nascent urban states in highland Oaxaca dating roughly to the Late Formative; most of these would have collapsed in their infancy, but their interaction catalyzed this transition across much of the southern highlands of Mexico.

73. The "long view" of Mixtec cities found at the end of this chapter is drawn from an unpublished conference paper, Balkansky 2006a, from Kowalewski et al. 2009, 331–49, and from Spores 2003c [1983]. Winter 1994a and 2005 summarizes what little is known of the Mixteca Baja in this period. Balkansky 1998b, 2012; Blanton et al. 1999; Marcus and Flannery 1996; and Spencer and Redmond 2004 among others discuss the Formative at Monte Albán.

74. Cowgill 2004, 542, defines urbanism with reference to regions and macroregions that "rather than individual settlements, are, for many purposes, better units of study." He adds that comparative research, rather than generating new typologies, could be improved by specifying more variables, among them population estimates, physical boundaries, walls and fortifications, planning, degree of spatial segmentation, scale and configuration of civic-ceremonial architecture, durability of the built environment, and division of labor among others. This approach emphasizes the evident variation among ancient cities but allows for their comparative investigation. Our

view of the Mixtec community as it evolved during Ramos times fits this scheme and is one of the reasons we consider it a variant form of urbanism.

75. Marcus 1983, 51.

76. Plunket 1983; Robles 1988; Spores 1972, 1974a, 1984, 24–28, and 2003c [1983]; and Winter and Hernández 1977.

77. We mention again the existence in prior centuries of a native Mixtec gray ware tradition; see Balkansky and Croissier 2009, Spores 1972. Spencer et al. 2008 discuss the dispersal of Valley Zapotec gray ware styles during this time.

78. Meissner et al. 2012 discuss this phenomenon at length for the Tayata figurine collection, linking the intentional burning and mutilation of figurines to "symbolic death"—but regardless of what these acts symbolized, we have in the Mixteca figurine assemblages yet further evidence for continuities crossing the pre-urban and urban periods.

79. Balkansky et al. 2000; Kowalewski et al. 2009, 32–35; Pérez Rodríguez 2008; and Spores 1972, 2003c [1983]. Cerro Jazmín is currently the focus of intensive survey and selective excavation by Verónica Pérez Rodríguez and associates. The results of this investigation are providing important new information, not only on developments in the city of Cerro Jazmín, but, as well, with respect to the study and understanding of the urbanization process in the greater Mixteca, Oaxaca, and Mesoamerica.

80. This site is reported in Spores 1996a and will eventually form part of Stephen Kowalewski's final report on the Coixtlahuaca survey. Loma Sandage was about 1.5 square kilometers in size and seems to have been an Early Ramos phenomenon.

81. Martí 1965a, 1965b; Spores 1996a.

82. Acosta 1965; Acosta and Romero 1992; Balkansky et al. 2004; Byland and Pohl 1994, 52–56; Caso 1938; Flannery 2003b [1983]; Geurds and Jansen 2008; Kowalewski et al. 2009, 63–76; Marcus and Flannery 1996, 165–69; and Spores 1984, 24–28. There is a long history of research at Monte Negro, and certainly an extended history of commentary; for the primary empirical contributions see Acosta and Romero 1992 (excavation) and Balkansky et al. 2004 (survey).

83. Balkansky et al. 2004; also Spencer et al. 2008.

84. Caso 1938, 1942; Guzmán 1934.

85. Burgoa 1989 [1674], I, 275–76; and as translated in Spores 2003h [1983], 230.

86. Balkansky et al. 2004; Kowalewski et al. 2009, 71.

87. Burgoa 1989 [1674], I, 275–76.

88. See comparative discussions of the temples and other architectural features in Balkansky et al. 2004; Geurds and Jansen 2008; Marcus and Flannery 1996, 165–69; and Redmond and Spencer 2008.

89. Kowalewski et al. 2009, 72.

90. Balkansky 1998a; Caso and Gamio 1961; Gamio 1957; Gaxiola González 1984; Kowalewski et al. 2009, 165–74; Spores et al. 1995; Spores 1996a; and Winter et al. 1991.

91. Balkansky 1998a; Kowalewski et al. 2009, 165–74.

92. Gaxiola González 1986.

93. Winter et al. 1991.

94. The Huamelulpan monolith is shown in Caso 1965b and Paddock 1966. Other out-of-context carved stones from Huamelulpan are shown in Caso 1956.

95. Joyce et al. 2006 conclude that gray wares found in the Mixteca were in some instances manufactured in the Valley of Oaxaca but in others were made locally in the Mixteca. This has been a point of emphasis for Spores since the 1960s. Our view is that many, probably most, gray wares found in the Mixteca were in fact of local manufacture. Spores 1972 based his view on visual inspection of clays, tempers, and surface treatments, in effect the "ware" that in many instances was "difficult to relate to the Monte Albán typology" (38). Balkansky and Croissier 2009 have quantified those observations via mineralogical studies using X-ray diffractometry and refiring experiments. For the most part, Mixteca tan wares and gray wares have similar mineralogical compositions, but technological differences, including tempering agents and firing programs, yielded reduced or smudged-ware pots from what would otherwise have been tan ware vessels. Gray wares, especially the decorated varieties, are significant primarily for dating comparable phases in different sites and regions but do not by themselves indicate the nature of interaction; see also Balkansky 1999, 2002, 79–80; Balkansky et al. 2004, 51–55.

96. Gaxiola González 1984, 51–52.

97. Balkansky 1998a; Spores 1996a.

98. Balkansky 1998b; Marcus 1992b; and Marcus and Flannery 1996, 195–207.

99. Joyce 2010, passim.

100. De Cicco and Brockington 1956; Brockington et al. 1974; and Joyce 1991, 2010. The area of full-coverage survey from the Río Verde region is limited to 152 square kilometers, none of which is published in monograph form. This level of coverage and the accessibility of the data do not compare favorably to the highlands of Oaxaca, and in consequence we know much less about the coast at this critical juncture.

101. Marcus and Flannery 1996, 195–207, argue that Monte Albán's political territory included San Francisco de Arriba. Their view is based on changing settlement patterns, pottery styles, and a stone monument from Monte Albán that refers to either a conquest or tribute obligation from the Tututepec/San Francisco de Arriba area on the coast of Oaxaca. Workinger 2002, 80–89, excavated about 140 square meters in various parts of San Francisco de Arriba, mainly long trenches, in which no complete structures were uncovered and "much of the material" was fill. The research design and results in this instance do not compare favorably to excavated results from the highlands of Oaxaca and are insufficient to evaluate a hypothesis of this magnitude. The subject of Monte Albán contact with the coast and other regions of Oaxaca

nonetheless remains contentious, with considerable need of new archaeological con-tributions from the coast; see bibliography of recent literature in Sherman et al. 2010.

102. Balkansky 1998a, 1998b; see Spencer 2010.

103. See Marcus and Flannery's 1996, 139–54, discussion of "the Monte Albán synoikism."

104. Balkansky et al. 2004; Wright 2006.

105. Balkansky 1998a, 2006a; Marcus 1983. These patterns are most fully developed at the longer-lived Late Ramos cities of Huamelulpan and Yucuita.

106. See discussions of Ramos-period architecture in Balkansky 1998a; Balkan-sky et al. 2004; and Spores 2003c [1983].

107. Geurds and Jansen 2008 link institutional, political, and religious practices they see reflected in the Mixtec codices to specific buildings at Monte Negro. Byland and Pohl 1994, map 19, identify prominent structures from Tilantongo as the literal "Temple of Heaven" from the Mixtec codices. These kinds of identifications are intriguing but must be seen as hypotheses to be tested with archaeological excavation.

108. Byland and Pohl 1994; Spores 1976, 2003h [1983].

109. The city-state concept, after Lind 2000 for the Mixtec, conflates the commu-nity with the *cacicazgo*, entities that we have endeavored to keep separate in this book.

110. Marcus 1992a, especially 57–67; Mary E. Smith 1973, passim.

111. See especially Caso 1951, 1956, 1965a, and 1977–79, I, 169–91.

112. Rivera Guzmán 2008a.

113. Spores 1972, 1974a; Winter and Hernández 1977.

114. Caso and Gamio 1961; Gaxiola González 1984, 77, passim; and Marcus 1992a, 57–67, 2003b [1983].

115. Caso 1928.

116. Marcus 2003b [1983].

117. Joyce Marcus, personal communication 2007.

118. Marcus 2003b [1983].

119. Ibid., 125.

CHAPTER 3

1. Verenice Heredia 2008 found differences in monumental building plans and access to goods even at lower-order sites in the Mixteca Alta; thus the residents of some sites and subregions were "wealthier" than others, or at least had greater access to quality goods, presumably through markets. Nochixtlan, for instance, shows up as being well connected to market and exchange activities prehistorically, just as in more recent times. Other sources for aspects of urban variation in the Mixteca include Balkansky 2006a, 2006b; Balkansky et al. 2000; Kowalewski et al. 2009; and Charlotte A. Smith 2002.

2. Balkansky 1998b, 1999; Spores 2003d [1983].

3. Cowgill 2008; Demarest et al. 2004.

4. Caso et al. 1967; and noting the changing regional settlement patterns and substantial reorganization at Monte Albán, see Balkansky 2002, 90; Marcus 1992b.

5. See discussions of site histories in Balkansky 1998a, 1998b, and 2012; Joyce 2010; and Winter 1994a.

6. See Flannery's 1986 discussion of causation. Marcus 1998b and Blanton et al. 1996 model the long-term "ups and downs" of cities and their hinterlands.

7. Marcus 1992b.

8. The Classic collapse and the origins of the Postclassic in Oaxaca are discussed in Balkansky 1998b, 2012; Byland and Pohl 1994; Casparis 2006; Jansen et al. 1998; Joyce 2010; Kowalewski et al. 1989, 301–305; Lind and Urcid 2009; Marcus 1989; and Winter 1989a. None of these authors are in complete agreement. The contributors to the recent volume by Blomster 2008 likewise offer a range of fundamentally incompatible views. The source materials include Monte Albán and other excavated sites, survey data from various regions, codices, and even oral histories, and these different sources are emphasized more or less than others depending on the author.

There is also the "IIIb–IV problem" arising from similar-looking pottery collections of the Epiclassic period. We do not, in consequence, always know which sites were really contemporary or went into decline at a given juncture. We agree with Marcus and Flannery 1990 that the solution to this problem is to work at complementary sites spanning the relevant time frame, a research program that will take twenty years to finish. The scattered efforts to date do not meet this standard, nor are we on a clear path toward getting there. Most such discussions concern Monte Albán and the Valley of Oaxaca, but there is a parallel issue in the Mixteca.

9. Hirth 1984; Jiménez Moreno 1966. We are separating a long "Classic" from an "Epiclassic," usually taken to mean the period of instability following Teotihuacan's decline, as a means of simplifying the regional comparisons and glossing over the chronological uncertainties. This also reflects what we have found for the Mixteca Alta and that may prove true elsewhere in Oaxaca, that by the later Classic period considerable areas of settlement were largely or entirely abandoned. Thus the onset of the Classic collapse in the Mixteca appears to have been quite early, and might have coincided with the revised "early" dates for Teotihuacan's collapse; see Cowgill 2008.

10. Rice and Rice 2004.

11. Balkansky 1999; Spores 1984, 40, 47–48.

12. Balkansky et al. 2000; Heredia et al. 2008; Kowalewski et al. 2009, 305–14; Rivera Guzmán 2000; Spores 2003d [1983], 1996a; and Winter 1994a.

13. Joyce 2010, 239–40.

14. Kowalewski et al. 2009, 35–39, figures 2.5 through 2.9; Spores 1984, 30–41, 2003a [1983].

15. Ibid.; Caso 1938.

16. The Mixteca gray-ware tradition goes back to the Formative period and seems to have arisen in parallel with the Valley of Oaxaca. We view the Classic period gray wares in the Mixteca Alta and Baja as being of mixed local and Valley of Oaxaca origin that regardless of source were likely distributed via market activity. In many instances the Mixteca gray wares are slipped orange, consistent with the Classic orange-slipped tan wares and orange wares that are typical of this period; see Kowalewski et al. 2009, 372–79, and Spores 1972.

17. Spores 2003d [1983].

18. Laura Stiver Walsh, personal communication 1999.

19. See data presented in Blanton 1978 and Marcus 1992b. Balkansky 1998b, 1999, and Casparis 2006 argue that Monte Albán lost control over the Valley of Oaxaca during the Classic period, becoming one of several competing centers prior to its collapse.

20. Kowalewski 2003a.

21. Balkansky et al. 2000, figure 11; Flannery 2003a [1983]; Kirkby 1972; Pérez Rodríguez 2006; Rincón Mautner 1999; and Spores 1969.

22. Donkin 1979; Treacy and Denevan 1994.

23. Balkansky 2012; Spores 2003d [1983].

24. Amadio 2010; MAFP.

25. Cerro Encantado is described in detail in Heredia Espinoza 2008; Kowalewski et al. 2009, 255–67, passim; and Spores 1996a.

26. Compare the sloping hill-sign elements from Tayata with Mary E. Smith 1973, 39, chart 3, and figures 48, 79, and 81; see also variant forms shown in 2003a [1983], 2003b [1983]. This is one of the best examples of a direct tie between Early Classic iconography and similar forms in the Postclassic codices.

27. Brockington et al. 1974; Brockington and Long 1974; and some particularly striking examples photographed in Berlin 1947.

28. Urcid and Joyce 2001.

29. Paddock 1965, 1966, and 2003 [1983]; also Moser 1977; Rodríguez Cano 1996.

30. Archaeological reports to date include Rivera Guzmán 2008b; Winter 1994a, 2005, and sources cited within (this volume).

31. Balkansky 1998b; Martí 1965a, 1965b.

32. Rincón Mautner 1995.

33. Rivera Guzmán 2000; Winter 1994a, figure 11.

34. Caso 1928, 79–80.

35. Marcus 1992a, 238.

36. Marcus 1989, 1992a, and 2003c [1983].

37. Spores 1997a. See Moser 1977 for the most comprehensive catalog of imagery.

38. Balkansky et al. 2000; Kowalewski et al. 2009, passim.

39. Matadamas Díaz 1996, 2001; and see Urcid 2008.

40. See, for example, Marcus 2002 on Zapotec writing from the region of Sola de Vega.

41. The "IIIb–IV Problem" has received recent attention in the Valley of Oaxaca (Lind and Urcid 2009; Martínez López et al. 2000), but no similar work is yet contemplated for the Mixteca Alta or Baja. Interested parties should communicate with Stephen Kowalewski, who could readily identify a dozen or so sites where research of this kind should begin.

42. Balkansky 2012; Marcus and Flannery 2003 [1983]; Pohl 2003a, 2003b; and Spores 1967, 2003b [1983], and 1984, 64–96.

43. Kowalewski et al. 2009; Lind 2000; Redmond and Spencer 1994; and Spores 1984, 74–80.

44. Terraciano 2001, 158.

45. Marcus 2003d [1983], 360.

46. Terraciano 2001; Spores 1974b.

47. Bernal 1965; Paddock 1966.

48. Marcus and Flannery 2003 [1983]; Flannery and Marcus 2003 (1983); and Spores 1974b.

49. Flannery 2003c [1983]; Kowalewski 2003b [1983]; and Marcus 2003e [1983].

50. Jansen and van Broekhoven 2008; Mary E. Smith 1973.

51. See, for example, Bernal 1949; Byland and Pohl 1994.

52. See also, among many others, Gutiérrez Mendoza 2003; Joyce et al. 2004; Kröfges 2004; Spores and Robles García 2010; and Whittington 2003.

53. Kowalewski et al. 2009, 315–29; Spores 1972, 2003e [1983].

54. Kowalewski et al. 2009, 82–96; Spores and Robles García 2007; and Stiver 2001.

55. This is a complicated issue owing to the difficulties of identifying the period of construction for buildings at sites with multiple components or occupations, and further complicated by the reuse of earlier ceremonial spaces during Postclassic times. Yucundaa-Teposcolula is, however, by almost any measure for any period, an extraordinarily monumental site.

56. Kowalewski et al. 2009, 75–76, 91–96, and 196–202; Kowalewski et al. 2008; and Spores 1972, 1996a.

57. Balkansky et al. 2000; Spores 1972; and Kowalewski et al. 2009, 39–43.

58. Similar observations apply to the Valley of Oaxaca during Monte Albán V, especially in the vicinity of Mitla, Monte Albán/Cuilapan (Sa'a Yucu), and Macuilxochitl. Kowalewski et al. 1989, 317, call these agglomerations "a nearly continuous belt of discontinuous settlement."

59. A point of clarification is in order. In the Mixteca Alta, the customary Postclassic settlement pattern was a segregated core, often relatively small such as at Achiutla, Yanhuitlan, or Tlacotepec, that was the seat of power, surrounded by extensive residential

areas. In survey reports, the segregated cores, or *cabeceras*, and their surrounds often appear as separate "sites," something that is done to facilitate data control and future analysis but does not reflect the actual place of residence as ancient inhabitants would have understood it. These "sites," moreover, are often separated by little more than erosion cuts or zones of pre-Hispanic agricultural terracing that are themselves cultural artifacts (although we do not include agricultural areas in the site size or population estimates).

When comparing site-size and population estimates, this reporting practice systematically makes capital centers look smaller than they really were. It is therefore not an especially rewarding analysis to pull site sizes from a published data table without understanding this background. One would be forced to reach absurd conclusions—for example that Achiutla's capital center, measuring only 14 hectares with a population of one thousand, was unimportant despite its immense presence in historical documents. Tilantongo, likewise, seems rather small until you start adding together the cluster of immediately adjacent "sites." This understanding of pre-Hispanic settlement dynamics and the "emic" perception of place mirrors the notion of *altepetl*, or the indigenous state among the Nahuas of central Mexico, described in Lockhart 1992, 14–15, and that was present as well among the Mixtec, e.g. Terraciano 2001.

60. Burgoa 1989 [1674] I, 275.

61. Kowalewski et al. 2009, 318 and table 10.2, analyze the relationship of the Yanhuitlan Beds to settlement patterns, finding a strong association between Postclassic urbanization and soil fertility. Lorenzo 1958b first made the link between these soil formations and the region's characteristic erosion. Kirkby 1972, 6, describes the Yanhuitlan Beds as being "highly erodible" and "the dominant influence on the physical environment of the Nochixtlan area."

62. Kirkby 1972.

63. The midrange population estimate for the central Mixteca Alta is 228,000; see Kowalewski et al. 2009, 317. This is, roughly speaking, 140 persons per square kilometer. Extrapolated over the entire Mixteca of western Oaxaca, eastern Guerrero, and southern Puebla, this yields an estimated 7,000,000 residents at the time of the Conquest. This is considerably higher than historically derived figures, e.g. Cook and Borah 1968. Both sets of sources have their inherent problems, but even a lower-range estimate, based on the archaeological surveys and accounting for zones less densely settled, is astonishing to contemplate. With these factors in mind, an estimate of between 1,000,000 and 1,500,000 inhabitants at the time of the Conquest is entirely feasible, and probably conservative.

64. Balkansky et al. 2000; Byland and Pohl 1994, passim; and Spores 2003e [1983].

65. Kowalewski et al. 2009, 322.

66. Marcus 1992a, 373–87.

67. Burgoa 1989 (1674) I, 275.

68. Stiver 2001. It is also true that terrace walls almost always serve multiple purposes, and this one may have functioned primarily as a ritual causeway.

69. Kowalewski et al. 2009, 324.

70. Burgoa 1989 [1674] I, 392–95. Gay 2000 [1881], 96–109, offers a romanticized account of this alliance.

71. Burgoa 1989 [1674] I, 352–53; translation by Mary E. Smith 1973, 85, 179.

72. Kowalewski et al. 2009, 199.

73. Elam 1989; Feinman and Nicholas 2004.

74. Marcus 2003f [1983], table 8.6.

75. Burgoa 1989 [1674] I, 319, refers to the Mixtecs' reputed warlike tendencies.

76. Barlow 1949.

77. Acuña 1984; Flannery 2003c [1983].

78. Bernal 1949; Kowalewski et al. 2009, 385; and Spores 1996a.

79. Brockington et al. 1974; Brockington and Long 1974; de Cicco and Brockington 1956; Joyce 2010, 270; and O'Mack 1990.

80. Spores 1993.

81. Excavated houses are described in Lind 1979; Pérez Rodríguez 2006; Spores 1974a; and Spores and Robles García 2010.

82. Pérez Rodríguez 2003, 2006; Spores and Robles García 2010.

83. Lind 1987; Pohl 2003; Spores 1972; Spores 2007; and Spores and Robles García 2010.

84. See Nicholson 1961 and related publications on the Mixteca-Puebla concept.

85. Hernández Sánchez 2005; Pohl 2003; and see Michael Smith 1986.

86. Lind 1987, Table 29; Kowalewski et al. 2009, 327–28; and Pérez Rodríguez 2006.

87. Caso 1977–79; Jansen and Pérez Jiménez 2007; Marcus 1992a; Pohl 1994; and Mary E. Smith 1973 among other works.

88. See Marcus 2003b [1983] on genealogical registers used by the Valley Zapotec, as well as our prior discussions of writing in chapters 2 and 3, this volume.

89. See Caso 1949, 1959, and subsequent publications; his review of a book by Philip Dark is perhaps the clearest statement of this perspective.

90. Byland and Pohl 1994, 7–10; Monaghan 1990; and Mary E. Smith 1973, 20.

91. Reyes 1976 [1593], 11.

92. Herrera y Tordesillas 1947 [1601–15] and as discussed in Mary E. Smith 1973, 27.

93. Whallon 1992.

94. See, for example, Balkansky 2006b; Balkansky et al. 2000; and Kowalewski et al. 2009, 315–29.

95. The primary historical sources are summarized in Spores 1993; the most recent archaeological materials are provided in Joyce 2010 and Joyce et al. 2004.

96. Eight Deer's life and times are summarized clearly, succinctly, in Marcus 1992a, 380–87, aspects of which are found in commentaries dating from Clark 1912 until the present.

97. Kowalewski et al. 2009; Spores 1996a; Spores and Robles García 2010; Stiver 2001; and the full spectrum of results from the CMASPP and HHYP.

Chapter 4

1. Dahlgren de Jordán 1954, 91–99.

2. Burgoa 1989 [1674], I, chapter 23 and passim; and discussed in Dahlgren de Jordán, 1954; Pastor 1987.

3. We view the eroded landscape as primarily post-Hispanic; see Kirkby 1972. Melville's 1994 environmental history, where the "plague of sheep" follows native depopulation in central Mexico, is a useful comparative case. See also Cook 1949, who correlated, correctly, erosion with pre-Hispanic population density, although we disagree with his explanation of the causes.

4. Kowalewski et al. 2009, 347; Pérez Rodríguez 2003, 1.

5. Spores 1967, 9–14, 164–71; AGN Civil 516; AGN Tierras 220, pt. 1; and AGN Tierras 400.

6. APJO, Teposcolula Civil, legs. 1–40, passim; AGEO, Asuntos Agrarios, leg. 1304, exp. 2. Extremely revealing for Tututepec is AGEO, Asuntos Agrarios 1304, exp. 2.

7. Herrera y Tordesillas 1947 [1601–15], déc. 3, lib. 3, caps. 12–13; Burgoa 1989 [1674], I, 274–396; and AGN Tierras.

8. Spores 1967, 9–14, 164–71; AGN Civil 516; AGN Tierras 221, pt. 1; AGN Tierras 400; and *Relaciones geográficas* in Acuña 1984; Paso y Troncoso 1905–1906, vol. 4; and *RMEH*, vols. 1–2.

9. Ibid.

10. Monaghan 1994; Pastor 1987, 43–44; and Spores 1967, 5–7.

11. Garvin 1994 examines adaptations to the high sierra.

12. Dahlgren de Jordán 1954, 127–42; Spores 1965, 1967, 9–14; and Spores and Flannery 2003 [1983].

13. Spores 1974a, 2003b [1983].

14. Dahlgren de Jordán 1954, 145–66; Spores 1965, 1967, 9–14, and 2003b and h [1983].

15. AGN Civil 516; AGN Tierras 400; AGN Tierras 985–86; AGN Tierras 2692, exp. 16; and Spores 2003h [1983].

16. Herrera y Tordesillas 1947 [1601–15] déc. 3, lib. 3, cap. 13; Dahlgren de Jordán 1954, 160.

17. Spores 1984, 72–74.

18. Spores 1967, 131–54, and 1974b.

19. This complex process has been deduced from several sixteenth-century *procesos* involving Yanhuitlan and a "separatist" *sujeto*, Tecomatlan, and a *pleito* between Tlaxiaco and the subject community of Atoyaquillo (Teita). See AGI Escribanía de Cámara 162; AGN Tierras 400; AGN Tierras 985–86; and AGN Tierras 44. Although these cases occurred in Colonial times, underlying pre-Hispanic practices are discernible.

20. AGN Tierras 24, exp. 6; AGN Tierras 34, exp. 1.

21. Spores 1974b.

22. Spores 1967, 131–54, and 1974b.

23. Byland 1980; Lind 1979; Spores and Robles García 2010.

24. Spores 1974a.

25. Pérez Rodríguez 2006.

26. Vaillant 1941 and Soustelle 1961 view the *calpolli* as egalitarian kin groups, but Lockhart 1992, 16, based on the lack of affirmative references supporting that view in the Nahuatl documents, argues that this was not the case.

27. Caso 1977–79; Spores 1967, 1974b; and chapter 6, this volume.

28. Rulers were designated (masculine) *yya, yya canu, cacique,* and *señor natural* and (feminine) *yyadzehe* and *cacica.*

29. AGN Civil 516; Burgoa 1989 [1674], I, 387. Subject populations were normally referred to as *tay ñuu, tayndahi,* or *nandahi* in Mixtec and as *sujetos* in Spanish.

30. Paso y Troncoso 1905–1906, vol. 4, 73–74.

31. Spores 1993.

32. Burgoa 1989 [1674], I, 392–95.

33. Ibid., 395.

34. Ibid., 387.

35. Ibid.; Bernal 1962.

36. Caso 1960, 38–42, and 1966; Clark 1912; and Mary E. Smith 1963. In recent years, traditional interpretations and dating correlations, particularly those provided by Alfonso Caso, have been questioned by some students of the codices. These studies have dealt almost exclusively with analysis of style, personal and place-glyph identification, and dating. Notable are the extensive commentaries of Maarten Jansen in recent editions of codices *Vindobonensis, Nuttall,* and *Egerton-Becker II,* and the chronological revisions of Emily Rabin.

37. Such an extended patrimony existed in 1764 when Don Martín Villagómez and his *cacica* wife held title to thirty-one *cacicazgos* distributed throughout the Mixteca from the Pacific coast to Acatlan, Puebla. AGN Indios 48, exp. 155; AGN Tierras 400, exp. 1; and AGN Tierras 985–86.

38. Burgoa 1989 [1674], I, 376.

39. Spores 1969.

40. Kirkby 1972.

41. Pohl et al. 1997.

42. Kowalewski et al. 2009, 324.

43. Paso y Troncoso 1905–1906, vol. 4; Bernal 1962; Spores 1984, passim; and Winter 1984.

44. Amadio 2010; Balkansky and Croissier 2009; and Duncan et al. 2008.

45. Bedard and Balkansky n.d.; Sisson 1989; and Winter 1989b.

46. Balkansky and Croissier 2009; Blomster et al. 2005; Joyce et al. 2006; and Spores 1984, passim.

47. Potsherds selected for sourcing studies tend to be those that are already suspected of being foreign; surveyors likewise collect the most ornate examples, since they tend to be the best chronological markers, while leaving veritable oceans of Mixteca tan ware, orange ware, and cream ware in the field.

48. Balkansky and Croissier 2009.

49. Lind 1987; Hernández Sánchez 2005.

50. Spores 1984, 80–84; Burgoa 1989 [1674], I, 376.

51. Barlow 1949.

52. Burgoa 1989 [1674], I, 276–78; AGN Inquisición 37.

53. Our discussion of Mixtec religion relies on AGN Inquisición 37, exps. 5, 7, 8, 9, 10, 11; Burgoa 1989 [1674], I, 274–79; Paso y Troncoso 1905–1906, vol. 4; *RMEH*, vol. 2; Acuña 1984; Jiménez Moreno 1962 [1593]; Jiménez Moreno and Mateos Higuera 1940; Romero Frizzi and Spores 1976; Herrera y Tordesillas 1947 [1601–15]; as well as HHYP, MAFP, and VNVP.

54. Alvarado's *Vocabulario* defines *ídolo* as *dzahui*, indicating that the term was generalized beyond its specific meaning of "god of rain."

55. AGN Inquisición 37, exp. 7; Paso y Troncoso 1905–1906, vol. 4.

56. *RMEH* 2, 135–42.

57. Bernal 1962.

58. Paso y Troncoso 1905–1906, vol. 4, 37.

59. Ibid., 84.

60. Burgoa 1989 [1674], I, 256–66; Herrera y Tordesillas 1947 [1601–15], déc 3, lib. 3, caps. 12–13; and Spores 1967, 22–27.

61. AGN Inquisición 37, exp. 11; Paso y Troncoso 1905–1906, vol. 4.

62. AGN Inquisición 37, exp. 7, and as quoted in Jiménez Moreno and Mateos Higuera 1940, 45–46.

63. Ibid.

64. Ibid.

65. AGN Inquisición 37, exp. 5.

66. Ibid.

67. Ibid.

68. Ibid.

69. Ibid. For detailed discussion of archaeological investigations at Yucundaa-Teposcolula, see various references to Spores and to Spores and Robles García in the bibliography.

70. Caso 1977, 1979.

71. Amadio 2010; Duncan et al. 2008.

72. Meissner et al. 2012 and MAFP.

73. Bellas 1997.

74. Caso 1960; Jiménez Moreno and Mateos Higuera 1940; and AGN Inquisición 37, exp. 5. See also *Relaciones geográficas* from Teozacoalco-Mitlatongo, Tejupan, Nochixtlan, Tilantongo, and Juxtlahuaca.

75. Duncan et al. 2008; Gaxiola González 1984; Lind 1979; Pérez Rodríguez 2003; Spores 1972, 1974a; and Spores and Robles García 2010.

76. AGN Inquisición 37, exp. 5.

77. "People came to this cave to consult the *demonio* and to request that water be provided in times of need." *RMEH*, vol. 2.

78. AGN Inquisición 37, exp. 5.

79. Ibid.

80. Herrera y Tordesillas 1947 [1601–15] describes burial in caves among other locations in déc. 3, lib. 3, cap. 13. Spores 1984, 84–95, and HHYP.

81. Spores 2003i [1983].

82. AGN Inquisición 37, exp. 5.

83. Herrera y Tordesillas 1947 [1601–15] déc. 3, lib. 3, cap. 13; Spores 1967, 24.

84. Burgoa 1989 [1674], I, 274–75; Reyes 1976 [1593].

85. Anders et al. 1992, 123–28; also Caso 1950; Furst 1977, 1978; and Williams 2009, 65–68.

86. Anders et al. 1992, 156–75; also Jansen and Pérez Jiménez 2007, 85, 90, who associate the west with the place sign for "Ash River." This could be a river in the general vicinity of the Oaxaca-Guerrero border, but following the discussion in Mary E. Smith 1973, 60–62, "Ash River" could instead reference Acatlan, Puebla. This location would in fact be the furthest west of the presumptively identified places.

87. Yanhuitlan-Nochixtlan and the northern Mixteca Baja are the zones that appear to have remained populated during the Epiclassic, and from which the foundational royal dynasties of the Postclassic would have emerged; see chapter 3, this volume.

88. Culhua-Mexica religion is discussed in Caso 1958b; Durán 1971 [1574–79]; León-Portilla 1963; Nicholson 1971; and Sahagún 1950–82, especially vols. 1–5.

CHAPTER 5

1. Spores 1964, 1967, and 1984, 97–121.

2. Lockhart 1992, 4. Rice and Rice 2005 describe late-surviving indigenous Maya in the Petén Lakes region of Guatemala.

3. Restall 2004.

4. Lockhart 1992, 5.

5. Various comparative studies come to mind. Taylor 1979 describes Colonial-era violence as situational, normative, and generally confined within the new institutional framework. Crosby 2004 describes the "biological expansion of Europe," where the perspective of environmental history shows the New World landscape remade and articulating with newly introduced social and economic systems.

6. The persistence of native forms of government and territorial organization, and the extent to which Spanish administration adhered to this template, is reported in Gibson's 1964 observations about Tlaxcallan and Mexican states; Spores 1964 and Terraciano 2001 describe a similar pattern for the Mixtec.

7. López de Gómara 1943 [1552], cap. 90; Oviedo y Valdés 1851–55 [1535], lib. 33, cap. 9; Herrera y Tordesillas 1947 [1601–15], déc. 3, lib. 9, cap. I.

8. Gayangos 1866, 51–157.

9. López de Gómara 1943 [1552], I, 330; Díaz del Castillo 1955 [1580], cap. 132.

10. Díaz del Castillo 1963, 310.

11. Herrera y Tordesillas 1947 [1601–15], déc. 3, lib. 3, cap. 9.

12. Ibid., déc. 3, lib. 3, cap. 9.

13. Simpson 1950; Zavala 1935.

14. González de Cossío 1952.

15. Simpson 1950; Zavala 1935.

16. Spores 1967, 75–81.

17. AGI Justicia, 117, núm. I.

18. Jiménez Moreno and Mateos Higuera 1940, 13.

19. Ibid., 15.

20. González de Cossío 1952, 58.

21. A carga in these cases was the amount of wood or fodder an individual could carry on his or her back.

22. Paso y Troncoso, I, 131.

23. Borah and Cook 1958.

24. AGN Tierras, 2941, exp. 28.

25. APJO, Tep. Civ. legajos 1–3, passim; AGN Mercedes, passim; AGN Tierras, passim.

26. Borah 1943, 24–25.

27. Ibid.

28. Ibid., 26–31.

29. Ibid., 25.

30. Ibid., 51–52.

31. Ibid., 31.

32. Ibid., 94.

33. Lee 1948, 462.

34. Ibid., 472.

35. Ibid.

36. Ibid., 451, 464.

37. Gómez de Cervantes 1944, 164.

38. Miranda 1958, 794–95.

39. Ibid., 796.

40. Burgoa 1989 [1674], I, 286.

41. The Inquisitorial investigation of 1544 is of unusual importance; see AGN Inquisición 37; and see Burgoa 1989 [1674], passim.

42. Spores and Robles García 2007; and Spores and Robles García 2010.

43. Jiménez Moreno 1962 [1593]; Jiménez Moreno and Mateos Higuera 1940.

44. Ibid., 22.

45. Scholes and Adams, 1961, 297–302.

46. Kubler, 1948, 390.

47. Burgoa 1989 [1674], I, 291–92.

48. Kubler 1948, 390.

49. Burgoa 1989 [1674], I, 292.

50. Kubler, 1948, 535; Burgoa 1989 [1674], 293.

51. AGN Tierras 29, exp. 1; Burgoa 1989 [1674]; Herrera y Tordesillas 1947 [1601–15], déc. 3, vol. 3, cap. 9; Berlin 1947; Mary E. Smith 1973, 84–88; and Spores 1967, 68–70.

52. Spores 1998.

53. Spores and Robles García 2007; Spores and Robles García 2010.

54. Spores 1998.

55. AGN Civil 726, exp. 7.

56. Romero Frizzi 1990, 218.

57. Ibid.

58. Bernal 1962; Paso y Troncoso 1905–1906; González de Cossío 1952; García Pimentel 1904; and *RMEH* 1927–28, vols. 1–2.

59. By way of comparison, the complex story of Spanish society and economy in the Colonial countryside has been treated in detail by María de los Angeles Romero Frizzi. One fundamental dynamic was the constant Spanish presence in the countryside, and the extent to which this presence facilitated economic integration with cities and, by extension, the larger world. Spanish residents of the Mixteca countryside, however, represented more a socioeconomic appendage of Oaxaca, Puebla, or Mexico cities than a socially integrated component of Mixtec life.

60. Spores and Robles García 2007; Spores and Robles García 2010.

61. Spores 2005.

62. Kowalewski et al. 2009, 263–67; Spores 1996a. The Spores 1996a survey zone covers a wider area around Tlaxiaco, making it necessary to consult both sources for reconstructing Tlaxiaco's late pre-Hispanic and early Colonial settlement history.

CHAPTER 6

1. See Spores 1967, 1984; Terraciano 2001.

2. Source materials are described in chapter 1, this volume.

3. Spores 1964.

4. Gibson 1966, 90–111; Haring 1947; and Zavala and Miranda 1954.

5. Spores 1984, 165–86.

6. Gibson 1964.

7. López Sarrelangue 1965.

8. Chapter 5, this volume.

9. Often a *cacique* held title to several communities acquired through inheritance or marriage, but he was permitted to serve as *gobernador* in only one community. See Spores 1967, 155–88.

10. Although natives, particularly *principales*, served religious *mayordomías*, belonged to *cofradías*, and otherwise functioned in the church, there is no evidence of the civil-religious hierarchical rotation described for other areas of Mesoamerica; see Carrasco 1961.

11. Gibson 1966, 90–111; Haring 1947; and Zavala and Miranda 1954.

12. Fisher 1929; Haring 1947, 144–48.

13. Spores 1967, 119–30, 171–84.

14. AGN Inquisición 37, exps. 5–11; AGN Tierras 220, 985–86; AGN Mercedes 3, exp. 454; AGI Escribanía de Cámara 162; and Burgoa 1989 [1674], I, 277.

15. AGN Civil 516.

16. Ibid.

17. Ibid.

18. Terraciano 2001, 105–17.

19. AGN Civil 516.

20. AGN Tierras 400, exp. 1.

21. AGI Escribanía de Cámara 162; AGN Tierras 400; AGN Tierras 985–86; and see Spores 1967, 140; Terraciano 2001, 126–30.

22. AGN Tierras 24, exp. 6.

23. Ibid.

24. AGN Tierras 29, exp. 1.

25. AGN Vínculos 272.

26. AGN Tierras 400, exp. 1.

27. APJO Administrativa Tep. Civ. ATC no. 2 (Legajo viejo 32, exp. 22): Inventario de los bienes de Don Felipe de Castilla, Cacique de Teposcolula en 1563.

28. AGN Tierras 29, exp. 1.

29. AGN Tierras 400, exp. 1.

30. AGN Indios, exp. 540.

31. Herrera y Tordesillas 1947 [1601–15], déc. 3, lib. 3, cap. 12.

32. AGN Civil 516.

33. AGN Tierras 24, exp. 6.

34. Ibid., 34, exp. 1.

35. Ibid., 59, exp. 2.

36. *RMEH* 2, 142–46.

37. Ibid. 2(5): 135–46.

38. AGN Tierras 29, exp. 1; ibid., 46, exp. 2; AGN, Vínculos, 272; Burgoa 1989 [1674], I, 335; and Berlin 1947.

39. AGN Civil 516.

40. Herrera y Tordesillas 1947 [1601–15], déc. 3, lib. 3, cap. 13.

41. Jiménez Moreno and Mateos Higuera 1940.

42. AGI Escribanía de Cámara 162.

43. Caso 1966.

44. AGN Civil 516.

45. Caso 1966.

46. AGN Civil 516.

47. AGI Justicia, leg. 117, no. I.

48. AGN Civil 516.

49. Caso 1966.

50. Ibid.

51. Ibid.

52. AGN Civil 516.

53. AGI Escribanía de Cámara 162.

54. AGN Inquisición 37, exp. 9.

55. AGN Civil 516.

56. Ibid.; AGN Tierras 985.

57. Ibid.; Jiménez Moreno and Mateos Higuera 1940, 36.

58. AGI Escribanía de Cámara 162.

59. AGN Civil 516; AGN Tierras 400, exp. I.

60. AGN Tierras 400, exp. 1; Jiménez Moreno and Mateos Higuera 1940, 34–36.

61. AGI Escribanía de Cámara 162.

62. AGN Tierras 400, exp. 1.

63. Ibid., cuad 21, ff. 55–75.

64. Ibid.

65. AGN Vínculos 272.

66. Ibid.

67. AGN Tierras 24, exp. 6.

68. *Codex Nuttall*; *Codex Bodley*; Burgoa 1989 [1674], I, 275–77, 369–75; Caso 1977–79, passim.

69. Balkansky et al. 2000; Kowalewski et al. 2009, 75–76.

70. AGN Tierras 24, exp. 6.

71. Ibid.

72. Ibid.

73. APJO Tep. Civ. legs. 5–6, exps. 564, 577, 597, 774, ff. 49v–52 and passim.

74. Ibid.

75. AGN Civil 516; AGN Tierras 400, exp. 1; ibid., 985–86, 1433; AGN General de Parte 2, exp. 1053; AGN Indios 6, 2a parte, exp. 3; and ibid., exp. 212.

76. Ibid.

77. AGN Tierras 34, exp. 1; Paso y Troncoso 1905–1906, IV, 53–57.

78. AGN Tierras 24, exp. 6.

79. Caso 1949, 1951, and 1960; and see Emily Rabin's (2002) revised chronology.

80. AGN Civil 516; AGN Tierras 3343, exp. 12; Paso y Troncoso 1905–1906, IV, 82–87.

81. AGN Tierras 44.

82. AGN Civil 726, exp. 7.

83. Paso y Troncoso 1905–1906, IV, 77–82.

84. Caso 1949.

85. AGN Indiferente General.

86. Ibid., 24, exp. 6.

87. Ibid., 59, exp. 2.

88. AGN Tierras 655, exp. 2.

89. Spores 1967, 110–54.

90. APJO Tep. Civ. 121.

91. APJO Huajuapan, Ramo Civil, Cajas 1–2, Provisionales.

92. Spores 1993.

93. AGN Tierras 29, exp. 1; AGN Vínculos 272.

94. AGN Tierras 24, exp. 6.

95. Ibid., exp. 4.

96. APJO Tep. Civ., Administrativa; Romero Frizzi and Spores 1976.

97. AGN Tierras 2948, exp. 28; AGN Indios 1, exp. 157; Spores 1967, 222–23.

98. AJT 7, exp. 2.

99. ARMT, Inventario de expedientes, 1843.

100. Spores 1967, figure 3.

101. Romero Frizzi and Spores 1976: AJT 7, exp. 2; APJO, Tep. Civ., no clasificado.
102. Ibid.

Chapter 7

1. For a detailed study of Spanish Colonial government and/or relations between the royal, viceregal, and provincial levels of government see chapter 6, this volume, and Clarence Haring, *The Spanish Empire in America*; Charles Gibson, *The Aztecs Under Spanish Rule*; Andrés Lira and Luis Muro, "El siglo de la integración," in *Historia general de México*; Lillian Fisher, *The Intendent System in Spanish America*. For indigenous government and local political structure, see Silvio Zavala and José Miranda, "Instituciones indígenas en la Colonia," in *Métodos y resultados de la política indigenista*.

2. Fisher, op. cit.: Haring, op. cit.: Gibson, op. cit.

3. Spores 1990a, 1990b.

4. Spores 1990c.

5. Lieberman 1970; Timmons 1963.

6. Abundant documentation of this type is housed in the AGEO and APJO, Oaxaca City.

7. Robertson 1952.

8. Vázquez-Gómez 1997.

9. Lynch 1986; Miller 1985.

10. AGEO Asuntos Agrarios 865, exp. 6.

11. APJO Teposcolula Civil 25.

12. Ibid., exp. 2041.

13. AGEO Conflictos 54, exp. 23.

14. APJO Teposcolula Civil, registros de protocolos y instrumentos públicos, passim. APJO Huajuapan Civil, passim.

15. APJO Huajuapan Civil, legs. 1 and 2.

16. Spores 1984, 64–66, 99–100, 119.

17. APJO Teposcolula Civil 25, exp. 2041.

18. AGEO Conflictos 54, exp. 1485.

19. Many contracts of this kind dating from the sixteenth to the nineteenth century are available in APJO Teposcolula Civil, passim.

20. This important, long-enduring institution has never been adequately studied. Although formal documentation is quite scarce, there were until recently a few older citizens in the Mixtecas who participated in the management of these herds and were quite willing to relate their experiences and to discuss the operation of the *haciendas*.

21. APJO Huajuapan Civil 1, exp. 21. Also see, APJO Huajuapan Civil 1, exps. 7, 9, and 14. For extensive discussion of nineteenth- and twentieth-century Mixtec *caciques*, their activities, status, and holdings, see Monaghan 1997; also Monaghan, Joyce, and Spores 2003.

22. APJO Huajuapan Civil 1, exp. 1.

23. APJO Huajuapan Civil 1 and 2, passim.

24. APJO Huajuapan Civil 1–5, passim; Monaghan 1997.

25. AJPO Huajuapan Civil 1–2, passim; Monaghan 1997.

26. McNamara 2007 is interesting for its Oaxacan point of view.

27. Monaghan 1994; Pastor 1987, 43–44; Spores 1967, 5–7.

28. For the late nineteenth century, see AGEO Gobernación. Informes de Jefes Políticos, 1890; AGEO Gobernación. Catastros, 1892.

29. AGEO, Gobernación, 1828, s.n. "Número de habitantes que se compone . . ."; Estadística del Departamento y Gobierno de Teposcolula que comprende el Partido del mismo nombre y los de Nochixtlan y Tlaxiaco, año de 1827 (EDGT), Plan Estadístico del Departamento de Teposcolula, 1826 (PEDT); Cuestionario de don Antonio Bergoza y Jordán (Huesca et al.), 2 vols., Oaxaca, AGEO, 1984. The total population of the state of Oaxaca in 1828 was 456,515; AGEO, Gobernación, 1828, s.n. "Número de habitantes de que se compone en sus respectivos Departamentos y cálcula de la fuerza que le pertenece para la milicia cívica"; AGEO; Legajos encuadernados, box 71, Decretos, 1826 F.

30. Relevant sources include AGEO, Gobernación, 1828, s.n., Oaxaca. Correspondencia del Señor Intendente don José María Murguía relativa a su Plan Estadístico del Estado de Oaxaca, 1827. Oaxaca had 456,515 inhabitants in 1828; AGEO, Gobernación, 1828 s.n. "Número de habitantes de que se compone en sus respectivos Departamentos y cálculo de la fuerza que le pertenece para la milicia cívica"; AGEO, legajos encuadernados, caja 71, Decretos, 1826 F. At this time Teposcolula and Nochixtlan had fifty-six pueblos and sixty-three pueblos respectively. AGEO, Gobernación, 1828, s.n. "Número de habitantes que se compone . . . ," op. cit.; Estadística del Departamento y Gobierno de Teposcolula que comprende el Partido del mismo nombre y los de Nochixtlan y Tlaxiaco, año de 1827 (EDGT); Plan Estadístico del Departamento de Teposcolula, 1826 (PEDT); Cuestionario de don Antonio Bergoza y Jordán (Huesca et al.), 2 vols., Oaxaca, AGEO, 1983.

31. Estadística del Departamento . . . , 1827, op. cit.; Plan Estadístico . . . , 1826, op. cit.

32. AGEO, Tesorería, 1827a, s.n. Aduana de Huajuapan, enero de 1827. Noticia de los cargamentos procedentes de ella y de los que pasan con dirección unos a la general del estado, otros a sus subalternas, y otros a varios puntos en el mes de la fecha (enero y febrero de 1827); AGEO, Tesorería, 1827b, s.n., Alcabala, Huajuapan.

33. AGEO, legajos encuadernados, Tesorería, caja 113, Tesorería, 1830a, Tehuantepec. Extracción de sal, año de 1830. AGEO, Tesorería, 1827, s.n., Tehuantepec, Aduanas, 31 de marzo de 1827. AGEO, Gobernación, 1828, s.n., Oaxaca. Correspondencia del Señor Intendente don José María Murguía relativa a su Plan Estadístico del Estado de Oaxaca, 1827.

34. Estadística del Departamento de Oajaca, 1827, op. cit.; Plan Estadístico del Departamento . . . , 1826, op. cit.; Cuestionario de don Antonio Bergoza y Jordán, op. cit.; AGEO, Legajos Encuadernados, Alcabalas, 1829d, Teposcolula, año de 1829. Libro manual de alcabalas de la Administración de Teposcolula.

35. For a detailed analysis of these activities during the Colonial period, see Romero Frizzi 1990.

36. Crop production figures are presented in Cuadros Estadísticos 6–10 and 12.

37. Spores 1990a, 1990b.

38. AGEO, ramos de Gobernación, Tesorería, and Fomento passim. There are no systematic guides, indices or inventories to these large, important documentary collections, which must be reviewed and consulted through a laborious page-by-page process.

39. Dalton 1971, 20–21.

40. These trends are reflected in the census and civil registry records of the period 1880 to 1900 currently found in the ARMT, AGEO, and APJO. These very infrequently list *ausentes*, or persons absent, and they show an extremely high level of community endogamy at levels often at or near 100 percent.

41. Spores 1990a, 1990b.

42. Population grew from 65,000 in the mid-1820s to 153,098 in 1895; see Cuadros Estadísticos 1.

43. Wolf 1957, 4.

44. Cuadros Estadísticos 5.

45. Cuadros Estadísticos 1, 3–4.

46. Cuadros Estadísticos 4.

47. AGEO Gobernación, Catastros.

48. Cook 1982, 241–68.

49. Marroquín 1957, 173–86; ongoing observation since 1963/1993 by the authors of this book; and see Warner 1975.

CHAPTER 8

1. Butterworth 1975; Dennis 1987; Greenberg 1989; and Paddock 1979.

2. Taylor 1979, 27, makes a comparable point about the Zapotec and other groups in the Colonial period.

3. Nagengast et al. 1992.

4. Bartolomé and Barabas 1986, 28–29.

5. De la Fuente 1949, 23.

6. AGEO, Memoria Administrativa presentada por el Gobierno. Informe administrativo rendido por el Gobernador del Estado, General Manuel García Vigil, Septiembre, 1921.

7. ARMT, Presidencia, unclassified, correspondence of Dr. Leovigildo Vásquez to Presidente Municipal Benjamín Bolaños Jiménez, August 31, 1935, and from Bolaños Jiménez to Vásquez, September 9, 1935.

8. ARMT, Presidencia, sin clasificación, correspondence of Julio Santiago to Presidente Municipal of Tlaxiaco, February 15, 1937.

9. ARMT, Presidencia, unclassified, Acta between merchants of Tlaxiaco and Delegado de la Liga, Max Cenobio Robles, February 12, 1937.

10. ARMT, Presidencia, 1959, unclassified, letters from Hernández Hernández to Adolfo López Mateos, June 8 and June 28, 1959.

11. ARMT, Presidencia 1959, correspondence from Hernández Hernández, January 26 and February 24, 1959.

12. AGEO Gobernación, Correspondencia del Gobernador, sin clasificación, 1975. Correspondence dated June 13, July 24, August 8, and August 19, 1975.

13. ARMT, Presidencia, unclassified, Estatuos de T.R.V.M, undated.

14. ARMT, Presidencia, sin clasificación, correspondence between representatives of T.R.V.M. and the Presidente Municipal of Tlaxiaco, May 7, 1982; June 7, 1982; January 13, 1984; December 8, 1984.

15. Cruz 1986, 437–42.

16. Barth 1969, 10–11.

17. Bartolomé and Barabas 1986.

18. Hernández Hernández 1965, 50–52; see also Kearney and Nagengast 1989.

19. Eriksen 2002.

20. Butterworth 1962, 1975; Orellana 1973.

21. This discussion of economy depends heavily on participant observation since 1960 by Spores as well as Cederström 1990; Marroquín 1957; de la Peña 1950; and Warner 1975.

22. Dalton 1971, 12.

23. Spores 1996b.

24. The Marroquín study mentions the importance of the penetration of the area in the 1950s by roads linking the Mixteca to the major economic capitals of the Republic, its present and predicted effects on marketing activity in the Mixteca, the shift in the mix of market products, and, at least implicitly, the growing dependency of the market on outsiders.

25. Bernal 1966; Burgoa 1989 [1674]; Gay 1982 [1881]; and Kowalewski et al. 1989.

26. Saville 1920.

27. APJO Civil, legs. 1–8; Criminal, legs. 1–10, passim.

28. Butterworth 1975; Colby 1998; Edinger et al. 1996; Stephen 2007; and Velasco Ortiz 1990, 1992, 2005.

29. The literature on Mixtec migration is extensive. Although detailed consideration cannot be provided in the present book, it is essential to refer especially to

the works of Colby 1998; the contributions in Corbett et al. 1992; Cornelius et al. 2009; the work of Edinger and associates; Stephen 2007; Velasco Ortiz 2005; and the numerous publications of Michael Kearney and associates.

30. Herrera-Sobek 1979 provides some background, but formal studies of the *braceros* are limited despite the obvious relevance to current policy debates over migrant workers.

31. Colby 1998.

32. Edinger and others 1996 describe in intimate detail the pervasive effect of migration by the Mixtecs of San Juan Mixtepec to numerous locations in the north. Although not entirely positive, the results of migration, for the most part, have been favorable for individuals and families involved and for the community as a whole as well.

33. Velasco Ortiz 2005, 2.

34. Ibid., 3.

35. Ibid., 3.

36. Ibid., 3–4.

37. Stephen 2007, 306, citing Cano 2005, has noted the exceptional growth since the 1980s of these international multiethnic coalitions in Oaxaca as well as in the western United States. In 2005 the FIOB met in Oaxaca and declared that its mission was "to contribute to the development and self-determination of the migrant and non-migrant indigenous communities, as well as struggle for the defense of human rights with justice and gender equity at the binational level."

38. Stephen 2007.

39. Ibid., passim.

40. We apply the term "transnationalism" in our description of Mixtecs settling in the United States and Canada, wherein social networks span international borders and otherwise separate societies are conjoined. This approach compares favorably with Cohen et al. 2009, Kearney 2000, Velasco Ortiz 2005, and other studies of Mixtec transnational migrants.

41. There are fundamental issues of migration, ethnicity, exchange, and the anthropological uses of "diaspora" that we cannot begin to work through in this overview, although Croissier 2007 is interesting for an archaeological approach that crosses subfield boundaries.

42. Kiracofe 1996.

43. The "Canción Mixteca" was written in 1915 by José López Alavéz during a sojourn away from Oaxaca. We recommend the Lila Downs version recorded on her album *La Sandunga*.

BIBLIOGRAPHY

ARCHIVAL SOURCES

Archivo General de Indias, Seville (AGEO)
Archivo General de la Nación, Mexico City (AGN)
Archivo General del Poder Ejecutivo del Estado de Oaxaca (AGI)
Archivo Histórico del Poder Judicial del Estado de Oaxaca (APJO)
Archivo del Instituto Nacional de Antropología e Historia, Mexico City (AINAH)
Archivo del Juzgado de Teposcolula, Oaxaca (AJT)
Archivo del Municipio de Teposcolula, Oaxaca (AMT)
Archivo del Museo Nacional de Arqueología, Historia, y Etnografía, Mexico City (AMINAH)
Archivo Regional de la Mixteca del Municipio de Tlaxiaco (AMMT)

PUBLISHED WORKS

Acosta, Jorge R. 1965. "Preclassic and Classic Architecture of Oaxaca." In Wauchope and Willey, *Archaeology of Southern Mesoamerica*, 814–36.
Acosta, Jorge R., and Javier Romero. 1992. *Exploraciones en Monte Negro, Oaxaca: 1937–38, 1938–39 y 1939–40.* Mexico City: INAH.
Acuña, René, ed. 1984. *Relaciones geográficas del siglo XVI: Antequera.* 2 vols. Mexico City: UNAM.
Aguirre Beltrán, Gonzalo. 1953. *Formas de gobierno indígena.* Mexico City: INI.

Ahern, Frances. 1993. Pottery Stylistic Variation among Coastal Mixtec and Amuzgo: An Ethnoarchaeological Study. Ph.D. dissertation, State University of New York at Stony Brook.

Alvarado Tezozomoc, Fernando de. 1944. *Crónica mexicana* [1598]. Mexico City: Editorial Leyenda.

Amadio, Ayla Martine. 2010. Ritual Use of Animals at Formative Period Tayata: A Comparative Perspective. M.A. thesis, Southern Illinois University Carbondale.

Anders, Ferdinand, Maarten Jansen, and G. Aurora Pérez Jiménez. 1992. *Origen e historia de los reyes Mixtecos. Libro explicativo del llamado Códice Vindobonensis.* Mexico City: FCE.

Balkansky, Andrew K. 1998a. "Urbanism and Early State Formation in the Huamelulpan Valley of Southern Mexico." *Latin American Antiquity* 9:37–67.

———. 1998b. "Origin and Collapse of Complex Societies in Oaxaca (Mexico): Evaluating the Era from 1965 to the Present." *Journal of World Prehistory* 12:451–93.

———. 1999. "Settlement Pattern Studies in the Mixteca Alta, Oaxaca, 1966–1996." In *Settlement Pattern Studies in the Americas: Fifty Years since Virú*, ed. Brian R. Billman and Gary M. Feinman, 191–202. Washington, D.C.: Smithsonian Institution Press.

———. 2002. *The Sola Valley and the Monte Albán State: A Study of Zapotec Imperial Expansion.* Memoirs 36. Ann Arbor: Museum of Anthropology, University of Michigan.

———. 2006a. Mixtec Urbanism. Paper presented at the annual meeting of the Society for American Archaeology, San Juan, Puerto Rico.

———. 2006b. "Surveys and Mesoamerican Archaeology: The Emerging Macroregional Paradigm." *Journal of Archaeological Research* 14:53–95.

———. 2012. "Oaxaca." In *The Cambridge World Prehistory*, Part IV: *The Americas*, ed. Colin Renfrew and Paul Bahn. Cambridge: Cambridge University Press, in press.

Balkansky, Andrew K., and Michelle M. Croissier. 2009. "Multicrafting in Prehispanic Oaxaca." *Archeological Papers of the American Anthropological Association* 19:58–74.

Balkansky, Andrew K., Stephen A. Kowalewski, Verónica Pérez Rodríguez, Thomas J. Pluckhahn, et al. 2000. "Archaeological Survey in the Mixteca Alta of Oaxaca, Mexico." *Journal of Field Archaeology* 27:365–89.

Balkansky, Andrew K., Felipe de Jesús Nava Rivera, and María Teresa Palomares Rodríguez. 2008. "Huamelulpan y Tayata, Oaxaca." *Arqueología Mexicana* 15 (90): 36–37.

———. 2009. "Los orígenes de la civilización Mixteca." *Arqueología Iberoamericana* 2:25–33.

Balkansky, Andrew K., Verónica Pérez Rodríguez, and Stephen A. Kowalewski. 2004. "Monte Negro and the Urban Revolution in Oaxaca, Mexico." *Latin American Antiquity* 15:33–60.

Barlow, Robert H. 1949. *The Extent of the Empire of the Culhua Mexica.* Ibero-Americana 28. Berkeley: University of California Press.

Barth, Fredrik. 1969. "Introduction." In *Ethnic Groups and Boundaries: The Social Organization of Culture Difference,* ed. Fredrik Barth, 9–37. Oslo: Universitetsforlaget.

Bartolomé, Miguel A., and Alicia M. Barabas. 1986. "La pluralidad desigual en Oaxaca." In *Etnicidad y pluralismo cultural. La dinámica étnica en Oaxaca,* ed. Alicia M. Barabas and Miguel A. Bartolomé, 13–95. Mexico City: CONACULTA and INAH.

Beaumont, Fray Pablo. 1932. *Crónica de Michoacán* [1778–80]. 3 vols. Mexico City: Editorial Porrúa.

Bedard, Justin, and Andrew K. Balkansky. N.d. Tayata Obsidian Sources: Characterization via XRF from the Formative Mixteca Alta. Manuscript.

Bellas, Monica L. 1997. The Body in the Mixtec Codices: Birth, Purification, Transformation, and Death. Ph.D. dissertation, University of California, Riverside.

Berlin, Heinrich. 1947. *Fragmentos desconocidos del Códice de Yanhuitlán y otras investigaciones Mixtecas.* Mexico City: Antigua Librería Robredo de José Porrúa e Hijos.

Bernal, Ignacio. 1948–49. "Exploraciones en Coixtlahuaca, Oax." *Revista Mexicana de Estudios Antropológicos* 10:5–76.

———. 1965. "Archaeological Synthesis of Oaxaca." In Wauchope and Willey, *Archaeology of Southern Mesoamerica,* 788–813.

———. 1966. "The Mixtecs in the Archaeology of the Valley of Oaxaca." In Paddock, *Ancient Oaxaca,* 345–66.

———. 1969. *The Olmec World.* Berkeley: University of California Press.

———. 1992. *Arqueología oaxaqueña.* Mexico City: La Colección Vidzu.

———, ed. 1962. "Relación de Guautla." *Tlalocan* 4 (1): 3–16.

Besserer, José Federico. 1999. *Moisés Cruz. Historia de un transmigrante.* Culiacán: Universidad Autónoma de Sinaloa; Mexico City: Universidad Autónoma Metropolitana Unidad Iztapalapa.

Blanton, Richard E. 1978. *Monte Albán: Settlement Patterns at the Ancient Zapotec Capital.* New York: Academic Press.

Blanton, Richard E., Gary M. Feinman, Stephen A. Kowalewski, and Linda M. Nicholas. 1999. *Ancient Oaxaca: The Monte Albán State.* Cambridge: Cambridge University Press.

Blanton, Richard E., Gary M. Feinman, Stephen A. Kowalewski, and Peter N. Peregrine. 1996. "A Dual-Processual Theory for the Evolution of Mesoamerican Civilization." *Current Anthropology* 37:1–14.

Blomster, Jeffrey P. 2004. *Etlatongo: Social Complexity, Interaction, and Village Life in the Mixteca Alta of Oaxaca, Mexico.* Belmont, Calif.: Wadsworth.

————, ed. 2008. *After Monte Albán: Transformation and Negotiation in Oaxaca, Mexico.* Boulder: University Press of Colorado.

Blomster, Jeffrey P. 2004, Hector Neff, and Michael D. Glascock. 2005. "Olmec Pottery Production and Export in Ancient Mexico Determined through Elemental Analysis." *Science* 307:1068–72.

Borah, Woodrow. 1943. *Silk Raising in Colonial Mexico.* Ibero-Americana 20. Berkeley: University of California Press.

Borah, Woodrow, and Sherburne F. Cook. 1958. *Price Trends of Some Basic Commodities in Central Mexico, 1531–1570.* Ibero-Americana 40. Berkeley: University of California Press.

Brockington, Donald. L., María Jorrín, and J. Robert Long. 1974. *The Oaxaca Coast Project Reports: Part I.* Nashville, Tenn.: VUPA 8.

Brockington, Donald L., and J. Robert Long. 1974. *The Oaxaca Coast Project Reports: Part II.* Nashville, Tenn.: VUPA 9.

Burgoa, Fr. Francisco de. 1989. *Geográfica descripción* [1674]. 2 vols. Mexico City: Editorial Porrúa.

Butterworth, Douglas S. 1962. "A study of the Urbanization Process among Mixtec Migrants from Tilantongo in Mexico City." *América Indígena* 22:257–74.

————. 1975. *Tilantongo: Comunidad mixteca en transición.* Mexico City: INI/SEP.

Byland, Bruce E. 1980. Political and Economic Evolution in the Tamazulapan Valley, Mixteca Alta, Oaxaca, Mexico: A Regional Approach. Ph.D. dissertation, Pennsylvania State University.

————. 1984. "Boundary Recognition in the Mixteca Alta." In Josserand et al., *Essays in Otomanguean Culture History*, 65–108.

Byland, Bruce E., and John M. D. Pohl. 1994. *In the Realm of 8 Deer: The Archaeology of the Mixtec Codices.* Norman: University of Oklahoma Press.

Cano, Arturo. 2005. "El camino del FIOB y su apuesta por el desarrollo: Los indios sin fronteras." *La Jornada*, April 3, 2005.

Carneiro, Robert L. 1981. "The Chiefdom: Precursor of the State." In *The Transition to Statehood in the New World*, ed. Grant D. Jones and Robert R. Kautz, 37–69. Cambridge: Cambridge University Press.

Carrasco, Pedro. 1961. "The Civil-Religious Hierarchy in Mesoamerican Communities: Pre-Spanish Background and Colonial Development." *American Anthropologist* 63: 483–97.

Caso, Alfonso. 1928. *Las estelas zapotecas.* Mexico City: SEP and Talleres Gráficos de la Nación.

————. 1938. *Exploraciones en Oaxaca: quinta y sexta temporadas, 1936–1937.* Publicación 34. Mexico City: Instituto Panamericana de Geografía e Historia.

————. 1941. *Culturas mixteca y zapoteca.* Mexico City: Ediciones Encuadernables de El Nacional.

———. 1942. "Resumen del informe de las exploraciones en Oaxaca durante la 7a y la 8a temporadas, 1937–1938 y 1938–1939." *Actas del XXVII Congreso Internacional de Americanistas* 2:159–87.

———. 1949. "El mapa de Teozacoalco." *Cuadernos Americanos* 8:145–81.

———. 1950. "Explicación del reverso del Códice Vindobonensis." *Memoria de El Colegio Nacional* 5 (5): 9–46.

———. 1951. "Base para la sincronología mixteca y cristiana." *Memoria de El Colegio Nacional* 6 (6): 49–66.

———. 1956. "El calendario mixteco." *Historia Mexicana* 5 (20): 481–97.

———. 1958a. "History and Science." *Boletín de Estudios Oaxaqueños* 3:1–4.

———. 1958b. *The Aztecs: People of the Sun.* Norman: University of Oklahoma Press.

———. 1959. Review of *Mixtec Ethnohistory: A Method of Analysis of the Codical Art*, by Philip Dark. *American Anthropologist* 61:147–51.

———. 1960. *Interpretation of the Codex Bodley 2858.* Mexico City: Sociedad Mexicana de Antropología.

———. 1965a. "Mixtec Writing and Calendar." In Wauchope and Willey, *Archaeology of Southern Mesoamerica,* 948–61.

———. 1965b. "Sculpture and Mural Painting of Oaxaca." In Wauchope and Willey, *Archaeology of Southern Mesoamerica,* , 849–70.

———. 1966a. "The Lords of Yanhuitlán." In Paddock, *Ancient Oaxaca,* 313–35.

———. 1969. *El tesoro de Monte Albán. Memorias* 3. Mexico City: INAH.

———. 1977–79. *Reyes y reinos de la Mixteca.* 2 vols. Mexico City: FCE.

Caso, Alfonso, Ignacio Bernal, and Jorge R. Acosta. 1967. *La cerámica de Monte Albán. Memorias* 13. Mexico City: INAH.

Caso, Alfonso, and Lorenzo Gamio. 1961. Informe de exploraciones en Huamelulpan. Report on file. Mexico City: INAH.

Casparis, Luca. 2006. Early Classic Jalieza and the Monte Albán State: A Study of Political Fragmentation in the Valley of Oaxaca, Mexico. Ph.D. dissertation, Université de Genève.

Cederström, Thoric Nils. 1990. "Migrant Remittances and Agricultural Development." *Culture and Agriculture* 40:2–7.

Chance, John K. 1978. *Race and Class in Colonial Oaxaca.* Stanford, Calif.: Stanford University Press.

———. 1989. *Conquest of the Sierra: Spaniards and Indians in Colonial Oaxaca.* Norman: University of Oklahoma Press.

———. 2004. "La casa noble mixteca: una hipótesis sobre el cacicazgo prehispánico y colonial." In *Memoria de la Tercera Mesa Redonda de Monte Albán. Estructuras políticas en el Oaxaca antiguo,* ed. Nelly M. Robles García, 1–25. Mexico City: INAH.

———. 2009. "Marriage Alliances among Colonial Mixtec Elites: The Villagómez Caciques of Acatlan-Petlalcingo." *Ethnohistory* 56:91–123.

Clark, James Cooper. 1912. *The Story of "Eight Deer" in Codex Colombino*. London: Taylor and Francis.

Clark, John E. 2004. "Mesoamerica Goes Public: Early Ceremonial Centers, Leaders, and Communities." In *Mesoamerican Archaeology: Theory and Practice*, ed. Julia A. Hendon and Rosemary A. Joyce, 43–72. Oxford: Blackwell Publishing.

———. 2007. "Mesoamerica's First State." In *The Political Economy of Ancient Mesoamerica: Transformations during the Formative and Classic Periods*, ed. Vernon L. Scarborough and John E. Clark, 11–46. Albuquerque: University of New Mexico Press.

Coe, Michael D. 1965. *The Jaguar's Children: Pre-Classic Central Mexico*. New York: The Museum of Primitive Art.

Cohen, Jeffrey H., Bernardo Ríos, and Lise Byars. 2009. "The Value, Costs, and Meaning of Transnational Migration in Rural Oaxaca, Mexico." *Migration Letters* 6:15–25.

Colby, Catherine. 1998. Return Migration from Canada and the United States: Its Effects in the Mixteca Alta of Oaxaca, Mexico. Ph.D. dissertation, Vanderbilt University.

Cook, Scott. 1982. *Zapotec Stoneworkers: The Dynamics of Rural Simple Commodity Production in Modern Mexican Capitalism*. Washington, D.C.: University Press of America.

Cook, Sherburne F. 1949. *Soil Erosion and Population in Central Mexico*. Ibero-Americana 34. Berkeley: University of California Press.

Cook, Sherburne F., and Woodrow Borah. 1968. *The Population of the Mixteca Alta, 1520–1960*. Ibero-Americana 50. Berkeley: University of California Press.

Corbett, Jack, Murad A. Musalem Merhy, Othón Ríos Vázquez, and Héctor A. Vázquez Hernández, eds. 1992. *Migración y etnicidad en Oaxaca*. Nashville, Tenn.: VUPA 43.

Cornelius, Wayne A., David Fitzgerald, Jorge Hernández-Díaz, and Scott Borger, eds. 2009. *Migration from the Mexican Mixteca: A Transnational Community in Oaxaca and California*. San Diego: University of California Center for Comparative Immigration Studies.

Covarrubias, Miguel. 1944. "La Venta: Colossal Heads and Jaguar Gods." *DYN* 6:24–33.

Cowgill, George L. 2004. "Origins and Development of Urbanism: Archaeological Perspectives." *Annual Review of Anthropology* 33:525–49.

———. 2008. "An Update on Teotihuacan." *Antiquity* 82:962–75.

Croissier, Michelle M. 2007. The Zapotec Presence at Teotihuacan, Mexico: Political Ethnicity and Domestic Identity. Ph.D. dissertation, University of Illinois at Urbana-Champaign.

Crosby, Alfred W. 2004. *Ecological Imperialism: The Biological Expansion of Europe, 900–1900*. 2nd edition. Cambridge: Cambridge University Press.

Cruz, Victor de la. 1986. "Reflexiones acerca de los movimientos etnopolíticos contemporáneos en Oaxaca." In *Etnicidad y pluralismo cultural. La dinámica étnica en Oaxaca*, ed. Alicia M. Barabas and Miguel A. Bartolomé, 421–45. Mexico City: CONACULTA and INAH.

Dahlgren de Jordán, Barbro. 1954. *La Mixteca: su cultura e historia prehispánicas.* Mexico City: UNAM.

Dalton, George. 1971. *Economic Anthropology and Development: Essays on Tribal and Peasant Economies.* New York: Basic Books.

Dark, Philip. 1958. *Mixtec Ethnohistory: A Method of Analysis of the Codical Art.* New York: Oxford University Press.

Dávila Padilla, Agustín. 1955. *Historia de la fundación y discurso de la Provincia de Santiago de México . . .* , 3rd edition [1596]. Mexico City: Editorial Ac. Literaria.

de Cicco, Gabriel, and Donald Brockington. 1956. *Reconocimiento arqueológico en el suroeste de Oaxaca.* Informe 6. Mexico City: INAH.

Demarest, Arthur A., Prudence M. Rice, and Don S. Rice, eds. 2004. *The Terminal Classic in the Maya Lowlands: Collapse, Transition, and Transformation.* Boulder: University Press of Colorado.

Dennis, Philip A. 1987. *Intervillage Conflict in Oaxaca.* New Brunswick, N.J.: Rutgers University Press.

Díaz del Castillo, Bernal. 1955. *Historia verdadera de la conquista de la Nueva España*, 4th edition [1580]. Mexico City: Editorial Porrúa.

———. 1963. *The Conquest of New Spain.* New York: Penguin.

Diehl, Richard A. 2004. *The Olmecs: America's First Civilization.* London: Thames and Hudson.

Donkin, R. A. 1979. *Agricultural Terracing in the Aboriginal New World.* Viking Fund Publications in Anthropology 56. Tucson: University of Arizona Press.

Drennan, Robert D. 1976. *Fábrica San José and Middle Formative Society in the Valley of Oaxaca.* Memoirs 8. Ann Arbor: Museum of Anthropology, University of Michigan.

———. 2003. "Radiocarbon Dates from the Oaxaca Region." In Flannery and Marcus, *Cloud People*, 363–70.

Duncan, William N., Andrew K. Balkansky, Kimberly Crawford, et al. 2008. "Human Cremation in Mexico 3,000 Years Ago." *Proceedings of the National Academy of Sciences* 105:5315–20.

Durán, Fray Diego. 1971. *Book of the Gods and Rites and the Ancient Calendar* [1574–79]. Translated and edited by Fernando Horcasitas and Doris Heyden. Norman: University of Oklahoma Press.

Earle, Timothy K. 1997. *How Chiefs Come to Power: The Political Economy in Prehistory.* Stanford, Calif.: Stanford University Press.

Edinger, Steven T, Evan N. Edinger, James M. Guerin, and Ann E. Mason, eds. 1996. *The Road from Mixtepec: A Southern Mexican Town and the United States Economy.* Fresno, Calif.: Asociación Cívica Benito Juárez.

Eriksen, Thomas Hylland. 2002. *Ethnicity and Nationalism: Anthropological Perspectives.* 2nd edition. London: Pluto Press.

Feinman, Gary M., and Linda M. Nicholas. 2004. *Hilltop Terrace Sites of Oaxaca, Mexico: Intensive Surface Survey at Guirún, El Palmillo and the Mitla Fortress.* Fieldiana, Anthropology New Series 37. Chicago: Field Museum of Natural History.

Fernández de Miranda, María Teresa, Morris Swadesh, and Robert W. Weitlaner. 1959. "Some Findings on Oaxaca Language Classification and Culture Terms." *International Journal of American Linguistics* 25:54–58.

Ferrusquía-Villafranca, Ismael. 1971. Geology of the Tamazulapan-Teposcolula-Yanhuitlan Area, Mixteca Alta, State of Oaxaca, Mexico. Ph.D. dissertation, University of Texas at Austin.

Finsten, Laura M. 1996. "Periphery and Frontier in Southern Mexico: The Mixtec Sierra in Highland Oaxaca." In *Pre-Columbian World Systems*, ed. Peter N. Peregrine and Gary M. Feinman, 77–95. Madison, Wis.: Prehistory Press.

Finsten, Laura M., Kent V. Flannery, and Barbara Macnider. 1989. "Preceramic and Cave Occupations." In *Monte Albán's Hinterland, Part II: Prehispanic Settlement Patterns in Tlacolula, Etla, and Ocotlán, The Valley of Oaxaca, Mexico*, by Stephen A. Kowalewski, Gary M. Feinman, Laura Finsten, et al., 39–53. 2 vols. Memoirs 23. Ann Arbor: Museum of Anthropology, University of Michigan.

Fisher, Lillian E. 1929. *The Intendant System in Spanish America.* Berkeley: University of California Press.

Flannery, Kent V. 1972. "The Cultural Evolution of Civilizations." *Annual Review of Ecology and Systematics* 3:399–426.

———. 1986. "A Visit to the Master." In *Guilá Naquitz: Archaic Foraging and Early Agriculture in Oaxaca, Mexico*, ed. Kent V. Flannery, 511–19. New York: Academic Press.

———. 2003a. "Precolumbian Farming in the Valleys of Oaxaca, Nochixtlán, Tehuacán, and Cuicatlán: A Comparative Study." In Flannery and Marcus, *Cloud People*, 323–39.

———. 2003b. "Monte Negro: A Reinterpretation." In Flannery and Marcus, *Cloud People*, 99–102.

———. 2003c. "Zapotec Warfare: Archaeological Evidence for the Battles of Huitzo and Guiengola." In Flannery and Marcus, *Cloud People*, 318–22.

———, ed. 1976. *The Early Mesoamerican Village.* New York: Academic Press.

———, ed. 1986. *Guilá Naquitz: Archaic Foraging and Early Agriculture in Oaxaca, Mexico.* New York: Academic Press.

Flannery, Kent V., Andrew K. Balkansky, Gary M. Feinman, et al. 2005. "Implications of New Petrographic Analysis for the Olmec 'Mother Culture Model.'" *Proceedings of the National Academy of Sciences* 102:11219–23.

Flannery, Kent V., and Joyce Marcus. 1994. *Early Formative Pottery of the Valley of Oaxaca.* Memoirs 27. Ann Arbor: Museum of Anthropology, University of Michigan.

———. 2000. "Formative Mexican Chiefdoms and the Myth of the 'Mother Culture.'" *Journal of Anthropological Archaeology* 19:1–37.

———, eds. 2003a. *The Cloud People: Divergent Evolution of the Zapotec and Mixtec Civilizations* [1983]. Clinton Corners, N.Y.: Percheron Press.

———. 2003b. "An Editorial opinion on the Mixtec Impact." In Flannery and Marcus, *Cloud People,* 277–79.

———. 2005. *Excavations at San José Mogote 1: The Household Archaeology.* Memoirs 40. Ann Arbor: Museum of Anthropology, University of Michigan.

Flannery, Kent. V., and Ronald Spores. 2003. "Excavated Sites of the Oaxaca Preceramic." In Flannery and Marcus, *Cloud People,* 20–26.

Fuente, Julio de la. 1949. *Yalálag. Una villa zapoteca serrana.* Serie Científica 1. Mexico City: Museo Nacional de Antropología e Historia.

Furst, Jill Leslie. 1977. "The Tree Birth Tradition in the Mixteca, Mexico." *Journal of Latin American Lore* 3:183–226.

———. 1978. *Codex Vindobonensis Mexicanus I: A Commentary.* Albany: Institute for Mesoamerican Studies, State University of New York.

Gamio, Lorenzo. 1957. Zona arqueológica de San Martín Huamelulpan. Manuscript. Mexico City: Archivo del Instituto Nacional de Antropología e Historia.

García Pimentel, Luis, ed. 1904. *Relación de los obispados de Tlaxcala, Michoacan, Oaxaca y otros lugares en el siglo XVI . . .* Mexico City: En Casa del Editor.

Garvin, Richard D. 1994. Modern and Prehispanic Agriculture in the Sierra Mixteca, Oaxaca, Mexico. Ph.D. dissertation, University of Calgary.

Gaxiola González, Margarita. 1984. *Huamelulpan. Un centro urbano de la Mixteca Alta.* Colección Científica 114. Mexico City: INAH.

———. 1986. "La arquitectura mixteca de Huamelulpan." *Cuadernos de Arquitectura Mesoamericana* 7:71–74.

Gay, José Antonio. 2000. *Historia de Oaxaca* [1881]. Mexico City: Editorial Porrúa.

Gayangos, Pascual de, ed. 1866. *Cartas y relaciones de Hernán Cortés al Emperador Carlos V.* Paris: Imprenta Central de los Ferro-Carriles.

Gerhard, Peter. 1993. *A Guide to the Historical Geography of New Spain.* Revised edition. Norman: University of Oklahoma Press.

Geurds, Alexander, and Maarten E. R. G. N. Jansen. 2008. "The Ceremonial Center of Monte Negro: A Cognitive Approach to Urbanization in Ñuu Dzaui." In *Urbanism in Mesoamerica / El urbanismo en Mesoamérica,* vol. 2, ed. Guadalupe Mastache, Robert Cobean, Ángel García Cook, and Kenneth G. Hirth, 377–421. Mexico City: INAH; University Park: Pennsylvania State University.

Gibson, Charles. 1964. *The Aztecs Under Spanish Rule: A History of the Indians of the Valley of Mexico, 1519–1810.* Stanford, Calif.: Stanford University Press.

———. 1966. *Spain in America.* New York: Harper and Row.

Gómez de Cervantes, Gonzalo. 1944. *La vida económica y social de Nueva España al finalizar el siglo XVI.* Mexico City: Antigua Librería Robredo de José Porrúa e Hijos.

González de Cossío, Francisco, ed. 1952. *El libro de las tasaciones de pueblos de la Nueva España, siglo XVI.* Mexico City: AGN.

Greenburg, James B. 1989. *Blood Ties: Life and Violence in Rural Mexico.* Tucson: University of Arizona Press.

Grove, David C. 1981. "The Formative Period and the Evolution of Complex Culture." In *Supplement to the Handbook of Middle American Indians.* Vol. 1: *Archaeology,* ed. Jeremy A. Sabloff, 373–91. Austin: University of Texas Press.

———. 1997. "Olmec Archaeology: A Half Century of Research and its Accomplishments." *Journal of World Prehistory* 11:51–101.

Gutiérrez Mendoza, Gerardo. 2003. "Territorial Structure and Urbanism in Mesoamerica: The Huaxtec and Mixtec-Tlapanec-Nahua Cases." In *El urbanismo en Mesoamérica/Urbanism in Mesoamerica,* vol. 1, ed. William T. Sanders, Alba Guadalupe Mastache, and Robert H. Cobean, 86–118. Mexico City: INAH; University Park: Pennsylvania State University.

Guzmán, Eulalia. 1934. "Exploración arqueológica en la Mixteca Alta." *Anales del Museo Nacional de Arqueología, Historia, y Etnografía* 1:17–42.

Haring, C. H. 1947. *The Spanish Empire in America.* New York: Harcourt Brace Jovanovich.

Heredia Espinoza, Verenice Y. 2008: *Cities on Hills: Classic Society in Mesoamerica's Mixteca Alta.* Oxford: British Archaeological Reports S1728.

Heredia Espinoza, Verenice Y., Stephen A. Kowalewski, and Verónica Pérez Rodríguez. 2008. "Cerro Jazmín: The Morphology of an Urban Center in the Mixteca Alta." In *Urbanism in Mesoamerica/El urbanismo en Mesoamérica,* vol. 2, ed. Guadalupe Mastache, Robert Cobean, Ángel García Cook, and Kenneth G. Hirth, 423–46. Mexico City: INAH; University Park: Pennsylvania State University.

Herman Lejarazu, Manuel. 2008. "Los códices de la Mixteca Alta." *Arqueología Mexicana* 15 (90):48–52.

———. 2009. "Los códices mixtecos." *Arqueología Mexicana,* edición especial 31:68–93.

Hernández Hernández, Manuel. 1965. *Informe de Trabajos de 1964 y 1965, Coalición de los Pueblos Mixtecos Oaxaqueños.* Mexico City: CPMO.

Hernández Sánchez, Gilda. 2005. *Vasijas para ceremonia. Iconografía de la cerámica tipo códice del estilo Mixteca-Puebla.* Leiden, The Netherlands: CNWS Publications.

Herrera y Tordesillas, Antonio de. 1947. *Historia general de los hechos de los castellanos en las islas y tierra firme del Mar Océano...* [1601–15]. 15 vols. Madrid: Academia de la Historia.

Herrera-Sobek, María. 1979. *The Bracero Experience: Elitelore versus Folklore*. Los Angeles: UCLA Latin American Center Publications.

Hirth, Kenneth. 1984. "Xochicalco: Urban Growth and State Formation in Central Mexico." *Science* 225:579–86.

Hopkins, Nicholas A. 1984. "Otomanguean Linguistic Prehistory." In Josserand et al., *Essays in Otomanguean Culture History*, 25–64.

Huesca, Irene, Manuel Esparza, and Luis Castañeda Guzmán, ed. 1984. *Cuestionario de don Antonio Bergoza y Jordán . . .* 2 vols. Oaxaca City: AGEO.

Jansen, Maarten, Peter Kröfges, and Michel Oudijk. 1998. *The Shadow of Monte Albán: Politics and Historiography in Postclassic Oaxaca, Mexico*. Leiden, The Netherlands: CNWS Publications.

Jansen, Maarten, and Gabina Aurora Pérez Jiménez. 2007. *Encounter with the Plumed Serpent: Drama and Power in the Heart of Mesoamerica*. Boulder: University Press of Colorado.

Jansen, Maarten E. R. G. N., and Laura N. K. van Broekhoven, eds. 2008. *Mixtec Writing and Society. Escritura de Ñuu Dzaui*. Amsterdam: KNAW Press.

Jiménez Moreno, Wigberto. 1966a. "Mesoamerica before the Toltecs." In Paddock, *Ancient Oaxaca*, 1–82.

———, ed. 1962. *Vocabulario en lengua Mixteca, por Fray Francisco de Alvarado* [1593]. Reproducción facsimilar con un estudio de Wigberto Jimenéz Moreno. Mexico City: INI and INAH.

Jiménez Moreno, Wigberto, and Salvador Mateos Higuera, eds. 1940. *Códice de Yanhuitlán*. Edición en facsímile con un estudio preliminar. Mexico City: INAH.

Josserand, J. Kathryn, Marcus C. Winter, and Nicholas Hopkins, eds. 1984. *Essays in Otomanguean Culture History*. Nashville, Tenn.: VUPA 31.

———, 1984. "Introduction." In Josserand et al., *Essays in Otomanguean Culture History*, 1–24.

Josserand, J. Kathryn, Maarten E. R. G. N. Jansen, and María de los Ángeles Romero. 1984. "Mixtec Dialectology: Inferences from Linguistics and Ethnohistory." In Josserand et al., *Essays in Otomanguean Culture History*, 141–63.

Joyce, Arthur A. 1991. Formative Period Occupation in the Lower Río Verde Valley, Oaxaca, Mexico: Interregional Interaction and Social Change. Ph.D. dissertation, Rutgers University.

———. 2010. *Mixtecs, Zapotecs, and Chatinos: Ancient Peoples of Southern Mexico*. Malden, Mass., and Oxford: Wiley-Blackwell.

Joyce, Arthur A., Hector Neff, Mary S. Thieme, et al. 2006. "Ceramic Production and Exchange in Late/Terminal Formative Period Oaxaca." *Latin American Antiquity* 17:579–94.

Joyce, Arthur A., Andrew G. Workinger, Byron Hamann, et al. 2004. "Lord 8 Deer 'Jaguar Claw' and the Land of the Sky: The Archaeology and History of Tututepec." *Latin American Antiquity* 15:273–97.

Kearney, Michael. 2000. "Transnational Oaxacan Indigenous Identity: The Case of Mixtecs and Zapotecs." *Identities* 7:173–95.

Kearney, Michael, and Carole Nagengast. 1989. *Anthropological Perspectives on Transnational Communities in Rural California*. Davis, Calif.: California Institute for Rural Studies.

Kiracofe, James B. 1996. Architectural Fusion and Indigenous Ideology in Early Colonial Mexico. A Case Study of Teposcolula, Oaxaca, 1535–1580, Demonstrating Cultural Transmission and Transformation Through Negotiation and Consent in Planning a New Urban Environment. Ph.D. dissertation, Virginia Polytechnic Institute and State University, Blacksburg.

Kirkby, Michael. 1972. *The Physical Environment of the Nochixtlán Valley*. Nashville, Tenn.: VUPA 2.

Kowalewski, Stephen A. 2003a. "Backcountry Pots." *Ancient Mesoamerica* 14:65–75.

———. 2003b. "The Archaeological Evidence for Sa'a Yucu." In Flannery and Marcus, *Cloud People*, 289.

———. 2008. "Regional Settlement Pattern Studies." *Journal of Archaeological Research* 16:225–85.

Kowalewski, Stephen A., Andrew K. Balkansky, Laura R. Stiver Walsh, et al. 2009. *Origins of the Ñuu: Archaeology in the Mixteca Alta, Mexico*. Boulder: University Press of Colorado.

Kowalewski, Stephen A., Luis A. Barba Pingarrón, Jorge Blancas, et al. 2008. Proyecto urbanismo temprano y tardío en Coixtlahuaca, Oaxaca. Informe técnico final. Report on file. Consejo de Arqueología and Centro INAH Oaxaca.

Kowalewski, Stephen A., Gary M. Feinman, Laura Finsten, et al. 1989. *Monte Albán's Hinterland, Part II: Prehispanic Settlement Patterns in Tlacolula, Etla, and Ocotlán, The Valley of Oaxaca, Mexico*. 2 vols. Memoirs 23. Ann Arbor: Museum of Anthropology, University of Michigan.

Kröfges, Peter C. 2004. Sociopolitical Organization in the Prehispanic Chontalpa de Oaxaca, Mexico. Ethnohistorical and Archaeological Perspectives. Ph.D. dissertation, State University of New York at Albany.

Kubler, George. 1948. *Mexican Architecture of the Sixteenth Century*. 2 vols. New Haven, Conn: Yale University Press.

Lackey, Louana M. 1991. *The Pottery of Acatlan: A Changing Mexican Tradition*. Norman: University of Oklahoma Press.

Lee, Raymond. 1948. "Cochineal Production and Trade in New Spain to 1600." *Americas* 4:449–73.

León-Portilla, Miguel. 1963. *Aztec Thought and Culture: A Study of the Ancient Nahuatl Mind*. Translated by Jack Emory Davis. Norman: University of Oklahoma Press.

Lieberman, Mark. 1970. *Hidalgo: Mexican Revolutionary*. New York: Praeger Publishers.

Lind, Michael D. 1979. *Postclassic and Early Colonial Mixtec Houses in the Nochixtlán Valley, Oaxaca.* Nashville, Tenn.: VUPA 23.

———. 1987. *The Sociocultural Dimensions of Mixtec Ceramics.* Nashville, Tenn.: VUPA 33.

———. 2000. "Mixtec City-States and Mixtec City-State Culture." In *A Comparative Study of Thirty City-State Cultures: An Investigation Conducted by the Copenhagen Polis Centre,* ed. Mogens Herman Hansen, 567–80. Copenhagen: The Royal Danish Academy of Sciences and Letters.

Lind, Michael D., and Javier Urcid. 2009. *The Lords of Lambityeco: Political Evolution in the Valley of Oaxaca During the Xoo Phase.* Boulder: University Press of Colorado.

Lira, Andrés, and Luis Muro. 1976. "El siglo de la integración." In *Historia general de México,* vol. 2, ed. Daniel Cosío Villegas, 83–181. Mexico City: El Colegio de México.

Lockhart, James. 1992. *The Nahuas After the Conquest: A Social and Cultural History of the Indians of Central Mexico, Sixteenth Through Eighteenth Centuries.* Stanford, Calif.: Stanford University Press.

Longacre, Robert E., and René Millon. 1961. "Proto-Mixtecan and Proto-Amuzgan-Mixtecan Vocabularies: A Preliminary Cultural Analysis." *Anthropological Linguistics* 3:1–44.

López de Gómara, Francisco. 1943. *Historia de la conquista de México* [1552]. 2 vols. Mexico City: Editorial Pedro Robredo.

López Sarrelangue, Delfina E. 1965. *La nobleza indígena de Patzcuaro en la época virreinal.* Mexico City: UNAM.

Lorenzo, José Luis. 1958a. *Un sitio precerámico en Yanhuitlán, Oaxaca.* Dirección Prehistoria Publicación 6. Mexico City: INAH.

———. 1958b. "Aspectos físicos del Valle de Oaxaca." *Revista Mexicana de Estudios Antropológicos* 7:49–63.

Love, Michael W. 2007. "Recent Research in the Southern Highlands and Pacific Coast of Mesoamerica." *Journal of Archaeological Research* 15:275–328.

Lynch, John. 1986. *The Spanish American Revolutions 1808–1826.* 2nd edition. New York: W. W. Norton and Company.

MacNeish, Richard S. 1964. "Ancient Mesoamerican Civilization." *Science* 143:531–37.

MacNeish, Richard S., Melvin L. Fowler, Angel García Cook, Frederick A. Peterson, et al. 1972. *The Prehistory of the Tehuacán Valley.* Vol. 5: *Excavations and Reconnaissance.* Austin, University of Texas Press.

MacNeish, Richard S., Frederick A. Peterson, and Kent V. Flannery. 1970. *The Prehistory of the Tehuacán Valley.* Vol. 3: *Ceramics.* Austin: University of Texas Press.

Marcus, Joyce. 1974. "The Iconography of Power among the Classic Maya." *World Archaeology* 6:83–94.

———. 1976. "The Iconography of Militarism at Monte Albán and Neighboring Sites in the Valley of Oaxaca." In *The Origins of Religious Art and Iconography in*

Preclassic Mesoamerica, ed. Henry B. Nicholson, 123–39. Los Angeles: University of California at Los Angeles, Latin American Center.

————. 1983. "On the Nature of the Mesoamerican City." In *Prehistoric Settlement Patterns: Essays in Honor of Gordon R. Willey*, ed. Evan Z. Vogt and Richard M. Leventhal, 195–242. Albuquerque: University of New Mexico Press.

————. 1989. "From Centralized Systems to City-States: Possible Models for the Epiclassic." In *Mesoamerica After the Decline of Teotihuacan A.D. 700–900*, ed. Richard A. Diehl and Janet Catherine Berlo, 201–208. Washington, D.C.: Dumbarton Oaks Research Library and Collection.

————. 1992a. *Mesoamerican Writing Systems: Propaganda, Myth, and History in Four Ancient Civilizations*. Princeton, N.J.: Princeton University Press.

————. 1992b. "Dynamic Cycles of Mesoamerican States." *National Geographic Research and Exploration* 8:392–411.

————. 1998a. *Women's Ritual in Formative Oaxaca: Figurine-Making, Divination, Death and the Ancestors*. Memoirs 33. Ann Arbor: Museum of Anthropology, University of Michigan.

————. 1998b. "The Peaks and Valleys of Ancient States: An Extension of the Dynamic Model." In *Archaic States*, ed. Gary M. Feinman and Joyce Marcus, 59–94. Santa Fe, N.M.: School of American Research Press.

————. 2002. "Carved Stones from the Sola Valley, Oaxaca." In Andrew K. Balkansky, *The Sola Valley and the Monte Albán State: A Study of Zapotec Imperial Expansion*, 103–21. Memoirs 36. Ann Arbor: Museum of Anthropology, University of Michigan.

————. 2003a. "The Genetic Model and the Linguistic Divergence of the Otomangueans." In Flannery and Marcus, *Cloud People*, 4–9.

————. 2003b. "The Style of the Huamelulpan Stone Monuments." In Flannery and Marcus, *Cloud People*, 125–26.

————. 2003c. "Changing Patterns of Stone Monuments after the Fall of Monte Albán, A.D. 600–900." In Flannery and Marcus, *Cloud People*, 191–97.

————. 2003d. "A Synthesis of the Cultural Evolution of the Zapotec and Mixtec." In Flannery and Marcus, *Cloud People*, 355–60.

————. 2003e. "Monte Albán's Tomb 7." In Flannery and Marcus, *Cloud People*, 282–85.

————. 2003f. "Aztec Military Campaigns against the Zapotecs: The Documentary Evidence." In Flannery and Macrus, *Cloud People*, 314–18.

Marcus, Joyce, and Kent V. Flannery. 1990. "Science and Science Fiction in Postclassic Oaxaca: Or, 'Yes, Virginia, There is a Monte Albán IV.'" In *Debating Oaxaca Archaeology*, ed. Joyce Marcus, 191–205. Anthropological Papers 84. Ann Arbor: Museum of Anthropology, University of Michigan.

————. 1996. *Zapotec Civilization: How Urban Society Evolved in Mexico's Oaxaca Valley*. London: Thames and Hudson.

———. 2003. "An Introduction to the Late Postclassic." In Flannery and Marcus, *Cloud People*, 217–26.

———. 2004. "The Coevolution of Ritual and Society: New ^{14}C Dates from Ancient Mexico." *Proceedings of the National Academy of Sciences* 101:18257–61.

Marcus, Joyce, and Judith Francis Zeitlin. 1994. *Caciques and Their People: A Volume in Honor of Ronald Spores.* Anthropological Papers 89. Ann Arbor: Museum of Anthropology, University of Michigan.

Marroquín, Alejandro. 1957. *La ciudad mercado (Tlaxiaco).* Mexico City: Imprenta Universitaria.

Martí, Samuel. 1965a. "¿Ciudad perdida de los mixtecos? Nueva zona arqueológica en la Mixteca Alta. Acrópolis de las ruinas de Diquiyú." *Cuadernos Americanos* 138:157–66.

———. 1965b. "Diquiyú. Un señorío zapoteco-mixteco ignoto." *Cuadernos Americanos* 139:219–31.

Martínez López, Cira, Robert Markens, Marcus Winter, and Michael D. Lind. 2000. *Cerámica de la Fase Xoo (Época Monte Albán IIIb-IV) del Valle de Oaxaca.* Proyecto Especial Monte Albán 1992–1994. Contribución 8. Oaxaca City: Centro INAH Oaxaca.

Matadamas Díaz, Raul. 1989. Informe al INAH sobre excavaciones en Yucunama en 1988–1989. Report on file. Centro INAH Oaxaca.

———. 1996. Informe al INAH sobre excavaciones en Yucunama en 1995 y 1996. Report on file. Centro INAH Oaxaca.

———. 2001. "Pictografías del norte de Oaxaca. ¿Escritura periférica zapoteca?" In *Memoria de la Primera Mesa Redonda de Monte Albán. Procesos de cambio y conceptualización del tiempo,* ed. Nelly M. Robles García, 183–201. Mexico City: INAH.

McNamara, Patrick J. 2007. *Sons of the Sierra: Juárez, Díaz & the People of Ixtlán, Oaxaca, 1855–1920.* Chapel Hill, NC: University of North Carolina Press.

Meissner, Nathan J., Katherine E. South, and Andrew K. Balkansky. 2012. "Figurine Embodiment and Household Ritual in an Early Mixtec Village." *Journal de la Société des Américanistes,* in press.

Melville, Elinor G. K. 1994. *A Plague of Sheep: Environmental Consequences of the Conquest of Mexico.* Cambridge: Cambridge University Press.

Miller, Robert Ryal. 1985. *Mexico: A History.* Norman: University of Oklahoma Press.

Miranda, José. 1958. "Orígenes de la ganadería indígena en la Mixteca." In *Miscellanea Paul Rivet, Octogenario Dictata,* vol. 2, 787–96. Mexico City: Congreso International de Americanistas, UNAM.

Monaghan, John D. 1990. "Performance and the Structure of the Mixtec Codices." *Ancient Mesoamerica* 1:133–40.

———. 1994. "Irrigation and Ecological Complementarity in Mixtec Cacicazgos." In Marcus and Zeitlin, *Caciques and Their People,* 143–61.

———. 1995. *The Covenants with Earth and Rain: Exchange, Sacrifice, and Revelation in Mixtec Sociality.* Norman: University of Oklahoma Press.

————. 1997. "Mixtec Caciques in the Nineteenth and Twentieth Centuries." In *Códices, caciques, y comunidades*, ed. Maarten Jansen and Luis Reyes García, 265–81. Cuadernos de historia latinoamericana 5. Leiden, The Netherlands: Asociación de Historiadores Latinoamericanistas Europeos.

Monaghan, John D., and Jeffrey H. Cohen. 2000. "Thirty Years of Oaxacan Ethnography." In *Supplement to the Handbook of Middle American Indians*. Vol. 6: *Ethnology*, ed. John D. Monaghan, 150–78. Austin: University of Texas Press.

Monaghan, John D., Arthur A. Joyce, and Ronald Spores. 2003. "Transformations of the Indigenous Cacicazgo in the Nineteenth Century." *Ethnohistory* 50:131–50.

Moser, Christopher L. 1977. *Ñuiñe Writing and Iconography of the Mixteca Baja*. Nashville, Tenn.: VUPA 19.

Nagengast, Carole, Rudolfo Stavenhagen, and Michael Kearney. 1992. *Human Rights and Indigenous Workers: The Mixtecs in Mexico and the United States*. San Diego: Center for U.S.-Mexican Studies.

Nicholson, Henry B. 1961. "The Use of the Term 'Mixtec' in Mesoamerican Archaeology." *American Antiquity* 26:431–33.

————. 1971. "Religion in Pre-Hispanic Central Mexico." In *Archaeology of Northern Mesoamerica (Handbook of Middle American Indians)*, ed. Robert Wauchope, Gordon F. Ekholm, and Ignacio Bernal, 395–446. Austin: University of Texas Press.

Nuttall, Zelia. 1902. *Codex Nuttall. Facsimile of an Ancient Mexican Codex Belonging to Lord Zouche of Harynworth, England*. Cambridge: Peabody Museum of American Archaeology and Ethnology, Harvard University.

O'Mack, Scott. 1990. "Reconocimiento arqueológico en Tututepec, Oaxaca." *Notas Mesoamericanas* 12:19–38.

Orellana, Carlos. 1973. "Mixtec Migrants in Mexico City: A Case Study of Urbanization." *Human Organization* 32:273–82.

Oviedo y Valdés, Gonzalo Fernández de. 1851–1855. *Historia general y natural de las Indias* [1535]. 4 vols. Madrid: Imprenta de la Real Academia de Historia.

Paddock, John. 1953. "Excavations in the Mixteca Alta. *Mesoamerican Notes* 3:1–50.

————. 1965. "Current Research: Western Mesoamerica." *American Antiquity* 31:133–36.

————. 1966a. *Ancient Oaxaca: Discoveries in Mexican Archaeology and History*. Stanford, Calif.: Stanford University Press.

————. 1966b. "Oaxaca in Ancient Mesoamerica." In Paddock, *Ancient Oaxaca*, 83–242.

————. 1979. "A New Look at the Problem of Human Violence." In *Social, Political, and Economic Life in Contemporary Oaxaca*, ed. Aubrey Williams, 1–22. Nashville, Tenn.: VUPA 24.

————. 2003. "The Rise of the Ñuiñe Centers in the Mixteca Baja." In Flannery and Marcus, *Cloud People*, 208–11.

Palerm, Ángel, and Eric R. Wolf. 1957. "Ecological Potential and Cultural Development in Mesoamerica." In *Studies in Human Ecology: A Series of Lectures Given at the Anthropological Society of Washington*, 1–37. Social Science Monographs III. Washington, D.C.: Pan American Union.

Parsons, Jeffrey R. 1971. *Prehistoric Settlement Patterns of the Texcoco Region, Mexico.* Memoirs 3. Ann Arbor: Museum of Anthropology, University of Michigan.

Paso y Troncoso, Francisco del, ed. 1905–1906. *Papeles de Nueva España. Segunda serie*, vols. 1, 3–4. Madrid: Sucesores de Rivadeneyra.

———. *Epístolario de Nueva España, 1505–1818.* 1939–42. 16 vols. Mexico City: Antigua Librería Robredo de José Porrúa e Hijos.

Pastor, Rodolfo. 1987. *Campesinos y reformas: La Mixteca 1700–1856.* Mexico City: El Colegio de México.

Peña, Moisés T. de la. 1950. *Problemas sociales y económicos de las Mixtecas.* Memorias del Instituto Nacional Indigenista 2(1). Mexico City: INI.

Pérez Rodríguez, Verónica. 2003. Household Intensification and Agrarian States: Excavation of Houses and Terraced Fields in a Mixtec Cacicazgo. Ph.D. dissertation, University of Georgia.

———. 2006. "States and Households: The Social Organization of Terrace Agriculture in Postclassic Mixteca Alta, Oaxaca, Mexico." *Latin American Antiquity* 17:3–22.

———. 2008. Investigaciones en Cerro Jazmín: un estudio sobre el urbanismo y el paisaje aterrazado de la Mixteca Alta, Oaxaca. Report on file. Centro INAH Oaxaca.

Pérez Rodríguez, Verónica, Kirk C. Anderson, and Margaret K. Neff. 2011. "The Cerro Jazmín Archaeological Project: Investigating Prehispanic Urbanism and its Environmental Impact in the Mixteca Alta, Oaxaca, Mexico." *Journal of Field Archaeology* 36:83–99.

Pike, Kenneth L. 1948. *Tone Languages: A Technique for Determining the Number and Type of Pitch Contrasts.* . . . University of Michigan Publications in Linguistics 4. Ann Arbor: University of Michigan Press.

Plunket, Patricia S. 1983. An Intensive Survey in the Yucuita Sector of the Nochixtlán Valley, Oaxaca, Mexico. Ph.D. dissertation, Tulane University.

Pohl, John M. D. 1994. *The Politics of Symbolism in the Mixtec Codices.* Nashville, Tenn.: VUPA 46.

———. 2003. "Ritual Ideology and Commerce in the Southern Mexican Highlands." In *The Postclassic Mesoamerican World*, ed. Michael E. Smith and Frances F. Berdan, 172–77. Salt Lake City: University of Utah Press.

Pohl, John M. D., John Monaghan, and Laura R. Stiver. 1997. "Religion, Economy, and Factionalism in Mixtec Boundary Zones." In *Códices y documentos sobre México: segundo simposio*, vol. 1, ed. Salvador Rueda Smithers, Constanza Vega Sosa, and Rodrigo Martínez Baracs, 205–32. Mexico City: INAH and CONACULTA.

Pool, Christopher A. 2007. *Olmec Archaeology and Early Mesoamerica*. Cambridge: Cambridge University Press.

Rabin, Emily. 1979. "The War of Heaven in Codices Zouche-Nuttall and Bodley: A Preliminary Study." *Actes du XLII Congrès International des Américanistes* 7:173–82.

———. 2002. "Toward a Unified Chronology of the Historical Codices and Pictorial Manuscripts of the Mixteca Alta, Costa and Baja: An Overview." In *Homenaje a John Paddock*, ed. Patricia Plunket, 101–36. Puebla: Universidad de las Américas.

Redmond, Elsa M. 1983. *A Fuego y Sangre: Early Zapotec Imperialism in the Cuicatlán Cañada, Oaxaca, Mexico*. Memoirs 16. Ann Arbor: Museum of Anthropology, University of Michigan.

Redmond, Elsa M., and Charles S. Spencer. 1994. "The Cacicazgo: An Indigenous Design." In Marcus and Zeitlin, *Caciques and Their People*, 189–225.

———. 2008. "Rituals of Sanctification and the Development of Standardized Temples in Oaxaca, Mexico." *Cambridge Archaeological Journal* 18:239–66.

Restall, Matthew. 2004. *Seven Myths of the Spanish Conquest*. Oxford: Oxford University Press.

Reyes, Fray Antonio de los. 1976. *Arte en lengua mixteca* [1593]. Nashville, Tenn.: VUPA 14.

Rice, Don S., and Prudence M. Rice. 2005. "Sixteenth and Seventeenth-Century Maya Political Geography and Resistance in Central Petén, Guatemala." In *The Postclassic to Spanish-Era Transition in Mesoamerica: Archaeological Perspectives*, ed. Susan Kepecs and Rani T. Alexander, 139–60. Albuquerque: University of New Mexico Press.

Rincón Mautner, Carlos. 1995. "The Ñuiñe Codex from the Colossal Natural Bridge on the Ndaxagua: An Early Pictographic Text from the Coixtlahuaca Basin." *Institute of Maya Studies Journal* 1 (2): 39–66.

———. 1999. Man and the Environment in the Coixtlahuaca Basin of Northwestern Oaxaca, Mixteca Region, Mexico: Two Thousand Years of Historical Ecology. Ph.D. dissertation, University of Texas at Austin.

Rivera Guzmán, Angel Iván. 2000. "La iconografía del poder durante el Clásico en la Mixteca Baja de Oaxaca. Evidencia iconográfica y arqueológica." *Cuadernos del Sur* 6 (15): 5–36.

———. 2008a. "Los inicios de la escritura en la Mixteca." In Jansen and van Broekhoven, *Mixtec Writing and Society. Escritura de Ñuu Dzaui*, 109–44.

———. 2008b. "El proyecto arqueológico de la Mixteca Baja, Oaxaca, México. Algunos resultados y perspectivas." *Itinerarios* 2 (2): 115–39.

Robertson, William S. 1952. *Iturbide of Mexico*. Durham, N.C.: Duke University Press.

Robles García, Nelly M. 1988. *Las unidades domésticas del preclásico superior en la Mixteca Alta*. Oxford: British Archaeological Reports 407.

Rodríguez Cano, Laura. 1996. El sistema de escritura ñuiñe: Análisis del corpus de piedras grabadas de la zona de la Cañada en la Mixteca Baja, Oaxaca. Tesis de licenciatura, Escuela Nacional de Antropología e Historia, Mexico City.

Romero Frizzi, María de los Ángeles. 1990. *Economía y vida de los españoles en la Mixteca Alta: 1519–1720.* Mexico City: INAH and Gobierno del Estado de Oaxaca.

———. 2008. *Teposcolula. Aquellos días del Siglo XVI.* Oaxaca City: CONACULTA, Gobierno del Estado de Oaxaca, and Fundación Alfredo Harp Helú.

Romero Frizzi, María de los Ángeles, and Ronald Spores. 1976. *Índice del Archivo del Juzgado de Teposcolula, Oaxaca. Época colonial.* Cuadernos de los Centros 32. Mexico City: INAH.

Ruiz Medrano, Ethelia. 2010. *Mexico's Indigenous Communities: Their Lands and Histories, 1500–2010.* Boulder: University Press of Colorado.

Sahagún, Fray Bernardino de. 1950–82. *Florentine Codex: General History of the Things of New Spain* [1575–77 or 1578–80], ed. Arthur J. O. Anderson and Charles E. Dibble. 13 vols. Santa Fe, NM: School of American Research; Salt Lake City: University of Utah Press.

Sanders, William T. 1965. The Cultural Ecology of the Teotihuacan Valley: A Preliminary Report of the Results of the Teotihuacan Valley Project. Manuscript on file. Department of Anthropology, Pennsylvania State University, University Park.

Sanders, William T., and David Webster. 1988. "The Mesoamerican Urban Tradition." *American Anthropologist* 90:521–46.

Saville, Marshall H. 1920. *The Goldsmith's Art in Ancient Mexico.* Indian Notes and Monographs 7. New York: Museum of the American Indian, Heye Foundation.

Scholes, France V. 1952. "Franciscan Missionary Scholars in Colonial Central America." *The Americas* 8:391–416.

Scholes, France V., and Eleanor B. Adams, eds. 1961. *Cartas del Licenciado Jerónimo Valderrama y otros documentos sobre su visita al gobierno de Nueva España, 1563–1565.* Mexico City: José Porrúa e Hijos.

Seler, Eduard. 1892. "Notice sur les langues Zapotèque et Mixtèque." *VIII Congrès International des Américanistes,* 550–55. Paris: Ernest Leroux.

Sharer, Robert J. 2007. "Early Formative Pottery Trade and the Evolution of Mesoamerican Civilisation." *Antiquity* 81:201–203.

Sherman, R. Jason, Andrew K. Balkansky, Charles S. Spencer, and Brian D. Nicholls. 2010. "Expansionary Dynamics of the Nascent Monte Albán State." *Journal of Anthropological Archaeology* 29:278–301.

Simpson, Lesley Byrd. 1950. *The Encomienda in New Spain: The Beginning of Spanish Mexico.* Berkeley: University of California Press.

Sisson, Edward B. 1989. "El comercio de la obsidiana en el Cacicazgo Postclásico de Coxcatlan, Puebla." In *La Obsidiana en Mesoamérica,* ed. Margarita Gaxiola

González and John. E. Clark, 331–44. Colección Científica 176. Mexico City: INAH.

Smith, Benjamin Thomas. 2005. "Anticlericalism and Resistance: The Diocese of Huajuapam de León, 1930–1940." *Journal of Latin American Studies* 37:469–505.

Smith, C. Earle, Jr. 1976. *Modern Vegetation and Ancient Plant Remains of the Nochixtlán Valley, Oaxaca*. Nashville, Tenn.: VUPA 16.

Smith, C. Earle, Jr., and Joseph W. Hopkins III. 2003. "Environmental Contrasts in the Otomanguean Region." In Flannery and Marcus, *Cloud People*, 13–18.

Smith, Charlotte A. 2002. Concordant Change and Core-Periphery Dynamics: A Synthesis of Highland Mesoamerican Survey Data. Ph.D. dissertation, University of Georgia.

Smith, Mary Elizabeth. 1973. *Picture Writing from Ancient Southern Mexico: Mixtec Place Signs and Maps*. Norman: University of Oklahoma Press.

———. 1994. "Why the Second Codex Selden Was Painted." In Marcus and Zeitlin, *Caciques and Their People*, 111–41.

———. 2003a. "The Earliest Mixtec Dynastic Records." In Flannery and Marcus, *Cloud People*, 213.

———. 2003b. "The Mixtec Writing System." In Flannery and Marcus, *Cloud People*, 238–45.

———. 2003c. "Codex Selden: A Manuscript from the Valley of Nochixtlan?" In Flannery and Marcus, *Cloud People*, 248–55.

———. 2003d. "Regional Points of View in the Mixtec Codices." In Flannery and Marcus, *Cloud People*, 260–66.

Smith, Michael E. 1986. "The Role of Social Stratification in the Aztec Empire: A View from the Provinces." *American Anthropologist* 88:70–91.

———. 1989. "Cities, Towns, and Urbanism: Comment on Sanders and Webster." *American Anthropologist* 91:454–60.

———. 2009. "Editorial—Just How Comparative is Comparative Urban Geography? A Perspective from Archaeology." *Urban Geography* 30:113–17.

Sousa, Lisa Mary. 1997. "Women and Crime in Colonial Oaxaca: Evidence of Complementary Gender Roles in Mixtec and Zapotec Societies." In *Indian Women of Early Mexico*, ed. Susan Schroeder, Stephanie Wood, and Robert Haskett, 199–214. Norman: University of Oklahoma Press.

Soustelle, Jacques. 1961. *Daily Life of the Aztecs on the Eve of the Spanish Conquest*. Stanford, Calif.: Stanford University Press.

Spencer, Charles S. 2010. "Territorial Expansion and Primary State Formation." *Proceedings of the National Academy of Sciences* 107:7119–26.

Spencer, Charles S., and Elsa M. Redmond. 2004. "Primary State Formation in Mesoamerica." *Annual Review of Anthropology* 33:173–99.

Spencer, Charles S., Elsa M. Redmond, and Christina M. Elson. 2008. "Ceramic Microtypology and the Territorial Expansion of the Early Monte Albán State in Oaxaca, Mexico." *Journal of Field Archaeology* 33:321–41.

Spinden, Herbert J. 1935. "Indian Manuscripts of Southern Mexico." *Annual Report of the Board of Regents of the Smithsonian Institution . . .* , 429–51. Washington, D.C.: U.S. Government Printing Office.

Spores, Ronald. 1964. "The Genealogy of Tlazultepec: A Sixteenth-Century Mixtec Manuscript." *Southwestern Journal of Anthropology* 20:15–31.

———. 1965. "The Zapotec and Mixtec at Spanish Contact." In Wauchope and Willey, *Archaeology of Southern Mesoamerica*, 962–87.

———. 1967. *The Mixtec Kings and Their People*. Norman: University of Oklahoma Press.

———. 1969. "Settlement, Farming Technology, and Environment in the Nochixtlán Valley, Oaxaca." *Science* 166:557–69.

———. 1972. *An Archaeological Settlement Survey of the Nochixtlan Valley, Oaxaca*. Nashville, Tenn.: VUPA 1.

———. 1973. "Ethnohistorical Research in Mexico." In *Research in Mexican History*, ed. Richard E. Greenleaf and Michael C. Meyer, 25–48. Lincoln: University of Nebraska Press.

———. 1974a. *Stratigraphic Excavations in the Nochixtlan Valley, Oaxaca*. Nashville, Tenn.: VUPA 11.

———. 1974b. "Marital Alliance in the Political Integration of Mixtec Kingdoms." *American Anthropologist* 76:297–311.

———. 1976. "La estratificación social en la antigua sociedad Mixteca." In *Estratificación social en la Mesoamérica prehispánica*, ed. Pedro Carrasco and Johanna Broda, 207–20. Mexico City: INAH.

———. 1984. *The Mixtecs in Ancient and Colonial Times*. Norman: University of Oklahoma Press.

———. 1990a. "La situación económica de la Mixteca en la primera década de la independencia." In *Lecturas históricas del estado de Oaxaca*. Vol. 3: *Siglo XIX*, ed. María de los Ángeles Romero Frizzi, 129–86. Mexico City: INAH and Gobierno del Estado de Oaxaca.

———. 1990b. "Relaciones gubernamentales y judiciales entre los pueblos, los distritos y el estado en Oaxaca (siglo XIX)." In *Lecturas históricas del estado de Oaxaca*. Vol. 3: *Siglo XIX*, ed. María de los Ángeles Romero Frizzi, 239–90. Mexico City: INAH and Gobierno del Estado de Oaxaca.

———. 1990c. "Los caciques de la Mixteca Alta, siglo XVI." In *Lecturas históricas del estado de Oaxaca*. Vol. 2: *Época colonial*, ed. María de los Ángeles Romero Frizzi, 101–49. Mexico City: INAH and Gobierno del Estado de Oaxaca.

———. 1993. "Tututepec: A Postclassic-Period Mixtec Conquest State." *Ancient Mesoamerica* 4:167–74.

———. 1996a. Informe final al Consejo de Arqueología del INAH del Proyecto Recorrido Arqueológico de la región mixteca central y oeste, 1993–1995, 1996. Report on file. Centro INAH Oaxaca.

———. 1996b. "Local Issues, Inter-group Conflict, and Ethnicity and the Formation of Mixtec Regional Coalitions." In *The Politics of Ethnicity in Southern Mexico*, ed. Howard Campbell, 33–40. Nashville, Tenn.: VUPA 50.

———. 1997a. "Arte antiguo en la Mixteca." In *Historia del arte de Oaxaca*. Vol. 1: *Arte prehispánico*, ed. Margarita Dalton Palomo and Verónica Loera y Chávez, 61–77. Oaxaca City: Gobierno del Estado de Oaxaca.

———. 1997b. "Mixteca *Cacicas*: Status, Wealth, and the Political Accommodation of Native Elite Women in Early Colonial Oaxaca." In *Indian Women of Early Mexico*, ed. Susan Schroeder, Stephanie Wood, and Robert Haskett, 185–97. Norman: University of Oklahoma Press.

———. 1998. "Differential Response to Colonial Control among the Mixtecs and Zapotecs of Oaxaca." In *Native Resistance and the Pax Colonial in New Spain*, ed. Susan Schroeder, 30–46. Lincoln: University of Nebraska Press.

———. 2001. "Estudios mixtecos, ayer, hoy y mañana: ¿dónde estábamos, dónde estamos, hacia dónde vamos?" In *Memoria de la Primera Mesa Redonda de Monte Albán. Procesos de cambio y conceptualización del tiempo*, ed. Nelly M. Robles García, 165–81. Mexico City: INAH.

———. 2003a. "Yucuñudahui." In Flannery and Marcus, *Cloud People*, 155–58.

———. 2003b. "Postclassic Mixtec Kingdoms: Ethnohistoric and Archaeological Evidence." In Flannery and Marcus, *Cloud People*, 255–60.

———. 2003c. "Ramos Phase Urbanization in the Mixteca Alta." In Flannery and Marcus, *Cloud People*, 120–23.

———. 2003d. "Las Flores Phase Settlement Patterns in the Nochixtlán Valley." In Flannery and Marcus, *Cloud People*, 152–55.

———. 2003e. "Postclassic Settlement Patterns in the Nochixtlán Valley." In Flannery and Marcus, *Cloud People*, 246–48.

———. 2003f. "Origins of the Village in the Mixteca (Early Cruz Phase)." In Flannery and Marcus, *Cloud People*, 46.

———. 2003g. "Middle and Late Formative Settlement Patterns in the Mixteca Alta." In Flannery and Marcus, *Cloud People*, 72–74.

———. 2003h. "The Origin and Evolution of the Mixtec System of Social Stratification." In Flannery and Marcus, *Cloud People*, 227–38.

———. 2003i. "Mixtec Religion." In Flannery and Marcus, *Cloud People*, 342–45.

———. 2005. "El impacto de la política de congregaciones en los asentamientos coloniales de la Mixteca Alta, Oaxaca: el caso de Tlaxiaco y su región." *Cuadernos del Sur* 11 (22): 7–20.

———. 2007. *Ñuu Ñudzahui. La Mixteca de Oaxaca. La evolución de la cultura mixteca desde los primeros pueblos preclásicos hasta la Independencia.* Oaxaca City: Instituto Estatal de Educación Pública del Estado de Oaxaca.

———. 2008. "La Mixteca y los mixtecos. 3000 años de adaptación cultural." *Arqueología Mexicana* 15 (90): 28–33.

Spores, Ronald, Andrew Balkansky, and Frank Crohn. 1995. Informe final al Consejo de Arqueología del INAH del Proyecto: recorrido arqueológico de la región mixteca central y oeste, 1993–1995. Report on file. Centro INAH Oaxaca.

Spores, Ronald, and Kent V. Flannery. 2003. "Sixteenth-Century Kinship and Social Organization." In Flannery and Marcus, *Cloud People,* 339–42.

Spores, Ronald, and Nelly M. Robles García. 2007. "A Prehispanic (Postclassic) Capital Center in Colonial Transition: Excavations at Yucundaa Pueblo Viejo de Teposcolula, Oaxaca, Mexico." *Latin American Antiquity* 18:333–53.

———, eds. 2012. *La ciudad mixteca Yucundaa-Pueblo Viejo de Teposcolula, Oaxaca y su transformación prehispánica-colonial.* Oaxaca City: Fundación Alfredo Harp Helú and INAH.

Stephen, Lynn. 2007. *Transborder Lives: Indigenous Oaxacans in Mexico, California, and Oregon.* Durham, N.C.: Duke University Press.

Steward, Julian H. 1942. "The Direct Historical Approach to Archaeology." *American Antiquity* 7: 337–43.

Stirling, Matthew W. 1943. *Stone Monuments of Southern Mexico.* Bureau of American Ethnology Bulletin 138. Washington, D.C.: U.S. Government Printing Office.

Stiver, Laura R. 2001. Prehispanic Mixtec Settlement and State in the Teposcolula Valley of Oaxaca, Mexico. Ph.D. dissertation, Vanderbilt University.

Swadesh, Morris. 1960. "The Oto-Manguean Hypothesis and Macro Mixtecan." *International Journal of American Linguistics* 26:79–111.

Taylor, William B. 1979. *Drinking, Homicide, and Rebellion in Colonial Mexican Villages.* Stanford, Calif.: Stanford University Press.

Terraciano, Kevin. 2001. *The Mixtecs of Colonial Oaxaca: Ñudzahui History, Sixteenth through Eighteenth Centuries.* Stanford, Calif.: Stanford University Press.

Timmons, Wilbert H. 1963. *Morelos: Priest, Soldier, Statesman of Mexico.* El Paso: Texas Western College Press.

Treacy, John M., and William M. Denevan. 1994. "The Creation of Cultivable Land Through Terracing." In *The Archaeology of Garden and Field,* ed. Naomi F. Miller and Kathryn L. Gleason, 91–110. Philadelphia: University of Pennsylvania Press.

Troike, Nancy. 1978. "Fundamental Changes in the Interpretation of the Mixtec Codices." *American Antiquity* 43:553–68.

Urcid, Javier. 2008. "An Ancient Story of Creation from San Pedro Jaltepetongo." In Jansen and van Broekhoven, *Mixtec Writing and Society. Escritura de Ñuu Dzaui,* 147–94.

Urcid, Javier, and Arthur A. Joyce. 2001. "Carved Monuments and Calendrical Names: The Rulers of Río Viejo, Oaxaca." *Ancient Mesoamerica* 12:199–216.

Vaillant, George C. 1941. *The Aztecs of Mexico: The Origin, Rise, and Fall of the Aztec Nation.* Garden City, NY: Doubleday.

van Doesburg, Sebastián, ed. 2009. *Pictografía y escritura alfabética en Oaxaca.* Oaxaca City: Instituto Estatal de Educación Pública de Oaxaca and Fundación Alfredo Harp Helú.

Vázquez-Gómez, Juana. 1997. *Dictionary of Mexican Rulers, 1325–1997.* Santa Barbara, Calif.: Greenwood Press.

Velasco Ortiz, Laura. 1990. "Los mixtecos: una cultura migrante." *México Indígena* 4: 46–49.

———. 1992. "Notas para estudiar los cambios del comportamiento migratorio de los Mixtecos." In *Migración y Etnicidad en Oaxaca,* ed. Jack Corbett et al., 79–86. Nashville, Tenn.: VUPA 43.

———. 2005. *Mixtec Transnational Identity.* Tucson: University of Arizona Press.

Warner, John C. 1975. "Estudio del sistema de mercados en el Valle de Nochixtlán y la Mixteca Alta." In *Mercados de Oaxaca,* ed. Martin Diskin and Scott Cook, 144–68. Mexico City: INI.

Waterbury, Ronald. 1975. "Non-revolutionary Peasants: Oaxaca Compared to Morelos in the Mexican Revolution." *Comparative Studies in Society and History* 17:410–42.

Wauchope, Robert, and Gordon R. Willey. 1965. *Archaeology of Southern Mesoamerica (Handbook of Middle American Indians).* Austin: University of Texas Press.

West, Robert C., and John P. Augelli. 1964. *Middle America: Its Lands and Peoples.* Englewood Cliffs, N.J.: Prentice-Hall.

Whallon, Robert. 1992. "A Statistical Analysis of Mixtec Nobles' Names." In Joyce Marcus, *Mesoamerican Writing Systems: Propaganda, Myth, and History in Four Ancient Civilizations,* 447–63. Princeton, N.J.: Princeton University Press.

Whitecotton, Joseph W. 1977. *The Zapotecs: Princes, Priests, and Peasants.* Norman: University of Oklahoma Press.

Williams, Robert Lloyd. 2009. *Lord Eight Wind of Suchixtlan and the Heroes of Ancient Oaxaca: Reading History in the Codex Zouche-Nuttall.* Austin: University of Texas Press.

Winter, Marcus. 1984. "Exchange in Formative Highland Oaxaca." In *Trade and Exchange in Early Mesoamerica,* ed. Kenneth G. Hirth, 179–214. Albuquerque: University of New Mexico Press.

———. 1989a. "From Classic to Post-Classic in Pre-Hispanic Oaxaca." *Mesoamerica after the Decline of Teotihuacan A.D. 700–900,* ed. Richard A. Diehl and Janet Catherine Berlo, 123–30. Washington, D.C.: Dumbarton Oaks Research Library and Collection.

———. 1989b. "La obsidiana en Oaxaca prehispánica." In *La Obsidiana en Mesoamérica,* ed. Margarita Gaxiola González and John E. Clark, 345–62. Colección Científica 176. Mexico City: INAH.

———. 1994a. "The Mixteca Prior to The Late Postclassic." In *Mixteca-Puebla: Discoveries and Research in Mesoamerican Art and Archaeology*, ed. H. B. Nicholson and Eloise Quiñones Keber, 201–21. Culver City, Calif.: Labyrinthos.

———. 1994b. "Los altos de Oaxaca y los Olmecas." In *Los Olmecas en Mesoamérica*, ed. John E. Clark, 129–41. Mexico City: Ediciones el Equilibrista and City Bank.

———. 1996. *Cerro de las Minas. Arqueología de la Mixteca Baja.* Oaxaca City: Casa de la Cultura de Huajuapan.

———. 2005. La cultura Ñuiñe de la Mixteca Baja: nuevas aportaciones. In *Pasado y presente de la cultura mixteca*, ed. Reina Ortiz Escamilla and Ignacio Ortiz Castro, 77–115. Mexico City: Universidad Tecnológica de la Mixteca.

Winter, Marcus, Margarita Gaxiola, and Gilberto Hernández. 1984. "Archaeology of the Otomanguean Area." In Josserand et al., *Essays in Otomanguean Culture History*, 65–108.

Winter, Marcus, and Gilberto Hernández. 1977. Informe preliminar de las excavaciones en San Juan Yucuita, Nochixtlán, Oaxaca. Report on file. Centro INAH Oaxaca.

Winter, Marcus, Alicia Herrera Muzgo T., Ronald Spores, and Vilma Fialko. 1991. Exploraciones arqueológicas en Huamelulpan, Mixteca Alta, Oaxaca. Informe temporada 1990. Report on file. Centro INAH Oaxaca.

Wittington, Stephen L. 2003. "El Mapa de Teozacoalco: An Early Colonial Guide to a Municipality in Oaxaca." *The SAA Archaeological Record* 3 (4): 20–22, 25.

Wolf, Eric R. 1957. "Closed Corporate Peasant Communities in Mesoamerica and Central Java." *Southwestern Journal of Anthropology* 13:7–12.

Workinger, Andrew G. 2002. Coastal/Highland Interaction in Prehispanic Oaxaca, Mexico: The Perspective from San Francisco de Arriba. Ph.D. dissertation, Vanderbilt University.

Wright, Henry T. 2006. "Early State Dynamics as Political Experiment." *Journal of Anthropological Research* 62:305–19.

Zárate Morán, Roberto. 1987. *Excavaciones de un sitio preclásico en San Mateo Etlatongo, Nochixtlán, Oaxaca, México.* Oxford: British Archaeological Reports 322.

Zavala, Silvio A. 1935. *La encomienda indiana.* Madrid: Centro de Estudios Históricos.

Zavala, Silvio A., and José Miranda. 1954. "Instituciones indígenas en la Colonia." In Alfonso Caso, Silvio Zavala, José Miranda, et al., *Métodos y resultados de la política indigenista en México*, 29–112. Memorias del Instituto Nacional Indigenista 6. Mexico City: INI.

Zorita, Alonso de. 1963. *Breve y sumaria relación de los señores de la Nueva España* [1566–70]. Mexico City: UNAM.

INDEX

Casa de Cultura, Santa Catarina Tayata, 70
Casa de la Cacica, *118*, 175. *See also* Palaces
Casa del Agua, 69
Casa religiosa, 153, 158. *See also* Monastery
Casado, 173. *See also* Tribute
Casas, Francisco de las, 144–48, 151, 179
Casas, Gonzalo de las, 147–48, 151–52
Caso, Alfonso, 101n89; archaeological
  surveys and excavations, 5n3, 6, 20,
  37, 57, 73–74; codices, 101, 104,
  136n36, 179; conjunctive-historical or
  convergent method, 5n3, 5; Instituto
  Nacional Indigenista (INI), 218; "Jaws
  of the Sky," 86; Monte Albán, 20;
  Monte Negro, 57, 88; Olmec, 51; royal
  succession, 184; Tilantongo, 184; Tomb 1,
  76; Tomb 7, 20; Yucuñudahui, 74, 76, 88;
  Zapotec writing, 37, 70
Casta linaje, 111. See also *Caciques;* Ruling
  class; *Yya toniñe;Yya tnuhu*
Castilla, Luis de, 144, 147, 153
Cattle, 150, 187, 208, 210. See also *Ganado
  mayor;* Pigs
Caudillos, 197
Caves, 29, 40, 93, 128; burials in, 133,
  135n80; Casa del Agua, 69; Coxcatlan,
  38, 40; filled by Spaniards, 135; "Great
  Causeway," 30, 135; hill signs and
  toponyms, 69, 102; near Mitla, 41; at
  Peñoles, 134n77; religious belief, 135;
  sacrifice in, 134–135; in Yucuita, 135; in
  Yucundaa-Teposcolula, 135
Ceramics, 164. *See also* Pottery
Cerro de las Minas, 38; archaeological
  surveys and excavations, 20, 33, 37, 84;
  mica, 20; Ñuiñe, 84, *86*; population, 72;
  settlement, 64; tombs in, 84; urbanism,
  75. *See also* Huajuapan
Cerro de la Virgen, 75
Cerro Encantado, 75, 81–83
Cerro Jazmín, *38, 56, 76*; archaeological
  surveys and excavations, 38n2, 40,
  55n79; architecture in, 75;
  coo-yuu terracing, 75; land in, 74;
  Nochixtlan Valley, 75; population, 74, 92;
  Religion, 75, 93; urbanism, 55–57, 60;
  Yanhuitlan, 92

Cerro Lagartija, 70, 80
Cerro Volado, 34, 58, 61–*62*. *See also*
  Huamelulpan
Chachoapan, 29; *aniñe* (royal housing),
  98, 117; archaeological surveys and
  excavations, 97, 134; commoners,
  98, 117; *coo-yuu* terracing, 55; plaza
  complexes, 162; projectile points, 40;
  religion, 134; relocation of, 163; royal
  succession, 180, 184–85
Chalcatongo, 56, 136, 182; archaeological
  surveys of, 24, 91; colonial settlement
  of, 145, 147, 158, 164; developments in,
  75; dialect of, 22; images of Dzahui in,
  81; Postclassic commoner houses in, 98;
  ritual in, 127; warfare in, 230
Chalcatzingo, 42
Charco Redondo, 42, 51
Charles V, 143
Chatino, 21, 26, 38, 75–76, 120, 235
Chazumba, 40; archaeological surveys of,
  64; carved monuments in, 83
Chert, 19–20, 123
Chert quarry, 75
Chicahuaxtla, 208; *encomiendas* and
  land ownership, 111, 145; language,
  206, 221; markets in, *126*; terracing
  in, 79
Chichicapan, 120
Chilapa de Díaz, 20, 227
Cholula, 141; colonial subjugation of, 143;
  polychrome pottery, 99, 127
Cicco, Gabriel de, 65
Closed corporate community, 212
Cochineal, 147–49, 163, 206, 208; *cochinilla*,
  206; *grana*, 149, 206, 208
Codex Bodley, 179, 182. *See also* Writing
Codex Borgia, 138. *See also* Writing
Codex Mendoza, 149, 237. *See also* Writing
Codex Nuttall, *103, 116, 118*, 182. *See
  also* Writing
Codex Vindobonensis, *130*, 136–*37*. *See
  also* Writing
Codex Yanhuitlan, *118*, 151, 178. See also
  Códice de Yanhuitlan; Writing
Códice de Yanhuitlan, 151, 178. See also
  Codex Yanhuitlan; Writing

www.ingramcontent.com/pod-product-compliance
Lightning Source LLC
Chambersburg PA
CBHW020824270326
41928CB00006B/436